The Right Fight

The

RIGHT FIGHT

BERNARD LORD *and the* CONSERVATIVE DILEMMA

JACQUES POITRAS

GOOSE LANE

Edited by Barry Norris.
Author photo by Tonë Meeg.
Cover and book design by Paul Vienneau.
Printed in Canada by Friesens.
10 9 8 7 6 5 4 3 2 1

Cover photographs: Front: Bernard Lord, Francine Dion; Richard Hatfield, October 1970, Provincial Archives of New Brunswick Richard Hatfield Photograph Collection, P282-12; Bernard Lord and Brian Mulroney, August 28, 2002, Noel Chenier/*The Telegraph-Journal*; Danny Cameron, September 1992, courtesy of Danny Cameron. Back: Richard Hatfield and Percy Mockler, February 1985, courtesy of Percy Mockler; Bernard Lord, Stephen Harper and Brian Mulroney, May 2004, *The Moncton Times-Transcript*; Dennis Cochrane, 1991, courtesy of Dennis Cochrane. Published by permission.

Library and Archives Canada Cataloguing in Publication

Poitras, Jacques, 1968-
    The right fight : Bernard Lord and the Conservative dilemma / Jacques Poitras.

Includes bibliographical references and index.
ISBN 0-86492-376-7

    1. Lord, Bernard, 1965-   2. Progressive Conservative Party of New Brunswick. 3. Conservatism — New Brunswick.   4. New Brunswick — Politics and government.   I. Title.

FC2478.2.P64 2004   971.5'105   C2004-904074-X

Published with the financial support of the Canada Council for the Arts, the Government of Canada through the Book Publishing Industry Development Program, and the New Brunswick Culture and Sports Secretariat.

Goose Lane Editions
469 King Street
Fredericton, New Brunswick
CANADA E3B 1E5
www.gooselane.com

To Giselle and Sophie

"I suspect that one hundred years from now, those who occupy this Legislature will still have to fight for equality. It may never be realized, but at least this Legislature will know that as of this time, it is the will of the people of New Brunswick that we work in that direction and we strive for that equality." — Premier Richard Hatfield, Legislative Assembly of New Brunswick, July 16, 1981

"The dimmer a party's prospects, the more numerous are its factions." — Dalton Camp, *Gentlemen, Players and Politicians*, 1970

Bernard Lord and Brian Mulroney, St. Thomas University, Fredericton,
August 28, 2002. NOEL CHENIER/*THE TELEGRAPH-JOURNAL*

Table of Contents

ELECTION DAY, 1991

LYNN MASON AWOKE EARLY on the morning of September 23, 1991. Summer was gone, and the air felt cool as he readied himself for what he knew would be a long day. He left his house on Preston Street, an ordinary, tree-lined lane of homes on Fredericton's north side, and set out for campaign headquarters.

Mason's polling station was around the corner from his house, at the Church of Christ on Bloor Street, but he had known it would be busy today, so he'd cast his ballot in the advance poll. When he reached the headquarters, in a small strip mall called York Plaza on Main Street, it was already filling up with volunteers. Mason — soft-spoken but intensely serious — began giving orders to the scrutineers, the men and women who would camp out at every polling station in the riding of Fredericton North to ensure all the ballots were counted properly. Mason had worked hard leading up to the campaign, especially once the election had been called, on signs, advertising and "anything that needed to be done." He wasn't going to let that effort go to waste now, on election day.

Mason had needed one scrutineer for each of Fredericton North's sixty-five polling stations, and he'd had no trouble finding them because the members of the Confederation of Regions party were on a mission. "They were incensed," Mason says today. "They saw a need for this party, and there was no difficulty getting people involved."

Mason was incensed, too. He'd come to COR to advance his pet issue — a solution to the mismanagement of government-owned woodlands by the forestry industry — and found an organization prepared to listen. He'd often voted Conservative in the past, but he liked the sound of this upstart party. For one thing, COR ran itself from the bottom up, its ideology reflecting its grassroots membership. Mason's philosophy of forest management had even found its way into COR's election platform.

Mason liked COR for another reason. The party was opposed to official bilingualism. "The expenditures involved were what pissed me off," he said. He'd watched Conservative premier Richard Hatfield blow huge amounts of cash on initiatives aimed at the one-third of New Brunswickers who were French-speaking. Hatfield had even flirted with the idea of duality — setting up separate, parallel government operations in each language. Only four per cent of francophones couldn't speak English, Mason reasoned, so why couldn't all the others go to school and work and deal with the government in the language of the majority? "I really don't believe in splitting cultures," Mason says. "English should be taught throughout the province, and the exact opposite of that was legislated bilingualism. It was politics more than anything else, not a benefit to the French community."

The new Liberal government of Frank McKenna had done no better, in Mason's view. McKenna had added another seven billion dollars to New Brunswick's public debt, and "I know for a fact two-thirds of that went to subsidizing bilingualism," Mason says. The Liberals were under pressure to write into the Constitution a piece of legislation, passed by Hatfield's government, that guaranteed the equality of the two linguistic communities. If that happened, the wasteful duality that so enraged Mason would become permanent. For those who felt as Mason did, it had to be stopped.

Across English New Brunswick, people who'd voted Conservative all their lives had concluded that the party had abandoned them. Their party, which had always spoken for the English-speaking majority, had bent to the Acadian vote. To fight back, they had created the Confederation of Regions party.

Mason had walked into COR's provincial office on Main Street one day, curious. He liked what the people there told him, not just about language or his ability to influence party policy, but about education, health care and a range of other issues. Soon, Mason was on the board of directors of the Fredericton North COR association, organizing a growing political machine of eleven hundred members. He got to know the party's provincial president, Ed Allen, a former Conservative MLA and cabinet minister, COR's biggest catch among the thousands of defecting Tories.

Now Allen's name was on the ballot in Fredericton North, not for the PCs but for COR. Lynn Mason's job was to get him elected.

* * *

Don Parent's job on election day — as much as it surprised him — was to make sure Ed Allen did *not* get elected.

Parent was a teacher and a Conservative who had loyally worked on Allen's campaigns over the years. Now, on September 23, 1991, Parent could hardly believe that he was on the ballot against his old ally. But that was the kind of campaign it had been. A week after Frank McKenna had kicked off the campaign, the Tories of Fredericton North had come to Parent, desperate. The party was in bad shape. Many of its volunteers had followed Allen to COR. They couldn't find a candidate. But COR was a fringe group, certain to lose, they told Parent. And the incumbent Liberal MLA, Jim Wilson, was vulnerable. They persuaded Parent that he could win.

The campaign persuaded him otherwise. "Even though Ed had been a defector, he still had a lot of respect," Parent says. "He could do no wrong." Now Parent was at his own campaign headquarters, on Maple Street, not far from Lynn Mason's home, watching the remnants of a once-powerful political organization straining to work its old magic. "It was obvious," Parent says, "that Ed was just invincible."

The Conservatives were fighting for survival, struggling to come back after losing every seat they'd had in the Legislature four years earlier. But as he waited out election day, Don Parent knew in his gut that Fredericton North was not coming home to the PC party.

* * *

For political volunteers, with so much to do in such a short time, the hours of election day pass in a flash. But for the men and women listed on the ballot, the day can feel like an eternity. The candidate must watch the minutes go by slowly, agonizing in the knowledge that, in polling stations across the riding, the collective judgment of the voters is taking shape, ballot by ballot. And the time in which it is possible to influence that judgment is draining away.

Election day 1991 was a particularly long day for Bob Simpson because he sensed he was losing.

Simpson spent part of the day visiting polling stations in York North, the sprawling riding he'd won for the Liberals in the famous 58–0 sweep of 1987. It ran from the village of Nackawic on the St. John River downstream to the farmlands of the Keswick Valley and the outskirts of Fredericton, then up the Nashwaak River to take in the village of Stanley, finally reaching the fabled Miramichi River in Boiestown.

Simpson had watched COR grow in York North and its message sink in with many of his constituents. "Everyone knew someone who couldn't get a job for this or that, and they'd fall back on the fact they weren't bilingual," says Simpson, who refused to pander to the sentiment. "I recognized the value of the government service being representative of the province's makeup. I didn't argue against it — I knew it was going to be a problem in my riding, but that's when principle meets pragmatism."

During the campaign, there had been media talk of a second straight Liberal sweep of all seats, a repeat of the historic 1987 win, but Simpson didn't believe it, especially when Premier McKenna made five visits to York North in the final week of the race. "I could tell by the way he was talking that he knew what was happening," Simpson says. The candidate knew, too, from his knocking on doors. "A lot of people were polite, but you could read into it that they were just being polite. Generally you'd get very few people who were nasty. But they did speak their minds. They would mention bilingualism, or jobs for their kids or, 'I've been told this' and 'I've been told that.' And when you left the door, you knew you didn't have their support."

Simpson's headquarters were near the COR campaign office on Main Street on Fredericton's north side, not far from where the ridings of York North and Fredericton North met. As the polls closed at eight p.m., he left the office in a gloomy mood to watch the results at his campaign manager's home.

* * *

The counting was starting as CBC's election night telecast went on the air. The pundits and the journalists talked briefly about COR, about whether this brand-new fringe party might possibly win a seat or two or, more likely, peel away votes from the Progressive Conservatives, threatening the PC comeback and allowing the Liberals to win big, perhaps giving them that second sweep.

The first result flashed on the screen at 8:07. In Carleton South, one of the most reliably Conservative ridings in New Brunswick, Liberal Bruce Smith was ahead of the Tory candidate, six votes to three. Moments later, Albert County, another Conservative fortress, reported a Liberal lead. Then, a glimmer of hope for the PCs: in the Tory heartland district of Kings East, Hazen (Hank) Myers — a former MLA and cabinet minister — was ahead. So was Mary Hatfield, niece of the late Tory premier Richard Hatfield, in his old riding of Carleton Centre.

As the trickle of numbers grew into a flood, the Liberals rapidly piled up leads across New Brunswick — ahead in seven seats, then a dozen, then twenty-four — but the Conservatives were leading in three, and it appeared the voters had chosen to restore the balance of the traditional two-party rivalry they'd known for a century.

Then a new colour popped onto the bottom of the screen — green, the colour of the COR party. It was leading in one riding, and that riding was Petitcodiac, where the Conservative leader, Dennis Cochrane, was trying to win a seat in the Legislature. A closer look showed COR running second to the Liberals in many other races.

Lynn Mason was watching the telecast at COR headquarters. His scrutineers were reporting back to him with good news that hadn't yet reached the CBC computers: Ed Allen was taking poll after poll after poll in Fredericton North. "We knew we were going to take seats," he says. "It really wasn't a sixth sense — you just knew. It was quite a feeling of satisfaction."

* * *

At 8:29, Dennis Cochrane was still trailing the COR candidate, Leona Geldart, in Petitcodiac. Cochrane, a polite, earnest school teacher, had taken over the PC leadership just two months before the election was called. He'd spurned previous invitations to seek the post, but this year, with the party shut out of the Legislature and still weak, he'd agreed to serve for one year — long enough to steer the party through the campaign and give it the Official Opposition status that it needed to begin a true rebuilding.

Now, though Cochrane himself was behind, it appeared on TV that his efforts for the party were succeeding:

Liberal 31   PC 5   COR 2

Under the rules of New Brunswick's Legislative Assembly, a party with five MLAs is officially recognized, meaning it gains extra funding, offices and staff, plus the right to participate in Question Period and name members to legislative committees. If the Tory results — five ridings and the second-highest number of seats — held, the party would form the Official Opposition.

Then the numbers changed again:

Liberal 32   PC 5   COR 4

"I think the Conservatives would like to stop the election right now if they could," Dalton Camp chuckled in the CBC election studio. He was right. At 8:35, the Tory claim to Official Opposition status was no longer clear:

Liberal 34   PC 5   COR 5

"COR is moving," announced CBC journalist Robert Jones, who was watching the trends developing and had noticed COR racking up an astonishing forty-one per cent of the popular vote in ten ridings around Fredericton. "They're moving in central New Brunswick, and it looks like they may have their breakthrough tonight."

More cascading numbers reveal the unthinkable:

Liberal 35   COR 6   PC 5

Races were tight and leads were changing all over the province: Cochrane was now ahead by eight votes, but Albert County had moved into the COR column by eleven. The standings were updated again:

Liberal 42   COR 8   PC 4

"We had a very tense evening in Moncton," says Brad Green, who worked as Cochrane's campaign manager. "It was clear we were going to have a significant challenge to win back the people who had voted COR."

For anglophone Conservatives like Green, COR's success represented a strategic problem. But on that election night, it represented something considerably more for francophones of any political stripe.

COR's rapid ascent was casting a shadow over Liberal triumphs in Acadian ridings like Shediac-Cap Pelé, where the government's star candidate, Bernard Richard, was cruising to an easy win. Richard had worked for the Société des Acadiens du Nouveau-Brunswick, and he'd been a passionate activist for francophone rights, including official bilingualism, all his life. As a young social democrat, he'd run for the left-wing Parti Acadien in 1974, but eventually he'd joined the Liberal Party, accepting the view that the mainstream parties were "big tents," where various interests could be brokered into a coalition that could bid for power, and where people like him could advance their goals in a spirit of tolerance and moderation.

Now, suddenly, COR was making a mockery of that notion. The backlash against bilingualism was coming into its own, and English New Brunswick was opting out of the "big tent." The sentiment "had been around forever," Richard says, "and you'd shake your head and say it's a small minority and it doesn't represent a lot of people."

But the numbers on the screen showed that it did:

Liberal 42   COR 9   PC 3

Ed Allen was leading in Fredericton North, and COR's leader, Arch Pafford was leading in Miramichi Newcastle. But unknown candidates were doing well, too, like Ab Rector in Oromocto-Gagetown and Bev Brine in Albert. "COR has an issue that nobody else wants," Dalton Camp commented, "and as long as it perturbs people and concerns people, there will always be a COR. Whether or not you can convert COR into some sustaining, ongoing force, such as the traditional parties — that's the challenge for COR."

At 9:24, the Liberals hit a new high for the night and the Tories plummeted to a new low:

Liberal 50   COR 6   PC 1   NDP 1

And then, as if to drive the point home, the CBC declared Greg Hargrove elected in York North — the first COR candidate to win a seat in the Legislature.

Bob Simpson left his campaign manager's home and headed to Hargrove's headquarters, also on Main Street in Fredericton North. "Congratulations and good campaign," Simpson told the winner as the COR campaign workers celebrated. "I was happy for them," Hargrove remembers now. "A lot of them took abuse, and I was happy that they got to rub a little nose."

A minute later, the COR band of volunteers down the street, among them Lynn Mason, erupted into cheers as well: Ed Allen was declared elected in Fredericton North. "He felt vindicated," says Allen's son Mike. Blown out in the Liberal sweep of 1987, Allen had ruminated about whether the voters were punishing him or the Hatfield government that he, too, had come to disdain. Now he had the answer: they wanted him to be their MLA again, and it didn't hurt that he'd tapped into their resentment about bilingualism.

In another part of the riding, though, Ed Allen's stock was dropping fast. "As a francophone in Fredericton, I felt kind of small," says Paul-Émile Thériault, a civil servant in the provincial tourism department who'd worked on Allen's Conservative campaigns. "It was disappointing to see that people in the community would elect someone like that. I wanted to vomit. All those years he played the game — he got a good job in government as a minister — and then he turned around and spit on us." Francophones in the capital began to wonder whether their neighbours and colleagues had voted for a party that wanted to repeal their rights. "You didn't know who to talk to anymore," Thériault says.

* * *

It was all but certain that COR would form the Official Opposition. "We are seeing the last days of the Conservative party in this province," said Don Desserud, a political science professor, on the CBC election broadcast. In Kings East, Hank Myers, maintaining his slim lead for the Tories, realized that his party had suffered a terrible blow. "It was severely damaged," he says. At his home near Moncton, Dennis Cochrane knew the other party leaders would soon head to their headquarters to deliver their speeches. But Cochrane felt paralyzed. "I didn't know what to say," he recalls. "I didn't know if I had my own seat at that point."

At 10:07, the CBC cameras — and the attention of the province — shifted to the rec center in Nordin, where Arch Pafford, the COR leader and architect of the day's surprising results, stepped onto a small stage. Party volunteers serenaded him with "For He's a Jolly Good Fellow" as he reached the microphone.

"We can be very, very proud of the results tonight," Pafford said. "The pollsters weren't that accurate, and the political pundits said we'd only end up with one seat at the most. But we've made an impact on politics in this province. . . . The COR party is here for a long, long time. Look at where we've come from in two short years — and we're just getting started."

Across the river in Chatham, the Liberal premier, Frank McKenna, was also moving to the stage. The night should have belonged to him — he'd scored a second landslide victory for his party — but the implications of COR's insurgency had blackened his mood. Two of his advisors, Steven MacKinnon and Maurice Robichaud, had hastily reworked the premier's victory speech, deciding it needed to reiterate emphatically the Liberal commitment to bilingualism. "New Brunswickers have voted massively for a province where all citizens are equal, French or English, north or south, wherever they may live," McKenna told the hundreds of Liberal workers. "Equality for all New Brunswickers is here to stay. We will not retreat."

Leaving the podium, McKenna donned a headset for an interview with the CBC, in which he brushed off questions about COR. "Most areas of New Brunswick went overwhelmingly Liberal," he said. "It strikes me that an intelligent analyst would say there's overwhelming support for the policies of the government rather than for a small minority of voters. If this was a referendum on language, the results are rather clear." As McKenna spoke, a party worker could be seen moving behind him to the large board listing all fifty-eight ridings; on it, Liberal wins had been colour-coded with large red panels affixed to the names. The worker pulled down the red panel from the row marked "Riverview."

During the interview, the CBC decision desk had reversed an earlier call awarding Riverview to Liberal incumbent Hubert Seamans. The very last poll to report had tipped it back to COR's Gorden Willden, giving the upstart party its fifth officially elected MLA — and status as the Official Opposition. It was heartbreaking for Seamans, whose 1985 by-election victory for the Liberals in the Tory fortress of Riverview had heralded the disintegration of the Hatfield government. He'd become minister of municipal affairs in the Liberal government. McKenna had warned him that COR was targeting Riverview, but Seamans had assumed the vote split would save him. "I was embarrassed to lose to the COR party," he'd remember. "I just felt they were people playing to peoples' darker side. It wouldn't have hurt so badly to lose to the PCs in a PC town."

At the same moment it declared Seamans defeated, the CBC also declared Cochrane elected in Petitcodiac, and the screen displayed the final party standings:

Liberal 46   COR 8   PC 3   NDP 1

In Fredericton North, Lynn Mason's day was winding down, and he was content. The voters had sent a message: twenty-one per cent of the electorate, or thirty per cent of English New Brunswick, had rejected the consensus on bilingualism the political establishment had put in place over the previous three decades. Policies designed to make francophones feel accepted were themselves unacceptable. "It was something to behold," Mason says. "It was a message being sent out by a third of the population that they just did not like the status quo."

Northeast of Fredericton, in a small Acadian fishing village perched where the mouth of the Miramichi River meets the Northumberland Strait, Jocelyne Durelle was watching the COR results, too, and understood the message.

Baie-Sainte-Anne was French-speaking, but its people shopped, worked and dealt with their provincial government in the Miramichi River towns of Chatham and Newcastle, where Arch Pafford had plotted the rise of the COR party and come so close to winning a seat in the Legislature himself.

Durelle, a government worker, was familiar with the hostility that COR was trading on. "I can't say it surprised me," she says. "We felt it. I worked in Newcastle, so I heard it when I'd answer the phone in both languages and they'd say, 'Speak white.'" In 1985, her three-year-old daughter had been transported by ambulance to hospital in Moncton with a possible case of meningitis. Durelle had not been allowed to ride in the ambulance, and the unilingual English-speaking ambulance attendants had not been able to communicate with the terrified unilingual French-speaking child for the entire ninety-minute trip. Afterward, Durelle had written a passionate plea for more services in French to a government committee studying bilingualism. But when she showed up at the committee's hearings in Chatham to present her brief, she'd felt a wave of resentment in the room. Now, that same resentment had elected eight MLAs whose sole mission was to strip away the language rights she already had. "You think you're accepted," Durelle says, "and then you're not sure anymore."

* * *

Dennis Cochrane appeared at his headquarters shortly before eleven p.m., just in time to speak to the CBC before its election show went off the air. All the questions were about COR. "They had one line that people bought," Cochrane said. "They didn't have much else on offer, but certainly I can't criticize the people who supported any other political party. What we've got to do as Conservatives is work to create a party that more people will support in the future."

Cochrane said this as if it was the most obvious, simple proposition in the world. But there was no easy path for the Progressive Conservative Party of New Brunswick to follow after election day. COR had earned twenty-one per cent of the vote, eclipsing, remarkably, the Conservatives' support. The PC popular vote had actually dropped below its low point in the wipeout of 1987. It was a dramatic illustration of the stark division in the party's long-time anglophone voting base.

Richard Hatfield, as premier, had sought for seventeen years to broaden that base, to transform it into a coalition that included French-speaking New Brunswickers. Now the coalition was shattered. Thousands of English voters had signalled that they wanted no part of Hatfield's vision. The only consolation among Hatfield's most ardent admirers was that the former premier had died in April and hadn't been forced to see this.

New Brunswick's Tories thought they'd hit bottom in 1987. But in 1991, a return to power and to the grand coalition building of the Hatfield days seemed farther away than ever. As they pondered their bitter defeat, they asked themselves two questions: How could this have happened? What would their party do to recover?

Part One

A NEW PARTY

Richard Hatfield receives a Valentine — a petition signed by francophone Conservatives supporting his leadership — from MLA Percy Mockler in February 1985. COURTESY OF PERCY MOCKLER

Chapter One

JIM PICKETT LIGHTS A MATCH

AS THE TRAVELER GLIDES OFF the Trans-Canada Highway and downhill to Perth-Andover, the noise and speed of the outside world give way to the soothing scene of the St. John River flowing serenely south. The little village that occupies the flat land on both banks is as quiet and calm as the current itself. At the bridge, drivers ease to a halt to yield the right-of-way to a neighbour or friend waiting to turn onto the narrow iron span.

Occasionally, when thick ice jams the river, or heavy snowfalls lead to large spring freshets, the water swells over its banks and spills into Perth-Andover's streets. Then the residents, as is their custom, press themselves into service to help each other out.

Tumult and upheaval are otherwise rare here. But late in the day of May 6, 1985, something was stirring.

Spring had come to Victoria County, but the air was cool, and there were occasional rain showers as Jim Pickett drove through the centre of town and out onto the highway. He accelerated north, ascending across the slender tail of the great spine of the Appalachian mountains, extending across the border from Maine. It would take Pickett less than half an hour to reach the New Denmark Recreation Centre, where the Victoria-Tobique Progressive Conservative riding association was holding its annual meeting in classic St. John River Valley style: a potluck supper, followed by some political speeches, then the business meeting itself.

As Pickett ascended the Four Falls hill and the great stone shape of St. Patrick's Roman Catholic Church came into view, the man in the passenger seat spoke up. "Jim Pickett," he said, "I understand you are up to something."

Pickett glanced over at his passenger and wasn't sure how much to say. It was true, he *was* up to something. But it might be awkward explaining his plans for the evening to the man in the passenger seat. Stewart Brooks, after all, had represented the riding of Victoria-Tobique as a Progressive Conservative member of the Legislative Assembly for more than two decades — from 1952, when he was part of Hugh John Flemming's surprise victory, through the Liberal 1960s, to 1976, when he retired from politics and was replaced in a by-election.

Pickett hadn't been much of a political person before Brooks came to his door to ask him to manage his final campaign in 1974. Pickett's father and uncle had attended the occasional meeting, and in the 1920s his grandfather had been an MLA for the United Farmers, a protest party that briefly appeared on and then vanished from the New Brunswick political scene. Maybe that was where Pickett got his rebellious streak: most valley people were deferential to their politicians to the point of being almost free of cynicism. "When I was growing up," Pickett explains, "when Hugh John Flemming's name came up at the dinner table, or Stewart Brooks or [federal MP] Fred McCain, there was no laughing or making fun or calling people jokers. This was politics. These people were respectable people."

Now Pickett had lost respect for the politician who mattered the most — to himself, to Brooks, who shared his feelings, and to the man in the back seat, a local road contractor named Bob Birmingham, who was known to land the occasional government highway job.

"All I'll tell you, Pickett," Brooks said, "is if Richard Hatfield gets a chance to respond, he will destroy you."

It was the last thing Pickett wanted to hear. He'd been agonizing for weeks over what he was going to do tonight. "Everybody wanted to do it," he says today, "but no one would do it. Most of them had government jobs. It was a personal thing. No one knew I was going to do it. I was planning it for about two weeks."

He had sat at his kitchen table, going over his list of insurance clients. "I tried to fathom if there was any way Richard Hatfield could destroy my insurance practice if I did this," he says. "I said, 'What is going to happen to my Tory clients?'" And so Jim Pickett pondered. The political climate in the PC party was hot and dry, and he proposed to light a match.

But what choice did he have? His premier — his leader — was spiralling out of control. Richard Hatfield had been charged with possession of marijuana the previous autumn, accused of carrying some weed in his bag during the visit of Queen Elizabeth to New Brunswick. No sooner had the premier recovered from that than two St. Thomas University students had accused him of using the government plane to ferry them to Montreal and supplying them with cocaine at his Fredericton home. The last straw had been an interview with Hatfield on CBC Radio following the premier's courtesy call to a US-based anti-drug caravan that had stopped in Fredericton. As Pickett recalls it today, when the reporter asked Hatfield why he had decided to visit the activists, he replied that he didn't know — that he had been told by advisors to be there.

Once Pickett had admired Richard Hatfield. "He seemed pretty astute. He knew how to get people to work. He had representation on every country road in the province. He was determined to get support from every person in the province, and he did a pretty good job of it." Lately, though, doubt had been setting in. It had started with Hatfield's initiative to expand the language rights of New Brunswick's French-speaking Acadians, who made up about a third of the province's population. The premier had given legal force to sections of the Official Languages Act that had not been implemented since the legislation became law in 1969.

"A lot of people didn't like it," Pickett says now. "I'm from Andover, and Andover's pretty English. In a year I wouldn't hear a word of French at church or at the bank. I understood what Hatfield was trying to do. I wasn't all that impressed with it, but that was the way the world was turning." Yet the premier seemed to be losing touch with the opinions of people like Pickett or another Tory member from the riding, Kevin Jensen. "French and English have lived in harmony and wouldn't do too badly if politicians would leave them alone," Jensen would say.

But Richard Hatfield wouldn't leave the language issue alone. He had recently commissioned a study, *Towards Equality of Official*

Languages in New Brunswick — better known as the Poirier-Bastarache report — that was now the subject of public hearings around the province. The report's recommendation of a dramatic expansion of the francophone presence within the civil service was threatening the old Tory view of English New Brunswick. And there was the absurd and expensive notion of requiring every last city, town and village — even overwhelmingly anglophone ones — to provide bilingual services. And so at the very moment the drug scandals exploded into the public consciousness, old-stock party members felt unsettled about their leader. Unsettled, yet unwilling or unable — precisely because of their conservative nature — to rock the boat.

Only if someone forced the issue might things change.

Pickett turned right at St. Patrick's and followed the Limestone Siding road back down into the valley of the St. John River, crossing a one-lane bridge, then hurrying along a country road toward New Denmark. The meeting was on the ground floor of the recreation centre, in a hall wider than it was long. The room was full that night. Pickett remembers it as "a real feast. It's a real opportunity when these farm families bring their potlucks."

The riding of Victoria-Tobique is English-speaking, except for some francophones along its northern edges, on the boundary with Grand Falls. That bilingual town is where the English Protestants of the St. John River Valley give way to the French Catholics of Madawaska County. New Denmark itself had started as a settlement of Danish immigrants, encouraged to move into the area to act as a buffer between the two groups. So it was an appropriate setting for an event that would set in motion a struggle within the Progressive Conservative party that was, at its core, a showdown over language.

As the Tories tucked into their meals, Pickett was still wavering on whether he would go ahead with his plans. He had lined up Kevin Jensen, a local farmer, to play a role in the drama that was about to unfold. But Jensen hadn't arrived yet. Pickett ducked out to find Jensen still at his farm down the road, finishing up some work in the field. He eventually arrived at the hall as the meal was wrapping up and the assembled Tories were preparing to move to the business meeting proper. But as Jensen entered the room, he was intercepted by three Tories, each with a vested interest in scuttling Pickett's plan.

There was Bob Birmingham, the beneficiary of government highway contracts, who had travelled up from Perth-Andover with Pickett and had gleaned a little of what was coming. There was Bernard DeMerchant — "a big-time Tory," as Jensen puts it — with strong connections to the party brass in Fredericton. And there was Mac Macleod, the universally respected MLA from Albert County and minister of agriculture in Hatfield's cabinet. "They sort of moved me into the corner and said, 'You can't do this,'" Jensen recalls. "They said, 'Nobody wants this to be done.' They put the push on. They tried to make it look like I was the only guy in the world who wanted to do this and it would be a terrible thing."

Jensen was unable to resist the strong-arm tactics of the three big Tories. "I told them I wasn't going to do it." Jim Pickett's carefully scripted drama was in trouble.

The meeting got rolling with preliminary remarks and routine business. As it proceeded, there was a bustle of activity back at the door. Tories glanced over to see Jean-Maurice Simard sweep into the room. Simard was Hatfield's French lieutenant, the premier's most trusted ally in the effort to win Acadian votes and one of the most powerful ministers in the PC government. "When he walked in, and he walked up along the wall to the front where Hatfield was sitting," Pickett says, still astonished eighteen years later, "there were 150 people sitting there, and they all started to boo. They *roared*."

These were Tories, loyal Tories, long-time Tories, jeering a fellow Tory. An *important* Tory.

A few days earlier, these English-speaking Progressive Conservatives of Victoria-Tobique had driven a half-hour upriver to Saint-Léonard, a French-speaking town in Madawaska County, to attend a federal PC meeting. Saint-Léonard was in a different provincial riding, but it was part of the same large federal constituency of Madawaska-Victoria as Perth-Andover and New Denmark. Simard, as the most prominent provincial Conservative in the federal riding, had addressed the crowd of mostly bilingual francophones and unilingual anglophones.

"He spoke well over an hour, and he never uttered a single word in English," Jim Pickett says. "We weren't very impressed with that."

Simard was hardly the kind of Tory the members in Victoria-Tobique were used to. Passionate, moody and stubborn, he had a shock of thick black hair and large, bushy eyebrows that gave him the appearance of an owl as he watched over the language issue from his perch in Fredericton. Simard was known to be from Quebec, and his temperament and his fiery speaking style were more suited to the personality-driven politics of his home province. His French-only speech in Saint-Léonard reinforced the mistrust many anglophone Tories felt toward him. "They didn't like him," Pickett says. "He seemed to be running the Hatfield government. It seemed like Hatfield was giving him free rein." So when the provincial riding executive in Victoria-Tobique scheduled their annual meeting for English-speaking New Denmark, they opted not to invite him.

Now, in typically brazen fashion, Simard had shown up anyway. For Jim Pickett and his plan, which had come so close to being de-railed by Macleod, DeMerchant and Birmingham, Simard's appear-ance was fortuitous. Simard was a polarizing figure in the PC party, and he polarized everyone in the room to Jim Pickett's side. "If Simard had not come there that night," Pickett says, "this thing would not have happened."

As Hatfield addressed the crowd, Pickett settled into a seat about two-thirds of the way toward the back of the room. He took an envelope from his pocket, placed it on his knee and began jotting down notes as the premier spoke. He saw Jensen, standing near the back of the hall. When the premier finished, Pickett leapt to his feet, abandoning his plan for Jensen to make the first move, unaware that his farmer friend had chickened out anyway.

"I was pretty involved with myself," Pickett admits. "I felt pretty confident I could say something. I wasn't going to let it not hap-pen." The chairman of the meeting acknowledged Pickett, and the premier turned his attention to the insurance agent.

Pickett glanced down at his notes and took a breath. What he was about to do had been done several times before in political parties, but only when they had been in opposition, when there was an ar-gument to be made that the party leader could not win. No one had yet attempted it against a leader with a track record of success, in a party in the midst of governing. But Jim Pickett looked up at Richard Hatfield. Then in his fifteenth year in power, on track to become New Brunswick's longest-serving premier, Hatfield had led the Tories to four consecutive majority governments and scored unprecedented victories for the party in French-speaking New Brunswick.

Jim Pickett told the chairman that he wished to move a resolution: that the Victoria-Tobique riding association request that the provincial PC party, at its next annual meeting, review the leadership of Richard Hatfield so as to remove him as leader and as premier of New Brunswick.

* * *

Revolution was in the air that spring in New Brunswick, even among those who seemed the very antithesis of revolutionaries.

Bev Harrison was the MLA for Saint John Fundy. A Newfoundlander and a monarchist, he felt a kinship with his Loyalist constituents; descendants of the colonists who had opposed the American Revolution out of devotion to the King, they had fled to the safety of British North America. Harrison also rejected the "rights revolution" of Pierre Elliot Trudeau — the 1982 patriation of the Constitution and the creation of the Charter of Rights and Freedoms, which protected linguistic minorities in Canada, including New Brunswick Acadians.

More recently, Harrison had been fighting revolution in the government civil service. The Poirier-Bastarache report, which had so angered the Tories in Victoria-Tobique, had alarmed Harrison as well. Its stated goal of increasing the number of Acadians holding government jobs seemed to break the unwritten understanding that had been reached with English New Brunswick: make your children bilingual through French immersion, and they will be able to get jobs in the public service. But hiring bilingual anglophones, capable of serving both language groups, didn't satisfy Poirier-Bastarache.

"This report is saying you must hire Acadians. For me to be bilingual, my promotional possibilities would be stifled," Harrison had told the Saint John *Telegraph-Journal* the previous December, when the report was just beginning to stir controversy. "Because there's a period of time when you must have affirmative action for Acadians. You've got to get the percentage up. And to do that, you've got to slow down the anglophone promotions to zero."

Yes, Harrison opposed revolutions. Yet he himself was now bringing one right into the Conservative caucus.

For Harrison was the chairman of caucus, the man whose job it was to strive for unity among MLAs. Instead, he was stoking conflict. Like other Tories, his concerns about Hatfield had begun with Poirier-Bastarache and were now inflamed by the premier's personal scandals. Both ran counter to — and seemed to outright offend — the prim, proper conservative way of seeing the world that had prevailed in the PC party before Richard Hatfield came along.

The same night Pickett stood up and called for Hatfield's ouster to the premier's face, Bev Harrison rose to speak to the PC riding association in his constituency of Saint John Fundy.

He pointed to the party's defeat in a by-election in Riverview the week before, a defeat many blamed on the premier's drug scandals, but also one that had unfolded in a traditionally Conservative riding where hostility to Poirier-Bastarache was high. Harrison "was very forceful," remembers Hank Myers, the MLA for the adjacent riding of Kings East. "He was very serious. He said the premier was bringing disgrace to the party — to the effect that if the premier cared about the party, he would resign."

A stunned silence fell over the room. Bev Harrison, the very image of the loyal British gentleman, was starting a revolution against Richard Hatfield.

* * *

That same night, a hundred miles east, Irène Guerette, a francophone from Saint John, was taking a breather from the grim task of studying the divisions in New Brunswick society.

Guerette co-chaired the committee studying the object of Bev Harrison's contempt, the Poirier-Bastarache report. After spending the fall at information sessions designed to spread the word about the report's contents, the committee was now soliciting feedback from citizens on the merits of the recommendations.

Irène Guerette was losing her faith in the ability of French and English to live in harmony in New Brunswick.

The committee was on friendly ground on the night of May 6. At the hearing in Bouctouche, a mostly francophone town in coastal Kent County, people reacted well to the recommendations. But within days, the committee would move on to Moncton, historically a crucible of English-French tension. Guerette had been reading some of the briefs submitted in advance.

"Destroying a province to satisfy a few Acadian fanatics is next to a sin," wrote Mrs. Fern Hutt of Moncton in a typical letter. "My French friends and neighbours were beautiful all those years ago. Today I feel differently towards them, and I blame these changed feelings on this very stupid, unnecessary and unwarranted Poirier-Bastarache report."

Mrs. Hutt was not unusual in claiming anglophones and francophones got along much better back in the days when there were no French-language schools, courts or government offices — or rights. Such letter-writers claimed to be open and welcoming to Acadians, except when their demands became unreasonable. But the prevailing definition of "reasonable" seemed to harken back to the nineteenth century. Many letters urged not only trashing the Poirier-Bastarache report but also repealing the 1969 Official Languages Act that had first guaranteed rights to the Acadian minority.

And there were more sinister missives.

"Mr. Porior [sic], you asked to hear from the silent majority, well here is one and no doubt you will hear from the majority," said one anonymous letter. "You and Bastarache have really started something that is going to take years to die down. People are going to get violent. You, Bastarache, Simard and Hatfield should head for Quebec where you will be safe. Most English speaking people would like to speak several languages but they don't like French rammed down their throats, which only brings on hatred, call it off before it is to late. There could be bloodshed."

More revealing of the depth of the problem facing Richard Hatfield and his beloved Progressive Conservative party were comments like those of T. Majensky. "I've voted Conservative for the last time," he wrote on a comment card he had filled out at an information session the previous autumn. Majensky lived in River-view, a once-safe Tory riding where Hatfield's candidate had just lost a by-election to the Liberal. No one doubted that Poirier-Bastarache had helped drive the Tories of Riverview to vote against their own party.

The PC base in New Brunswick was in revolt. Kathryn Barnes, president of the Moncton North provincial PC association — and one of Hatfield's candidates in the 1982 election — wrote in her brief to the committee that the report was "frightening" and "certainly not in the best interest of the majority of this province." She questioned the need for bilingual judges and suggested throwing the whole issue to a referendum, where, of course, anglophones would have two-thirds of the vote. "After all, is that not what democracy is all about — the wishes of the majority?"

The dissent reached right into Richard Hatfield's cabinet. In early April, his minister of social services, Nancy Clark Teed, had said publicly that she would resign if Poirier-Bastarache were implemented. "It is hard to believe that supposedly sincere and democratic-minded people wrote this strident, divisive and false impression of both French and English-speaking New Brunswickers," she had told Guerette's committee. Later that month, Clark Teed's Conservative cabinet colleague, Fisheries Minister Jean Gauvin, forcefully and publicly rebutted her arguments, mocking her assertion that English and French had got along fine until the notion of language rights had ruined everything. "We Acadians know what must be done to preserve 'harmony,' 'understanding' and 'friendship,'" Gauvin said sarcastically. "To maintain these values, we need merely bow our heads, be submissive and above all, of course, speak English. Those, very often, are the only conditions necessary to preserve this sentimental climate. I refuse to accept such a myopic perspective."

Such a public split between two cabinet ministers could only mean one thing: Richard Hatfield's government was breaking apart along language lines.

Members of the anglophone wing of the party, like fellow MLAs Keith Dow and Eric Kipping, would soon join Harrison in declaring openly that Hatfield had to go. Others would scheme in the shadows, never revealing their part of the plot. Meanwhile, francophones, determined to hang on to the influence Hatfield had given them, would muster their forces to strike back. They would deploy their considerable organizational talents — the ability to sell memberships, pack meeting rooms and, above all, motivate people — not to defeat Liberals but to beat back their fellow Conservatives. And they would do it because they loved the most hated man in English New Brunswick.

"This is the francophone culture," explains Percy Mockler, who, along with Gauvin and other francophone MLAs, would sit on a secret "Save Hatfield" committee once the review fight was on. "They're very respectful. They're very loyal after you've demonstrated that you're one of them. Richard Hatfield had become one of us."

* * *

Hatfield sat at the front of the hall in the New Denmark Recreation Centre and watched Jim Pickett call for a leadership review. After Pickett sat down, the premier turned to look at the chairman, who had just been elected that night and had never run a meeting before. The nuances of procedure were unknown to the young man, who froze, unsure what to do. There was a stunned silence in the hall as Tories waited to see what would happen next.

Jim Pickett remembers it clearly: "Hatfield looked up to the young man and said, 'Put the motion on the floor.' So he said, 'All those in favour,' and my God, there was a big roar. And he said 'Any against,' and there wasn't a peep.'"

Pickett's fears about revenge would prove unfounded; he did not lose a single one of his Tory insurance clients for having moved against the premier. Instead, people congratulated him when they ran into him in Perth-Andover because, in the days that followed, Jim Pickett became a well-known person in New Brunswick. Journalists connected his motion and Harrison's statement, both coming on the same night, and see evidence of a growing problem for Richard Hatfield. There was no conspiracy at first, but Pickett and Harrison would eventually join forces to build an organization with the sole objective of driving Hatfield from office.

The drug scandals had broken only the loyalties that had already been frayed by Hatfield's language initiatives. Over the summer and leading into the Saint John convention, the most vociferous advocates of review would be MLAs like Bev Harrison and Keith Dow, vocal opponents of Poirier-Bastarache. And the premier's strongest defenders would be the Acadian MLAs who had joined his government because of his embrace of French New Brunswick.

"It was easy to implicate these other issues," Keith Dow says today. "An English-French split, a Protestant-Catholic split, a cultural split. There's a certain validity to that. There's a certain veracity."

Richard Hatfield's dream of a grand coalition within his cherished Conservative party was coming apart at the seams.

Chapter Two

THE ACADIAN VOTE

RICHARD HATFIELD once reportedly told a small group of people that, until he was twenty, he thought that Acadia was simply a university located in Wolfville, Nova Scotia.

The story rings true; by what means *would* a young Richard Hatfield have learned the story of the Acadians, the first French settlers in North America, caught between two great eighteenth-century powers in a struggle for control of a continent? The tale of their violent expulsion from fertile lands in Nova Scotia and what is now New Brunswick would not have been part of the daily discourse in the village of Hartland, where Hatfield was born on April 9, 1931.

Hartland sits along one of the great bends of the St. John River, at the very centre of Carleton County. Covered in rich soil, dotted with solidly built white churches and swathed in the gleaming ribbon of the river, Carleton County was a pillar of Conservatism in New Brunswick — English and Protestant to the core. When Hatfield was born, it had already produced one Tory premier, James Kidd Flemming, and it would soon produce another — Flemming's son, Hugh John, who in 1952 would end seventeen years of Liberal rule in Fredericton.

Hatfield's father, Heber, who ran a potato chip company and was a federal Member of Parliament, named his son Richard Bennett to honour R.B. Bennett, the only New Brunswicker to become Prime Minister of Canada — albeit after moving to Calgary to live his adult life and build his fortune. One of young Richard's earliest political memories was of meeting Bennett in July 1938, at the federal Conservative convention in Winnipeg, where the former prime minister handed over the party leadership to his successor.

It was a memorable moment for seven-year-old Richard, but another encounter left a more profound impression on him and probably contributed far more to the future premier's eventual political legacy.

He would tell his biographers, Michel Cormier and Achille Michaud, of climbing down off the train in Ottawa, where he was accompanying his father to a sitting of the House of Commons, and meeting on the platform a shoeshine man and his young boy. It was like staring into some sort of cultural funhouse mirror, for here were Heber Hatfield, MP, and his son Richard face to face with a humble shoeshiner and his own son. In every way — bearing, attire, grooming — the Hatfields were clearly more affluent, more success-ful, more worldly. Yet young Richard would remember that both the shoeshine man and his child were francophones who nonetheless spoke English. How could it be, he would wonder, that this im-poverished French boy on the platform had mastered two languages while he, son of an MP and successful businessman, could speak only one?

Another Carleton County youth might not have wondered at all, but Hatfield was different. Eric Kipping, an acquaintance of Hat-field's in his student days at Acadia University, detected even then a personality not bound by the normal restraints of tradition but open to new experiences and different perspectives. "He was very broad-minded. You could see that his mind was ranging. He was very fair-minded."

The two tendencies in Richard Hatfield — openness of spirit and love of politics — began to converge in the late 1950s, in a way that would defy the expectations of the little village where he was born. Back in Hartland working for the family potato chip company, Hat-field travelled New Brunswick as a sales representative. On those long, circuitous journeys, he would meet Acadians, and naturally the talk would turn to politics. They would tell him that Hugh John Flemming's Conservative government was doing nothing for them. Hatfield, his political instincts already beginning to sharpen, would report back to his father's Tory friends that Acadians were practically crying out for attention from the Progressive Conservative party. But the power brokers assured Richard there was no point in reaching out: francophones didn't vote Tory and they never would.

That explanation wasn't enough for Richard Hatfield.

* * *

"There were demographic distinctions in the Conservative community," Dalton Camp wrote in *Gentlemen, Players and Politicians*, his memoir of his early years as a Tory strategist for Hugh John Flemming, Robert Stanfield and John Diefenbaker. "Few were Roman Catholics, fewer still were French-speaking." Yet this reality, like many other patterns in New Brunswick politics that seemed to date back to the distant past, had not always been true.

Once upon a time, as recently as the early decades of the twentieth century, Conservatives were often elected in predominantly francophone constituencies. In those days, Canada was young and its political parties were loosely organized mechanisms for state-building — exploiting the prerogatives of political power, particularly patronage, to build coalitions that bound the young federation together.

Thus, parties were the forum for political brokerage, with prime ministers and premiers trying to assemble caucuses from as broad a base as possible and drawing their cabinets from those caucuses. Regional ministers would seek consensus that would cut across geographic and cultural lines. The rewards of power — jobs and contracts for supporters, along with a general sense of belonging — added an incentive for accommodation among a variety of interests and communities, allowing them to overcome differences and fuse into a single, cohesive polity. "There is . . . no basis for the systemic exclusion of any group if its interests can be incorporated into the definition of politics used by the party," David Smith wrote in "Canadian Political Parties and National Integration." "Numbers, not principle, are the currency of electoral politics."

In New Brunswick, the effort at accommodation focused on one line above all others. That line ran diagonally from Grand Falls in the northwest through the centre of the province to Moncton in the southeast. Above it, generally, lived francophone, Catholic Acadians, who made up one-quarter of the population by 1912; below it lived the anglophone Protestants, dominant in numbers, wealth and power. (Important exceptions to this diagonal divide, like the Irish of Miramichi or the non-Acadian French-speakers of Madawaska, only proved the rule.) The English in the south, by backing a single party, could elect a government on their own, while francophones could not. A party that could draw on a base of support among both groups — above and below that diagonal line — would be more likely to hold power.

Yet it took decades for Acadians to realize that they could actually benefit from this raw political calculus, that parties might be willing to offer rewards in exchange for the key to power. Before the late 1800s, the focus of Acadian activism was the Catholic church, whose hierarchy included few francophones. The fight for an Acadian bishop at the end of the nineteenth century gave this impoverished, scattered people their first sense of political unity and eventually led to the creation of secular organizations to represent their interests. By 1884 their élites had gathered in two Acadian congresses to choose August 15, the Feast of the Assumption in the Catholic calendar, as their national day, and the French tricolour, with a star in the blue panel to represent Our Lady of the Assumption, as their flag.

Education was the battleground on which Acadians first confronted the established political order. They protested an 1871 provincial law requiring newly non-religious schools to use texts prescribed by the province — English texts, in other words. If French parents wanted a Catholic education for their children in their language, they would be forced to provide it outside the school and at their own expense. After the law sparked a riot in Caraquet in 1875, English Protestant voters responded by seeing to it that the province's only Acadian MP was defeated in the next election by an English-speaking Liberal. Even then, though, the impetus for brokerage was emerging: to avoid further bloodshed, factions in the provincial legislature struck a compromise that allowed priests who passed an examination to teach children — including some religious lessons in French after school. It was not equality, but it would have to do for decades.

Leading into the new century and up to the Great War, loose coalitions in the Legislature began to evolve into disciplined Liberal and Conservative party organizations — both of them excluding

Acadians from positions of power. Though the Conservatives were heavily influenced by Orangemen, and francophones leaned to the Liberals because of the federal leader, Wilfrid Laurier, Conservative candidates still had a fighting chance in some French areas. The Tories elected MLAs in solidly Acadian Kent County in 1908 and 1912, for example. But Robert Borden's introduction of conscription eroded that support. Many Acadians resisted the idea of taking up arms for the same British Crown that had deported their ancestors.

Into this moment of political opportunity stepped Pierre-Jean Veniot, a journalist and Liberal organizer from Bathurst, who may have been the first New Brunswick politician to glimpse the potential of mobilizing the Acadian vote. "Let's be proud to be Acadians," he once said. "The more frankly Acadian and French we are, the more the English will respect us." In advancing the cause of his people, Veniot would also bind their political allegiance to the Liberal Party for decades to come.

Veniot was born in Richibucto, Kent County, with the family name Vigneau. But when his father Étienne moved the family to Pictou, Nova Scotia, a Scottish school headmaster who couldn't get his tongue around the French spelling changed it to Veniot, and Pierre-Jean became Peter John. Educated in English, Veniot would lose his French completely, only to regain it as an adult when he returned to New Brunswick and got involved in journalism and politics. He was passed over for the party leadership in 1914 precisely because he was French, but the slight did nothing to dampen his enthusiasm for the Liberals — or for mixing his ambitions with the party's. He worked the Acadian ridings non-stop in the election campaign of 1917. In typically alarmist tones, the Fredericton *Gleaner* interpreted Veniot's message: "Now is the time to take control of the government, the English voters are away fighting the war, and if you vote the [Tory] Murray government out now, while you have a chance, the new government will be ours, and we can run the country to suit ourselves as they do in Quebec."

The ethnic divide resonated through the campaign. There were rumours in Acadian communities that returning soldiers and British immigrants would settle in French areas so as to dilute and assimilate francophones. The *Gleaner* responded by urging its readers to "remove forever the menace that has been threatening our government, our institutions and our people." Acadians, feeling under siege, voted *en masse* for the Liberals. By holding on to a few of its English seats, the Liberal party formed the government with twenty-seven members, while the Conservatives elected twenty-one.

Veniot, as public works minister, the second-most powerful man in the Liberal cabinet, moved quickly to exploit the sudden Acadian influence in the government. He went on a road-building spree in the north, improving the lot of isolated communities and, not coincidentally, cementing Liberal electoral gains. The road construction binge came under attack by the Conservative opposition, which naturally further solidified Liberal support in those areas. In 1920, francophones rewarded the Liberals by voting *en bloc* for them again. Combined as in 1917 with some English Liberal seats, this French support paved the way to victory in twenty-four ridings altogether, compared with fourteen for the Conservatives and six for the United Farmers.

Veniot, however, paid a price for establishing a new political cleavage in New Brunswick politics. In 1923, when Walter Foster resigned to enter federal politics, Veniot became the first Acadian to move into the premier's chair. The prospect of a French premier was more than English New Brunswick could accept. So when Veniot called an election in 1925, voters in the south rallied to the one instrument with which they could defeat him: the Conservative party. Anti-Catholic sentiment burst into the open, with Tories campaigning on the slogan, "A Vote for Veniot Is a Vote for the Pope of Rome."

It worked. On election day, the Liberals failed to elect a single MLA in English Protestant ridings — which made up a majority of the Legislature — and were reduced to eleven seats in only four counties: Gloucester, Kent, Madawaska and Victoria. In Woodstock, someone burned a cross in celebration, a vivid illustration of the hardening divide in New Brunswick politics. The Conservatives were the party of English Protestant power, while, as historian Arthur Doyle has noted, "After Veniot, the Liberal party in New Brunswick had an almost monolithic block of 'safe' Acadian seats — support the party usually found essential for electoral success."

The consequences for Acadians became clear three years later, in 1928, when Conservative Premier John Baxter set out to allow bilingual education, an entirely reasonable notion from the perspective of today but a radical step at that time. Baxter's Regulation 32 would have given local school boards the freedom to adopt bilingual education if they'd wished. But it soon fell victim to political reality: anglophone Tories could not accept any French in any schools, even if the school authorities themselves in francophone areas wanted it. Had the Tories of the day been a truly provincial party, Baxter might have been able to face down the revolt. But he had no real base of support in Acadian New Brunswick and only one francophone minister in his cabinet — hardly enough to champion the cause in the face of an English backlash. The premier retreated and scrapped his plan. Regulation 32 became a victim of the political divide in New Brunswick, a divide that would endure, with minor exceptions around the margins, for another six decades.

Numbers tell the story. From 1900 to 1960, the Tories elected forty-seven MLAs, the Liberals seventeen in the English Protestant St. John River Valley. In solidly Baptist Albert County, the Tories won five of six races between 1900 and 1925. (Five straight Liberal victories there from 1930 to 1948 have been attributed to Baxter's repeal of the Temperance Act, another modernizing move — like bilingual education — that showed that he was either brave or politically tone-deaf. Albert returned to the Conservative fold in 1952.) In contrast, in each of the largely francophone counties of Kent and Gloucester, the Liberals won eleven of thirteen seats from 1903 to 1960. Even in the Tory sweeps of 1952 and 1956, Kent and Gloucester remained solidly Liberal. Straddling this chasm were the counties of Sunbury, Queens and York, whose English voters tended to shift between Liberals and Tories and thus decided many elections.

So the Liberals dominated French New Brunswick — but paradoxically, French New Brunswick hardly dominated the Liberal party.

Francophones had a hard time making it into Conservative cabinets, there was only one French-speaking minister after each of the Tory wins in 1908, 1912, 1925 and 1930. They did not fare much better when they helped bring about Liberal majorities. There was one French-speaking minister in each of the Liberal cabinets of 1935 and 1939, two in that of 1940, and three in that of 1949 — paltry representation for a people whose votes formed the foundation of the party's success. Premier Dysart is reported to have once promised a campaign audience in Hartland that there would be no second Acadian minister in his cabinet if the Liberals were returned to power.

Given the chance through the middle of the century to correct francophone under-representation in the Legislature, Liberal premiers did nothing. When Dysart took office in 1935, English-dominated counties had fifty per cent of the population but fifty-eight per cent of the seats. French counties had twenty-three per cent of the population but only twenty-one per cent of seats, while counties with mixed populations were home to twenty-six per cent of New Brunswickers yet had only twenty-one per cent of the seats. Correcting this would have helped more Liberals get elected, yet Liberal premiers ignored the opportunity during the seventeen years they held office until 1952, a sign that the Liberals, though happy to get their votes, didn't necessarily want to give francophones more clout. Though francophones continued to vote Liberal along the lines established by Pierre-Jean Veniot, the notion of "Acadian power" was still a foreign concept.

So, as Premier Hugh John Flemming prepared to call an election in 1960 and coast to what everyone expected would be an easy third majority, the essential electoral math of New Brunswick remained unchanged: the English elected mostly Tories and the French elected almost exclusively Liberals.

It would be another decade before Richard Hatfield would set out to change that. First, there was one more grand Acadian-Liberal bargain to come.

* * *

More than forty years ago, surveying the province for his book *Politics in New Brunswick*, historian Hugh Thorburn wrote, almost in passing, "The dramatic election of 1960 is not covered — although I do not think it calls for any significant modifying of my conclusions."

History would prove him wrong. Louis J. Robichaud, the Liberal premier elected that year, unleashed a political and social revolution in New Brunswick that altered rural life — particularly Acadian life. He built institutions and legislative protections that moved French New Brunswick into the mainstream of political discourse. Acadians established a direct relationship with their government, unfiltered by English politicians and bureaucrats unable to relate to their concerns. Acadians' old élite networks, devoted to cultural survival, became more public, more political and more able to participate at the centre of power. "One man, Louis Robichaud, not always consciously and sometimes against his will, came to embody the aspirations and contradictions of a historical community," wrote sociologist Joseph-Yvon Thériault.

Robichaud was born in Saint-Antoine, a small Kent County village where his father ran a sawmill. Young Louis took to politics, keeping a scrapbook of political figures. At age twelve, he borrowed a friend's bicycle to pedal six miles to the next village, Notre-Dame, to hear Premier Dysart speak at a picnic. Louis showed an interest in the politics of the present, not of the past. There was little talk of Acadian history in the Robichaud home; they did not dwell on the Deportation.

Robichaud attended Laval University in Quebec and studied under Rev. Georges-Henri Lévesque, the dean of social sciences and a critic of the Catholic church's social conservatism. Lévesque was a reformer and an advocate of economic justice for the poor and the unemployed. It was in Quebec that Robichaud came to realize that Acadians had to be freed from the isolated, Catholic, subsistence life they had known. After graduating, he returned to New Brunswick.

In 1952, Robichaud became a lawyer and was asked to seek the Progressive Conservative nomination in Kent County. He chose instead to run for the Liberals and placed first among six candidates seeking the three seats in Kent under the old county system.

Robichaud's elevation to party leader six years later, at the age of thirty-three, seemed a bold move by the Liberals, given the party's reluctance to accord francophones real clout. In fact, the selection was coldly calculated: party power brokers saw Robichaud as a decent enough interim leader who would put up a fight against Flemming and lose, then make way for an English leader who could aim for power in 1964. But Robichaud was a formidable campaigner. More than any other party leader in the past, he threw himself into the contest, criss-crossing the province to attend countless nominating conventions even before the campaign began.

In 1917, Veniot had found conscription. Similarly, in 1960, Robichaud, another strong personality, found a compelling issue. Flemming was proposing to charge all New Brunswick families, rich or poor, a fifty-two-dollar hospital premium to cover rising health care costs. The premium ($338 in 2002 dollars) proved unpopular enough that a critical number of voters in English New Brunswick registered their protest by voting Liberal. The Tory vote in the south dropped six percentage points from where it had been four years earlier, enough to shift several marginal seats to the Liberals. Thirty-one Liberals were elected against only twenty-one Tories, and Robichaud became the first Acadian premier with a mandate to govern.

And govern he would, pressing forward in each of his three terms in office with a major reform that would cement his place in history.

In his first term, Robichaud responded to financial troubles at church-run colleges by consolidating publicly funded universities — including creating the French-language Université de Moncton. By graduating future generations of Acadian political and business leaders, the university became a self-perpetuating legacy.

In his second term, Robichaud broke the old repressive system of county governance that saw a starkly uneven distribution of local services, with wealthy areas availing themselves of good roads and schools while poorer areas — among them most francophone counties — suffered a lack of essential infrastructure. In Saint John County, home of the province's industrial base and much of its wealth, the county budget was $180.79 per capita. In Restigouche County, in the francophone north, far from the centre of power, it was only slightly more than one-tenth of Saint John's — $19.06. It was the kind of inequity Robichaud had determined to correct as a student at Laval, and he did so by centralizing the property tax system and busting the old political cliques and cabals in the county seats. This guaranteed at least an approximately just distribution of government funding for services. The tax reforms were opposed in the 1967 election by K.C. Irving, who deployed his media holdings and his wealth in an attempt to unseat the Liberals. Robichaud nonetheless hung on to his majority, now a caucus with a majority of francophones. The cabinet, too, was mostly French-speaking, which only deepened anglophone suspicion.

In his final mandate, Robichaud's centrepiece was a reform more overtly cultural, more explicitly designed for his own people: the Official Languages Act. The premier moved cautiously by proclaiming only some sections of the law, those allowing either French or English to be used in the Legislature, for example, or permitting a municipal council to choose to use either language or both. Despite his decision to defer more far-reaching and expensive sections, many considered the law radical. "Your senseless, degenerate and ruinous official language act is one of the worst evils anyone ever tried to perpetuate [sic] on the citizens of this province," a member of the Canadian Loyalist Society wrote to Robichaud.

The legislation passed unanimously, a historic moment for New Brunswick. But a sense of *fin de régime* was descending on the Liberals in the Assembly. In May 1969, the minister of municipal affairs and MLA for Edmundston, Fernand Nadeau, was convicted of tax evasion, but Robichaud, rather than drop him from cabinet, merely shuffled him into another job.

Other challenges began to mount, some from forces Robichaud had unleashed himself. Students at the Université de Moncton, politicized thanks to Robichaud's reforms, were now demanding he move even faster on their issues. They wanted Moncton's City Hall to adopt bilingualism, but their protests met with resistance from the mayor, Leonard Jones, whose name would become a synonym for linguistic intolerance in the community.

Moncton was becoming the crucible for English-French tension. A consolidation of school districts had left anglophones and francophones in the city served by a single district with a single board. Anglophones — or the growing number who no longer opposed French education outright — wanted bilingual schools because they hoped, reasonably, that their children would learn French from francophone classmates. But Acadian parents feared that exposing their children to English classmates day after day was a recipe for assimilation, so they began lobbying for their own schools. Robichaud resisted demands for a separate French board, fearing a precedent that would negate the point of his consolidation of local school authorities into larger regional boards. But his stance made him appear suddenly unsympathetic to Acadian needs.

Robichaud faced the same paradox when a network of community-based regional development agencies in northern New Brunswick evolved into explicitly nationalist organizations. The agencies had hired young field workers who adopted militant positions, putting them at odds with the premier, who felt they owed him gratitude, not grief. Robichaud responded by setting up a committee to look at abolishing the committees.

In the twilight of his years in power, Robichaud thus faced accusations of compromising and even misrepresenting the Acadian cause that he had spent a decade advancing. No one could claim, though, that political power was exclusively anglophone anymore. In fact, journalist Michel Cormier argued in 1999, while at work on a biography of Robichaud, that the premier's efforts may have prevented Acadian nationalism from descending into ethnic sectarianism by showing that "French power" could be deployed independently of, and differently from, nationalism. "Political power in New Brunswick after the 1960 election could no longer be conceived in the same way again," Cormier said at a 1999 symposium examining the Robichaud legacy. "From that point on it was shared, according to the calculus of election results, between the anglophone majority and the francophone minority, and no political leader could afford to ignore this new equation if he or she hoped to be elected."

Indeed, Robichaud had empowered his people to such an extent that they would soon feel confident enough to break their bonds to the party that had taken them for granted since 1917. They were becoming aware of themselves as a political force — and Richard Hatfield was taking note. In creating Acadian power, Robichaud set in motion a reshaping of New Brunswick's political dynamic that is still underway today.

In his lifetime, Robichaud was elevated to the status of icon, his name evoked across partisan lines by Liberals and Tories alike anxious to claim they were the true heirs to his legacy. But in 1970 the political realities were not so kind. Louis J. Robichaud was battered, exhausted and limping toward electoral defeat. "A change was inevitable," he told his biographer, Della Stanley. "I'd done too much for the Acadians and the English wanted a break."

Much to their surprise, they weren't going to get it from Richard Hatfield.

* * *

Frédéric Arsenault doesn't remember the exact date, but it was sometime after June 19, 1961, the day voters in Carleton went to the polls in a by-election to choose a replacement for defeated premier Hugh John Flemming. Arsenault, an Acadian from Mont-Carmel, Prince Edward Island, was a student at Collège Saint-Joseph, a Catholic-run French institution in Moncton.

He was summoned to the office for a phone call. "He said he was an MLA," Arsenault recalls. "Fine. But when he said Hatfield, that struck a bell."

The caller at the other end of the telephone line introduced himself to Arsenault as Richard Hatfield, the newly elected member of the Legislative Assembly for Carleton. Arsenault knew the Hatfield name because of Richard's father's potato chip company. But the young politician wasn't calling to talk about spuds. He had heard that Arsenault was active in student affairs and was politically minded; he wanted to come to Moncton, meet with him and ask him some questions about the Acadian community. "If you're a student at that time and someone who's an elected person calls you and wants to talk, you go," Arsenault says.

Arsenault remembers it vividly. They met at Cy's, a famous Moncton seafood restaurant. Arsenault ate chicken in a basket; Hatfield picked up the tab. "The agenda was open," he recalls of the conversation, which lasted hours. "That was the first thing that struck me. He had one or two things to talk about, and otherwise it was open. It was really an open-ended discussion."

After the lunch, Arsenault would have sporadic contact with Hatfield: a phone call out of the blue or an unannounced visit, always devoted to the MLA's insatiable desire for more information, more context about the francophone reality. "He was actively trying to learn, and he was open, not only to the Acadian community but to all communities," Arsenault says. "And I happened to be part of the Acadian community."

Today, Arsenault demurs when asked about his influence on Hatfield's future activities as PC leader and premier. "I looked at it as: someone asked a question and I gave an answer. Someone asked what I thought and I gave an opinion." He does not claim to have been Hatfield's only "resource person" on Acadian issues. In fact, he suspects that Hatfield was having discreet meetings and conversations with a wide variety of people.

Hatfield called again in the spring of 1963, but this time he wanted more than information. He asked Arsenault to spend his spring break in Fredericton translating Conservative documents for the coming election campaign. Arsenault was put up at the Lord Beaverbrook Hotel, which to him seemed extravagant and luxurious. He ended up doing more than translating. He wrote much of the campaign material, including a platform plank committing a PC government to setting up a French-language normal school — a training college for teachers — in Moncton.

Returning from studies at Oxford, Arsenault became executive assistant to then-PC leader Cy Sherwood, a job arranged by Hatfield. Arsenault remembers Sherwood as a sympathetic figure, well-meaning and principled but also profoundly challenged by the political changes of that decade. He was the last pre-modern party leader in New Brunswick, a politician of an earlier era who had missed his time and was devastated by his electoral defeat in 1963. When the mercurial Charlie Van Horne took over as leader in 1967, Arsenault drifted away from the provincial party and ran as a federal PC candidate in the 1968 election, where he was crushed by Trudeaumania. He ended up working for the Société Nationale des Acadiens (SNA) in Moncton, where he was able to watch Richard Hatfield continue to manoeuvre his party into position to win Acadian votes.

The young MLA was making appropriate noises: in 1967, Hatfield spoke during a debate on a motion by Van Horne to recognize the status of French in the legislature. (The Liberals, preparing their own motion and unwilling to recognize French alone, opposed the motion.) "Many people can get by . . . in a second language," he told the Assembly, "but our native language is the one in which we express our hopes, our views, our desires and our aspirations. It is the language we use to express things which are important to us, and more than that our native language is the one that expresses our being."

Two years later, as Opposition leader, Hatfield was somewhat less poetic but no less generous as he endorsed Robichaud's Official

Languages Act. "The spirit of this Act is to encourage and enhance understanding and good will in our province of New Brunswick," Hatfield said in a legislative committee session on April 11, 1969, "and I think it is important that those who are responsible for its implementation and administration recognize that it will take all their efforts and all their skill to assure that no one in this province is treated unfairly. I think this Act allows for the growth and continued good will and understanding in our province, and once it is passed the challenge is in the hands of those who are responsible for its administration and implementation."

True, there was a caveat there, a bone thrown to anglophones who worried about losing out to the French. But Hatfield was supporting the bill and bringing his entire caucus along with him. Somehow, remarkably, the staid old Tory party of English New Brunswick had been persuaded to vote for official bilingualism — despite MLAs' fears that it would cost them their seats. "It was my first great political challenge," Hatfield would say years later.

And it was only the beginning. Soon he promised to maintain those radicalized community development agencies that Robichaud was planning to abolish. "Hatfield had established an early credibility with these groups," Arsenault says. The new leader also deftly moved in to take political advantage of the Moncton school board debate. The SNA had been leading the charge on the issue from its Moncton office until the day one of Robichaud's cabinet ministers, André Richard, called. According to Arsenault, he told the SNA staff they were playing the Conservatives' game, their demands going beyond what the premier could provide without spending more political capital. They had to stand with Robichaud, he argued, rather than embarrass him to the benefit of a Tory party that was not sympathetic to francophone aspirations.

The SNA bought Richard's arguments, and Moncton's Acadian élite backed off. "Suddenly the steam came out of the protest," Arsenault says. But parents weren't ready to give up as easily as the professional activists. They felt betrayed by the power play, and they paid attention when Richard Hatfield came to the city to promise them their French-language school board. Some even began to wonder if they should remain part of a monolithic Liberal voting bloc.

On the surface, the 1970 election campaign appeared to cut along the same old lines. In most francophone regions, voters remained loyal to the Liberals, while many anglophones, unaware that some militant Acadians now saw Robichaud as too cautious and too moderate, perceived French conspiracies everywhere. There were revelations of subsidies from France for the Moncton-based Acadian newspaper *L'Évangéline,* and rumours of separatists infiltrating the Université de Moncton. In mid-campaign the October Crisis exploded in Quebec. New Brunswick Liberals braced for a vote split along language lines that would restore the Tories to power on the strength of anglophone votes.

And that is what the voters appeared to deliver — but closer examination reveals a different story. The Conservatives won the election, 31-27, picking up just six new seats. In Sunbury, two Conservatives ousted Liberals as voters punished the provincial party for Pierre Trudeau's defence cuts. In Edmundston, citizens rebuked Robichaud for not firing Nadeau after his tax conviction by electing a Conservative, an accountant named Jean-Maurice Simard.

In Moncton, three critical seats switched hands, as anglophones apparently sought revenge on Robichaud for his language initiatives. But something else happened in Moncton. Acadians calculated that on the school board question, the Conservatives might actually be able to do more for them — with less opposition — than the Liberals. They were responding to the overtures from the new young leader of the PC party, a lawyer from Hartland who nonetheless appeared to sympathize with Acadian concerns. "What happened in 1970," says Frédéric Arsenault, "was [that] the Acadian vote was not as one-sided as it was in 1967." Maybe this Richard Hatfield was a different kind of Tory.

In other areas of New Brunswick, however, the results deepened each party's links to its historic constituency. The Liberals gained votes in French areas, while the Tories were stronger than before in counties like Albert, Carleton, Charlotte, Kings and York. Voters in the Tory heartland had had enough of the Acadian power they equated with Liberalism. But that Acadian power had done something in Moncton. Quietly, subtly, it had sensed that it might have found another vehicle.

It wasn't much, but for Richard Hatfield, it was a beginning.

* * *

On November 12, 1970, Richard Hatfield presented his cabinet of seventeen MLAs to be sworn in by Lieutenant-Governor Wallace Bird. One by one, they advanced to the front of the chamber of the Legislative Assembly to place their hands on the Bible. Loyal Tories, thrilled to be back in power, watched them come. They recognized the stalwarts, of course: John Baxter, an MLA since 1962 and son of Premier Baxter, became minister of justice. Wilfred Bishop, first elected in Flemming's upset of 1952, took the oath to become minister of natural resources.

And there were new faces, none newer than Jean-Maurice Simard, the accountant and former party president from Edmundston. Simard would be minister of finance — a job no francophone had held before in New Brunswick. Richard Hatfield was making his move.

Suddenly, Simard stopped. There was a problem with the Good Book on which he was asked to place his hand. It was an English Bible, and Simard would not swear his oath on it. The ceremony came to an abrupt halt as aides scrambled off to find a French Bible.

Arsenault chuckles at the memory. "You can see that this did not fit what people in the party would expect, traditionally," he says. "He was the type of politician most people in New Brunswick were not used to."

Watching the scene unfold, Richard Hatfield might have been privately delighted to see old English Tory feathers ruffled by Simard's stubbornness. The new premier had found a francophone as determined as he to build a new Progressive Conservative party.

Chapter Three

THE FRENCH LIEUTENANT

AS HE SET OUT to remake his party, the new premier of New Brunswick called on the lessons of history.

Richard Hatfield must have sensed that only an anglophone like himself, bred in the Tory heartland of the St. John River Valley, could persuade the PC party to embrace Acadian power. But he also knew that he needed a francophone ally within his caucus to carry that effort into French New Brunswick. He had only to think of the great partnerships that had shaped Canada: Baldwin and La-Fontaine, Macdonald and Cartier. Or, more recently, King and St-Laurent. Hatfield would eventually gain his own political capital among Acadians, but in those early days of his premiership, he needed a French lieutenant.

There were only three francophones in his caucus. Joseph Ouellette, elected in Victoria County thanks to the francophone votes around Grand Falls, would stay on the backbench. Jean-Paul LeBlanc, the beneficiary of Hatfield's school promises in Moncton, became municipalities minister. And Jean-Maurice Simard was elevated to the powerful position of finance minister, symbolizing Hatfield's attempts to make his government a partnership between the two cultures.

Simard was different from the patrician figures that had dominated Tory politics until then. Large, charcoal eyes blazed beneath thick dark eyebrows, an image reinforced by his thick black hair. His voice was not the deep baritone his demeanour might have suggested. Instead, it could, and often did, reach a high pitch that could grate on the listener — particularly when Simard became animated, which was often.

Fuelled at times, it seemed, by a burning rage and an impatience to expand francophone power, Simard would be labelled by his opponents inside the party and among Tory voters as a closet separatist, a Quebec agent, a French puppeteer pulling Richard Hatfield's strings. To this day, Tories of the Hatfield era can be situated on the language spectrum based on their views of Jean-Maurice Simard.

For anglophone Tories like former MLA Eric Kipping who eventually revolted over the language issue, Simard had too much control. "When it came to matters of bilingualism and Acadians, [Hatfield] was taking his direction from Simard. Looking at it from the outside, I wouldn't have said he was a Conservative. I would have said he was part of the Parti Acadien."

For francophones who came to the PC Party because of Hatfield, Simard's influence has been overstated. "Simard could say what he wanted," insists Yvon Poitras, a former MLA and minister. "If it wasn't all right with the premier, it didn't happen. The premier wasn't a yes man for Simard." And for Acadians less influenced by the pair's aggressive tactics, like Omer Léger, the truth is somewhere in the middle: "Simard was a different type. It was good to have one in a crowd like him. Too many Simards might have been dangerous."

Simard was born in the tiny community of Rivière-Bleue, in the Témiscouata region of Quebec, where the backroads of the St. Lawrence River's south shore give way to the great north woods of Maine and the Madawaska panhandle of New Brunswick. His father Évariste, a sawmill operator, had switched from the Liberals to the Union Nationale after the 1939 election following a dispute with the local Member of the National Assembly over woodcutting rights on provincial land. Jean-Maurice grew up in a household in which politics were a passion and Liberals were the enemy.

He carried this with him in 1959 to Edmundston, where he set up his accounting business. At first he didn't act on it. "I had made a vow that I would get my professional life and business operating on solid ground before I touched politics," he recalled in a series of interviews for the Provincial Archives of New Brunswick. He poured his considerable energy into the firm, opening satellite offices in Grand Falls and Rivière-Bleue and often working from all three in the same day.

But politics proved hard to resist. When his brother ran in Témiscouata in the 1966 Quebec election, Jean-Maurice was his campaign manager. A year later, during the New Brunswick campaign, he hosted a radio show in Edmundston on which provincial candidates debated the issues. "My style, my nature, was that I wanted a challenge, and certainly you could get a challenge by siding with the PCs," Simard said years later. Like fellow Hatfield confidants Fred Arsenault and Dalton Camp, he offered as a Conservative candidate in the 1968 federal election, losing by a respectable 285 votes, a margin that caught the attention of Richard Hatfield.

Hatfield wasn't yet the party leader in the fall of 1968, but, having already run once for the leadership against Van Horne, he was widely seen as the heir apparent. He was certainly contemplating his next moves on the political chessboard, and he wanted Simard in position. So Hatfield persuaded him to come to Fredericton to seek the party's presidency at its annual meeting.

Anticipating an opponent, Simard prepared a speech. "I said as a francophone I would encourage other francophones to get involved in the provincial Tory party. But I set conditions: would we be equal?" As it turned out, Simard was acclaimed. "When I left the meeting, many older ladies and senior citizens laughed at my speech. I was offended. But Richard Hatfield understood what had to be done to make the Tory party a successful party. . . . He wanted to build a Tory party, a *new* party, with francophones and anglophones. With no conditions. His dream. My dream."

So, when Hatfield came to Edmundston in 1970 to ask Jean-Maurice Simard to be his candidate, the fiery orator and new Tory convert agreed. His motivation was simple: political brokerage — membership in a coalition that could collect and distribute the spoils of power.

"I wanted Edmundston to get its share of the proverbial pie. I thought the Liberals just ignored Edmundston and took Edmundston — as the most traditional Liberal French riding — for granted and didn't have to do anything." There were skeptics among Simard's friends. "God knows how many times people said, 'What are you doing in the Tory party? You'll never get elected!' But I said, 'If by some accident — and I repeated that so many times from '68 to '70 — if by accident the Tory party is elected without francophones, would you like that?' I said, 'I wouldn't want that.'"

Simard understood that the French vote could be harnessed and delivered to the party willing to accommodate francophone concerns. "New Brunswick is Liberal," he said. "I mean, the Acadians are Liberal. . . . As a democrat, I can't accept that, you know. I always felt that . . . if we have two parties and we play one against the other, that's how we're going to get things." So Simard set out to "play" the PC party, and to play a leader willing to be played. He would always insist, though, that their motives went beyond victory for its own sake. "He wanted power *to do things*! Richard Hatfield knew that he needed power to improve the lot of New Brunswickers. *All* New Brunswickers. That takes seats."

But Simard faced a hurdle in becoming Richard Hatfield's candidate in Edmundston, and to overcome it, he adopted a strategy of brinkmanship that would become his trademark.

Guy Charest, a lawyer whose office was next door to Simard's in downtown Edmundston, decided in 1970 that he, too, wanted the PC nomination. Charest had lost the 1968 federal nomination to Simard and had disputed the convention result for three weeks, hampering Simard's campaign and, perhaps, costing him the seat. "I told Richard Hatfield I was not prepared to fight another nomination convention against Guy Charest. I had to tell [him] three times in the space of two or three months. Finally I called him three days before the nominating convention. . . . I gave Richard Hatfield one hour to call Guy Charest and [make him] disappear. He did that." Charest bowed out of the contest.

Simard easily won the nomination against a single, less formidable opponent, and was ready when Robichaud called the election. Simard "ran a very personal campaign in Edmundston," Fred Arsenault says. "He ran a very aggressive campaign. He wouldn't know how to run any other kind. A lot of radio ads. He was a very hard worker. Very dynamic." On election day, Simard triumphed with 3,065 votes against

2,490 for the Liberal, Fernand Picard — a comfortable majority of fifty-five per cent for a Tory candidate in what had been a safe Liberal seat.

Hatfield met with Simard after the election to discuss cabinet positions. Now it was Hatfield's turn to impose conditions. In those days of smaller government, MLAs and even ministers traditionally served on a part-time basis, holding on to their regular jobs as teachers, lawyers and businessmen. But Hatfield insisted his ministers be full-time cabinet members and sell off any business holdings they had. "I never had any second thought or hesitated," Simard would recount. But, he added, "It was not easy to give up that life that I'd built. I had no idea what I'd gotten myself into."

Neither had the PC party of New Brunswick.

* * *

The early years of the Richard Hatfield government are remembered more for their scandals than for the premier's efforts to build the new party he wanted. The Bricklin fiasco, a costly failed attempt to establish a car manufacturing plant in New Brunswick, and the Atkinson affair, a scandal that revealed a system of political kickbacks, dominated headlines. Few noticed the careful spadework that Hatfield — always supported by his French lieutenant — was doing in what had been considered safe Liberal territory.

The first test came quickly, before the premier had even had the chance to reach out to Acadians in any coherent, policy-oriented way. In 1971, Louis Robichaud accepted a federal appointment and resigned his Kent County seat, setting up a by-election race that everyone was certain the Liberals would win. "I thought it was going to be a thank-you vote to Louis Robichaud," says Omer Léger, the PC candidate. Léger says his party "was not well-known. . . . You had to have courage to be a Conservative. It was so easy to be Liberal."

But local issues played to Léger's argument that the area needed someone on the government side. Roads were unpaved, and the Bookmobile — a library housed in an old school bus — wasn't making many stops in Kent County. And the candidate himself had a profile. "If you said 'Vote Conservative,' no way. But if you said

'Vote for Omer,' well, that was something. So I told Liberals, 'Don't change parties. Just vote for Omer.'"

Léger's brochures added a splash of red to the traditional blue of the Tories, blurring party lines. More important were his photographs: Léger on the steps of the Legislature, Léger with the minister of transportation. The message helped Léger trounce his Liberal opponent 6,682 votes to 4,610 — and Hatfield and Simard knew they had a winning strategy in French New Brunswick. Find a well-respected person in the community, play down the Tory name and play up the connection to power. It worked again in 1972, when the mayor of Caraquet, Lorenzo Morais, became the first Conservative elected in Gloucester County since Wesley Coffyn squeaked out a ninety-four-vote victory in a 1931 by-election. By September 1974, Hatfield had doubled 1970's number of francophone Tory MLAs from three to six — after Fernand Dubé captured Campbellton in a by-election by adding French votes to the bilingual city's anglophone Tory bloc.

By then, Richard Hatfield had boldly and explicitly embraced the Acadian cause. At first, his attention seemed to focus on the arts. There was the official trip to Paris, where Hatfield persuaded the prestigious *Le Monde* to review Antonine Maillet's play *La Sagouine*, then in performance in the city. He appeared in Bathurst at an avant-garde exhibition mounted by young Acadian artists. "He found them fun-loving and possessed of a great *joie de vivre*," says his former executive assistant, Win Hackett. "He also found them to be talented, interested and hard-working. . . . His motivations were first and foremost to make them equal as citizens of the province and secondly to break the traditional voting patterns of English Conservative and French and Irish Catholic Liberal voting."

To achieve that, Hatfield had to do more than embrace Acadian artists. He had "*to do things,*" as Simard later put it. And he had one advantage over John Baxter, the premier who in 1925 had attempted to allow more French education in New Brunswick. Hatfield had a bloc of francophone MLAs backing him in caucus — and carrying the battle into cabinet.

The francophones' support was needed for initiatives that fell broadly into two categories. First, there was the old-fashioned delivery of government largesse. In 1972, for example, the premier announced that, with the help of funding from Ottawa, the province would create the Village Historique Acadien, a simulated eighteenth-century community near Caraquet, aimed at tourists. It would be a francophone counterpart to the popular King's Landing historic village outside Fredericton, and it would create permanent jobs in the area.

Bureaucrats in Fredericton would often resist these types of projects. Frédéric Arsenault remembers shepherding through the bureaucracy a proposal for a Marine Centre in Shippagan — only to have the deputy minister of tourism, during a meeting with the town mayor and the premier, suggest it go to St. Andrews instead. "It was not easy," Omer Léger would say. "We had to have our files pretty tight and pretty well documented. We had to argue harder. When we got the Hillsborough railroad for Albert County, with Mac Macleod, it was not that hard."

The second thrust of Hatfield's Acadian strategy, in addition to dividing these spoils of power, was the delivery of power itself.

Louis Robichaud had failed to proclaim many sections of the Official Languages Act before leaving office; now Hatfield would finish the job. On July 26, 1972, sections permitting motions and other documents in the Legislature to be submitted in English or French became law. On December 20 came an even more significant step when the sections giving any New Brunswicker the right to a court trial in English or French took effect. That same year, Hatfield fulfilled his election promise to the Acadians of Moncton by giving them their own separate French-language school board.

Some Conservatives began to wonder what had happened to the Hatfield they knew. He was now giving speeches on bilingualism that sounded curiously like those of Pierre Trudeau. This was worrying enough, but leading up to the 1974 election, Hatfield went farther. All his efforts before that year, however sincere, could be written off as craftily political. But when Richard Hatfield chose to champion the cause of Acadians in the very heart of the resolutely staid, conservative and very English city of Fredericton, no one could accuse him of opportunism. Some, in fact, suggested he was committing political suicide.

Official bilingualism was slowly transforming the character of the provincial capital: more and more francophones had come to

Fredericton to work in the civil service. When they arrived, they discovered an appalling lack of French-language education for their children. Hatfield had learned from the Moncton experience that education is at the very core of any minority's quest for cultural survival. From the moment children are immersed in another language, they begin to lose their own. School them in their mother tongue, though, and they will have a bulwark against assimilation. In Fredericton, Acadians had been forced to build that bulwark themselves, setting up a private school to educate their children in French — until the Robichaud government was finally embarrassed enough to fund a French school under the authority of the English school district in the city.

It was a half-measure. The school was located in former military barracks that were in poor repair. It moved to a vacant building on Montgomery Street in 1971, but the school board refused to change its name to École Sainte-Anne — to honour the Acadian community that had existed on the site of modern Fredericton until the Expulsion of 1755. A committee of francophones eventually adopted the ambitious goal of a large complex that would house the school, a community centre, office space for francophone community associations, and rooms for the growing number of French classes being held for anglophone civil servants. With the federal government's financial support, Hatfield announced in January 1974 that the province would build the facility.

The reaction in Fredericton was swift and hostile. Anglophones couldn't understand why their community needed a French-only school. Within the Tory caucus, Simard and other advocates watched as old-time Conservative MLAs such as Dr. Everett Chalmers of Fredericton South fought the plan. A resolution even came before Fredericton's city council that it register its opposition to the school. "I didn't think we needed it," says Len Poore, a Tory who was then a city councillor and later became a leader of anti-bilingualism groups. "Not only was there going to be a school, but they were going to have a school with everything in it — a gym and everything."

When Hatfield learned of the council resolution, he decided to act. True, the resolution would not change anything. But symbols are important to minorities, too, and the symbolism of a municipal council — in a capital city that belonged to all New Brunswickers

— condemning French-language education was too much for the premier to accept. He would respond with a symbolic gesture of his own: he himself would go before Fredericton city council to argue against the motion.

The very idea was so bizarre as to be incomprehensible. The premier — whose power over the city's more junior form of government allowed him to dissolve the municipality at will — would plead with the council not to pass a toothless resolution. Several people close to him, including fellow Carleton County MLA Charles Gallagher, urged him not to lower himself. But the advice went unheeded. "There was no point telling him," Gallagher remembers. "He had his mind made up."

The meeting turned into a circus. Two hundred and fifty people attended, including members of a group calling itself the Dominion of Canada English Speaking Association, based around Moncton and Sussex. Most councillors tiptoed around the language question, preferring to rely on economic arguments. "I feel it's a luxury we can't afford," Councillor Carl Howe told Hatfield. Len Poore was more direct: he failed to understand why Acadians needed to come to Fredericton in the first place, and suggested it might be better for everyone if they would simply learn and speak the language of the English majority.

Hatfield rejected this notion of majority, or mob rule. "If you think we're going to make all of our decisions on the basis of so many fors and so many againsts," he told the council, "that the ones with the most numbers are going to win, I'm telling you you're not going to have that kind of luxury. That kind of mathematical application of government decision-making leads to chaos, riots, wars and everything else. I can't accept that."

But Hatfield's vision of a democracy that protected its minorities was lost on the councillors. They passed their resolution, which failed to stop the eventual construction of the community centre and school. The opposition within the PC caucus faded as the fall election approached and divisions gave way to the discipline of power. "I remember Chalmers," Simard said. "It was obvious he didn't agree with Richard Hatfield's policies and overtures towards francophones . . . [but] like me, he hated Liberals. That's why he listened to Richard Hatfield. He wanted to win. He wanted to beat Liberals."

Francophones were listening to Richard Hatfield, too. Claude Bourque, editor of the Moncton daily *L'Évangéline*, wrote after the council confrontation, "Premier Hatfield, in the eyes of the Acadian people, has well and truly earned his spurs."

* * *

The results of the 1974 election were never in doubt. Voters in New Brunswick rarely throw a government from office after one mandate. The suspense, then, was about whether Richard Hatfield's efforts would allow him to keep the francophone seats he won in 1970 and in subsequent by-elections — and pick up even more.

He had a new electoral map he hoped would work in his favour. Previously, elections were fought over multiple seats in each county. In a county with three seats, each voter got three votes, and the top three vote-getters were elected. Occasionally, voters would "split the ticket" and send MLAs from different parties to Fredericton, but generally they would send a full contingent of only Liberals or only Tories to the Legislature. The county system was replaced by fifty-eight individual ridings for the 1974 election, however, so that a particularly strong candidate from a specific area could defy a county's traditional party loyalty and win a seat. Tories thus nabbed seats in Liberal counties and vice versa, giving Hatfield a net gain of two seats: thirty-three Conservative MLAs and twenty-five Liberals.

French New Brunswick remained almost unchanged. Three francophones held their ridings: Simard was re-elected easily in Edmundston, while Dubé kept Campbellton and Léger hung on in Kent South. Two Conservative gains were narrow: in Madawaska-les-Lacs, next to Edmundston, Jean-Pierre Ouellet defeated the Liberal incumbent by ninety-five votes; in Nigadoo-Chaleur, Roland Boudreau won by 180 votes. Balancing those victories, however, was the loss to the Liberals of two seats whose PC MLAs — Lorenzo Morais in Caraquet and Joe Ouellette in Grand Falls — chose not to run again. And in Moncton, the Acadians who had elected Jean-Paul LeBlanc turned on him for being a less than forceful advocate for their cause. "I'm not bad-mouthing him, but he was not interested," Simard said. "He didn't understand them. He came from Moncton. Some people would say — I'm not saying I agree with it — he was assimilated and so on." Omer Léger agreed: "Nice guy, but he was not perceived as being a defender of the faith for Acadians."

Still, the results were not discouraging. Three seats held, three lost, two gained. A net loss of only one meant Hatfield had five francophone MLAs, a good base to build on. The more significant change was in cabinet: the French lieutenant, Jean-Maurice Simard, was out, sitting instead on the backbenches. Simard would claim that he asked to be freed from the constraints of power to "patch up my financial situation. . . . I got involved in a bad investment in Rimouski in '72 and it got worse and worse, because, being finance minister, I had strangers looking after that." The long hours and the stress, he added, were harming his health.

Back home, Simard suffered for his exile from cabinet. "The people in Edmundston were very disappointed. They didn't understand. . . . People would make sure they didn't meet me on the sidewalk. They would cross the street not to be seen with me, because I was disgraced, according to them." For six months, Simard recalled, he second-guessed his decision. Then he joined a legislative task force looking at regional development and began travelling the province, particularly across the north. "I started meeting people, some of my morale came back and my strength came back, and I could see the light at the end of the tunnel."

Simard was propelled toward the light by the premier. "Richard Hatfield helped solve my financial problem in 1975 and '76," Simard revealed in one of his Provincial Archives interviews. "I had a mortgage on a motel in Rimouski. About fifty or sixty thousand dollars. Through the help of Richard Hatfield, the Tory party bought my mortgage. This is the first time I've talked about it. That helped me solve, and pay off, at discount, some loans I owed people."

Simard returned to cabinet in 1976 with a new job, president of the Treasury Board, and a new outlook. As a Madawaskan, he had embraced the push for francophone rights because they were good for his constituents. Now, after his travels to Acadian areas of the province, he could see beyond the rivalries that often divided far-flung francophone communities. He was developing a pan-francophone vision of New Brunswick that went beyond basic bread-and-butter language rights.

"Why do you bother with all these people, the Acadians?" an assistant asked him at the time. "Your first duty is to Edmundston."

"Yes," Simard replied, "but you know, I think I'm part of a bigger group here."

He would later explain in the Provincial Archives interview, "I realized then that, after five or six years, Edmundston and my riding stood to benefit if we could . . . [get] our share, and at the same time do battle for the other French parts of New Brunswick. I thought we should. I certainly realized the weakness that we suffered . . . because we were split at least three ways, northwest, northeast, southeast. So I said, 'If we get together and associate, and travel and try to espouse a similar cause, we could get somewhere.' I could, I suppose, have decided to listen to people who said, 'Don't bother with the rest, get everything for Edmundston,' but I felt that I could, without neglecting Edmundston, fight in the name of the other communities. And it proved to be right."

On July 1, 1977, the final sections of the 1969 Official Languages Act were proclaimed law. These required that proceedings and reports of the Legislature, government documents and the *Royal Gazette* be published in both English and French, and that a child's mother tongue would determine the language of his or her schooling — paving the way for the eventual creation of autonomous French and English schools and boards of education, not just in Moncton but across New Brunswick.

Simard's influence was clear — and not altogether welcome in English New Brunswick, where some Tory MLAs began to sense their supporters chafing at the ongoing broadening of francophone rights.

"I was told quite often in those days because of my support for official bilingualism that I would never be elected again," says Les Hull, who represented York South, a riding that began on the southwest edge of Fredericton and sprawled out into the far-flung rural reaches of the county south and west of the city. As a teacher, Hull understood, for example, that a French school was important in attracting talented Acadian civil servants to the capital. His constituents didn't always see it that way, nor did his right-hand man in the riding, Danny Cameron. But Hull's access to power usually allowed him to soothe the anger with patronage.

Charles Gallagher, the MLA from Carleton North, remembers addressing the Royal Canadian Legion in Woodstock on Remembrance Day, 1976. Having just joined cabinet as education minister, he decided to speak about the expanding French immersion program and was promptly booed. "It wasn't easy," he says now, "but the changes had to be done at that time by an English premier for it to be accepted. It wouldn't have been accepted by a French premier." That was Hatfield's calculus: if he could reach out to French New Brunswick while maintaining the loyalty of English New Brunswick — an occasional bit of chafing notwithstanding — he could expand the base and create his new PC party.

Yet, in 1978, when Hatfield went to the polls again, when the Liberals appeared on the verge of taking power away from the Tories, it was that reliably solid rock of Conservatism — English New Brunswick — that rescued Hatfield's career and gave him another four years to pursue his dream.

In 1978, the budget surplus was gone. The plan to build the Bricklin plant had fallen apart. The costs of construction at the Point Lepreau nuclear power plant were soaring to double the original estimate. Richard Hatfield had been in office for eight years — perilously close to the natural political lifespan of a typical New Brunswick premier. "He was supposed to lose, according to the polls," Fred Arsenault says. "He won by the skin of his teeth."

And he did it by letting the old voting patterns re-emerge one last time.

The Liberals' new leader, Joseph Daigle, had stepped down as a Provincial Court judge in Kent County to lead the party back to victory. As a government lawyer, Daigle had undertaken the massive job of translating the provincial acts and statutes into French to bring them into compliance with the Official Languages Act. This gave him credibility among Acadians. Some heralded him as a new Louis Robichaud.

But that kind of appeal had its limitations. In English New Brunswick, memories of the tumult of the 1960s were still fresh and not altogether welcome. Hatfield tailored his campaign to those sentiments, seizing on Pierre Trudeau's musings on reducing the Queen's role in Canada to tar Daigle as an anti-monarchist. If Daigle was going to rally the francophone vote to the Liberals, Hatfield needed to consolidate English New Brunswick around the Tories. And no issue served that purpose better than the Queen. Tellingly, Daigle chose not to campaign in Saint John — the province's biggest and most Loyalist city — during the 1978 campaign.

Then Daigle made one of the legendary gaffes of New Brunswick politics. Eight days before the election, in response to Hatfield's labelling him — in reference to Trudeau — a "second-hand rose," the Liberal leader responded by calling the premier "a faded pansy." That kind of slur just wasn't acceptable, at least not in English New Brunswick, where politics was still seen as a genteel activity.

And so the old cleavage emerged on election night, October 23. English New Brunswick lined up behind Richard Hatfield and French New Brunswick came out solidly for the Liberals. There were exceptions on both sides, but there was no mistaking the split for anything but what it was. Two Acadian Tory cabinet ministers were defeated, including Omer Léger, who was bumped out of his seat by Daigle. Hatfield's francophone contingent was knocked back to four — exactly what it had been in 1972. The Tories barely hung on, with thirty seats to twenty-eight for the Liberals.

Acadian Tories were discouraged. Hatfield's eight years of trying to build a francophone base for the party had yielded little. "All the time he spent — is there something?" Arsenault asked himself. "What is the result?" The French lieutenant had survived, to be sure — Simard won Edmundston with fifty-seven per cent of the vote, almost identical to his percentages in the last two elections, but Hatfield's dream had suffered a terrible setback.

And a new obstacle had emerged on election night.

In 1972, a group of activists, meeting in Bathurst, had created the Parti Acadien. They were young veterans of the new francophone militancy, some of them field workers for those community development agencies created by Robichaud and saved by Hatfield. At the outset, the party's goals were economic. Its quasi-socialist philosophy aimed to help forestry workers and fishermen keep more of the wealth they created. Its founders disavowed any sympathies with the separatist Parti Québécois. "We want to unite, not separate,

Acadians and others who feel they are being left out by the present political parties," said the party's first president, Euclide Chiasson.

By 1978, the party had adopted a more explicitly nationalist platform, espousing a dramatic decentralization of government administration and services to the regions of the province, particularly the north, to pave the way for the eventual creation of a separate Acadian province. Some Acadians were intrigued or, at least, unconvinced that the two existing parties had anything better to offer. That year, the Parti Acadien earned twelve per cent of the vote in the twenty-three ridings where it fielded candidates, a threefold increase in support over 1974.

Mainstream New Brunswick was startled, alarmed, disturbed. But not the French lieutenant. As he looked over the vote totals for the Parti Acadien, Jean-Maurice Simard did not see trouble. He saw opportunity.

He was drawn particularly to the results in Restigouche West, where the Liberal incumbent, Alfred Roussel, squeaked back into office with 2,174 votes compared with 2,003 for the Parti Acadien candidate, a Catholic priest named Armand Plourde. The Tory, Jean-Guy Raymond, ran third with 1,576 — a seemingly hopeless result.

But Simard looked at those 2,003 votes for the Parti Acadien, votes that were not Liberal but that were cast for a party with no chance, really, ever to take power and do anything for its supporters. What if those votes had been cast for the Conservatives, who *could* win elections? Added to those who actually voted PC, the total would have been enough to crush the Liberals in Restigouche West.

At that moment, Simard had the outlines of his strategy for the next election. Moncton was too complicated a mix of French and English: Jean-Paul LeBlanc had shown how difficult it was to be a forceful activist for his people in a majority anglophone city. No, the key was not Moncton but the francophone north, a Liberal fortress that suddenly appeared vulnerable.

The Parti Acadien had shaken loose those Liberal votes. Now Simard would go out and get them — by convincing francophones that voting Conservative was the nationalist thing to do.

Chapter Four

"ENCORE PLUS FORT"

SAINT-QUENTIN LOOKS like an Old West town dropped — with a few gaudy neon signs thrown in — onto a plateau in the middle of deep forest in an isolated corner of French-speaking northwest New Brunswick. Approaching the village from north or south, the visitor looks straight down the main road, lined with one- and two-storey buildings, all the way to the opposite end of the village and beyond, to the highway that disappears into the infinity of the trees.

In 1981, the most important francophones in the government of Richard Hatfield travelled that road. Jean-Maurice Simard, Omer Léger, and Jean-Pierre Ouellette all made their way to Saint-Quentin to visit a local businessman named Yvon Poitras, who had been raised in Grand Falls but had moved to the village to open a Home Hardware franchise. They wanted him — they *needed* him — to be their candidate in Restigouche West.

Poitras, heavy-set, round-faced and plain-talking, was the perfect fit for the electoral strategy of Hatfield and Simard. He was well-known, well-liked, not overtly political, and thus highly credible in his community. In fact, the Conservatives had first seen his potential four years before, when they were recruiting for the 1978 election.

But the very basis of Poitras's appeal — his community involvement in the form of his role in the Knights of Columbus — led him to spurn the PC entreaties the first time. In 1978, Poitras was in line to become state deputy for the Knights, the top ranking man in the

New Brunswick organization. He had no intention of passing that up — not even for something that might have given him considerably more influence in his community.

So, in 1981, Tories beat a path to his door again.

Besides Ouellette, Léger and Simard, there came Roger Carron, a party worker from nearby Campbellton and a personal friend of Poitras. One evening, the two men sat down at Poitras's kitchen table, and Carron began answering the prospective candidate's questions. When he couldn't answer them, he would pick up the telephone and call someone in Fredericton who could. Gradually Poitras came around.

In 1981, Knights of Columbus chapters all over North America prepared to mark the order's centennial. In New Brunswick, they would gather in Chatham, a convention Poitras — state deputy at last — was organizing. "[Hatfield] had sent someone to our convention every year, but he had never come himself," Poitras says. This time, someone from the premier's office called Poitras looking for more information. He sent a book on the history of the Knights, and, to his delight, the premier flew to Chatham on the government plane. Hatfield wowed the crowd — and the state deputy — with a speech that showed his knowledge of the organization. "He talked about the Knights of Columbus as if he'd known them all his life," Poitras says, still amazed at the man's political savvy. "He'd read the book cover to cover."

A few months later, Poitras was invited to attend a PC nominating convention in Beresford and was assigned the job of driving Hatfield back to the airport in nearby Bathurst. The premier used the trip to continue his lobbying. Poitras told Hatfield about the committee he sat on in Saint-Quentin that was trying to secure funding to finish building an arena in the village. "No way am I going to run if that isn't fixed," he told the premier. A week later, Jean-Maurice Simard came to Saint-Quentin and handed over a cheque, and Yvon Poitras agreed to become the Conservative candidate in Restigouche West.

Simard's formidable reputation for acquiring the spoils of power served as a powerful recruitment tool across northern New Brunswick in late 1981 and early 1982. In Madawaska South, where Percy

Mockler was considering signing up, Simard's ability to deliver was leveraged in a different way.

"Jean-Maurice Simard was a very powerful minister, and he was very well respected, but he had this *'Edmundston d'abord'* [Edmundston first]," says Mockler, then chairman of the newly created French school board in the Grand Falls area. "Simard was basically sponging every government office he could to Edmundston. He was sponging Grand Falls. He was sponging Saint-Léonard." Saint-Léonard was Mockler's hometown, the community from which he had risen out of poverty to become a well-known civic leader, once taking over a local school with the minister of education inside to prevent its closure.

Now Mockler — small, stocky, excitable and full of energy — wanted to fight for Saint-Léonard again. He had gone to Héliodore Côté, the local Liberal MLA, and asked him to stop the bleeding of jobs and services to Simard's riding. But Côté was in opposition, powerless to intervene. So Mockler met with Simard to tell the minister to his face that he was destroying Saint-Léonard. "Get elected," Simard told Mockler, "and after you get elected you'll have the same privilege as I do. You can knock on the premier's door."

So Percy Mockler joined the Tory team — another respected community leader who would lend credibility to the PC party's 1982 campaign in French New Brunswick.

* * *

Good candidates were important, but Richard Hatfield and Jean-Maurice Simard needed more if they were going to have their breakthrough in French New Brunswick. They needed to point to a record of achievement on behalf of francophones.

Despite the setback of the 1978 election and the tiny French contingent in the caucus, they pushed ahead to fashion such a record. They finally implemented autonomous francophone and anglophone school districts across the province, giving French New Brunswickers their own educational institutions a century after the Caraquet riots. They showered the francophone north with job-creation projects: roads, bridges, government offices, schools, hospitals, provincial parks and museums. Simard faced long fights over his shifting of money to those ridings, and his appointing more people from the region to government boards and committees. Some in the south argued that people in the north ought not to get such appointments because they would have such a long drive to Fredericton.

Hatfield and Simard moved ahead with the creation of a provincial civil service that would comply with the Official Languages Act by providing bilingual service to New Brunswickers — despite the headaches that would create for MLAs from traditional anglophone Conservative ridings.

Hank Myers, of Kings East, and other members walked a fine line in supporting their government on the language issue. "There were people who had convinced themselves that if we hadn't had a bilingualism policy, they'd be able to work for the government," Myers says now. "In most cases they wouldn't have got those jobs anyway — but that was their excuse. We had to fight that all the time. . . . It was very hard to convince people that wasn't true, and we didn't devote enough efforts to that." Sometimes the complaints were ridiculous. When the Department of Transportation installed a *cul de sac* sign at the end of a road in the town of Sussex, "the president of the Orange Lodge was in my office frothing at the mouth," Myers recalls. "I tried to explain to him that *cul de sac* was a word used in London, England. It was like talking to a tree."

Other times, Myers had to agree that the policy was going too far. He remembers a posting for a job as a New Brunswick Power linesman based in Sussex, the heart of his constituency. The job required fluency in both languages. "This virtually eliminated every applicant in my riding," Myers says. "Although we had francophones in my riding, they had jobs better than an NB Power linesman. So it meant we were going to have to bring someone in from elsewhere in the province." Myers went to Jean-Maurice Simard, who, as Treasury Board president, had power over government hirings. Simard saw to it that the bilingualism requirement was dropped, and Myers was able to assure himself that a constituent would get the job.

Simard may have been flexible, but the small band of francophones in the caucus and cabinet were suspicious of MLAs like Myers and the constituencies they represented. "This . . . was a real cloud over the province," says Jean Gauvin, the fisheries minister and MLA for Shippagan-les-Îles, who was first elected in 1978. "There are some people who believe that if you give something, you're losing something on your side."

Gauvin knew perfectly well that bilingualism requirements in the civil service would, in fact, hurt the careers of some unilingual employees. A cabinet memo from 1981, explaining a proposed change to the designation of language requirements for government jobs, stated bluntly: "Career opportunities for some applicants not meeting the language requirements of Departments could be reduced." By publicly denying the obvious logic found in their very own briefing materials — instead of arguing *why* the ability to function in French was as essential as any other — Hatfield's ministers may have harmed their own credibility in English New Brunswick.

Still, individual rights and equality are central to conservatism and were to Progressive Conservatism, and the Official Languages Act, with its emphasis on a person's right to be served in his or her own language, was arguably consistent with those ideals. It could, at least, be wedged into the framework of a conservative ideology. But in the late 1970s, with basic individual rights secured in law, a competing idea was gaining favour among francophone thinkers: collective rights — the recognition of a *group*'s entitlement to protection and promotion.

Collective rights were high on the agenda of the Convention d'orientation nationale des Acadiens, held in Edmundston in 1979. With the strong showing of the Parti Acadien in the previous year's election and a coming referendum on independence in neighbouring Quebec, Acadian community leaders, artists and activists were seeking a common goal. They debated a variety of options in Edmundston, all emphasizing the collective rights of francophones to manage their own affairs. Almost half the delegates favoured a separate Acadian province, while other options — like dual, autonomous English and French government departments — enjoyed broad support. The only consensus was that the status quo was no longer acceptable.

Simard paid close attention to the proceedings, aware of the opportunity they presented. In his speech to delegates, he embraced the philosophy of collective rights and promised, as he would later put it, *to do things* — to pass new legislation recognizing the equality of the two linguistic communities of New Brunswick.

It was an easy promise to make. Delivering Bill 88 would come only after an eighteen-month battle inside the civil service, the Conservative caucus and the cabinet. Simard bypassed the legislative drafters at the Department of Justice and brought in outsiders, including Michel Bastarache, a professor of law at the Université de Moncton and an expert on linguistic rights. "That bill was discussed for more hours and . . . more time," Simard recalled, "than any other piece of legislation that I'm aware of. And it was such a short bill, but there were people who didn't like the comma in that place, society versus community, and so on for a year and a half."

Then came the political pressure. "First the anglophones were criticizing it," Simard said. "I was preaching separatism, according to them. And the Acadians didn't want it. They said it didn't go far enough. It was useless [in their view because] we had the Official Languages legislation, although we explained so often that we're not talking about individual rights, we're talking about collective rights. So we were getting it from both sides . . ."

Within the government, the battle unfolded. "God knows how we had to fight in caucus and in cabinet and so on!" Simard said. "Because people said, 'We don't need to recognize [them], we know they exist.' Well, I said, 'If we exist, let's officially recognize it.' . . . So I was really down after about six or seven months, until I said, 'Well, if you don't want it, I guess we'll can the damn thing!' And then somebody called Richard — I think one of CBC's French fellows — and said, 'What do you think, Richard, as the premier?' He said, 'No sir, we're not going to kill it. We're not going to let it die. We're going to pass it!'"

Echoes of that long internal fight were heard in the Legislative Assembly on July 16, 1981, during the final debate on the bill. Simard, practised in the tactical arts of brinkmanship, raised the spectre of Acadian nationalism — the very cause he was tacitly embracing in the bill — as a threat to social order, pointing out that the 1969 Official Languages Act hadn't been enough to blunt the rise of the Parti Acadien. "Granting individual rights that are limited to relations between the government and the citizen no longer guarantees peace and social stability, regardless of linguistic community," he told the chamber. He pointed to the duality within the Department of Education — separate administrative branches for the French and

English school systems — as a system that had, in fact, eliminated fights over language.

To those who argued Bill 88 would create linguistic ghettoes, Simard had an even more dire warning. "Ghettoes usually spring up when a particular group feels it has been wronged in some way, and not when it can take its rightful place free of prejudice and discrimination. . . . We must keep in mind that a government has to ensure social stability and security, and it is a hundred times better to use public funds now to guarantee the stability and security than to be obliged to use them later to calm social tensions which could arise if we do not act immediately. . . . If certain francophones speak about creating an Acadian province it is because, rightly or wrongly, they have difficulty feeling at home in New Brunswick. Let us not delude ourselves. These problems exist now . . . and it is in an attempt to solve them that we are proposing this recognition of the equality of the two linguistic communities."

But Simard's arguments appeared lost on some of his own Conservative colleagues. In his speech, John Baxter, the MLA for Kings West, avoided any reference to the underlying philosophy of collective rights. Falling back on the traditional conservative concept of individual rights — which the bill did not address — Baxter, either confused or disingenuous, sought only to persuade his own constituents that the bill wouldn't hurt them and that he had tried his best to acknowledge their fears: "I feel an attempt should be made to assure unilingual anglophones and even unilingual francophones that they will not be refused employment in our province, and I have debated this principle within our government and within my own political party. . . . I feel equal status carries with it the right to employment here in New Brunswick and that a person should not be refused employment simply because he is not bilingual."

Hatfield himself straddled both arguments, adopting Simard's threats of anarchy by pointing to Northern Ireland — "the essence of their problem is a refusal to accept equality" — while trying to assure anglophones that Bill 88 was, in fact, less radical than Simard intended. "I am not going to reveal any caucus secrets," he said, "but I want to say that this bill was debated, argued, discussed and beaten about, but I believe that a better bill came out of it." It was the only way to put a positive spin on the knowledge that there was a fissure inside the caucus over language policy.

More eloquently, Hatfield made an appeal to history: "It is not easy to bring about equality. It is not easy to make it happen. As a matter of fact, I suspect . . . that we will fail to bring about equality. I suspect that one hundred years from now, those who occupy this Legislature will still have to fight for equality. It may never be realized, but at least this Legislature will know that, as of this time, it is the will of the people of New Brunswick that we work in that direction and we strive for that equality."

* * *

Jean-Maurice Simard had joined Hatfield "*to do things*," and Bill 88 might have been the perfect swan song for his career. But in the early months of 1982, an election year, the French lieutenant realized an even greater opportunity had arrived. "The time had come," he would re-call, "for Richard to harvest some of the things he had done."

The forces that had blocked the PC party's push into French New Brunswick — that had stopped the harvest Simard and Hatfield had been longing for — were falling by the wayside. The Liberals were divided, in part because of Joe Daigle's uncertainty about Bill 88. Hoping to win support in English New Brunswick, Daigle had opposed it at first, only to frustrate his francophone MLAs, who favoured the bill. He reversed his stance to vote for it in the end, but it was too late. "I think it's one of the things that may have cost Joe Daigle his job," Simard said later, referring to a 1982 caucus revolt led by the ambitious Liberal MLA from Tracadie, Doug Young.

Meanwhile, the Société des Acadiens du Nouveau-Brunswick, the main nationalist lobby group, had lost its federal funding after sup-porting the Yes side in the 1980 Quebec referendum, and the Parti Acadien, which had caused so much alarm in 1978, was sputtering toward irrelevance. Torn apart over whether to back the Yes forces, the party postponed its 1982 leadership convention because no one wanted to run. When its activists drifted away and sought a new home, Jean-Maurice Simard was waiting. "All these things had accumulated, including Bill 88, that showed that they had no *raison d'être* anymore. These people were coming to us."

It was time to reap the harvest. Rather than bow out of politics with Bill 88 as his legacy, Simard prepared an electoral campaign the likes of which New Brunswick had never seen before — and most of the province didn't even notice it.

"I went over to Hatfield's residence in July 1982," Simard recounted in his Archives interviews. "Richard Hatfield had known that I would serve — because I told him in 1974 — ten years maximum. In 1982 it had been twelve years. I was ready to quit. I considered myself tired of government. He encouraged me to stay for another election. So I put some conditions, in a manner of speaking. I realized the Richard Hatfield government, in my eyes, deserved to win more Acadian seats. We deserved to harvest French seats. . . . I put the condition that I would organize the Grand Ralliement in Shippagan. First condition: the Tory party would finance [this event]. Second condition: the Tory party under Richard Hatfield would let me and the French members have a French [election] platform, taking [into account] the interests of the French regions. Third condition: [we would] have our own slogan, song, organization.

"Richard Hatfield was a bright man," Simard said. "He accepted my conditions."

* * *

The weather was typical for late August in New Brunswick: warm during the day, cooler in the evening. Louis Léger, in 1982 the vice-president of the New Brunswick PC Youth Federation, scanned the passengers arriving at the Moncton Airport. Jean-Maurice Simard had sent him to greet a very important visitor. Yves Dupré finally appeared, his kindly, wise face resembling that of a priest or a philosopher or a mysterious guru. "I knew that he was from Montreal and he was going to help with the francophone campaign," Léger says. "He told me what he was doing, but it wasn't really clear. He was coming on a reconnaissance mission, basically, to go to the Grand Ralliement and find out what francophones wanted."

Léger — who would later become a communications consultant himself — didn't yet know that he was playing chauffeur to the man who was then the star of political strategists in Quebec. Educated in sociology, Dupré had started his marketing and communications career in the private sector, then founded his own company, Groupe BDDS, in 1979. He made his mark in 1981 when his strategy helped re-elect, against long odds, the Parti Québécois government of René Lévesque — the victory coming despite the previous year's defeat of independence, the PQ's sole reason for existence. Simard, impressed by the victory, had contacted Lévesque's staff and had gone to Montreal to meet with the PQ brain trust. He was told that Dupré was the man he really wanted to talk to.

Léger didn't know it when he picked up Dupré at the airport that August night, but the Montreal consultant already had been working for Simard and the PC party for months. His first gambit, a poll of francophone New Brunswickers, seemed to show that no Tory harvest was possible. "It would be utopic to hope for gains," Dupré remembers concluding. Francophones didn't dislike Hatfield, nor did they have a reason to vote for him. They recognized Bill 88 as significant and were pleased but surprised that the Tories had passed it, but they needed to be told and shown that they had clout with the PC party.

Dupré had some ideas on how to do that, but he told Simard, "I can't do this from my desk. I have to see things up close." And so he and Simard conceived the Grand Ralliement, part symposium, part pep rally, part focus group.

Simard and Jean Gauvin, who represented Shippagan, would invite Acadian leaders to the fishing town for three days of consultations that would allow Dupré to measure more directly what was on the minds of francophones and how their aspirations might be folded into an election strategy. "We positioned it as a chance to consider post-Bill 88 — 'where do we go from here?' — so it allowed the Acadian élite to attend without appearing that they were taking part in a political event," Dupré says. "They knew the PC party was going to benefit from it, but they were benefitting from Bill 88, so they calculated that it was good for the party but it was good for them, too."

The slogan of the event was *Mon pouvoir j'y crois* — I believe in my power. And all the Progressive Conservative candidates in francophone ridings, including Mockler and Poitras, were there to draw the clear connection between that power — Acadian power — and PC power. With the exception of Hatfield, most of the anglophone

Tory MLAs stayed home, suspicious. "They were saying 'my power' meant Simard power," Simard explained. "Some MLAs and cabinet ministers were spreading it that it was my attempt to take over the Tory party."

For three days, the 450 delegates from francophone cultural, educational and labour organizations discussed and debated policy side-by-side with PC party members and candidates. Some resolutions advocated going even farther than Bill 88, but workshop leaders finessed procedure to ensure that they didn't reach the final plenary session. Still, the image of Acadian leaders co-operating with the Progressive Conservative party of New Brunswick was powerful. "When we saw they were there — they were participating and they weren't fighting — we knew we had it won," Dupré says.

For francophone Tories who first came to the party in 1982, the Grand Ralliement remains a vivid memory. "That was the crossroads," says Percy Mockler, "when people said, 'We can trust Richard Hatfield. We have tangible examples of success.' You had names. You had faces. It wasn't just the Liberal party that could give this to people. They could touch it. They could feel it. They could feel the power."

Though Omer Léger, who in 1982 was attempting to make a comeback after losing his seat in 1978, recalls the Grand Ralliement as "highly" political, functioning as a giant focus group for Yves Dupré with some substance thrown in for good measure, Léger's son Louis sees it above all as a symbol. "You can say that it was just clever strategy, but for francophones in the Conservative party, it was like a coming of age. That's how I felt. It was a big deal. The symbolism of it was understood, and francophones in the party were very proud of it. But the beauty of it was that it worked."

Hatfield called the election on September 2, scarcely ten days after the closing of the Grand Ralliement. In the first week of the campaign, Louis Léger attended a rally for his father at the firemen's hall in Saint-Antoine and saw the campaign material. It included the slogan *Encore plus fort avec Hatfield*, which Dupré had created for Hatfield, who arrived by helicopter. "That's when it dawned on me that that was the result of the Grand Ralliement," Léger says.

The premier and his campaign team had given Simard what he wanted: full autonomy in francophone ridings to create posters, advertisements and slogans. In anglophone ridings, the strategy was to link the abrasive new Liberal leader, Doug Young, to Pierre Trudeau's dismal record on the economy, while in French New Brunswick, voters were reminded of Hatfield's close co-operation with Trudeau in the patriation of the Constitution, which included guarantees of New Brunswick's bilingual status.

The separate strategies led to some friction with the people who had traditionally run the PC campaign in New Brunswick and who now found themselves relegated to the English areas of the province. Norm Atkins, then the head of Dalton Camp's Toronto ad agency, recalls battles over camera crews and other resources. "There were some difficult times in co-ordinating what Jean-Maurice wanted to do and what the general strategy was for the campaign."

"Some people [in Fredericton] opposed it ferociously," Dupré recalls. "They felt it was separatist to have a separate campaign." He and Simard even prepared for the possibility that journalists from English New Brunswick would make an issue of the distinct strategies. Simard's line with reporters would be that the campaign "reflects the reality" of the province — which Dupré says was true. "When we looked at all the ridings, what would work in one area would hurt in another. If one group wants green and one group wants white, you give one green and one white. If we tried to mix them, we wouldn't please anybody. . . . It wasn't two solitudes, it was two communities with a wall between them."

Dupré and Simard needn't have worried that an enterprising journalist would discover, never mind make an issue of, the two-pronged campaign. Reporters, voters and even Conservative candidates in English New Brunswick remained blissfully unaware. "This wasn't common knowledge at all in Kings East," says Hank Myers. "It didn't make the media here. It didn't raise alarm bells." Myers admits, a little sheepishly, that he didn't find out about the French campaign himself until after the election.

New Brunswickers voted on October 12, and all the elements — the strong candidates, the record of action, including Bill 88, the symbolism of the Grand Ralliement, and a mid-campaign government bailout of the Acadian newspaper *L'Évangéline* — came together precisely as Hatfield and Simard had hoped in francophone ridings. The Parti Acadien vote evaporated, and Simard's new recruits — among them Percy Mockler and Yvon Poitras — were elected in five ridings.

In Kent South, voters ended Omer Léger's four-year exile from the Legislature. Simard was returned, as were Jean Gauvin in Shippagan-les-Îles, Jean-Pierre Ouellette in Madawaska-les-Lacs and Fernand Dubé in Campbellton. Nine francophones helped give the Conservatives a total of thirty-nine seats, more than double the Liberal tally of eighteen and the largest Tory majority since 1912.

The harvest Hatfield had worked so long to reap was his. Now he had to decide what to do with it.

* * *

The exhilaration of election night was not shared by all Tories.

In the Saint John area, Conservative candidates campaigning door to door had found their loyal supporters in a foul mood. "People were telling me, 'This is the last time I'll vote for you unless you get rid of Hatfield,'" says Eric Kipping, who was seeking his second mandate from the voters of Saint John North. When Kipping probed a little deeper, he discovered that voters felt that initiatives such as Bill 88 were proof that Hatfield was "soft" on Acadians — and on Jean-Maurice Simard. "People said, 'If Richard's letting him get away with this, something is wrong.'"

Kipping had managed to soothe his constituents in the past, but this time it was more difficult. A few days after winning re-election, he told Hatfield about the ominous comments he'd heard at the doorsteps.

"He looked me straight in the eye and said, 'Thank you, Eric.' And that was it. No discussion. And that's when I realized Richard was changing."

Chapter Five

THE MIDDLE GROUND IS LOST

RICHARD HATFIELD LOOKED forward to 1984. His federal party had elected a new leader, Brian Mulroney, who appeared poised to seize power in Ottawa. Pope John Paul II was scheduled to make a stop in New Brunswick during his visit to Canada later in the year. The Queen, whom Hatfield adored, was also planning a trip to the province. But what excited Hatfield the most was that 1984 would mark the bicentennial of New Brunswick — it was two hundred years since the colony that would become a province had been carved out of the larger territory of Nova Scotia.

Hatfield was always looking for things to celebrate, and he poured millions into marking the bicentennial. There were grants and scholarships and medals. There would be a new coat of arms. The Queen herself would join in the celebrations. But most of all, the premier hoped to use the occasion to cement the idea of a New Brunswick identity, a common feeling of belonging that would transcend the old English-French cultural division. It would be the crowning moment of his public life — and a powerful legacy for his political party.

But 1984 would not be kind to Richard Hatfield.

Already known for skipping cabinet and caucus meetings, the premier was becoming even less visible in Fredericton. "He wasn't leading," says Keith Dow. "He was being irresponsible." Eric Kipping says Hatfield "went quite wonky" and speculates that the brain tumour that killed Hatfield in 1991 was there as early as 1984. "That's medically possible, isn't it?" Kipping asks, as if hopeful his theory would be confirmed. "That it was affecting a part of his brain?"

Those who tried to defend Hatfield from Eric Kipping, Keith Dow and Bev Harrison concede now that the premier's absences left the government without direction. But they also say the trio of Saint John MLAs held too narrow a view of the province. "There were a lot of people in Fredericton, Moncton and Saint John who had never gone [north] beyond the Chatham bridge," complains Jean Gauvin. "And it's pretty hard to understand the north when you've never met its people."

The earliest sign of trouble, the first blow to Richard Hatfield's hopes for 1984, was over a symbol — in retrospect, a seemingly minor affair compared to what followed. But, as Hatfield should have known, symbols are rarely minor in New Brunswick.

The year 1984 marked not only the province's bicentennial, but also the centennial of the creation of the Acadian flag. Acadians saw the flag, which had first been adopted at an Acadian National Congress in Miscouche, Prince Edward Island, as a turning point in their effort to survive as a people and the beginning of their attempts to secure their rights. Many francophones, among them Pierre Godin, the Liberal MLA for Nigadoo-Chaleur, felt the anniversary should be commemorated.

"You are putting much more emphasis on our province's bicentennial than on the centennial of our flag, and that is unforgivable," Godin told Hatfield when he rose in the Legislature on April 3. "Over the last two hundred years, other governments have ignored our people. Now you are following in their footsteps." No informed, objective observer could claim that Hatfield and Simard had "ignored" the Acadians. But Godin berated the premier at length, then moved a resolution that the flag fly on the Legislature building for the rest of the year. For good measure, Godin dared the Conservatives to vote against the motion.

This was too much for Hatfield, who recognized the trap Godin was laying. He told the chamber that the government "wishes to announce in some detail its policy with regard to *le drapeau acadien*," but he asked for an adjournment. A week later, the premier fired back at Godin, calling his speech "mean and partisan." He refuted Godin's assertions — as Hatfield paraphrased them — that Acadians had "nothing to celebrate." And he laid his own trap for the Liberals: "I do feel that this motion as proposed is insufficient in that it would only have the flag fly in front of the Legislature for one year," he said, as his intentions became clear to stunned MLAs, "and since the government was proceeding in the direction of making provision to fly other flags on other provincial government buildings, I thought that the Acadian flag should be added as well." It would fly at *all* government buildings, at *all* times, the only qualification being the line "where appropriate."

Flabbergasted, the interim Opposition leader, Raymond Frenette, began raising procedural objections to what Hatfield was doing, without endorsing or rejecting the substance of the amendment. Former Liberal leader Doug Young, normally so smooth but now perplexed, sputtered picky questions about the height of the flagpoles and other details before finally, reluctantly, thanking Hatfield for his "generous" amendment. And Godin, who had so vociferously denounced the government for giving his people nothing to celebrate, ended up presenting the premier with an Acadian flag he could raise at the Legislature.

In the excitement of that bipartisan moment, Eric Kipping, the MLA for Saint John North, joined the debate to praise the Acadian people. He spoke of their courage, their energy and their determination to be "full-fledged partners in our province." He digressed into a tribute to the British Commonwealth and its tolerance of diverse cultures, but eventually he returned to the question at hand, asking, "If we have no respect for a symbol, how can we have respect for the people it represents?" He declared his support for the motion, which passed unanimously. But he would soon have second thoughts.

"I knew it was not an actual flag in heraldry," he says now. "It was a symbol, a well-known symbol, of course, and it had been around for a long time." But Kipping was attached to another symbol: the Red Ensign, Canada's flag before the Maple Leaf was adopted in 1965. He'd opposed that change, skeptical of the argument that Canada had to be less visibly British to make Quebecers feel welcome. But if that had been the principle in 1965, he felt it also had to apply in 1984: "I thought it's only fair that if they wanted to remove colonial symbolism, they should also remove the Acadian flag — because it was the French flag with a star on it." Hatfield's former executive assistant Win Hackett says MLAs were consulted, but Kipping asserts otherwise. "That kind of subject was not brought up in caucus very often. That was one of my criticisms of Richard. When it came to matters of bilingualism, he was taking his direction from Simard." (Simard was away in Florida during the flag debate and would claim to have played no role. "I heard about it when I came back to Fredericton," he said.)

As angry constituents called their MLAs and wrote letters to the editor, two of Kipping's Saint John colleagues went public with their opposition. "He was overdoing it," says Keith Dow. "It seemed to be silly to have the Acadian flag all over the province and no Union Jack when the Queen was coming. . . . The Acadians were very close to him and most people in caucus had no problem with that. Just have balance and perspective."

Dow and Harrison warned that they weren't simply speaking for themselves. The tolerance for overtly pro-Acadian initiatives was wearing thin among their constituents. "What [Hatfield] didn't understand was there was an undercurrent there that was about to rise to the surface for the first time, really, in New Brunswick history," Harrison says, positioning himself as a moderate. "People like me were trying to keep a lid on it, because some of my colleagues were quite bigoted."

The flag may have been a symbol to Acadians, but Hatfield's decision became a symbol to many English New Brunswickers that he was being unduly influenced by his francophone MLAs. Saint John, accustomed to having the biggest bloc in any Tory cabinet, now had fewer ministers — having ceded some seats to make room for francophones from the north. Kipping himself had been in cabinet but now found himself on the backbench.

And there were the bilingualism horror stories. Dow remembers two driver examiner jobs posted in Saint John, both requiring fluency in English and French. A constituent, a retired RCMP officer, applied for one position and was disqualified for not being bilingual. "This fellow went ballistic," Dow says. "Talk about a red neck, or becoming a redneck. . . . That was when unilingual anglophones could be negatively affected and turn that into deeper feelings." Dow couldn't get the requirement changed, and it became one of many small provocations to English New Brunswick that created a resentment ready to be harnessed.

Len Poore stepped in to harness it.

Within days of the flag decision, Hatfield's old nemesis from Fredericton City Hall — the man who had opposed the École Sainte-Anne in 1974 — was sitting in the bar of the Lord Beaverbrook Hotel, chatting with friends, when a francophone went by wearing a t-shirt bearing the name of an Acadian association and a picture of that troublesome flag. "I said, 'We should start an association, and bang, that was it, right there. So we put an ad in the paper," Poore recalls. In no time at all, they'd formed the New Brunswick Association of English-Speaking Canadians and were protesting the flag decision at the Legislature. One night, one of its members crept onto the roof of the Lord Beaverbrook Hotel, tore down its Acadian flag and threw it in the river. "I didn't tell them to do it," Poore says now. But, he adds, grinning, "they told me they were going to do it, and I certainly didn't stop them."

Hatfield eventually relented, agreeing to fly the Acadian flag mainly in francophone areas and in the capital. At the Legislature itself, rather than remove the flag, he would dilute its offence with yet another banner. "He gave in [and flew the Union Jack], which is why we have a circus tent up there now," says Harrison.

Hatfield likely assumed that, with the flag matter settled, he could get back to enjoying the bicentennial. But things had changed for the premier. Three MLAs had flexed their muscles. Tories had begun to wonder if their leader had lost his instincts. And Len Poore now had an organization in place that could be mobilized at a moment's notice. The flag flap, just a minor affair over symbols, turned out to be a dress rehearsal for the real drama to come.

* * *

Of the many miscalculations that doomed *Towards Equality of Official Languages in New Brunswick*, better known as the Poirier-Bastarache report, few were as deadly as its timing.

The document had been a long time coming. In 1979, when the Official Languages Act was ten years old, bureaucrats, including Bernard Poirier, the head of the government's language office, had proposed a sweeping review of how the government was living up to the principles of the law. He led a study group and recruited Michel

Bastarache, former dean of law at the Université de Moncton, to research and write a report. The pair — Poirier a bespectacled former journalist and civil servant, Bastarache an intense intellectual — decided not to fret about political sensitivities. "It would have been easy to have taken the point of view of bureaucrats or politicians in attempting to explain and to justify the deficiencies or the lack of action by government on certain files relating to language rights," Poirier would recount in his memoirs. "The committee believed it better to play it straight, to describe the situation as it was in 1982 in New Brunswick, come what may!"

Bastarache finished the report in 1982, and Hatfield promised, when he addressed the annual meeting of the Société des Acadiens du Nouveau-Brunswick that May, that officials would study the recommendations to sort out how to implement them. He also committed to a public consultation, which — because of the 1982 election and other priorities — was delayed for more than two years. A new committee of respected New Brunswickers would hold two rounds of meetings: an initial series of information sessions to explain the report, following by hearings to find out what New Brunswickers had to say.

By the fall of 1984, when the information sessions finally got underway, the flag debacle of the spring was still fresh in the minds of anglophones, now wary and alert to any special government favours for francophones. Adding to their irritation, Simard had announced in October that he would cut 1,200 to 1,800 civil service jobs (out of a total of 10,000) through attrition — while vowing to get more francophones, including unilingual francophones, into government jobs in Fredericton. To make matters worse, later that month, Hatfield was charged with possession of marijuana after a small bag of grass was found in his bag during the Queen's visit. This scandal, unrelated to language, nevertheless widened the chasm between the premier and the sense of propriety held by his traditional Tory supporters in English New Brunswick.

The report's timing was undeniably bad, but there was also the substance of the report itself. Surveying the attitudes of seventy-seven influential New Brunswickers and writers of letters to newspaper editors, Bastarache found a "persistent intolerance" among anglophones toward francophone rights. He concluded that some "paranoid" anglophones saw the French as losers in the great colonial struggles of 1759 to 1763 and bilingualism as their revenge. Even the more generous stereotype of the easy-going, fun-loving Acadian ran contrary to the Protestant ethic of thrift and hard work, he wrote.

More troubling to Bastarache was that many English-speakers rejected the view of Acadians as a "founding people" and believed, incorrectly, that they had arrived in the area *after* the English, and therefore had a lesser claim to land, wealth and rights. Some anglophones wished openly that the British had outlawed the French language after 1763 and saw francophone demands for language rights as outside the aspirations of the Acadian mainstream. Francophone civil servants were considered beneficiaries of favouritism and not as competent or as well trained as their anglophone colleagues.

"One must conclude that the Official Languages Act is not, by itself, sufficient to promote the equality of the two official language groups," Bastarache wrote. "Attitudes have not evolved as they should have, and existing dissatisfaction shows that the improvisation we have seen, in the final analysis, has had unfortunate consequences on the level of social relations."

In the face of these overwhelmingly negative attitudes, Bastarache advocated not a retreat, not the status quo, but a further dramatic expansion of francophone rights that amounted to the creation of a fundamentally new order of government. He said the provincial government should adopt a model of duality — parallel branches of each department, one operating in English, another in French — that would allow anglophones and francophones to work in their own mother tongues without having to become bilingual. Only bureaucrats at the highest level, charged with co-ordinating the efforts of the French and English work units, would need to be bilingual.

Duality was already in effect in the Department of Education, where distinct administrations oversaw distinct school systems. But for other government departments, it was a radical idea with radical implications. Senior civil servants who did not become bilingual would not advance. "While civil servants already in positions have acquired rights in job security," Bastarache wrote, "they do not have the same vested rights in promotion."

The thrust of the report echoed the nationalist, collective-rights ideas espoused by the Parti Acadien and debated at the Convention d'orientation nationale des Acadiens in 1979. Bastarache suggested some government departments and agencies with particular relevance to francophone regions, such as the Department of Fisheries, be moved out of Fredericton altogether and into areas like the Acadian Peninsula. He also urged an affirmative action program for the hiring of francophones, saying bilingual anglophones "cannot truly be counted as representatives of the francophone population of New Brunswick." This recommendation, in particular, was seen as a betrayal of goodwill by anglophones who had enrolled their children in French immersion classes so that they might become bilingual government employees someday.

The tone of the report was also a problem. References to the "Orangeman atmosphere" of Saint John and to the "English language of Shakespeare" were taken as sneeringly sarcastic. It may have been the way educated Acadian nationalists talked among themselves about anglophones, but it was something else to use such terms in a publicly funded report for a government that placed a premium on consensus.

All of the report's elements — timing, content and tone — combined in November 1984 to shake that consensus as the first round of information sessions began in a high school auditorium in Fredericton. Sometimes the meeting felt like a replay of the École Sainte-Anne debate of a decade earlier, with angry residents showing their hostility and attacking the high cost of bilingualism. "It's a bit like giving starving Ethiopians a colour TV set instead of food," one man complained. Others laughed and jeered when members of the committee responded that they had no mandate to consider the financial cost of duality. Len Poore was there that night to allege that unilingual anglophones were victims of discrimination and to recruit more members into his New Brunswick Association of English-Speaking Canadians.

The tension increased at the next session in Saint John. Committee members were greeted by catcalls and protests. A chorus of people yelled, "Go home!" When francophones spoke, some anglophones picked up newspapers and loudly rustled the pages to drown them out. "I couldn't believe these were Saint John people," Irène Guerette, a committee co-chair and prominent Saint John francophone, told a reporter at the meeting. "Maybe that was the first time people had a forum to explain their feelings on it," she says today.

The growing backlash would quickly claim its first victim. During a scheduled break in the first round of sessions, Guerette's co-chair, Horace Hanson, a respected Fredericton lawyer and the son of one-time federal Tory leader R.B. Hanson, resigned. Hanson's letter to Hatfield claimed the committee was inefficient, spending money needlessly, and that many of its members supported the Poirier-Bastarache report even though they were supposed to be neutral. The first two information sessions had caused "frustration and anger among interested groups and persons from the English speaking community" and were "disruptive and divisive," he wrote. But Hanson's most serious charge was that bureaucrats in the Official Languages office, "which is composed entirely of bilingual francophone civil servants," were trying to "manipulate" the committee. He refused to identify them.

The impact was severe. Hanson, highly respected among old-stock Fredericton Tories, seemed to be confirming their most profound fears about Poirier-Bastarache: the fix was in, and a secret cabal of francophones was plotting domination of the government.

Those who knew Hanson through the committee insist that he supported the basic thrust of bilingualism. Irène Guerette guesses he simply resented having to share the chairing duties. He may also have been upset by Hatfield's marijuana scandal, she speculates, or he may have learned that he had cancer. Fred Arsenault has another explanation: "He was a very correct person, and if he got involved in something that was unruly, he would probably ask himself what he was doing there." But Bernard Poirier, in his memoirs, questions whether Hanson simply couldn't accept that francophone civil servants, on loan as support staff, were so involved in the committee's work.

Whatever the reason, Hanson's departure was the first damaging blow to Poirier-Bastarache to come from within the political establishment. Len Poore delivered the second from the outside.

"Our strategy was to hold more and more public meetings," he says now. Poore had quickly discovered that all he had to do was explain the contents of the report — "they were preaching what had to happen and what was going to happen" — and people would sign up to his cause. So confident was he that the document itself would anger people that he ordered two thousand copies to distribute to his members.

Poore may claim today he let the report speak for itself, but a newspaper account at the time shows he also used smear tactics to drive the point home. One columnist described a meeting at which Poore had referred to Jean-Maurice Simard as "that dark fellow." He also told his audiences, absurdly, that English had been banned in Caraquet. He facetiously endorsed the idea that the Acadian Peninsula be made a special administrative area for government services: "I think they should get that, fence it in and keep those sons of guns behind the fence and don't let them out." The tactics worked: the English-Speaking Association gained more and more members all the time, and the Poirier-Bastarache process spun out of control.

Then, on December 6, another New Brunswicker with considerably more mainstream credibility delivered a third setback to both the report and the consultative committee. In an interview with the Saint John *Telegraph-Journal*, former premier Louis Robichaud urged that the meetings be cancelled. "The situation is highly emotional at the moment," he told a reporter. "It's time for people to come back to their senses." Robichaud denounced Poore, but he also denounced the government — not just for Poirier-Bastarache, but for the flag policy, which he blamed for upsetting "the whole applecart. It's a heck of a nice flag. I have my own and I'm proud of it, but the premier should never have allowed it to fly on provincial buildings."

With those comments, Robichaud gave political cover to the growing backlash. If the father of Acadian rights felt Poirier-Bastarache went too far, then opposition to the report must surely be rational, reasonable, moderate and mainstream.

With Len Poore and Louis Robichaud attacking from opposite ends of the language spectrum, the middle ground on which Poirier-Bastarache could rest was shrinking rapidly. Bev Harrison had been right: an undercurrent was rising to the surface, disturbing the political consensus on language. Now it would roil the coalition supposedly built on that consensus — the Progressive Conservative government of Richard Hatfield.

* * *

The caucus had been stewing for weeks. Len Poore says today that Ed Allen, the MLA for Fredericton North and Hatfield's minister of supply and services, was outraged by the Poirier-Bastrache recommendations, though cabinet solidarity dictated that he publicly support whatever the government decided. Allen died in 2002, but other MLAs leave no doubt that emotions were running high. "It created a chasm, no question, and the flag issue, too," says Keith Dow. "It exacerbated latent feelings beneath the surface."

On one side of the chasm were English MLAs who argued that they were not against francophone rights themselves, but that the government had to take into account that opposition existed. "The masterminds who were doing this probably knew they should have been going slower," Kipping says. "The Acadians had a good case but they couldn't get there fast. Of course they'd been here several hundred years. But you have to watch your pace, and they didn't, and naturally that caused resentment."

But the advocates of going slow found themselves painted as bigots — or apologists for bigotry. "Arguments that counselled caution and care were often misunderstood," says David Clark, then the MLA for Fredericton South. "The people who were really upset were not used to seeing a French commission going around the province, articulating rights and a sharing of power," says Win Hackett, then Hatfield's assistant. Hackett nonetheless admits that the proposed duality within government departments would have been unworkable.

Other supporters of Poirier-Bastarache are philosophical, acknowledging the report put MLAs from staunchly English areas in a political bind. "An MLA can only be a reflection of the people he represents," Jean Gauvin says. "They were going home on the weekends and coming back to Fredericton on Mondays with all the comments their constituents had." David Clark agrees: "More than one member of the caucus lived in a state of conflict between the practicality of personal electoral prospects and doing the right thing." Clark adds, though, that Dow, Harrison and Kipping were not merely reflecting popular will. "My belief is that when they argued against legislative action on language, they argued their convictions and did not simply act as advocates for the interests of their constituents." Hank Myers of Kings East says there were five MLAs — whom he will not name — who were "anti-French out of fear, or because of the fear of their constituents." The rest, Myers says, simply recognized that Poirier-Bastarache, however valid its recommendations, threatened the consensus in the province and in the party. "I felt some of the positions that were being taken and the ideas being put forward would create exactly the situation that was created."

The internal dissent also fed existing suspicion toward francophones within the party. Ministers like Jean Gauvin, Jean-Pierre Ouellet and Fernand Dubé had run up huge expense claims for purchases that sometimes stretched the definition of "government business," offending the Tory sense of Protestant frugality. Some long-time members began to wonder if these ministers weren't just freeloaders. There were whispered suggestions that the Acadian shift of support to the Tories in 1982 had not been a reward for Hatfield's language policies but simply a realignment of convenience for francophones interested in the rewards of power.

Other Tories began to fear the rewards of power would disappear if the turmoil continued. At meetings of the provincial executive during the height of the Poirier-Bastarache controversy, party president Janice Clarke received the brunt of it. "Primarily the concerns were about the reports they were seeing in the media, that it would be harmful to the government, based on some of the incidents that were happening," she says.

And the incidents continued. In the second week of December, Irène Guerette and the committee travelled to Miramichi for another information session. There, one member was struck by an egg thrown from the audience. In Moncton, an English-speaking man pushed over a Radio-Canada TV light, then got into a shoving match with a francophone woman. To everyone's relief, that Moncton session marked the end of the first round. The committee would pause for the holidays before moving into the second round, the public consultations, early in the New Year.

By then, the dissent within the PC party was out in the open. The *Telegraph-Journal* had published a story by columnist Don Hoyt quoting anonymous MLAs who said there was a rift in the government. Hoyt reported that five MLAs — cabinet ministers Mabel Deware of Moncton, Mac Macleod of Albert, Bill Harmer of Petitcodiac, and backbenchers Bev Harrison and David Clark — were trying to "slow down" Jean-Maurice Simard and his Poirier-Bastarache agenda. The story said they were concerned about Hatfield's absences and, for the first time, the idea of dumping him as leader was raised. "It could reach that point," an anonymous MLA told Hoyt. "Some members would be quite prepared to do it."

The story shook the committee, whose members were already discouraged by what they were seeing at the information sessions. "It really was two solitudes," says Irène Guerette. "I was amazed at how much the two [groups] didn't know each other." The members themselves had talked about calling a halt, but, Guerette says, "if you had stopped in the middle of this, it would have looked bad for everybody." Now came reports that members of the government wanted to derail the process.

Hatfield's caucus was set to meet on Friday, December 13. The day before, caucus chairman Bev Harrison and MLA Keith Dow lobbed two more volleys at Poirier-Bastarache. Harrison, in a *Telegraph-Journal* interview, attacked what he called "the racial slurs" in the report and the "nationalist ideology" of Bastarache, and he labelled the hiring approach "affirmative action," saying it would "slow down the anglophone promotions to zero." Dow, quoted in a separate story, called on the government to cancel the second round of hearings. A third story quoted Yvon Poitras, now a cabinet minister, saying "maybe" the government would agree to postpone the hearings.

By the time MLAs emerged from the six-hour caucus, however, Harrison was describing "a mood of good camaraderie and solidarity," and he blamed journalists for raising the leadership issue. Kipping brushed aside the question of Hatfield's absences. "You know, it's just like someone you love," he said. "You want to be around them. Well, all right, we love him, we want him to be with us when we make our decisions and when we have to solve our problems. In general, the premier is present and he is leading. . . . You media people, really, are making something of this that does not exist."

Behind closed doors, Hatfield had vowed to respond to the growing anger in the province. Five days into the New Year, he appointed two new anglophone members to the committee, including a new co-chair, retired judge Lloyd Smith, giving it equal representation from the two language groups. And — explaining that the two new members needed to get up to speed — Hatfield postponed the second round by a month, pushing it into February. But there was no question of cancelling it altogether. "To end this public consultation because of these deplorable incidents would be a defeat for the democratic process and for the New Brunswick tradition of civility and mutual respect," he said. And he pleaded with more moderate anglophones to come forward and balance the extremists who had thrown eggs and heckled during the first round: "We ask fair-minded New Brunswickers to co-operate in this consultation with the people. It is the people's opportunity to ensure that government policy will have a firm foundation in a more democratic process."

Meanwhile, the government prepared a secret public-relations campaign. A confidential committee document, stored at the Provincial Archives, outlines a tender for a six-month "information campaign and implementation strategy" to help the committee "deal with hostile and/or difficult situations." Consultants would attempt to plant positive news stories on the Official Languages Act, on members of the committee, and on peoples' experiences speaking two languages. There was money for polling ($20,000), for a twenty-eight-minute documentary ($23,100) and to pay a "strategy consultant" for twelve days of work ($12,000). The total budget: $149,950.

The package included likely questions from reporters and possible answers, many of them designed to portray what was happening in New Brunswick not as a dangerous schism but as perfectly normal. "Disagreement has a place in decision-making" was the heading of one document, citing such examples as the adoption of the Canadian flag. "Tempers flare, people will and must let off steam. It is always a painful experience. But when the dust settles, reasonable people can and generally do make reasonable decisions." A second document was more pragmatic. Labelled "contingency plan," it outlined scenarios "to control noisy, grandstanding situations" during the second round. One tactic involved a hand signal from the chairman to the technician to turn off the microphone. Another option was described starkly as "cancel the process."

But no amount of strategy could contain what had been unleashed. Across English New Brunswick, in cities and small towns, along country backroads and in the homes and halls and churches that had long formed the electoral bedrock of the Progressive Conservative party, a considerable amount of energy waited to vent.

* * *

The file boxes sit on dusty shelves in a ramshackle old warehouse owned by the Provincial Archives. Inside, some briefs are neatly typed, articulate and well reasoned. Others are handwritten, marred by poor spelling and grammar, and verge on the ridiculous. Together they form a catalogue of the ethnic suspicion, fear and even hatred that manifested itself in New Brunswick in 1985. "The attitude that we took was that we were going to stay as cool as possible and hear everything [people] were going to say," Irène Guerette says of the second round. And as the briefs came in by the dozens and then the hundreds, New Brunswickers spelled out their divisions in black and white before her eyes.

"This Country was founded on violence and war and that is what you are going to get if you keep on this matter without a free vote," wrote a man in Minto. "The French people in the province sound like a bunch of Communists. I hate to think what is next if French is forced down the English people's throat. . . . I am afraid eggs was first, bullets may be next." An Oromocto couple said they "thought the dominance of French was settled on the Plains of Abraham. . . . Since when do the conquered people tell the conquerors where they get off at?"

Some briefs displayed a basic misunderstanding of the report's recommendations. Bastarache never suggested that small, over-whelmingly English towns and villages be forced to provide full bilingual services, yet that fear gripped mayors and councillors across English New Brunswick, and it pushed them to oppose the report. Mayor Charles Smith of the village of Harvey complained in his submission that requiring his tiny community to go bilingual would be too rad-ical and too costly. "All this expenditure and extra work would gain absolutely nothing," he wrote. "It is far more important for French speaking Canadians to learn to speak English."

Other New Brunswickers demonstrated a deeper ignorance. One complained that Poirier-Bastarache aimed to improve the economic lives of francophones. "Unfortunately, the Acadians settled areas that have fewer economic resources in today's environment," the man wrote, unaware that in 1755 the British had forcibly removed the Acadians from the more fertile regions of the Maritimes.

Occasionally, an opponent of expanded French services would unwittingly make the case for such services, as a Newcastle writer did when he condemned plans for a French community centre and school in his town. Oblivious to the francophones living there, he said the only French-speakers were in nearby villages — Rogersville, Neguac and Baie-Sainte-Anne — that already had their own schools. "No children from these areas go to school in Newcastle at the present time," he wrote, "with the exception of some from Bellefond [but] most of these people are French in name only, as their fathers and forefathers all went to high school in Newcastle."

Other writers were diligent researchers, scanning committee documents for ammunition. A.L. Laberge of Newcastle pointed out, correctly, that eleven of the fourteen researchers who contributed to the document were francophones. "This in itself is reason for questioning the credibility of the report and of those who contributed to it," he wrote. Laberge also warned that those surveyed for the report had also skewed its findings: "There are some most insidious French activists in the Miramichi area."

This was a repeated theme — nefarious militants were up to no good in their advocacy of French rights. The reality is more sobering. Like other francophones from English areas who filed briefs, Jocelyne Durelle of Baie-Sainte-Anne wasn't seeking power. She eloquently described her experience when her sick three-year-old daughter was transported alone to Moncton by unilingual Engilsh ambulance attendants. The inability of the paramedics to ask the girl in her own language if she was experiencing neck pain — a tell-tale sign of meningitis — made the lack of French service a life-and-death affair. "Can you imagine a child of that age, traumatized in that way, surrounded by people who can't communicate with her?" Durelle asked. "Any parent, whatever language they speak, can appreciate how my husband and I felt during those hours the trip took, knowing she had no one to console her or ever understand her."

Another letter spoke poignantly of assimilation. Leo Boucher of Minto wrote that he came from a family of thirteen children born to French parents. "The older ones speak French fairly well, the younger understand French but have a hard time to express themselves in French," he wrote. "As far as I know, none of us can read or write French, we had no choice but to go to English school." Add the children of the thirteen siblings and "here is 2 generations who have lost their Mother tongue. . . . I've never really thought about this that much. As you can probably tell I'm limited in being able to Express myself. However I hope you will get the main idea of what I'm trying to say. . . . I want to wish all of you who are trying so hard in wanting to have a better understanding Between French & English. . . . Both parties seem to have a Blind outlook only because, they want to live within their own circle, Yet there is so much to gain knowing another language. My wife and I both realize this. With all this, here I'm hoping my Daughter will take a French Course when she completes High School this year. May the Good Lord Bless You all in your endeavor."

But such articulate and eloquent statements of the need for equal services in both languages — and the consequences of not having them — were overwhelmed by others.

Many writers wanted not just to stop Poirier-Bastarache but to turn the clock back to before 1969. In response to a request printed in the Fredericton *Daily Gleaner*, dozens wrote letters to the commission, identically worded, asking not just that it shelve the report but that "immediate action be taken by the Provincial Government to have the 1969 Official Languages Act of New Brunswick and subsequent acts pertaining to it repealed." Meanwhile, members of Len Poore's New Brunswick Association of English-Speaking Canadians filed briefs in each English community where there would be hearings. One long-winded, heavily annotated treatise attempted to prove a French conspiracy: "The establishment of the French demand throughout Canada is not to be accomplished in one day, but by bits and pieces here and there innocently, while . . . the English-speaking . . . whether willingly or unwittingly see their future slowly eroded and wonder what it is that is happening."

Other writers wrote less cluttered letters. "The French people of New Brunswick," wrote Greg Hargrove, a young man from the Nashwaak Valley, north of Fredericton, "should have English forced on them through education from grade one."

These were the most forceful views. But even moderates found it difficult to support Poirier-Bastarache. Harold Culbert, the mayor of Woodstock and later a Liberal MP, wrote that he supported the 1969 Official Languages Act enthusiastically — but duality, as recommended by Bastarache, was untenable. Even the University of New Brunswick, no bastion of extremism under president James Downey, said there were too many unanswered questions about duality. "Left unresolved, it could create misunderstanding within the province, embarrassment before outside funding agencies, both public and private, and limit the technological competitiveness of New Brunswick."

UNB's brief went on to mount a devastating attack on the academic merits of the report — a particularly damning critique given that Bastarache, a former dean of law at another provincial university, was the lead author. The brief said the survey of attitudes, based on a few dozen opinion leaders and some letters to the editor, lacked credibility. "There is no place here for partisan or *a priori* analysis — the manipulation of data and rationalization of contrary evidence to justify a predetermined set of conclusions," the UNB brief said. "Yet Part One of this report is filled with historical, sociological and political inaccuracies and distortions, and with evidence of an *ad hoc* and amateurish research design. . . . Practically all of the questionable information serves to justify a single ideological premise, that legitimate francophone aspirations can never be respected within shared political institutions."

The briefs make one thing clear: "Fair-minded New Brunswickers," as Hatfield had called them, had not responded to his plea to pull Poirier-Bastarache from the edge and back to the middle ground. They could support something that made sense to them, such as government services in one's mother tongue. But duality — duplication of entire government departments in English and French — did not resonate with fair-minded New Brunswickers. Though they may have been troubled by the anti-French insults and the thrown egg from the first round, they could not quite embrace what the bigots were attacking, either. And so they remained silent, leaving the battle to those who wanted to roll back francophones' most basic rights and to Acadian leaders compelled to push for the report's adoption if only to make sure they retained what they already had.

As these two opposing forces came to occupy the field, with no moderating force in between, Poirier-Bastarache could not find solid footing in the mainstream of New Brunswick society. It was inevitable, then, that the middle ground would also be lost within the PC party, within the government caucus and within Richard Hatfield's cabinet.

Conservative party members participated in the second round, filing briefs and appearing at the hearings along with other New Brunswickers. The Moncton North PC association submitted a document opposing Poirier-Bastarache; the party's Caraquet association filed one supporting it. Hank Myers, MLA for Kings East, condemned "bitterness and animosity and even bigotry which have surfaced in recent months," but also lamented the attempts to "legislate culture." Pointing out that most bilingual New Brunswickers were francophone, "it does not require much imagination to decide who the authors think ought to run the province," Myers wrote.

The profound split in the party finally came into full view in April, when two cabinet ministers — normally bound by the conventions of the parliamentary system to show public unity at all times — offered starkly opposite views of the report.

Nancy Clark Teed, MLA for Saint John South, had already vowed to resign as minister of social services if Poirier-Bastarache were implemented as a whole. She repeated the threat before the committee on April 2. "This report turns a blind eye to the feelings of average people," she said. Its duality proposal was aimed at creating "a separate Acadian society." The minister lambasted the survey of anglophone attitudes. "The authors present a vision of a cold, unfeeling people which is blatantly false, if not outright racist." She also claimed Bastarache had falsely described "a collective Acadian mentality which in no way corresponds to the diversity and pluralism of thought, culture and business methods which today's New Brunswickers choose to follow. It is hard to believe that supposedly sincere and democratic-minded people wrote this strident, divisive and false impression of both French and English-speaking New Brunswickers."

Clark Teed claimed some knowledge of francophones' wishes. Based on her travels in the province, she concluded that bilingual services were not a high priority for Acadians. "My personal opinion is that their first concern is for livelihood, shelter, food, clothing and services, and the language they are provided in would be secondary," she said. "I have to say if I was in a car accident in Shippagan I really wouldn't care whether the ambulance driver spoke my language. I would care that he could get that vehicle to the hospital."

That language might actually affect care — as it threatened to do when Jocelyne Durelle's daughter couldn't tell the ambulance staff about her symptoms — seems not to have occurred to her. Nor did Clark Teed seem to be aware of the plight of francophones in the Saint John area. Albert Comeau, for instance, had complained to the committee of the absence of service in his language when he had been a patient in a provincial rehabilitation centre in 1980. Perhaps Nancy Clark Teed wasn't such an expert on francophone priorities after all.

That was Jean Gauvin's interpretation, his frustration building as he read news reports of Clark Teed's presentation. Gauvin, MLA for Shippagan-les-Îles on the Acadian Peninsula and Hatfield's minister of fisheries, was tired of fighting his fellow ministers behind closed doors in cabinet. "They thought that the province was like their ridings," he says of some anglophone members of cabinet. "It's pretty difficult when you don't understand the mosaic of the province." He wished in vain that Hatfield would take control of the agenda. "It was very clear there were no political 'lines' on that issue," he says. "There was no political direction that everyone should go one way."

So Jean Gauvin went his own way. He sat before the committee in Shippagan on April 30 to rebuke — implicitly yet publicly — his cabinet colleague, Nancy Clark Teed.

Gauvin said the reaction to Poirier-Bastarache appeared to corroborate much of the survey of attitudes. He dismissed the notion, espoused by Clark Teed and others, that everyone in New Brunswick had been perfectly happy, and would still be if only the report had not come along. "Does talking about linguistic rights . . . mean wanting to destroy the harmony, understanding, spirit of co-operation and goodwill between francophones and anglophones?" he asked. "Is merely talking about the delivery of services in French . . . enough to sow disunity?" Gauvin said it was still hard for Acadians in some cases to get provincial services in French, to work for the government in French, or to win jobs at the senior levels of the bureaucracy. "The Acadians are pressing for changes," he said, "and these demands are legitimate, because very often the current situation causes them to feel that they are second-class citizens."

Gauvin's comments revealed the schism in the government, but few saw the portents; the public relations strategy and the lack of disruptive antics at the hearings in the second round combined to move the Poirier-Bastarache story off the front page. Only those who were looking for the nuances understood the implications of Gauvin's remarks. "The gulf was widening," says Bev Harrison, a Bastarache skeptic and ally of Nancy Clark Teed. Harrison had found the story on Gauvin's appearance on page six of his *Telegraph-Journal*, just above something equally troubling to him: a photograph of Hubert Seamans, the winning Liberal candidate in a by-election held two nights before in the traditionally Tory riding of Riverview.

As Tories drew connections between the language controversy and the loss of Riverview, the crises converged. "Richard Hatfield should have been at his prime, at his strongest, at that point — to carry it, to balance it, to deal with it," says Louis Léger, who had watched the tremendous show of strength at the Grand Ralliement less than three years earlier.

Instead, Harrison says, "what you had was a very short period of time where it looked like his fourth term was going to hell in a hand-basket." Language divisions among the PC membership were in plain sight at the precise moment when Hatfield needed loyalty to face his drug scandal. But loyalty to the premier and to the party was based, as it is in every government, on access to power, and there was a palpable sense that power was slipping away from the Conservatives.

The Riverview by-election, coming just when these challenges were mounting, opened the floodgates. Keith Dow, two days after the vote, told a newspaper reporter that the party had to listen to "the very direct message" from the electorate. "There's no question that in the majority of the English-speaking ridings of the province, there is concern with respect to perceptions of government leadership," Dow said. "No question about that, it's a major factor."

Just days after the Riverview defeat, Jim Pickett went to New Denmark and saw his motion calling for a leadership review passed. The same night, Bev Harrison stood up at a meeting of his riding association and asked for Hatfield's resignation. The division in the party was now official. Francophone Conservatives saw their champion under attack because of his efforts on their behalf. Anglophone Tories were concluding that Hatfield had lost touch, and their irritation about language, the Acadian flag and Poirier-Bastarache was being validated by Dow, Harrison and others.

"It was something under the surface in the beginning," Janice Clarke, then party president, says with a sigh. "They were talking more about the personal difficulties. In hindsight, you can perhaps see that [language] was a larger motivating factor than what they were presenting."

As bad as 1984 had been for Richard Hatfield, 1985 was becoming much worse. The divisions in New Brunswick laid bare by Poirier-Bastarache would now consume the Progressive Conservative Party.

* * *

The consultative committee on Poirier-Bastarache handed in its report on June 19, 1986. To Hatfield's surprise, its eight members had agreed unanimously on the need for duality in the civil service and for decentralized administrative units of the government in franco-phone areas — two recommendations that followed closely those Poirier-Bastarache had suggested. Hatfield expressed his government's commitment to bilingualism and promised more progress in the future, then rejected both suggestions. "The work unit concept in the federal government has not achieved the results anticipated," he said in the Legislature. "Although some 'natural' work units have been and may be established in some departments and regions, we will not adopt this concept as a solution."

"I was disappointed it went on the shelf," Irène Guerette says. "But a report is a report. You hand it in and it's not yours anymore." Like others, she believes Hatfield was so exhausted by the 1985 leadership battle that he could not have implemented the recommendations even if he'd wanted to. "He was finished as a premier then. We could see the end of his reign. It was obvious."

Hatfield had at least proven wrong many of the anglophones who had predicted the government's mind was made up and their opposi-tion would be ignored. But it was too late to persuade them that their opinions mattered. He had always gambled that he could accom-modate French New Brunswick while retaining the support of the English Tory heartland. Now he was losing the bet.

"I thought at that particular time that we'd won a victory," says Len Poore, whose English-Speaking Association had played such a key role in stopping Poirier-Bastarache. And Poore had achieved some-thing else. At several meetings of the association, he and his cronies had talked about the need for a new political party that would represent the exclusive interests of the anglophone majority in New Brunswick. His association — full of long-time Progressive Conservatives who no longer felt at home in their old party — now stood ready to become the backbone of a new political force.

It was certainly not the legacy Hatfield had wanted to leave, and many in the Tory party would wonder precisely when the process had gone so badly wrong. Media coverage played a role by focusing on the worst examples of bigotry at the information sessions, though a survey of the hundreds of briefs suggests that such views were shared by a large number of people.

More fatal, perhaps, was the early decision by Bernard Poirier and Michel Bastarache not to consult the public *before* drafting their report. "At the outset, we rejected the idea of holding public hearings," Poirier wrote in his memoirs. "Our experience of public hearings offered no guarantee that the discussions would be calm and moderate. Such debates often became charged with emotion at a cost to the objectives." It's a startling admission: the two lead authors of the report, aware that there would be substantial opposition, chose to pretend it did not exist.

Other Tories blame not only the approach Poirier and Bastarache took but their selection in the first place. "It should have been Poirier-MacLellan or Poirier-Johnston," says Omer Léger. "It was a mistake to have two prominent francophone guys. Philosophically, it made sense. But you have to sell the product, and the customer is always right." Poirier himself would admit to the *Ottawa Citizen* in 1997 that the recommendations were out of touch with the political reality of the day. "It was, I suppose, too much to chew on at one time," he said.

Frédéric Arsenault — Hatfield's first Acadian confidant in 1961 and a deputy minister in 1985 — says there was another miscalculation. Arsenault was reading the report at home one night, not long after the meetings had turned ugly, when he detected something in the writing style of the inflammatory chapter on English attitudes.

Arsenault says he showed the document to his wife, who exclaimed, "It's the *mitraillette*." She recognized the writing style as that of René-Jean Ravault, a sociologist from France who had taught her at the Université de Moncton. His rapid-fire speaking style had earned him the nickname *mitraillette* — the machine gun.

Curious, Arsenault asked for the research studies Poirier and Bastarache had commissioned before they assembled the report. He found that the report's survey on English attitudes — including the hot-button phrases and the accusation of "persistent intolerance" — had come from René-Jean Ravault's research study, *Perception of Two Solitudes.*

Something else was in Ravault's study: a conclusion that Michel Bastarache had chosen not to quote.

"[T]he intervention of the provincial government in this area must — despite the most frequent Acadian demands — be founded on persuasion and not coercion," Ravault had written. He went on to say that coercive measures would be opposed by anglophones— who, as the majority, would trip up any government that adopted them. The English had only accepted bilingualism so far precisely because it had not been coercive, he continued. Anything more forceful risked a serious backlash.

Arsenault says he was stunned. Bastarache had been warned by his own hired expert that English attitudes required him to proceed with caution. Instead, he had ignored the warning and advocated the dramatic, even radical idea of duality. "I took the Poirier-Bastarache report on one side and the Ravault report on the other side and marked the parts that were copied in yellow," Arsenault says. "And the recommendations of Ravault — 'go slow' — were *not* copied. And I took it to Hatfield and said 'This could be the source of your problem.' Ravault said 'go slow' and Poirier-Bastarache said 'go for it.' . . . If you borrow someone's research and then discard their conclusion, that's quite something."

The premier had been prepared to adopt whatever Poirier-Bastarache recommended, Arsenault says, but ended feeling betrayed. "It appeared people had their minds set when they started. You had a two-person committee who agreed with each other to start with — and they weren't listening to other views that were coming in. You should try to ensure in your committee that all the points of view are reflected, so that if there's a dissenting point of view, it's reflected in the report, or in a dissenting minority report."

Instead, the dissent had to find its release outside the committee, with the resulting damage to the process and to English-French relations. To this day, the chapter on anglophone attitudes — based on Ravault's study but without his corresponding advice to go slow — are what people remember most about Poirier-Bastarache. "There are references that are excessively nationalist, bitter, accusatory and out of line," Keith Dow says. "I'm surprised that Michel Bastarache was appointed to our Supreme Court after expressing views like that."

Instead, Bastarache's 1997 elevation to the Supreme Court of Canada was greeted with near unanimous praise in New Brunswick. But by ignoring the hostility he knew was out there, by urging strong action against the advice of his hired expert, by suggesting that "attitudes have not evolved as they should have," Bastarache revealed a troubling disregard both for New Brunswickers who hadn't joined the élite consensus on bilingualism and for the politicians who had been legitimately elected to represent them.

Chapter Six

"ONE OF US"

AS RICHARD HATFIELD sought to measure, then outmanoeuvre, the forces lining up to remove him from the party leadership, he discovered that the political equilibrium that had guided him for a decade and a half had been turned upside down.

In his first three terms in office, "he was prepared to risk Carleton County attitudes in a quest for Acadian support," Bev Harrison says. "He thought, 'The English will be with me anyway.'" Now, in the spring of 1985, Hatfield had to rely on the near-unanimous backing of francophones. The real battle would be in the English-speaking ridings — down the St. John River into Fredericton and Loyalist Saint John, then east through Kings and Albert counties — that Conservative premiers had always taken for granted.

Members of the Legislative Assembly from those ridings had enormous, perhaps even decisive, influence on how grassroots Tories voted. Yet a clear accounting of their loyalties is difficult. Even now, almost two decades later, many are still reluctant to name names. "There were plots and counterplots, including people in cabinet who were going to go and spear Richard in his den," says Hank Myers. "Then we'd have a caucus meeting and everyone was fine."

Three of Hatfield's opponents are well remembered by all: the Saint John MLAs who went public and came to be known as "The Three Musketeers" — Bev Harrison, Keith Dow and Eric Kipping.

Of the three, Harrison's role was the most significant. As caucus chairman, his job was to bring MLAs together, not divide them. But the former school teacher had a contrarian streak. A history buff since childhood — "I would correct my teacher and all those things" — and a monarchist, he had opposed the patriation of the Constitution in 1982, an effort Hatfield had supported. The British North America Act, Harrison argues to this day, was better left in England, protected from meddlesome politicians. By writing things down in a Constitution and in a Charter of Rights, Pierre Trudeau and his accomplices, among them Hatfield, had abandoned the British tradition of common law and had gutted Parliament's supremacy. Initiatives such as Bill 88 and Poirier-Bastarache, with their emphasis on collective rights, proved to Harrison that the premier didn't understand the British system — an attitude Hatfield's advisors considered pompous. "I once heard him say 'I know more about the Constitution than Richard does,' a statement I found egregious," Win Hackett says.

Harrison's ally Eric Kipping, also first elected in 1978, was a Cape Bretoner who had known Hatfield at university and had served on Saint John common council. He came by his anglophile attitudes honestly: his father had fought in the First World War and two of his brothers had died in the Second. At sixteen, Eric had joined the Royal Canadian Corps of Signals as a high-speed Morse code operator in time to see the end of the war in Europe.

The third musketeer, Dow, was the son of a Conservative Baptist father from Woodstock and an Anglican Liberal mother from Saint John. He had become involved with the Saint John West PC riding association when Rod Logan was the MLA and minister of justice. Dow had thought that Hatfield's "political prudence" on language — proclaiming sections of the Official Languages Act "piecemeal" through the 1970s — had worked well. When Logan was named a judge just before the 1982 election, Dow won the nomination and the seat.

Three MLAs from three staunchly Loyalist Saint John ridings would become the public faces of the party revolt against Hatfield. But as the review movement gathered steam, others would join them, often from the shadows.

* * *

The rumblings had started early on, before the Poirier-Bastarache process had spun out of control and when the drug allegations against Hatfield were limited to some marijuana in his luggage. At the PC annual general meeting in Moncton in November 1984, Hatfield had been contrite. "I am used to the applause," he told delegates. "I am used to the support. I might say that I took it for granted." He admitted to being distracted by the bicentennial, the Papal and Royal visits and the drug possession charge, but he vowed to fight back and win the next election. Eight hundred delegates in the hall responded with a rousing show of support.

It proved the last unanimous endorsement Hatfield would enjoy from his party.

Two weeks later, the Conservatives won a by-election in Madawaska Centre, giving them a majority of francophone ridings for the first time. But that was overshadowed by a loss to the New Democrats in Saint John East the same day, a result that underscored for Tories Hatfield's strength in French New Brunswick and his decline in Saint John, that most Tory of cities.

Hatfield was acquitted of the marijuana charge in January 1985. But by then, the Saint John *Telegraph-Journal* had published Don Hoyt's story that three ministers and two backbenchers — Harrison and David Clark of Fredericton South — were trying to "put the brakes" on the Poirier-Bastarache report just as the province was bracing for the second round of hearings.

Then, just a few days after the marijuana acquittal, came the even more shocking allegation that Hatfield had invited two university students to his home for marijuana and cocaine, before flying them to Montreal with him on the government plane. The new accusations, though unsubstantiated, jolted the rebels back into action. Entering an early February caucus meeting two days after they were published, Kipping, citing phone calls from his constituents, told a reporter, "If he says they're true, he should quit in my opinion." Other skeptics of Poirier-Bastarache — Harrison, Dow and Clark — joined Kipping in demanding Hatfield come clean. "The charge simply reinforced other negative perceptions that some people held about the premier," Clark says. "Some New Brunswickers never got comfortable with the fact he was a unique human being."

Francophone Tories rallied — sometimes literally — to defend the man who had given them power and influence. The attachment they felt for him was deep, according to MLA Percy Mockler. "He had compassion. He listened to our concerns. He had become one of us." A meeting in Caraquet drew more than seven hundred party supporters, who sang and chanted their solidarity with their leader. A petition in the form of a Valentine's Day message — with Poirier-Bastarache still looming over everything — left no doubt about their views. "Premier Hatfield's attackers," the message said, "are the same people who are attempting to undermine our community by objecting to our rightful demands to share in the political power."

Hatfield responded to the accusations the day before Valentine's Day, admitting he was "unconventional" and "extremely gregarious" and that the two students had been to his home, where he often entertained. But he denied "completely and unequivocally" that he'd given them drugs. He said that the marijuana at the heart of the earlier charge had been planted in his bag, and that he would not quit over unsubstantiated accusations. His fate would be decided in the next election. "That is the only process which will remove me from this office," he said. It earned him a brief reprieve. The Liberal opposition stopped talking about the drug issue, calculating that the damage had been done and they should not appear too eager to profit from it.

Conservatives, too, retreated from the precipice — until April 28, 1985, when the voters of Riverview pushed them right back to the edge.

The riding's Conservative MLA, Brenda Robertson, a powerful minister in Hatfield's cabinet, had been appointed to the Senate a few months earlier, opening the seat for a by-election. Though a suburb of Moncton, Riverview was also an urban outpost of the rural, Baptist, and English Albert County, and some of its voters tended to gaze suspiciously across the Petitcodiac River at Moncton and its constant grappling with the language issue. The river had been a symbolic barrier to that turmoil, and Riverview had remained resolutely Tory — until Poirier-Bastarache forced its voters to confront the unpleasant reality that the PC party, which had stood for their interests for so long, had suddenly exposed them to the French fact.

The only other time voters in Riverview had abandoned the Conservatives in recent memory was when Premier John Baxter had seemed to endorse vice by repealing the Temperance Act. In 1985, Riverview's voters would still not endorse a premier who endorsed vice — or who embraced francophones. In electing the Liberal, Hubert Seamans, they endorsed those Conservatives — like Harrison, Kipping and Dow — who felt it was time to remove Hatfield from office.

* * *

Forest fires were burning out of control on the Miramichi in the spring of 1985. The night of Tuesday, May 6, the same night Jim Pickett made his motion in New Denmark and Bev Harrison his speech in Saint John, seventy men were trying to contain two blazes covering more than a hundred and fifty acres of woods west of Newcastle. Now another inferno spread quickly through the anglophone strongholds of the Progressive Conservative party.

A lot of Tories wanted Hatfield gone, but they weren't sure how to make it happen. There was no mechanism in the party constitution for a leadership review, and Jim Pickett's MLA, Doug Moore, told reporters the day after the Victoria-Tobique meeting that he wasn't sure the party should adopt one. Still, Moore felt he had to do something. "It was a clear direction from my constituents," he said of the vote in favour of Pickett's resolution. Other riding associations added their voices: Saint John North and three Moncton ridings soon called for review, while Bathurst and Dalhousie passed resolutions supporting the premier. In Sussex, Hank Myers persuaded his membership to vote down a review resolution 44-34.

Harrison didn't like the idea of a review mechanism either. He thought Hatfield should simply quit after the Legislature adjourned in July. "I think the system provides for a smooth transition, which means that when leaders feel they don't have the confidence of the public, they should resign and call a convention," he said. "That's the proper system to use and that's the one I'd like to see take place." Even in rebellion, Harrison hewed to tradition, preferring the Westminster model in which caucus retained the power to remove a leader.

Hatfield rejected that notion, repeating that he drew his legitimacy from the voters, not his MLAs. "I know I have the mandate to govern this province and I'm going to continue to do that," he told reporters. But Harrison was determined to have his British-style coup, and he, Dow and Kipping lobbied their fellow MLAs to come out against Hatfield.

Their first obstacle was the nature of Conservatism itself: tidy, gentlemanly, deferential. "I just told them I wasn't interested," says Les Hull, then MLA from York South. "I stayed behind the leader. Richard Hatfield had been very good to me, and I had major work to do in [my department]. I am still proud of the fact today that I stood by the leader." Charles Gallagher from Carleton County also spurned the Three Musketeers. "I had to judge by what I saw," he says. "[Hatfield] was accused of so many things — things I didn't see, and I worked closely with him. I did not want to undermine the things that had been done." Others simply dodged the musketeers. "I was being very obvious about avoiding them," Myers says. "I'd say hello in the corridor, but there were no more lunches or chitchats late in the evenings."

But others did lend their support, encouraging the musketeers quietly or speaking up behind closed doors in caucus while remaining reluctant to go public themselves. Win Hackett says Nancy Clark Teed, the minister from Saint John who had threatened to resign over Poirier-Bastarache, privately urged Hatfield to quit. Myers remembers York North MLA David Bishop asking the premier to resign in a caucus meeting. Yet Teed and Bishop were never identified publicly. And two of the musketeers say John Baxter — the son of Premier Baxter, respected minister of finance, and apparent Hatfield stalwart — was a key player in the plot from the beginning. "John Baxter was leading this," says Keith Dow. "He said Hatfield was a spent force." Dow adds that Baxter was "very, very slick" in keeping his name away from the revolt. Harrison confirms Baxter's role, and Myers names Baxter as another MLA who called for Hatfield to quit during a caucus meeting.

In fact, Dow says, there were really five musketeers at the core of the plot: the three who went public, plus Baxter and David Clark, MLA from Fredericton South. Clark's public role was limited to asking Hatfield to address the drug allegations. But according to Dow, he went well beyond that; he was pro-coup all the way.

If no definitive list of plotters is possible, one thing is clear: it was limited to anglophone MLAs. "We knew colleagues like Percy Mockler, Jean Gauvin and Jean-Maurice [Simard] were ardently, ardently pro-Hatfield," Dow says. "These things didn't bother them, him dancing the night away in New York or vacationing in Morocco. Maybe they were more worldly or sophisticated. I think they were just being practical: Hatfield brought them into the mainstream."

Kipping and the others did approach some of the francophone MLAs, particularly those first elected in 1982. Surely these rookie MLAs, with presumably tenuous holds on their seats, would listen to arguments that their futures were in jeopardy. But when Percy Mockler was told he, as a francophone, had to urge Hatfield to go, he refused. "I said I'd rather be defeated for the right reason than be elected for the wrong reason," Mockler says now. For Yvon Poitras, Hatfield's generosity — the Knights of Columbus speech, the Saint-Quentin arena, the cabinet appointment — outweighed his own desire for a second term. "I made it known very, very clearly that I would not work against Richard Hatfield. They said, 'He's going to go down and you're going to go down with him.' And I said, 'That's my problem.'"

Only one francophone MLA, Fernand Dubé of Campbellton, ever told Hatfield to quit, according to three caucus sources. It was the one breach of solid French support, and Dubé eventually paid for it. After the 1987 election debacle, when Dubé sought to be named interim leader by the party's executive council, the other francophone members got their revenge by voting against him, blocking his ambition to be the first francophone leader of the PC party. "He lost because of his caucus conduct against Richard Hatfield," says one member who voted against Dubé.

Caucus lobbying continued through the spring. Hatfield's mother died late in May; the premier attended the funeral. A few days later, at Jean-Maurice Simard's request, he persuaded Prime Minister Brian Mulroney to name Simard to the Senate. Then Hatfield disappeared from public view; many hoped he was planning his retirement.

The lobbying and the hopes came to naught: when Conservative MLAs gathered for a caucus retreat in late July at a resort on Long Lake in Victoria County, Hatfield did not quit. The musketeers didn't have the numbers they needed to force him out, and so they didn't even bother introducing a motion of non-confidence. Harrison's British-style coup fizzled.

But the revolt wasn't over. If the musketeers couldn't complete the revolution they'd started, other Conservatives would have to finish the job.

* * *

Jean Gauvin was able to claim, accurately, that many of Richard Hatfield's opponents within the PC party didn't understand the English-French mosaic of New Brunswick. But he wasn't able to say that about Eric Bungay. Bungay was from Moncton, where Tories had lived in close quarters with the French fact. Unlike their counterparts in Fredericton and Saint John, they actually saw and, in some cases, spoke to Acadians every day. They had seen the birth of Acadian nationalism in the streets of Moncton and on the campus of their new French-language university. Many of them believed Hatfield would rescue them from all that when he became premier in 1970, so their sense of betrayal was particularly acute.

Bungay did not share it. He didn't like that ugly side of Toryism, but he'd seen it when he supported Charlie Thomas, the one-time Tory Member of Parliament in Moncton. In 1974, Thomas faced an internal challenge for the federal party nomination from Moncton's mayor, Leonard Jones, a vocal opponent of francophone rights. Jones's bigotry had earned him the wrath of young Acadian students in Moncton — and a loyal coterie of anglophone supporters. Those supporters came to the convention, wrested the nomination from Thomas and handed it to Jones. "You could feel the hatred in the room that night," Bungay says.

Bungay could see that Jones still had "a lingering influence on the atmosphere" in Moncton. His supporters retained considerable clout within the local party organization: in 1984, they had seen to it that Dennis Cochrane, another mayor of Moncton and a former Jones acolyte, won the federal PC nomination, blocking Brenda Robertson's plans to run in what was seen as a rebuke of Hatfield's overtures to francophones. Yet, though he claims he was uncomfortable with their attitudes, Bungay — more concerned about the harm done by the drug allegations — made common cause with them, if only to force Hatfield out. "Leaders come and go and they don't mean a damn. The party is the thing. The party stays," he says. "It didn't take political genius to know that we couldn't win an election for dogcatcher at that time. All you had to do was get a consensus of the people you talked to on the street — and the people in the Tory party." As a former party vice-president and a retired travelling salesman, Bungay quickly plugged into his network of contacts to put together an organization dedicated to dumping Hatfield.

New Brunswickers first learned of its existence the morning of September 16, 1985, when *Telegraph-Journal* columnist Don Hoyt — now the chief chronicler of the coup plotters — revealed that twenty-five to thirty Tories from thirteen ridings had met in Penobsquis, near Sussex, to plan strategy for the PC annual meeting in November in Saint John. Among them were the Three Musketeers and a number of Tory stalwarts from the Fredericton area, Charlotte County and the St. John River Valley. Jim Pickett travelled down from Perth-Andover and found himself named co-chairman, with Bungay, of what they called "Leadership Initiative 85."

At first, they promised a diplomatic approach — polite requests to meet with the premier and the party executive to try to "resolve" the leadership issue. They hoped to persuade Hatfield to spare the party the ordeal of an open fight. But they'd misjudged his determination. "It was his life," Harrison says now. "There was an ego there — albeit not one that beats you up. An ego that says, 'I'm good for New Brunswick and New Brunswick can't do without me.'"

Hatfield remained true to his principle that it was up to the voters to toss him out. Fred Arsenault says he might have resigned after the highs of the Papal and Royal visits in 1984, but once the drug scandal broke, he would not leave under a cloud. And with Poirier-Bastarache roiling the party, he may have feared a leadership race would unleash a factional fight and threaten the new PC party he had tried to build. "I'm sure Hatfield knew what the outcome would be," says Kevin Fram, then a PC youth member who later befriended Hatfield. "He probably felt, if he left, he would have been turning the party over to forces who were anything but progressive. He'd be caving in to those forces."

* * *

As the Saint John convention approached, Hatfield showed that he had no intention of caving in, and he soon outflanked the coup plotters.

First came a cabinet shuffle. Hatfield dropped francophone Clarence Cormier of Dieppe, as a sop to the English. He promoted Nancy Clark Teed to health, tying a key Saint John MLA more closely to his own fate. He moved Jean Gauvin from fisheries to housing, giving him more time to organize francophone ridings for the convention. And he made David Clark minister of justice, neutralizing the fourth musketeer.

Dow is angry to this day at Clark for violating a pact that he claims Clark had proposed himself. "I remember David Clark saying to us, 'No question of any of us taking a cabinet position,' and he was the first to jump." Leading up to the shuffle, Harrison, Dow, Kipping and Clark were invited to individual meetings with Hatfield, who talked to them about possible ministerial appointments. Harrison, Dow and Kipping say they rejected Hatfield's brazen attempt to co-opt them — and assumed Clark would, too. Yet there he was, taking the oath and joining John Baxter, another secret coup plotter, as a minister in Hatfield's cabinet. "He bought them off," Dow seethes. "Clark called us [after the shuffle] and said, 'This is very important to me, boys. We'll have a beer and talk about it sometime,' and he hung up the phone."

Clark acknowledges in an e-mail interview that Hatfield's decision silenced him on the leadership question. "I continued to believe we were in serious political trouble, although I was much more circumspect about expressing such views. . . . I was alert to a new reality that I was now a member of the government and not just a member of the governing party and parliamentary caucus, and a much more stringent standard of behaviour applied." As for the pact, "I can't confirm or deny," Clark writes. "I remember no such conversation with Mr. Dow or anyone else. . . . I know of no pre-existing circumstance that would, should or could prevent me from joining cabinet." He angrily rejects charges that Hatfield purchased his loyalty. "The premier never, either directly or through agents, questioned my loyalty or demanded any promise of loyalty beyond my oath of office."

Clark attributes Dow's allegations to "bellyaching from the backbenches. . . . Backbenchers have no power and don't get to participate in government; consequently, they are prone to complaining about all manner of things." Clark — who himself had complained about Hatfield when he was a backbencher — says the Three Musketeers should have resigned if they felt so strongly about the premier. Dow says he was twice invited to join the Liberals, once by Frank McKenna himself, but he refused. "I had been a Conservative, I was elected as a Conservative, and I just couldn't do that," he says. "You just can't change your stripes." Besides, according to parliamentary convention, as a backbencher Dow had no obligation to support the government at all times.

With his new cabinet carefully chosen to blunt the leadership attack, Hatfield planned his next moves with the help of a secret committee that gathered in Fredericton on October 5, two days after the shuffle. Present were francophone members such as Jean Gauvin, Yvon Poitras, Omer Léger and Percy Mockler, as well as loyal anglophone members such as Charles Gallagher. Dalton Camp, Hatfield's long-time friend and advisor, attended, as did Jim Ross, a Fredericton businessman, and Bruce Hatfield, the premier's nephew and election campaign manager. Norm Atkins, Camp's brother-in-law and head of his Toronto advertising agency, also pitched in, as did Noel Kinsella, a Hatfield friend, and Hugh Segal, a fellow Red Tory from Ontario. "Politically, we were loyalists of Richard, and it was a natural thing for us to be there," Atkins says.

And, according to some members of the committee, someone else was there who gave their efforts an added organizational edge: Janice Clarke, the party president.

The Bungay group was preparing a formal request for a vote in Saint John to amend the party constitution and create a mechanism for a leadership review. Procedure and rules were becoming more important, and, as head of the party, Clarke might have been expected to remain neutral in the struggle. But Omer Léger says he remembers her attending the meetings. A second committee member also puts Clarke in the room — but quickly backpedals when it is pointed out that her presence might have violated notions of neutrality.

Clarke herself firmly denies attending: "I never met with any of those people." But was she neutral? "To a degree. As president of the party, my duty was to support the leader. I don't dispute that people were trying to assist, but as president I wasn't actively involved in anything of that nature." One coup plotter says, though, that Clarke had no duty to "support the leader," only to administer the process fairly — a principle he says the entire executive violated by throwing up roadblocks for Leadership Initiative 85. "The way that was set up, politically and ethically it was dreadful," he says. The party brass resisted the group's request that the vote be by secret ballot, until Hatfield himself said he had no objection. "Stupid us," Harrison says now. "We didn't insist that it be an *announced* secret ballot." That oversight would come back to haunt him.

With the procedural upper hand, the save-Hatfield committee adopted the model of the 1982 election, with distinct strategies for English and French New Brunswick. Among anglophone Tories, they hinted the premier probably would leave before the next election — but only if he won the vote in Saint John. "The issue was, and the point that had to be made, was that the vote had to be in favour of Richard so that he would have his options," Atkins says, recalling that he used that argument to win over former Fredericton South MLA Bud Bird. "A lot of people were hoping that if he got a confirmation of his leadership, that he'd make that decision," Atkins adds, admitting he was hoping for it himself.

In French New Brunswick, meanwhile, the tactics were a variation on *"Encore Plus Fort."* With Jean-Maurice Simard in the Senate, the job fell to Jean Gauvin to persuade francophone members that their influence in the party was at stake. Organizationally, Gauvin says, "It's just like a convention." Local organizers are called to get people out to riding meetings and ensure they vote for the right slate of delegates. Then the delegates are tracked by phone, reminded of their importance and cajoled to stay committed. The final step: get them to the convention and make sure they vote.

Gauvin had an extra motivation as he cranked up this machine: he wasn't just fighting for Richard Hatfield's future or for Acadian influence. His own future, his own influence, were at stake.

The previous year, Brian Mulroney had come to New Brunswick to recruit star candidates to run for the federal Conservatives. It was early summer when Mulroney's Lear jet touched down at the small airstrip in Pokemouche, on the Acadian Peninsula, where Gauvin was waiting. Louis Léger drove them to a PC rally in Shippagan. "Obviously, the only reason Mulroney was there was to make sure Gauvin was going to run for him," says Léger. Mulroney played to the crowd at the rally. "He said fishermen in Eastern Canada would 'have a voice' if I was elected," Gauvin remembers. "He didn't say cabinet, but you could read between the lines."

When he left the Acadian Peninsula, "Mulroney was absolutely convinced Gauvin was going to run," Léger says. But, as the summer unfolded, the new federal Liberal leader, John Turner, rose in the polls. "All of a sudden, people got scared, including Gauvin, and including his riding president and his executive. It was understandable, because for a long time Conservatives in that area had not had a minister in a provincial government. They were scared they were going to lose him, and then Mulroney would not win. Gauvin would be in opposition in Ottawa, and they would not have a minister in Fredericton." Hatfield applied his own pressure in an end-of-summer telephone conversation, and Gauvin decided not to run for Mulroney.

The decision angered Mulroney, who placed a premium on loyalty. The two men crossed paths at a Moncton hotel during the federal campaign. "When Mulroney saw Gauvin, he turned his head and kept on going," Léger says.

Unlike Simard, unlike Brenda Robertson, unlike countless other New Brunswick Tories now enjoying a taste of federal patronage, Gauvin had no favours from Ottawa to fall back on if Hatfield went down to defeat. As he began calling riding presidents in the north, Jean Gauvin knew he had to give the review fight everything he had.

And so did Hatfield himself. The premier began travelling the province, holding closed-door meetings with party members, trying to pull them back from the edge. Tories who spoke to reporters as they left the meetings delivered mixed verdicts. Some were dissatisfied and unmoved, but others were flattered by the attention and impressed with their leader's case. Revolution was in the air, but there was still a lot of good old-fashioned Tory gentility and deference at work. If Hatfield could coax it sufficiently to the fore, he might get a split in the anglophone south, which, combined with the solid support he knew he had in the francophone north, would be enough to save him.

* * *

On the eve of the convention, in the corridors of the Saint John Trade and Convention Centre and nearby hotels, the two factions shmoozed delegates and compared numbers. Hatfield's people said he needed a simple majority to survive; the coup plotters talked of having sixty per cent on their side. Everyone recalled, though, that their federal leader, Joe Clark, had resigned three years earlier with sixty-six per cent support. Bungay and others knew even a forty per cent vote for their amendment would probably spell the end for Hatfield.

Uptown Saint John was steeped in intrigue. The Hilton was the official hotel for the delegates, so Gauvin had booked the francophone delegates he controlled into the Delta, where it would be harder for the coup plotters to get to them — and easier for him to keep them disciplined. "It was strategy. When people are spread out in different hotels, it's hard to pass messages. It's easier to get to them if they're under the same roof." Meanwhile, the plotters gathered in Bungay's room. Jim Pickett remembers him saying, "We've done a lot of work. Don't get your hopes too high. I've been close to these things before, and something can go terribly wrong at the last minute to throw this thing terribly off track."

Early that Saturday afternoon, Hatfield forcefully told the delegates what was at issue: "I speak for the majority when I say their concern is to make the party one that represents all of New Brunswick, not parts of it, and their concern is that we continue to have a party where the power rests with the majority of its membership and nowhere else." He moved on to a robust defence of bilingualism, pointing out that — in law — it protects anglophones as well as francophones. "It is the overriding responsibility of every government to strive to protect all of the rights of all of its citizens, whether it's in the north or the south, anglophone or francophone, rich or poor, Conservative or Liberal." He closed with another attack on the dissidents, accusing them of wanting "to linger over the past" and vowing to defy their predictions by leading the party to another victory.

The thunderous standing ovation that greeted the end of the speech rattled the coup plotters. They were already scrambling after learning that they would not be allowed to have their own scrutineers for the ballot counting. The amendment to create an annual leadership review, they realized, was in trouble: too many party members feared it would lead to near-constant turmoil, and old-stock Tories hated turmoil. Without more MLAs lining up in support, the idea lacked legitimacy. They decided to withdraw the doomed amendment and substitute a straight motion of non-confidence in Hatfield, one that allowed people to render a verdict without sentencing the party to perpetual, untidy infighting.

But when one of the plotters, Rod MacKenzie of Saint John, went to the microphone to make the substitution, party president Janice Clarke ruled him out of order and shut off his microphone. "That one action right there sealed the win for Hatfield," Jim Pickett says. "By us not getting our motion on the floor first, we lost a lot of wallop."

"People came to the meeting expecting to vote on the constitutional amendment, and that had to proceed," Clarke explains coolly. "There was no mechanism to present another matter for a vote."

Debate proceeded on the amendment. The coup plotters were suddenly on the defensive, fighting for an amendment they had just attempted to withdraw. They told delegates that it would not lead to automatic leadership conventions and that it could be repealed the following year, an admission that they'd lost the day.

When Janice Clarke returned to the podium later in the afternoon to announce the result of the vote, no one was surprised to learn the amendment had failed. But Clarke did have one shock for the delegates: she would not reveal the vote numbers. The coup plotters sent someone to a microphone to demand them, but the microphones were already shut off again, and Hatfield's supporters were loudly celebrating the victory.

Confronted by reporters afterward, Clarke said, "Any figures that you hear, I can tell you they will be nothing but rumours and speculation."

"How many persons know the figures besides yourself?" a journalist asked.

"The accountants."

"Three people?" a skeptical television reporter asked. "Hermetically sealed for all time?"

"Indeed," Clarke said. "I've forgotten them already."

The results remain one of the great political mysteries of New Brunswick to this day and are a recurring subject of speculation for Conservatives. Jim Pickett, for one, is convinced that the amendment passed and Clarke simply lied. Others are more sanguine. "I'm convinced Mr. Hatfield and his supporters won the day on that," Keith Dow says. "But I think there was a significant amount of delegates voting for review. If it had been ninety-two to eight, what would be the point of holding that back?"

Almost twenty years later, with Hatfield dead and buried for more than a decade, Janice Clarke sticks to her story. "I was presented with a piece of paper with a number on it," she says. "I looked at it and I was satisfied with the result. I don't remember what the exact number was except that it was significant and the amendment was defeated." Surely, though, Clarke remembers the *range* of the numbers? "I was well satisfied that it was a clear decision," she says firmly.

It may have been clear enough for Clarke at the time, but the exact figure would have revealed something important: the precise equation — the combination of the solidly pro-Hatfield French bloc and anglophone deference — that saved Hatfield. Remove the francophone vote from the "No" total and the extent of anti-Hatfield sentiment in the English ridings would be clear. Had he won two-thirds of those heartland votes? Half? Or less?

But perhaps the numbers *were* irrelevant, some Tories must have thought to themselves as they left Saint John. After all, Hatfield's supporters had hinted that, if allowed to do so on his own terms, without being forced, the premier *would* resign for the good of the party.

"What we all tended to overlook," Janice Clarke says, "was he was a strong believer that you were elected by the people, and you were there until the people removed you."

Chapter Seven

WAITING

DURING THE YEAR-LONG struggle over his leadership, Richard Hatfield spoke confidently about winning a fifth mandate from New Brunswickers. He hinted that he would follow the traditional pattern and go to the people in the fall of 1986, roughly four years after the last election. There was speculation about a snap election immediately after the party convention in Saint John, but most Conservatives felt no strategic choice of dates would spare them. They could only wait for the inevitable. "We could feel it," Jim Pickett says. "I don't know why some people in the party closed their eyes to that."

Not long after Saint John, Hatfield met with Janice Clarke to assess the mood of the party and to ask what might happen if he stepped down. She reported that most members were telling her there was no obvious successor. "No one had been groomed," Clarke says. "No one was aspiring. And everyone believed in the Hatfield magic. Not everyone, of course, but that seemed to be the thing: 'He pulled this out four times — he'll do it again.'"

The belief was based on the premier's presumed popularity in the northern francophone ridings, whose PC members had saved his leadership in Saint John. One scenario had the party squeaking out re-election by sweeping those constituencies and holding on to a handful of Tory heartland seats in the south.

Early in 1986, that last hope for Tory survival was put to the test.

Three days before the deadline set by law, Hatfield called a by-election for Edmundston, Jean-Maurice Simard's old seat. The race would be critical, more so than the Riverview contest, and not just because of the northern sweep strategy. Edmundston's voters, always aware of how the wind was blowing and with a good dose of self-interest, had voted with the government for half a century. Hatfield played to that self-interest at the January nominating convention, declaring, "Edmundston needs an MLA on the side of the government, and I, as leader of that government, need an MLA from Edmundston."

But the voters' intuition was sharper than Hatfield imagined: usually they detected the provincial trend *during* an election; now they sensed it months *before* the next campaign. They voted almost two to one for Liberal candidate Roland Beaulieu. "Simard City Goes Liberal," blared the headline in the *Telegraph-Journal*, just in case anyone missed the symbolism of the result. The jubilant Liberal leader, Frank McKenna, called the riding "the Tory *Bismarck*," but the premier remained in denial, telling reporters, "If [the voters] wanted to be opportunistic, they would have voted for someone on the government side, because the government is going to remain the government, and I think they would have done that."

As Hatfield jetted off to Paris later in the month with Prime Minister Mulroney to attend the first summit of the Francophonie — a new international organization of states with historical ties to France — Tories back home began to panic. Self-interest wasn't unique to Edmundston; in Ottawa, New Brunswickers like Louis Léger, who had gone to work for the federal Conservative government, were receiving anxious phone calls from provincial party members. "People saw the ship going down, and they were scrambling," he says. "They wanted to be appointed to boards, they wanted this and that. They wanted things that were not possible."

The pessimism extended to the corridors of the Centennial Building, the nerve centre of provincial government power in Fredericton. There was no dynamism left, no energy and no one advocating new ideas. "You had a worn-out government," Fred Arsenault says. "You'd been there sixteen years, and it's very difficult for a government to renew itself from inside." In June, when Hatfield received Irène Guerette and Lloyd Smith's final report on Poirier-Bastarache, he quickly tossed it on the shelf. There was no stomach for bold initiatives and no political capital left to spend on them. "People had had enough of conflict and infighting in the party," Percy Mockler says. "People were tired, and Premier Hatfield was very, very wounded."

There was a feeling of letting the clock run down, but only the premier controlled the clock, and as summer turned to fall, Tories realized they would not have to fight an election in 1986 after all. Moreover, Richard Hatfield would not take his review victory and leave of his own accord. He was going to stay, and no one could contemplate another attempt to force him to do otherwise.

So, in that autumn of 1986, Tory party members had little to distract their attention other than one final aftershock of the leadership review battle, a last reminder of how badly divided and damaged their party was.

Brad Green had been elected president of the PC Youth Federation at the Saint John convention. Green jumped in as a student at Fredericton High School and had been elected to the Youth Federation executive in 1983, when he was eighteen. He soon joined his local riding association and volunteered at the party's provincial office downtown. That gofer job had allowed Green to play a bit part in the leadership review drama when the notice of Bungay's amendment motion arrived at the office the previous October. Rules required the party secretary, retired Anglican Archdeacon J.F.N. Jones of St. Andrews, to sign each copy of the notice that would be sent to the fifty-eight Conservative riding presidents. Green was dispatched to drive the documents from Fredericton to the resort town to collect the signatures. He sensed the momentous nature of his errand: though Bungay's amendment was technically a procedural mechanism, "everyone saw it for what it was," he says.

Like other Tories, Green was torn about Hatfield. "People were not blind to the situation that was developing," he says. "Many concerns were being expressed away from the cameras. Individuals and groups were expressing concerns about the direction in which we were headed." But Green himself chose to support Hatfield, voting in Saint John for a Youth Federation resolution backing the premier. "Here we had a leader who had led us to four consecutive majority governments, and I think for many party members, myself included, there was a feeling of loyalty to this man, given what he had achieved."

Some, though, felt Green had not been loyal enough — and for many francophone youth members, still bruised by the musketeers and looking for revenge, Green symbolized the stodgy old Tory heartland and therefore needed to be taught a lesson.

Those young francophones saw the PC office staff, including volunteers like Green, as suspicious of the French fact in the party and tepid in the support they showed for Hatfield's outreach to Acadians. "They weren't anti-French, but they were leery of these new members," says Kevin Fram, an anglophone who, in the fall of 1986, found himself the front man for the francophones — their candidate in a campaign to remove Green from the presidency of the youth wing. Green "was part of that little clique from Fredericton and Albert County and Kings County," Fram says. "I was of the view that Bradley V. Green, as he called himself, was rather staid and traditional. I felt the youth wing weren't doing enough in support of the premier. I guess you could say I was a bit of a zealot or a Hatfield nut. It's not to say [Green] didn't do a good job, but when you're not in the seat, you always think you can do a better job."

Fram was a member of the PC organization at Mount Allison University in Sackville, a campus club that had taken the lead in publicly endorsing Hatfield a year earlier. "It was a very progressive group of individuals who believed not only in blind loyalty to the leader but in what Hatfield stood for. The things he had done to modernize the Progressive Conservative party — dragging New Brunswick kicking and screaming into the twentieth century — those were the kinds of things we were into," Fram says with a chuckle.

Fram's enthusiasm for Hatfield — and the fact that he had no French roots himself — made him an ideal vehicle for the francophone youth members who were plotting revenge. Among them was Louis Léger, who had previously played chauffeur to both Yves Dupré and Brian Mulroney. Another was Louise Pelletier, a student from Edmundston who worked in the party office alongside Green. According to Fram, she was regarded by the old-stock Tory staffers as pushy and aggressive, particularly on language issues. Léger and Pelletier brought in other people to help Fram's insurgent campaign, including the president of the student council at the Université de Moncton, Bernard Lord, who worked on Fram's campaign literature. Though he never met Lord, Fram says he heard a lot about him. "Louise Pelletier was particularly infatuated with him. Everyone who spoke of Bernard Lord at that time thought he was a fantastic guy."

The youth federation battle was a sideshow, but even in 2003, during an interview in his ministerial office, the normally taciturn Brad Green became animated when asked about it. He was clearly irked by the suggestion that he wasn't fully behind Hatfield in the review fight. "The people around the premier who were making decisions around the campaign were not questioning my loyalty whatsoever," he says. He notes Hatfield's people asked him to address the full convention in 1986, knowing his speech would boost his chances of beating Fram and keeping the youth presidency. Green also says he, like other Tories, welcomed francophones in the party, even if some veterans thought their presence reeked of opportunism.

Yet Green acknowledges that Fram's bid to unseat him was an English-French fight. "Certainly the support between the two of us broke down on language lines," he says, adding he's at a loss to explain why. "Perhaps there were those who felt their own role in the party would be enhanced if they had someone they were closer to in a leadership role," he says.

Green won the day by a margin of eleven votes out of hundreds of ballots cast, the near-perfect split stark evidence of the persistence of the division of 1985. Fram, while admitting his attempt to unseat Green was brazen and presumptuous, blames the defeat on the widespread knowledge that he was the candidate of the French wing. "I had this rather menacing, dangerous francophone element behind me, and that was unacceptable," he says.

At the conclusion of an interview on the subject, Green remained irritated by Fram's suggestion that he wasn't loyal. It was clearly important to him to prove otherwise. He revealed that Bruce Hatfield, the premier's nephew and closest advisor, tacitly helped him in the 1986 youth campaign. And finally, he argued, a good measure of who was most loyal might be the two men's position in 2003: Green was a senior cabinet minister in the PC government in New Brunswick, while Fram had switched parties to become an assistant to a federal Liberal minister in Ottawa.

* * *

So 1986 came and went without the PC party's subjecting itself to the judgment of the voters. At the end of April 1987, Hatfield met Prime

Minister Mulroney and the other premiers to draft the Meech Lake Accord, a proposed constitutional amendment that would decentralize federal power and grant Quebec special status in return for the province's signature on the Constitution and the Charter of Rights, which it had refused to endorse in 1982.

To take effect, Meech had to be passed by all ten provincial legislatures and Parliament in Ottawa within three years. With an election certain in 1987, New Brunswick would be the first political testing ground for the agreement. Liberal leader Frank McKenna was promising to seek changes to better protect francophone minorities outside Quebec, a threat to the deal's fragile unanimity. Yet Hatfield opted against recalling MLAs over the summer to ratify Meech Lake — seemingly confident he would have all the time in the world to pass it in his *next* mandate.

And now the clock began to run out.

By late August, experts were consulting legal texts to calculate exactly when Hatfield would have to dissolve the Legislature and call an election. There was speculation in the media and among the opposition Liberals about when Lieutenant-Governor Gilbert Finn would be legally obliged to step in and do it if the premier did not. But Hatfield finally visited Finn on the morning of August 29 and set the election date for October 13. He had waited until almost the last moment — just two days before his mandate would expire — to put in motion a forty-five-day campaign, the longest allowable. It was as if he was determined to hold on to his job for as long as legally possible.

The language question, which Hatfield handled so deftly for three mandates then bungled so badly in his fourth, remained below the surface as the campaign unfolded. The Liberals knew it was potentially explosive. Their polling showed that fewer than half of the anglophones felt Acadians contributed to the good of the province, and a majority felt closer to English Canadians in other provinces than they did to francophone New Brunswickers. Support for bilingualism was below fifty per cent among anglophones, and seventy per cent were ready to support a reduction in French-language services. McKenna ignored the subject and focused on the economy and on jobs, hoping to craft a goal and a vision that both language groups could support.

It would have taken a gaffe of epic proportions to derail McKenna's campaign. His events seemed ever louder, more enthusiastic and bigger in numbers as the days went by, while Hatfield was greeted by tepid crowds. The Tories often ran late, causing reporters to miss filing deadlines, while the Liberals kept a tight schedule.

There were occasional glimmers of hope for the Conservatives, usually in the north. "I recall a rally we had in Tracadie," Jean Gauvin says. "Lots of people, lots of movement, lots of excitement. And one in Shippagan, too. Sometimes you dream."

But the bottom was rapidly falling out of the big dream for which Richard Hatfield and Jean-Maurice Simard had worked so hard.

In the southern ridings that had once been rock-solid Tory, people who had never imagined themselves voting Liberal were intrigued by Frank McKenna, this small-town farm boy from the Kings County heartland, whose values of thrift and self-help they could relate to. And he was anglophone to boot. In the north, the very argument that had brought Acadians to Hatfield's side — become a partner in power — was now working against him.

From his office in downtown Montreal, Yves Dupré watched on television as voters refused to shake Hatfield's hand. Feeling a tinge of nostalgia for the Grand Ralliement and the glory days of the 1982 election, Dupré dispatched a woman from his advertising department to New Brunswick to come up with some ads that might save a few seats in francophone areas. But it was too late.

"That's it — we're done," Jean-Maurice Simard said to Jean Gauvin when the senator appeared in Shippagan-les-Îles five days before the vote. "We're having a hard time to finish this thing." The party had no money left to pay the bills through to election day. Gauvin listened in horror as the original French lieutenant made a dire prediction: the Tories were going to lose every single seat in the province.

The possibility of a complete wipeout was dawning on other Conservatives around the province. Percy Mockler had created his own focus group in his riding of Madawaska-Sud: a mechanic, a hairdresser and a priest whom he would consult regularly about what they were hearing. The news wasn't good. "I'm defeated," Mockler told Hatfield during a conference call the Friday before the election. "Then I'm going to lose all fifty-eight seats," the premier replied.

That final weekend, Brad Green, Janice Clarke and two other Tory volunteers jumped in a van for a lightning tour of all the constituencies. "In riding after riding," Green says, "people were saying to us, 'We're okay here, but I'm worried about the riding next door.' The problem was, every riding was next door to someone.'"

Tory voters wanted to get rid of Richard Hatfield so badly that they weren't going to trust that job to anyone else. On election day, half the people who had voted Conservative in 1982 switched, and the Liberal sweep that Tories had talked about in hushed tones wiped out all thirty-seven Conservative incumbents. McKenna took sixty per cent of the popular vote, the PCs just twenty-eight per cent.

The collapse was as broad as it was deep: in the southeast, where the Tory vote dropped from fifty-one per cent to twenty-four per cent, cabinet minister Mabel Deware finished so badly in Moncton West that she lost her deposit. In Saint John, the Conservative share plunged from 45.8 per cent to 26.1, and Health Minister Nancy Clark Teed trailed both the Liberals and the NDP. In the francophone north, the numbers were just as decisive, though the Tory fall was not as precipitous: the party's share of the popular vote went from 40.5 to 28.8 per cent in the northeast; in Madawaska, where 48.2 per cent of voters had gone Conservative five years earlier, the party's support stayed above the thirty per cent mark. In Restigouche West, Yvon Poitras — the Knights of Columbus stalwart and the archetype of Hatfield's community-minded francophone recruit — came closest of any Tory to being elected, falling twenty-five votes short of being the sole survivor of the PC debacle.

* * *

Two days after the election, Percy Mockler went to Fredericton and wandered up to the second floor of the Centennial Building, where he found Richard Hatfield cleaning out his office. Mockler was despondent; this defeat was so deep, so broad, so far-reaching that it was hard to imagine the party could ever recover.

As Mockler tells it, Hatfield comforted him with words that sounded like prophecy: "You were not defeated. I was defeated. Someday, your people will ask you to come back under extraordinary circumstances, and you will win again." Hatfield's prediction soothed Mockler a little; surely the comeback the premier spoke of could not be any farther away than it was at that moment. Surely the Progressive Conservative Party of New Brunswick could not sink any lower than it had on October 13, 1987. Surely it had hit bottom.

But another challenge to the party appeared on the horizon, a challenge illuminated by Les Hull's explanation of politics in his former Tory heartland constituency of York South. For Hull, the careful distribution of the spoils of power had kept anti-French sentiment at bay in the riding. "We'd have pockets of people complaining that too much money was being spent on bilingualism," he says, "and then we'd get some money for a road or something."

In the fall of 1987, there were no longer any spoils of power for Tories to distribute. There was no longer any money "for a road or something." There was no longer anything for a brokerage party to broker *with*.

And that meant there was no longer any reason for opponents of francophone rights to buy into Richard Hatfield's dream of a modern Conservative party.

No, the Tories had not yet hit bottom.

Part Two

OPEN SEASON

Danny Cameron at the Confederation of Regions leadership convention, Campbellton, September 1992. COURTESY OF DANNY CAMERON

Chapter Eight

THE WEST COMES EAST

ANYONE WHO MET Elmer Knutson learned that behind the combed-back grey hair, beefy fingers and big, slightly zealous eyes, an unusual mind was at work, developing strange notions of how the world worked.

One of Knutson's most baffling political theories was that the Canadian Confederation was illegal, and thus that the country's very existence was null and void. After trying for years to persuade the federal Progressive Conservative party to understand this, Knutson went to London in 1983, where, he would claim, he found archival documents proving the British North America Act had no standing in Canada and that the 1931 Statute of Westminster granted sovereignty to the provinces but never united them into a single entity. "It's revolutionary thinking that I have," he once told a magazine interviewer. "Great Britain was in charge until 1931, and then for sixty years we've been deceived by parliamentarians." It was still possible in the late 1980s, Knutson reasoned, to deal with Canada's regional grievances by bringing the provinces together under a different constitutional framework — a Confederation of Regions, he called it, a philosophy which also provided the name of the political party he founded.

Knutson created his party in the years of Prairie populist protest directed at the federal Liberal government of Pierre Trudeau. The Saskatchewan-born Knutson, a war veteran, miner, baseball player and car salesman, had founded the Western Canada Foundation in Alberta in 1980 in response to Trudeau's hated National Energy Program. But his members bolted to the Western Canada Concept, an explicitly separatist provincial party. Knutson flirted with Social Credit before deciding to start COR in 1984.

Besides Knutson's unique take on the Constitution and the standard western resentment of official bilingualism and big government, COR also espoused his bizarre monetary policies. Knutson's plan was to charge foreign companies a tariff on everything they sold in Canada. Rather than collect the tariff as government revenue, the other country would use it as credit to buy Canadian products. "It was so involved and complicated that you could never sell it to people," says Jim Webb, a retired Canadian Pacific train dispatcher in Saint John who met Knutson in 1988. "There wasn't fourteen people out of 14,000 who understood what he was saying." Greg Hargrove, a labourer from the Nashwaak Valley, north of Fredericton, agreed: "It was over my head, what he was talking about."

Jim Webb and Greg Hargrove understood one thing about Elmer Knutson very well, however: he was angry. That was how he found them in the first place. Knutson was scouring the country for angry people — and there were a lot of them in New Brunswick.

Hargrove and Webb were among the thousands of Progressive Conservative voters disenchanted over Richard Hatfield's overtures to francophones. The coalition, the new party the premier had tried to build, wasn't for them. Hargrove had joined the New Brunswick Association of English-Speaking Canadians during the Acadian flag controversy, convinced there was a Quebec conspiracy to annex Atlantic Canada. "There was not really evidence of it, but there were things happening that led you to believe it was going to happen," says Hargrove, who had written the Poirier-Bastarache committee that francophones should be forced into English schools. Webb, fed up with Hatfield, joined the association, too. "He left Jean-Maurice Simard minding the store," Webb says. "Jean-Maurice Simard was the premier."

Out West, Elmer Knutson had reasoned that New Brunswick's English-Speaking Association might be a good fit with his prairie uprising. Early in 1988, having tracked down names and phone numbers, he invited a handful of the association's members, including Hargrove and Webb, to meet him in Ottawa. They agreed to set up an Atlantic wing of COR to run candidates in New Brunswick in the next federal election. Webb, charged with recruiting candidates, looked to disenchanted Tories like himself, people whose loyalties had been frayed by what they saw as pandering to francophones. Whether it was Poirier-Bastarache provincially or Meech Lake federally, old-stock Conservatives had no shortage of annoyances, and they resented those who were trying to usurp *their* party. Webb soon obtained the name of one such Tory in the community of Nordin, on the Miramichi River just downstream from the gritty, industrial town of Newcastle.

Arch Pafford was a transplanted Newfoundlander who ran the local office of a Fredericton company called Atlantic Rentals. He'd supported local Miramichi Conservatives such as former MLA Paul Dawson, a cabinet minister in Richard Hatfield's last government. But in his role as president of the local service district — a committee that monitored such provincial services as road maintenance in non-municipal areas of the province — Pafford was hearing complaints about official bilingualism. "It was affecting people overnight," he says. "I had letters. I had people crying to me on the phone. " He knew a woman who had been in line for a promotion a year or two earlier after working for CN for a decade. But as Pafford tells it, she lost out when the position was designated bilingual — and then suffered the indignity of having to train the francophone who won the job.

During the 1987 provincial election, Pafford had quizzed his local candidates about bilingualism. "They didn't want to talk about it," he says, including the Conservatives. "It was a hot potato. It was too controversial." Feeling abandoned by his party, Pafford was planning to run as an independent in the 1988 federal election when he got a phone call from Jim Webb and Dolores Cook, another of Knutson's new lieutenants in New Brunswick. Pafford hadn't heard of COR, but he agreed to meet with Webb and Cook. When they laid out the party's philosophy at his kitchen table — including its plan to eliminate official bilingualism — "right away, I said yes."

Pafford's ten per cent of the vote in the 1988 election was the best among the seven COR candidates running in New Brunswick — he came third, ahead of the NDP — but it was hardly a show of strength. (In Ontario, COR candidates sapped enough support from federal Conservatives in five rural ridings to help elect Liberals — the party's only real impact in that election.) So it was easy for the political mainstream to dismiss COR as a gang of rural, redneck, anti-French bigots, just as they dismissed Reform, another prairie protest party. Still, Webb and Hargrove believed they were onto something in New Brunswick. A lot of disaffected Conservative voters in English-speaking areas of the province had yet to settle on a new political home. Hargrove, Webb and a few other COR supporters met in Saint John with the president of the English-Speaking Association, Thane Robson, and agreed to fold the association into a provincial Confederation of Regions party.

A new party was a long shot, but it was worth a try. In 1988 Frank McKenna's Liberals had a virtual monopoly on political power in New Brunswick, holding all fifty-eight seats in the Legislature. The Tories had no leader and showed few signs of life. Hank Myers, the former MLA and cabinet minister from Kings East, had become president of his local Tory constituency organization after his defeat and soon learned that only eight Tory riding associations held annual meetings that year. "These ridings were just falling apart," he says. Not only had Tories lost access to the patronage that built party loyalty, but a party structure barely existed to make them feel valued. Thousands remained loyal, but thousands of others — after the trauma of Poirier-Bastarache and the leadership review — weren't certain they *wanted* to be Conservatives anymore.

Into this vacuum stepped Knutson's small band of followers — though their enthusiasm for their federal leader was waning, given his focus not on language rights but on his constitutional and monetary policies. "I couldn't see that anyone was that interested" in Knutson's views, Webb says. So COR became a convenient brand name for a New Brunswick crusade that otherwise bore little resemblance to the federal party. "We just found that to be an avenue to do what we wanted to do provincially," Webb continues.

The notion of an anti-bilingualism party had been broached before, but Len Poore, a founder of the English-Speaking Association who says he retained his Conservative membership the entire time he was badgering Richard Hatfield, had always rejected it. "It's got to be one or the other, fellas," he remembers telling his members. By 1988, many of them were impatient. Poore "said he wanted to run a protest group," Webb remembers. "We said protest groups don't get anywhere. You have to get at the table, there in the Legislature."

So the call went out, and people responded. Arch Pafford was at home one day in the spring of 1989 when his friend Amby Laberge, who had helped his federal campaign, telephoned. "Want to go to Moncton with me for a drive?" Laberge asked.

"What's going on there?" Pafford wanted to know.

"There's a COR meeting, and I want to see what's happening," Laberge answered.

What was happening was the dawn of something new in New Brunswick: the protest politics of the Prairie west were coming east. That old Tory deference was replaced by defiance. The province was entering what one political scientist would call "a populist moment."

When Pafford and Laberge arrived at the Lions Senior Citizens' Centre on St. George Street in Moncton, they were astonished to find the room packed with four hundred people from twenty-eight of the province's fifty-eight electoral ridings. Among them was Leonard Jones, the former Moncton mayor whose name had become synonymous with anti-French bigotry. Jones explained electoral law, telling the crowd that if COR could set up ten riding associations, it could register as an official political party. So they pulled out a map of New Brunswick's ridings, began building lists of names from the membership rolls of the English-Speaking Association and struck a committee to draft a constitution and bylaws.

Arch Pafford found himself elected as the party's first president. "Arch seemed to have a kind of magnetism with people," Webb says. "He had a charisma." With his angular features and snow-white hair, Pafford resembled the pop artist Andy Warhol more than a rabble-rousing populist. But his eyes, which glistened at times with kindness, also showed flashes of righteous anger, and it was not difficult to fathom his almost evangelical appeal to people wanting to believe. "I was on a mission, right from day one," he says, the fervour returning to his voice even in 2003. "I had to organize. It had to be done and it had to be done right."

The very next weekend, Pafford traveled to Perth-Andover to preside over his first COR meeting. Eight people attended, including journalists, and it appeared the party might suffer the same fate as other third parties in New Brunswick. But Pafford knew COR was different because of how bilingualism resonated. As the weeks rolled by, the meetings grew in size. "They were like a social event," he remembers. "At most meetings, by eight o'clock, eight-thirty, people want to get home. But at nine, nine-thirty, they were still there, milling around, talking, excited about what we were doing." Greg Hargrove was struck by how easily the new party built up its bank account. "We had no public funds," he says. "We would pass the hat to pay for our meetings, and I saw people in the front row dropping fifty dollars in the hat, and I thought, 'Holy cow. These people are inspired.' These were people who squeezed every penny."

The media treated COR as a curiosity, a transplanted Prairie protest movement of bigots who would vent their anger and quickly fade into obscurity. After all, populist uprisings just didn't happen in New Brunswick, particularly when they were based on seemingly extreme positions. "Once you're labelled, it's a hard obstacle to overcome," Pafford says. Jim Webb still bristles today at the party's racist image. "Everybody in COR was being described as hating the French people. We didn't hate French people, but it was how the language act was being applied. It's just like the Chinese," Webb continues, perhaps unaware that Chinese do not make up one-third of New Brunswick's population. "I don't have a problem with the Chinese, but I'd have a problem with their language. [French] is a fine language, but it's not the dominant language in the province."

Webb was echoing a sentiment common during the Poirier-Bastarache process among English-speaking New Brunswickers. He did not consider how francophones might feel about a party determined to roll back their fundamental rights because he, like other COR supporters, were convinced that Acadians themselves had been perfectly happy with their pre-1960s second-class status and had become troublesome to the majority only when provoked by Quebec separatist sympathizers like Jean-Maurice Simard. Webb and other COR supporters were confident that francophones wouldn't begrudge a return to "simpler" times; they could all remember a French friend who'd never been uppity, who'd never demanded equality, before Louis Robichaud and Richard Hatfield had gone and caused so much trouble.

It was a view more widespread than the Tory and Liberal political élites could understand, for the very reason that it was rarely expressed in the political arena, where both parties, striving to build broad coalitions, had forged a consensus on language. Now something revolutionary was happening: a new party, sparked by western anger but adapting quickly to eastern politics, was willing to question what everyone — or everyone who had shared in political power — had taken for granted.

COR was making its move just as attachments to the traditional parties were eroding. The election of 1987 had shaken loose long-time Conservatives, who voted Liberal that year to get rid of Hatfield. Their return to the Tory party was not certain, given that many of them were what political scientists Alain Gagnon and A. Brian Tanguay called "modernization losers": people who "see their familiar world being turned topsy-turvy by a welter of state-engineered programs and a bevy of militant interest groups . . . [and] feel most threatened by the epochal social and economic changes of the late twentieth century." In New Brunswick, they may have been ill-informed about francophones, unmoved by Hatfield's attempt to build a new PC party and quick to blame the French for their problems. But there were thousands of them, and their loyalty was up for grabs.

Through the summer of 1989, Arch Pafford persuaded more and more former Tories to join his mission. As he laid the groundwork for COR's first leadership convention, Pafford looked not just for passive followers but for leaders, people who knew how to take this upstart protest party to the next level. He needed Conservatives with experience as organizers, candidates and financial donors. "Many of them were leaning towards our policies," Pafford says. He sent out feelers to two of the anti-Hatfield musketeers, Bev Harrison and Keith Dow, but their suspicion of Poirier-Bastarache did not equate with the outright repeal of official bilingualism. "They would say 'We're not a single-issue party, we're not anti-French,'" Dow says, but he and Harrison rejected the overtures.

One Conservative more open to the anti-bilingualism message was Ed Allen, the former Conservative MLA for Fredericton North who had been Hatfield's minister of supply and services. Allen had been bitter when he was shuffled out of cabinet in 1985 to make room for Fredericton South MLA David Clark, as the premier tried to blunt the growing revolt in his caucus. Allen "put on a brave face about it," his son Mike says. "I think he was hurt initially because he probably felt he was the more seasoned of the group [of MLAs in Fredericton]."

Allen had opposed the expansion of official bilingualism within the PC caucus, though he'd voted along party lines on key legislation, including Jean-Maurice Simard's Bill 88. Mike Allen says his father understood the need for government services in French but felt the education system — particularly French immersion — would "take care" of the language issue over time, making legislated bilingualism unnecessary. "He was not a big proponent of it being forced," Mike says.

Mike suggested to his father that he run as an independent in the 1987 election to demonstrate his displeasure with the PC party. Allen was respected in Fredericton North for returning phone calls, accepting invitations to events and helping children find summer jobs regardless of their parents' political affiliation, and he might have had a chance had he left the Tories. But "he just couldn't," Mike says. "He was loyal and he was going to stick with it."

After losing his seat in the Liberal sweep, Allen, like other former MLAs, joined a caucus of non-elected Tory critics trying to hold the Liberals accountable. In that role, he told a journalist in February 1989 that the implementation of bilingualism had gone too far — and was promptly rebuked by PC party president Richard Johnston for deviating from a fundamental PC policy. Johnston felt there was no room for confusion: criticizing "implementation," he says now, "is code talk" for deeper opposition to francophone rights. "Once you opened that door, you allowed every wingnut to come out and say whatever they wanted to say."

Late that summer, Mike Allen found his father at his front door on a Saturday morning "with a sheepish look in his eyes." The previous evening, Allen had appeared unexpectedly at a COR meeting at the Kinsmen Centre on School Street, where the party was setting up its Fredericton North riding association. "He got all caught up in the emotion of it and joined the party on the spot," Mike says. Greg Hargrove remembers, "He was really what gave us our legitimacy. . . . It gave the green light to a lot of soft supporters." Don Parent, a Fredericton North Tory who remained loyal, calls Allen's switch to COR "probably the biggest shot in the arm they ever got."

A couple of weeks later, buoyed by Allen's defection, two thousand delegates streamed into Fredericton for COR's first leadership convention, where they faced the task of merging the amateurish politics of protest with a smoothly running professional party machine. It was COR's coming-out party on the provincial political scene, and everyone was waiting to see if it would be taken seriously.

Try as they might, however, organizers couldn't keep a lid on the roiling resentment. Jock Andrew, an author of conspiracy-theory books, told the convention that "the whole of the Canadian government is under French-Canadian control" and that there was a conspiracy to eliminate English. Journalists seized on the comments, which prominent COR members refused to refute. "I believe to a degree there is [a conspiracy]," Pafford said. "Until somebody tells me something concrete that's different, I'll continue to believe that." Ed Allen, elected the party president, told reporters, "You might have bigots in the party, I don't know. But what party doesn't have bigots?" He conceded Andrew's comments might have sounded extreme — then added, considerably less sheepishly than when he'd joined COR, "I hope and pray to the Almighty power above that we won't see the day when there will be complete Frenchification of Canada as he has said in his book."

Pafford won the party leadership on the first ballot with fifty-eight per cent of the vote. His spring and summer of political spadework around the province had made him the logical choice to lead COR. "New Brunswick now has a political party that will change the face of politics in this province and across Canada," he said triumphantly to cheering delegates. "We are going to be a force to be recognized and reckoned with in this province."

Despite the rough edges, the convention had been an impressive display of organizational strength. The COR party had clearly arrived. But there was still skepticism about its prospects. After all, anyone who understood anything about politics in New Brunswick knew it would take an extraordinary combination of political circumstances for the party even to come close to winning a single seat. "COR was marginal," says Steven MacKinnon, then a political assistant to Frank McKenna, who saw the language issue as a distraction, a mere "brushfire" and nothing more. Joining COR "wasn't the acceptable thing to do," he says. "It just seemed a little weird and a little backward, and not as big as it really was."

* * *

Frank McKenna's advisors could be forgiven for believing COR was "not as big as it really was." In late 1989 and early 1990, it was inconceivable that anything might threaten the Liberals' grasp of power.

The party's hold on every seat in the Legislature had turned Question Period — the daily queries to ministers that normally constitute parliamentary accountability — into a farce. Backbench Liberals lobbed softballs at ministers. One question at the height of the Meech Lake crisis was typical: "Since our Premier is the only First Minister with an open and flexible initiative, an initiative which can be the basis for positive building, and is a leader who inspires confidence on a national scale, does the Premier plan to provide an additional measure of leadership which will be so vital in the context of the current situation nationally?" McKenna, not surprisingly, said if it were necessary, he would.

Outside, citizens were restless. Brian Mulroney's Meech Lake Accord had become the focus of popular discontent with the political system. Early on, McKenna had felt Meech did not do enough to protect minority francophones in New Brunswick and called for changes. Though that put him at the opposite end of the spectrum from other Meech opponents, who condemned the accord's concessions to Quebec, McKenna was still the best vehicle they had. But early in 1990, with Meech heading for collapse, McKenna hatched a secret plan with Mulroney's officials to salvage the agreement. A so-called parallel motion in the New Brunswick Legislature would deal with some of his objections to Meech and allow opponents to ratify the accord. In return, Mulroney would entrench Jean-Maurice Simard's Bill 88, with its guarantee of equality for New Brunswick's two linguistic communities, in the Constitution. Entrenchment, which Acadian activists had been demanding, would give McKenna the minority-language protection he felt was missing from the original Meech deal.

In joining the rescue effort, however, McKenna was undercutting one of the key strategies he'd adopted in the 1987 election: avoid the potentially explosive language issue and focus on job creation, a vision that both language groups could support. Now McKenna was deep into the Constitution, inflaming the same voters who had caused headaches for Richard Hatfield.

Those voters thought they'd made themselves clear when they

dumped Hatfield in 1987. Now here was McKenna, embracing special status for Quebec on the national stage while favouring Acadians back home. Though he'd rejected many of its recommendations, Hatfield had promised in the wake of the Poirier-Bastarache report to continue enhancing bilingualism in the civil service. The bureaucracy continued its work on the file after McKenna took office, drafting a policy known ominously as "language profiling." It would measure the demand for minority-language service in each government office and determine how many employees were needed to provide it. It would then assess how many bilingual staff were needed — managers who supervised both anglophones and francophones, for example — to ensure all employees could *work* in the language of their choice, a considerable advance beyond bilingual service to the public.

Rumours spread that every government employee — right down to snowplow operators in the Nashwaak Valley, north of Fredericton — would soon be colour-coded according to language skills, surely a prelude to language-based layoffs. Backbench MLAs began taking heat. Andy Scott, then executive director of the provincial Liberal party, moved into the premier's office to deal with the growing backlash. "We simply weren't applying enough political sensitivity on this," Scott says. "The instrument was just too blunt." Ray Frenette, a cabinet minister, told McKenna's biographer Philip Lee, "We were moving just a little too fast on the language issue. When people see that any given policy of government might take some jobs away from A and transfer them to B because of language, you're going to have people reacting badly."

Scott's salvage mission consisted of drawing up giant organizational charts of each government department, with each employee included, then going through them to assess each position. Is it *really* necessary that this job be bilingual? Are there *enough* bilingual jobs here? "Once we got the substance right," Scott admits, "we recognized we had a huge communications problem." So Scott took his show on the road, attending public information sessions across the province. "You could tell it was a skeptical, arms-folded-in-the-back kind of crowd," he recalls.

Out in New Brunswick's English heartland, Scott delivered his pitch — a rehash of the standard consensus case for bilingual service. But that pitch had some competition. Many of the same people who listened to Scott were also hearing from a slight, charismatic white-haired man who didn't parrot the old Liberal-Conservative platitudes about language rights.

Sometimes Arch Pafford spoke in the very same community halls where Andy Scott had been. Often he journeyed further into the back country. "I went to meetings where there had never been meetings before," he says proudly. And people were paying attention.

* * *

In Frank McKenna's office on the second floor of the black-glassed Centennial Building, the COR party still wasn't registering as a political threat. But, as the next election approached, the lack of opposition in the Legislature certainly was. "If you had enough people deciding they wanted an opposition," Steven MacKinnon explains, "that could be a problem." So McKenna decided to create an opposition. He had given both the Conservatives and the NDP offices at the Legislature, use of the library and the right to submit questions to the Public Accounts committee. Now, he took the unusual step of inviting party leaders to appear at the bar of the Legislature to pose questions.

"It is an entirely new procedure," Speaker Frank Branch told the MLAs on March 15, 1990, the first day of the system, "and I ask for the forbearance, patience and cooperation of all honourable members and leaders of the political parties to ensure the success of this proceeding." At the bar, Arch Pafford — permitted to participate as the leader of a registered political party — looked down the rows of wooden desks and up at the chandeliers and the portraits of British monarchs past and present. He hadn't received a mandate from the voters, but there he was, bringing his mission onto the floor of the Legislative Assembly itself.

Pafford's first question was about Meech Lake. He demanded that McKenna — then in the midst of his jockeying to rescue the deal — submit any resulting constitutional resolution to a referendum. McKenna deflected the question, firing back that with fifty-eight of fifty-eight seats, "we have a fair chance of representing the majority of the people of the province of New Brunswick" and chastising Pafford for claiming to speak for the public. "Certainly, the pollsters do not bear that out," McKenna said. Then he turned the tables on COR. "While the leader is here and we have a chance to have close encounters of the third kind, I have a question I would like to ask him." The premier then read a statement Ed Allen had made at a COR meeting: "We are going to take away that life support to the terminally ill language and that terminally ill language will disappear, in North America at least." Facing Pafford, McKenna said, "What you are talking about is cultural genocide, my friend, and my question to you is whether or not you condone, and whether you associate yourself with, the comments of the president of the party."

Taken aback, Pafford managed to say that he didn't condone the remarks and that they had been taken out of context. But McKenna wasn't finished. Cheered on by his Liberal MLAs and ministers, he pounded on Pafford again, asking the COR leader if he agreed with the president of the Alliance for the Preservation of English in Canada that speaking French was like having AIDS. As Pafford stammered that he did not, McKenna struck again: "Has this person appeared at your meetings?"

Finally, the Speaker stepped in. "Somehow we have gotten this mixed up," he said. "The questions are supposed to come this way." Pafford, saved by the intervention, moved on to the subject of cost overruns at the construction of an NB Power plant near Bathurst.

Pafford was no better prepared for his next appearance, handing McKenna another opening by challenging the premier to back up his claim that COR was spreading untruths. McKenna pounced, demanding Pafford prove COR's claim that bilingualism was costing the province half a billion dollars — about one sixth of the entire budget. "If you are going to get into this debate, as you are determined that you are going to, arm yourself with the facts," McKenna admonished him. "Be careful in the use of those facts, because somebody may confront you, and you will find that you are not able to produce when those people sitting next to you demand to know where you are coming from."

It was clear to political veterans that McKenna had mopped the floor with the COR leader. "Pafford was a disaster," MacKinnon says. "He was weak. He was just awful. He wasn't polished." But Pafford saw it differently: he had won just by being there. "That was very important to us," he says. "That kept us in the limelight. It gave us legitimacy." He says the scrums with reporters afterward were "worth millions of dollars in advertising. All of a sudden we're on the political scene. We're right there in the fire."

Just as important for COR was who was not there in the fire with Pafford: the new leader of the Progressive Conservative Party, Barbara Baird-Filliter.

* * *

By late 1989, the Progressive Conservatives had shaken off the trauma of 1987, gathered their residual strength and got on with the job of holding a leadership convention. There had been two candidates: Barbara Baird-Filliter, a thirty-seven-year-old lawyer from Fredericton, and Hank Myers, the former two-term Kings East MLA and minister of agriculture under Hatfield. "It was a choice between someone who had been an MLA and a minister in the previous government," says Brad Green, then the provincial youth president, "and a new face, someone the public would not associate immediately with the Richard Hatfield years."

From a young age, Barbara Baird had believed herself destined to be a political success. Her grandfather, a friend of Lord Beaverbrook, and her father, a civil servant, had told her she would be New Brunswick's first woman premier. She played the piano, learned judo and attended the London School of Economics. In her law school graduation photo, she stands on a rail bed, a foot on one rail, and gazes boldly, defiantly, into the camera. "I was going to make tracks," she sighs, looking at the picture.

Though most influential backroom Tories opted for the new face, not everyone was so enthusiastic. Kevin Fram, who had sought the youth presidency in 1986 on a pro-Hatfield, pro-francophone platform, says Baird-Filliter was "fudging and hedging" on language when he met her. He says she talked of rebuilding in the traditional anglophone Tory ridings first. At the convention, which Baird-Filliter won in a landslide, she endorsed bilingualism but added that the policy should not leave anyone feeling like a victim of discrimination. That led delegate Louise Pelletier, Fram's ally in the youth campaign, to tell CBC Radio: "Her stands on linguistic issues . . . are very vague to say the very least.

I haven't heard any substance at all." Jean-Maurice Simard said in a Provincial Archives interview that Baird-Filliter fell victim to the view that Hatfield's Acadian overtures had led to his defeat in 1987. He recalled urging her to fight for the constitutional entrenchment of Bill 88, his cherished equality legislation that he'd pushed through the Legislature in 1981. In the midst of the constitutional debate, entrenchment had become the latest francophone cause, and Simard believed it was imperative that the PC party embrace that cause. Yet, he claimed Baird-Filliter "didn't know what Bill 88 was," and though she eventually backed entrenchment, Simard felt that she never made the case as forcefully as she could have.

Baird-Filliter — who doesn't recall that meeting with Simard — says she was always clear with party members about bilingualism. "It was here to stay," she says. "That was part of the essence of the Conservative party in this province. We'd embraced bilingualism with Richard and that wasn't going to change." She also refutes Fram's claims she focused on Tory English heartland ridings, saying she visited the Acadian Peninsula "all the time." She adds, however, that she knew her party was losing members to COR and that she had to assure those people she'd look out for their interests, too. Whenever she broached how to do that, she says, some francophone Conservatives would not hear of it. "You could not satisfy those two extreme positions."

The rise of COR was only one of her challenges. McKenna, the Liberal premier, remained popular, while her federal leader was increasingly loathed. She had to spend time away from the limelight, reviving the party by rebuilding riding organizations, setting up policy committees and raising money. A group of "old-guard" Tories, as she puts it, refused to accept a young woman leader with new ideas. She had proudly kept her birth name in her professional career but, at the urging of advisors, reluctantly appended her husband's when she became leader. She was criticized for spurning the invitation to appear at the Legislature in the spring of 1990, a decision she says was based on the advice of Conservative guru Dalton Camp. "The circumstances were monumental," she says. "Insurmountable."

Baird-Filliter appeared, belatedly, at the bar of the Legislature on October 30, 1990. "I wish to draw the attention of the House to the fact that we have with us a long-awaited visitor," Liberal MLA John McKay cooed sarcastically. "After these many months, it is proof of the old adage, 'Absence makes the heart grow fonder.'"

"Thank you, honourable member, for those kind words of introduction," Baird-Filliter replied gamely. "I feel somewhat akin to the person who has been invited to dinner; it is a question of who will eat or be eaten."

As it turned out, Barbara Baird-Filliter was eaten alive by her own party.

Brad Green blames the expectations of the membership, who, he says, "did not make the transition easily to being out of power and out of the Legislature. It requires a definite shift in mindset and that was difficult." Hank Myers says her inexperience and errors drove away veteran Conservatives like him. "The people who were advising her and helping her dropped out one by one," he says. Whoever was to blame, Baird-Filliter decided one day in the spring of 1991 — as hurtful, unfounded rumours about her personal life began making the rounds — that she could not go on. "You're just in this impossible situation constantly, and it just dawned on me that for the sake of the province, if I was the problem and I eliminated myself, maybe the party would stop bickering and get on with the job of winning some seats." She called an acquaintance at CBC Television and told him she had a story for him.

* * *

Dennis Cochrane was at his home on the outskirts of Moncton that night, watching the news with his wife, when Baird-Filliter appeared on the screen, reading a prepared statement. "Many party supporters have questions about the direction in which the party is heading," she was saying. She spoke of "self-appointed critics" who questioned her leadership "continually." She acknowledged mistakes but said they were not the reason for the party's situation. Regardless, she was quitting. "I believe it is the right thing to do," she said.

Cochrane turned to his wife. "I said, 'Oh no — we don't need this.'"

The former Moncton MP had been considered a potential replacement for Hatfield during the leadership review battle in 1985 and had been courted to run in 1989. Now he knew the party would come calling again, this time with an election expected within months. "I really didn't want to run," he says. "I was principal of a school. I lived four kilometres away. And I was happily married. Things were good." But Brad Green lobbied Cochrane hard. He got others to call. He lined up commitments of support. He built lists of organizers. He solicited invitations for Cochrane to speak at party events.

Cochrane's assets were obvious: he had experience in government, a reputation for decency, an effortless public speaking style learned in the classroom and a knack for diligent, methodical organizing.

But for francophones in the PC party, Cochrane had baggage.

Dennis Cochrane didn't come from the Hatfield wing of the PC party. He had ties to Moncton Tories whom Acadians regarded with suspicion, including the infamous Leonard Jones. Cochrane had supported Jones in 1974 in his famous fight for the federal PC nomination in Moncton, and was among the disaffected Tories in the city who had clashed with federal leader Robert Stanfield for vetoing Jones's nomination. Cochrane claims it wasn't about "an affiliation with Jones" but the principle that local riding associations should be free to choose their candidates. "What had happened offended my sense of what was fair. At that time, you're twenty-three years old and you're full of what's right and what's proper." But Eric Bungay, a Conservative who opposed Jones in 1974, says Cochrane's sympathies with the anti-French mayor were well known. "He was a young, young man," Bungay says, forgivingly. "He came under the influence of those people. He was a Len Jones man, strong." Two rival riding executives — one pro-Jones, one anti-Jones — were later elected in Moncton, with Cochrane in the pro-Jones camp. Still, he was courted to run provincially in 1978 and 1982, a sign, he says, that he was "accepted by Hatfield and became, basically, a mainstream Tory."

He may have been mainstream, but his battles with the progressive wing of the party continued. After serving a term as mayor, Cochrane decided to seek the federal PC nomination in Moncton in 1984 — as did Brenda Robertson, a Hatfield cabinet minister from Riverview. Robertson didn't want a fight for the nomination, so Cochrane was promised the patronage job of his choice to sit out the contest. He refused, and Robertson bowed out instead, bitterly concluding she could not beat Cochrane at a convention. His supporters in the Jones wing of the local organization were too strong.

"Brenda always said Dennis was supported by the wrong people," one Tory says.

Cochrane's federal career was brief, his one term as MP for Moncton marked by Ottawa's decision to close the CN repair shops, leading to the loss of hundreds jobs and his defeat. He would also be remembered for his refusal in 1988 to vote on his own government's Bill C-72, an updating of the federal Official Languages Act — another sign of Cochrane's lukewarm commitment to linguistic equality. He admits now that, with one eye on re-election and the CN issue hurting him, he was trying to pander to anti-French sentiment in Moncton. "I made the wrong decision," he says. "I should have voted for it. It was bad judgment on my part. I was probably trying to find a way to be all things to all people."

So Cochrane was hardly an ideal leader for a provincial party that had so recently sought to re-order the political map of New Brunswick by winning large blocs of francophone support. But he just might be the right man to appeal to traditional PC constituencies — whose voters were not all that keen on Acadian power anyhow — and win enough of them to put the party back in contention. He agreed to serve as leader for one year, to carry the party through the next election.

Cochrane found the Tories "in terrible shape" when he took over in June, barely three months before the expected election. There was no money and no platform, he says. "We had three or four nominated candidates when I became leader. I remember calling the Xerox guy and saying, 'We can't pay for this copier.' God love him, he took it back." When the party office applied for a credit card for his travel expenses, "I got a note from the bank manager saying, 'Dennis, I would suggest you apply for this card in your own name, not the party's name.' My credit rating was better than the party's credit rating."

It would soon dawn on Cochrane exactly where the volunteers, the organizers, the money and the candidates had gone.

* * *

The morning of August 21, the COR party's nominated candidates gathered at Pond's Resort, on the Miramichi River near Boiestown, for a final campaign preparation meeting. The party's official re-presentative, Don Sutherland, had already written to his riding counterparts explaining fundraising and advertising rules. "Now is the time to get rid of the kid gloves and start fighting a real battle. Remember, if we as COR-NB members don't react aggressively to this upcoming election and defeat the McKenna government, we will never again have a democratic opportunity to restore linguistic rights to the English-speaking majority in New Brunswick. If we allow ourselves to be defeated now, we, our children and grandchildren forever after will be second-class citizens in an English-speaking country."

The candidates took part in mock debates and attended workshops on advertising. Each received a copy of the COR election platform, "A Fair Deal for New Brunswickers," which promised the repeal of the 1969 Official Languages Act and of Simard's Bill 88, and the establishment of English as the language of work within the government. No other language would be banned from "oral communication," the document said, and the proceedings of the Legislature would still be translated, but bilingual government documents were "expensive and sometimes unnecessary" and, under a COR government, would be provided only on the basis of some undefined "need."

COR also made classic populist promises of lower taxes, smaller government, reduced debt, free votes in the Legislature, referendums and fixed election dates. The document also reminded candidates of the pecking order in a grassroots party: while MLAs would be obliged to support the leader on issues laid out in the platform, "an elected COR member will be responsible to, in order of precedence, the following: The Electorate, The Party, The Leader."

At two p.m., an excited party volunteer interrupted the meeting to give the candidates news from Fredericton: McKenna had called the election for September 23. "Cheers went up" from the candidates, Pafford remembers. "They were anxious to get out there."

Early on, COR seemed destined for failure. The campaign began quietly in that final week of August, just as the Liberals had planned, with the race coming into focus only after Labour Day. On September 7, the *Telegraph-Journal* carried a column by Don Richardson with the headline "Language issue not playing major role." It reported on a poll showing that only twelve per cent of voters considered language important, far behind the economy. COR's support was at fifteen per cent, well behind the Conservatives' twenty-two per cent. The Liberals were far ahead, their re-election assured.

The Tories' prospects weren't as encouraging out on the trail. Dennis Cochrane spent the campaign gamely bouncing around the province in a small, single-engine plane, rented by the hour and piloted by a Tory supporter's husband, who had a private pilot's permit and needed the hours to qualify for a commercial licence. "The first time I was in the plane, it felt like wrapping yourself in tinfoil, attaching an engine and heading off," says Brad Green. Late one night, after an evening rally in Carleton County, he and Cochrane were driven back to the remote, unlit airstrip where the plane was parked. A party volunteer drove his truck to the end of runway, turned around and flicked on his high beams. "The instructions to the pilot," Green says, "were, 'Aim for the headlights and be off the ground before you get there.'"

Candidate recruitment was likewise *ad hoc*: in several constituencies, the Tories had only paper candidates — names on the ballot that let the party claim to be running in all fifty-eight ridings. In Dieppe, it was Cochrane's volunteer driver. "There are ridings where you don't have any organization and you prop somebody up to run," he says.

In the TV leaders' debate, Cochrane was marginalized by angry exchanges between McKenna and Pafford. "It's not the language policy that is causing disunity, it's the people who are misrepresenting the language policy," the premier said. "You've had your head in the sand for the past four years," Pafford shot back. "I've been out there and I've listened to what the people are saying about the language issue." Pafford, so badly bruised at the Legislature the previous year, was now holding his own against McKenna — and in doing so was gaining more legitimacy in the eyes of voters.

At the outset of the campaign, political forecasters had looked at the parties challenging McKenna — the non-entity that was the NDP, the still-devastated Conservatives and the fringe, long-shot COR party — and, seeing a COR-PC split of whatever anti-government vote existed, speculated about a second consecutive Liberal sweep of all fifty-eight seats.

But civil servants, hospital workers, police officers were discreetly telling Arch Pafford they would vote COR. "I was out there every day," he says. "I had the pulse. To the naysayers, I ignored them and continued on my way." In Sunbury, near Fredericton, Max White, the former president of the PC riding association who had voted to remove Hatfield as leader, was now a COR candidate. "I knew within a week and a half of door to door," he says. "In the entire campaign, I had only one woman who blasted me. . . . I knew within a week that we were on the move."

Conservatives knew it, too. In Fredericton North, where Ed Allen was running for COR, the Tories could not find a candidate. A week into the campaign, they finally persuaded Don Parent to challenge the incumbent Liberal, Jim Wilson. "They kept saying I had to beat Jim Wilson, and just in the couple of weeks I had to knock on doors, I told them, 'Ed Allen is the guy I've got to beat,'" Parent remembers. "I was running against God in Ed Allen in Fredericton North."

Soon Liberals knew it, too. In York North, a sprawling, traditionally Conservative riding stretching from Nackawic to the outskirts of Fredericton and north to Stanley and Boiestown, Liberal Bob Simpson, elected in the 1987 sweep, felt his chances for a second term slipping away as COR's message — there would soon be no government jobs for unilingual anglophones — began to catch on. "As the campaign went on," he says, "I started hearing things at the door from many people. The depth of it became perfectly clear." In Riverview, Liberal cabinet minister Hubert Seamans — whose by-election win in 1985 heralded the end of the Hatfield era — was counting on a PC-COR split. But then he began to encounter strange reactions at the doorsteps: silence, noncommittal politeness, a lack of enthusiasm. His milkman, a francophone, told him that people were bragging they were working hard for COR. "I just couldn't believe how insensitive people could be to other people," he says.

In the final ten days of the campaign, Liberal strategists finally caught on and tailored McKenna's schedule accordingly. On a single day, for example, he hit five ridings where COR was considered a factor, darting through New Maryland, Burtts Corner, Riverside-Albert, Gagetown, Durham Bridge and Boiestown. In Burtts Corner, he told a hundred campaign workers at a breakfast for Bob Simpson to make sure they had an MLA they could be proud of. At the Albert County fair, he had a chance meeting with COR candidate Bev Brine. They exchanged pleasantries. "I'll talk to you in the Legislature," Brine said confidently as she moved off.

COR hadn't been registering in public opinion polls, but then, five days before the vote, a survey showed the party strongly in second place, at twenty-four per cent. The Tories were far behind, tied with the NDP at fourteen, while the Liberals led with forty-eight. COR's showing was immediately dismissed by the Liberals. "We had no other corroborating evidence of that," MacKinnon says. "We were all so parsimonious, we weren't polling. We were so confident."

In York North in the final week, Bob Simpson was anything but confident. His COR opponent, Greg Hargrove, was telling voters nightly that Bill 88's guarantee of equality for the two linguistic communities might someday give francophones an equal number of seats in the Legislature. But there was little Simpson could do to counter such fabrications. He greeted the dawn of election day, September 23, with apprehension. "I knew it might not even be close," he says, "and it wasn't."

Chapter Nine

HONOURABLE SKUNKS

ON THE MORNING OF September 24, 1991, New Brunswickers awoke to a changed politics. The two-party system they'd lived with and had understood for decades had been rattled; the consensus they thought had taken hold now seemed considerably less firm. COR was the Official Opposition, with twenty-one per cent of the popular vote, meaning one-third of the citizens in English New Brunswick had chosen the party committed to eradicating francophone rights. Based on that vote, the party that had passed the hat to survive was eligible for $180,000 in public subsidies, plus taxpayer-funded offices and staff at the Legislature. COR would benefit from the mechanisms that had seemed designed to keep fringe parties down and protect the old-line parties. Now one of those old-line parties, the Progressive Conservatives, seemed in danger of disappearing altogether.

The eight new COR MLAs, among them Greg Hargrove, might be seen as skunks at the establishment garden party, but they'd earned the status of *honourable* skunks. "We've impacted on the politics of New Brunswick and we're here to stay," Arch Pafford told reporters as he relaxed the morning after the election on the patio of his modest bungalow in Nordin.

Liberals grappled for explanations. At a news conference in Fredericton, Frank McKenna blamed angry civil servants. Earlier in the year, in an effort to trim $185 million from the government budget, McKenna had frozen the wages of ten thousand public sector workers.

Three thousand of them protested in Fredericton in April, and the Canadian Union of Public Employees staged demonstrations at Liberal nominating conventions through the spring and summer. McKenna suggested that COR had given those angry workers an outlet. But that was facile: COR did well in Fredericton, where many government workers lived and voted, but it also won in places where they did not.

McKenna was clearly irritated that the COR insurgency had taken away from his massive victory, though forty-six of fifty-eight seats was a landslide by any standard other than the one he'd set four years earlier. "The majority rules," he said at one point, reminding journalists that most New Brunswickers had voted for parties supporting official bilingualism. "Should voters in one or two or even eight ridings decide they don't support the policies of the government, that doesn't mean we'll alter our agenda to suit their wishes. We believe in [bilingualism] as Liberals as a matter of faith. I'm unswerving in my conviction — there will be no retreat."

Behind the scenes, McKenna's people were unsure how to react. COR's breakthrough underscored Canadians' willingness to cast aside the traditional parties and all their constitutional talk of "distinct" cultures. "We were very sensitive to how this would play across the country," Steven MacKinnon says. More personally, he and McKenna's other advisors realized gloomily that many of their neighbours in the capital, people they saw at the grocery store or at the Farmers' Market on Saturdays, had voted COR. "We all lived in Fredericton, and we felt very dirty going back there," MacKinnon says.

McKenna's advisors argued over whether to entrench Simard's Bill 88 in the Constitution. Some argued that the election results made it clear the premier should drop the politically dangerous subject. "This makes it all the more important to do it," answered McKenna. He'd been leery of the implications of Bill 88's granting of collective linguistic rights — and in no hurry to entrench it in his first mandate — but now he saw it as a bulwark against COR's rising influence, especially if the Conservatives won back those voters and returned to power by abandoning bilingualism. "It's all the more important that we never give ground on this," McKenna told his staff.

Left on the sidelines was the provincial PC party. The Tory popular vote — though it translated into three seats — was below COR's and actually down from 1987. The party's survival was in doubt, and even leader Dennis Cochrane had to admit it would take time to determine if COR was an aberration. COR had placed second in many races; in sixteen ridings, a combined PC-COR vote would have defeated the victorious Liberals. Cochrane knew those ballots should have been his — at any other historical moment, they would have been. "Obviously there's a problem out there," Cochrane said ominously, "and unless it's dealt with, COR will remain a factor for years to come." He would not completely rule out shifting the PC party's language policy to lure back COR voters. "The mind is never closed," he said, before quickly adding, "I don't think we'd ever mimic their position. It's not reasonable. It's not possible." But the fact that Cochrane would even speak of such an idea publicly revealed how profound the challenge was to Richard Hatfield's legacy.

* * *

The Confederation of Regions party had achieved its first goal: shock the political system. But as its eight "honourable skunks" gathered in Fredericton, they faced a serious problem: Arch Pafford, their kindly, charismatic leader, the self-proclaimed man on a mission, had failed to win his riding.

Pafford had felt obligated to be in other ridings during the campaign, so he hadn't spent enough time in Miramichi-Newcastle to win the close three-way race in his own riding. Still, as he journeyed to Fredericton to meet his new caucus, "I was still pretty happy," he says. He envisioned a scenario in which he'd appoint someone as house leader in the Legislature and stay on as party leader to continue building COR in the field, pulling in more traditional Tory voters — surely an easier task now that COR had momentum.

Pafford got a rude awakening when he met the new MLAs. "That was a very traumatic experience for me," he says. "I thought going into the meeting that I had a lot of support, but in the meeting it turned out otherwise." When he realized the caucus wanted its leader in the Legislature, Pafford says he urged Ed Allen to accept the interim position. But Allen's health was poor and he declined. Instead, the caucus chose Danny Cameron, the new MLA from York South. Pafford would stay on as a full-time employee of COR, Cameron told a news conference. "He will continue to play a major role in this party because he has pulled off politically what is pretty close to a miracle in two years."

Danny Cameron — sixty-six years old, dignified, patrician, with the stand-up-straight, chest-out bearing of the military man he had once been — was the obvious choice for leader. His life story was one that COR members could admire. He'd been born in poverty on a farm in Osgoode, Ontario, a village of ninety-nine people divided among Anglicans, Baptists and Presbyterians. "Life was in your face every day," Cameron would remember, "pretty raw and basic." The values of thrift and self-sufficiency he learned would stay with him the rest of his life. "Today, young people — and you can't blame them — see so many things in front of them, and they expect everything and they want it now," he told an interviewer. "We didn't have a 'now' list. We had a 'maybe' list."

Osgoode, Ontario also shaped Cameron's views on ethnicity. "Prejudice was something I learned about at an early age," he'd told a COR banquet audience in 1990. "We were taught Scottish clan prejudice. My cousin married a Campbell and there was hell to pay. My sister married an Anglican and my mother never forgave her to the day she died." The next village down the road was a mix of Irish and French Catholics. "The French farmers were very poor," Cameron remembered. "We felt sorry for them. They were poorer than we were, and if they were on the outs with either the parish priest or the political boss, they had no hope of getting ahead. That was my introduction to French politics."

Cameron left Osgoode at fifteen to make a living, starting with a six-dollar-a-week job at a Dominion grocery store in Ottawa, then working for a time in Montreal. "Loved the city," he'd recall, "and worked with a mixture of French and English — picked up a little more culture, I guess." In the Royal Canadian Air Force, he met French-speaking Quebecers with Scottish, Welsh and Irish names — examples of assimilation. "Are we complaining?" he'd ask. "Are they complaining? Not as far as I know." Later, running his Fredericton-based equipment rental company, he ordered up bilingual invoices and contracts for his customers in northern New Brunswick. "There was initial appreciation," he told the COR banquet in 1990, "but over a short time the forms fell into disuse because most understood and accepted the English version readily."

In the 1980s, Cameron, by then a self-made millionaire and Conservative bagman, had grown frustrated with Richard Hatfield, whose support for bilingualism seemed to fly in the face of the lessons Cameron had learned over a lifetime of hard work. As president of the York South provincial PC riding association and right-hand man to cabinet minister Les Hull, Cameron sympathized with Tories who were angry about Hatfield's overtures to Acadians. "His views were similar, but he never let it interfere with the work we were doing," Hull says. "He helped me tremendously." Cameron told his 1990 COR audience that his opinions did not mean he was anti-French. "I trust," he said, "that all those people sitting in judgment of me — and I am sure some of you here have similar stories to tell — will hesitate to automatically brand anyone who speaks out a bigot or a redneck. For over forty years, while supporting the PC party and contributing time, money and effort, I was never called such names. Am I one now?"

In 1988, despite his growing cynicism, Cameron sought the federal PC nomination in Fredericton. The favourite — Bud Bird, a popular former mayor and provincial cabinet minister — had decided not to run. Then Bird changed his mind, and the party brass urged the other candidates, including Cameron, to pull out. Most of them refused, and the contest became a pitched organizational battle, with Bird's troops setting up a massive phone bank to build lists of supporters. "They brought a lot of people in from Ottawa to put Bud in place," Cameron would say. More than two thousand Tories turned out for the convention, which Bird won on the first ballot. He went on to be elected MP for Fredericton in the 1988 federal election.

The following year, Cameron got a call from Arch Pafford, who had been the manager of his rental company's Miramichi office. Pafford was recruiting influential Tories to COR, and he made his pitch to his former boss. "I thought, what the heck — some of the things he said made sense, some of them didn't," Cameron said in a brief interview. According to documents in his files, Cameron bought a COR membership card on December 28, 1989.

His conversion from Tory to COR supporter was fervent: when he went public at that COR banquet in March 1990, he called for the repeal of federal bilingualism legislation and the shelving of Bill 88. "This madness must be brought to a halt," he said. "I will fight to my last breath to keep New Brunswick from becoming a second Quebec."

Cameron's philosophy mirrored that of many ex-Tories who liked Acadians better when they hadn't made a fuss. English and French people had got along just fine in New Brunswick before the advent of official bilingualism, he believed, and activists who had stirred up all the trouble did not represent most francophones. "We would not be suspicious and untrusting of one another if the politicians did not foment unrest, stonewall on issues, involve themselves in issues better left alone, ply us with unnecessary programs and procedures, and on and on and on, and pass you and me the bill," he said. "We are angry at government and politicians, not French people." For good measure, he called on the province to scrap plans to build a bridge to isolated Miscou Island off New Brunswick's northeast tip. Instead, he suggested, forcibly relocate Miscou's 1,400 Acadian residents to the mainland and turn the island into a bird sanctuary or a military firing range.

Pafford says Cameron, like countless other anglophone Tories whom Hatfield had taken for granted or ignored, was attracted as much by COR's commitment to genuinely democratic, grassroots politics as by its language policies. "He understood coming in that it was a party of the people, and that the executive had a lot more power in our party than in other parties, and that the leader was answerable to the people through the executive." But loyal Tories like Fred Beairsto, a long-time backroom organizer in Fredericton, couldn't understand the defection. "You know that people lean in a certain direction, but it's quite another thing to say 'We're going to do something about it and form a party,'" he says. "I don't know what those people thought. I guess they thought they could form the government. Danny Cameron's not a stupid guy, so you say, 'What in hell is he doing? What's he doing involved in *that*?'"

Whatever the motivation, Cameron's move was second only to Ed Allen's in importance, says Greg Hargrove. "He would show the business community they didn't have to be afraid. It would mean financial support and more prominence and more respectability."

Indeed, the selection of Cameron as interim leader helped COR appear less dangerous. "I look forward very much to the challenge of furthering the cause of the COR party in a moderate way," he said at that first news conference. "I'm a moderate person." Don Hoyt of the *Telegraph-Journal* lauded what he called Cameron's talk of seeking an English-French "compromise." Cameron told Hoyt he didn't have time for extremists and would put his own "stamp" on the party — which, he said, needed "to show more maturity than I've seen in the past."

Pafford claims Cameron appreciated COR's grassroots philosophy, but the new interim leader told Hoyt that he drew a clear distinction between the "political arm" of the party — the leader and the MLAs — and the "administrative arm," with which he said he wasn't familiar. Most notably, Cameron told Hoyt there were priorities other than language to focus on. "Our approach will be different" in the Legislature, he said, "and it's my prerogative to steer it in whatever direction I see, provided the people who support us agree."

Cameron would learn quickly that COR's supporters most definitely did *not* agree — and though his moderate tone may have pleased newspaper columnists, it was hardly acceptable to the party's rank-and-file members. They'd joined because they weren't the types to compromise.

Neither was Danny Cameron.

* * *

The trouble began almost immediately. Internal party correspondence reveals that soon after the election, COR party president Laurie Robichaud convened an "investigative committee" of the party, at Cameron's suggestion, to probe actions that were "detrimental to the success and smooth operation" of COR. "The mandate of this Committee is to put a stop to the infighting, backbiting, distrust and interference by individuals, of the [sic] progress and growth of this party," a memo said. "It must be brought to the Board in the context of the Party first, ahead of individual aspirations." Attached to the memo, discovered in Cameron's correspondence files, is a list of ten members, including MLA Brent Taylor and Georgina McArthur, an early ally of Jim Webb's. "Nothing concrete," said a handwritten note next to one person's name. Another said, "Deposition coming re his attitude."

There are few details about the committee in the documents. "It was supposed to investigate what had gone wrong in the election," says Arch Pafford, whose memories of the committee are dim. "I didn't like it at all." The process quickly collapsed when several participants backed out before the committee's scheduled meeting on October 26. The investigation "would have a negative effect both on the Party and the Caucus," Don Sutherland, the party's official representative, wrote to Robichaud.

Within weeks, Robichaud was voted out as party president at COR's annual general meeting. He was replaced by Pafford, suddenly in the odd position of administering the party apparatus that was in the process of hiring him as a staff employee, as Cameron had promised when he became leader. Robichaud complained that Pafford's dual role — running the organization while reporting as a staffer to Cameron — allowed Cameron to take complete control of the COR machine.

At the same time, some party members were alarmed at the moderate tone Cameron had struck with Don Hoyt. The party's board of directors called an "emergency informal meeting" to discuss his statements. A letter from one of Cameron's own constituents in York South, Malcolm MacNeil, reported that there was "vigorous verbal objection" to the remarks. "'I think there is compromise that should be studied,'" the letter paraphrased. "What compromise?" Another supporter, Glenna Cox of Lake Utopia, wrote to Cameron: "We do not need a PATRIARCH who thinks he knows best what others want. COR in the next while will certainly find the insincere power hungry and shallow people who cannot stick to the great policies that so many worked so hard for. Not even you have the right to construe them as you see fit."

As tempers rose within the party, Cameron abandoned his moderate tone and went on the attack over Frank McKenna's trip to Paris to attend the Francophonie summit, a gathering of leaders of countries with historical and cultural ties to France. "When did New Brunswick become a French nation/country?" Cameron demanded in a press release, wondering whether Acadian organizations were seeking independent status like Quebec. The criticisms were a reality check for Don Hoyt, who wrote a follow-up column saying he'd been had by Cameron's talk of compromise. The leader "has lost his nerve and become a prisoner of the hard-liners who see a French conspiracy under every rock. A wolf in sheep's clothing is still a wolf."

Cameron's hard-line tone created, in turn, another problem among COR's moderates. "I am english and have supported the C.O.R. party since its inception," said one anonymous letter writer. "I have a lot of good friends that are french and real nice people. They are part of our society and very well deserve a place in this province. After all, they do make up a large part of our population. I sometimes wonder if you and a few more are working full time to split this province down the middle and eventually we will be like Quebec. . . . I am to discusted to sign my name or to be called a member of the C.O.R. party."

Simultaneously, another front opened in the attacks on Cameron. He was criticized for the staffing decisions he'd made as Official Opposition leader. Several COR supporters were upset he'd hired Dorothy Brislain, his campaign manager in York South, as his executive assistant. They felt they had a right to positions like that — and many, apparently confused about the difference between being in power and sitting in opposition, assumed that Cameron and his MLAs would get to place their supporters in all sorts of government jobs.

"You can't really understand it until you experience it, what the demands are," Greg Hargrove says ruefully. "There were people who had worked for the party who felt their due was there — 'Where's my payoff for being a loyal party supporter?' Well, you know, this is the big leagues now. You've got to have people in your legislative office who are competent, who have the qualifications to do the job. You can't just take somebody because they're an old party hack, so it causes resentment. People are very naïve, you know: 'What the hell did we put you in there for?'"

All this relentless oversight, constant feedback, and bitter second-guessing was, for Cameron, a jarring change from the business world, where he'd run his companies the way he saw fit. Now there was no pleasing anyone.

Finally, on December 11, in a letter to the COR board of directors, he responded to his critics. He defended Brislain's qualifications and insisted he never used the word "compromise" with Don Hoyt. He attached two lists, which he called "my approach to my responsibilities." The first list, "Things I Will Do," was conciliatory, including promises to "work with the incoming board and executive to chart future direction" and "provide, with their input, the best, most acceptable political product to all the people of New Brunswick."

The second list reveals Cameron's frustrations after just two months on the job as interim leader of the COR party. It is labelled "Things I Will Not Do":

Referee personality clashes.

Participate in kangaroo courts.

Support empire builders.

Be commanded by armchair generals.

Allow caucus to be controlled by advocacy groups.

Comment on remarks made by nameless, faceless dissenters.

Provide a forum for bigots or racist elements.

Chase rumours and/or unfounded charges, or verbal accusations.

Be manipulated as a puppet.

Cameron was sending a message to the COR board that, even as interim leader, he expected the flexibility and the discretion to act as he felt necessary, without having to constantly seek grassroots approval. "The leader can't lead if he has to follow everyone else," he would tell a party board meeting a few days later. "The caucus can't function if we are being attacked by our own people." What Cameron wanted was the top-down style of the traditional political parties. But COR was supposed to be different: it was going to give voice to all those people whom Richard Hatfield and Jean-Maurice Simard had forgotten.

"Danny was a great businessman and a good leader," Hargrove sighs, shaking his head, "but a piss-poor politician."

* * *

Publicly, the Confederation of Regions party remained focused on bringing a dissenting voice on bilingualism into the Legislative Assembly. On Tuesday, February 11, 1992, COR's eight MLAs finally took their seats across the aisle from Frank McKenna's Liberal government.

"On a personal basis, they were nice people," recalls Bernard Richard, then the new Liberal MLA for Shediac-Cap Pelé, who found himself in the spillover government seats to the left of the Speaker, near the Opposition. "But it was a strange feeling, knowing they were elected because they opposed something I considered fundamental." The more Richard thought about the eight COR members as the Official Opposition, using taxpayer dollars to attack Acadian rights, the more he felt it was "a pretty sickening idea."

COR's reception in official Fredericton was mixed: the staff at the Legislature "were professional," Hargrove says, "but some of them did what they had to do and no more." Civil servants were soothed by the presence on the COR benches of Ed Allen, whom many of them had known as a minister. Some francophone Liberals, like the ambitious Kent South MLA Camille Thériault, were gracious; others, like Bernard Thériault of Caraquet and Pierrette Ringuette-Maltais of Madawaska-Sud, treated the COR MLAs with contempt. "I had Liberals say to me, 'You don't belong here,'" Hargrove remembers. "I said, 'Tell that to the voters.'"

Early in the session, COR's MLAs seemed anything but angry, populist or revolutionary. Cameron's reply to the Speech from the Throne — normally a chance for the Official Opposition to lay out its alternative vision in detail — was barely half the usual length and decidedly nonconfrontational in tone. "Our parliamentary tradition depends on reasoned and honest debate, and this opposition intends to rise above pettiness and partisanship to carry out the vital role given us by the voters," he said. The first Question Period was equally tame, with COR MLAs sticking to economic questions and not raising language.

The Liberals discovered that most of the COR MLAs were not tepid, they were simply not very good at their jobs. "McKenna was a very fast-moving target," remembers MLA Brent Taylor, who says Cameron set no overall Question Period strategy other than to react to the government. While Tory Jean Gauvin managed to reveal embarrassing government grants in the Assembly, COR committed gaffes. MLA Ab Rector, during a Public Accounts committee hearing, asked about a $17,000 Department of Labour payment to "Miss Lameque." "Who is this Miss Lameque, and why did we pay her?"

"Miss Lameque isn't a person," the deputy minister of labour answered. "She's a boat." As part of a training program, the government had subsidized the salaries of the crew.

"Having COR in the legislature made it easier," McKenna's aide Steven MacKinnon says. "We could lay things on the table." When a Liberal MLA from Moncton presented a committee report on what New Brunswick's constitutional position should be in forthcoming negotiations — including endorsement of the deeply resented "distinct society" status for Quebec — COR issued a press release saying it was "too early to comment on the entire document." Two days later, Cameron finally sent out a detailed critique. "I'm not slow," he would explain. "I'm careful."

It didn't help that COR's only experienced MLA, Ed Allen, was having health problems. "He found that legislative session tough," his son Mike says. "The work they had to do — to stay on their toes and be good critics — it was one of the toughest situations he ever had to work." Seated nearby, Dennis Cochrane would watch Allen struggle to his feet, often with a copy of that day's *Globe and Mail* in hand, and paraphrase a question from the headlines, frequently about a federal program such as gun control. "You'd sit there and ask, 'Where are they coming from? What is this about?'" Cochrane says.

Cochrane's small Conservative caucus of three soon began to eclipse COR. Finally, eight months after the election, "I had some faith we were back," Cochrane says. "I had a caucus. I had a francophone and an anglophone. I had one in the north, one in the south. They'd both been in the House. They'd both been ministers."

And they'd both achieved a measure of redemption: Jean Gauvin, after his disastrous spurning of Brian Mulroney's invitation to run federally in Gloucester in 1984, had wrested the PC nomination away from the sitting MP in 1988, only to lose in the election to the Liberals. So he'd re-entered the provincial arena, squeaking out a fifty-vote win in his old riding of Shippagan-les-Îles in 1991. Hank Myers, back as the MLA for Kings East, had been tainted as a leadership candidate three years earlier as too close to Richard Hatfield. Now, his government experience was a valuable asset in the Legislature.

And there was Cochrane himself, not only a master debater and a wise user of parliamentary procedure, but also a skilled organizer. He travelled the province, attending local PC meetings, raising money, cajoling more volunteers to help out — and it was working. At the party's annual meeting in April 1992, six hundred delegates heaped praise on him and his "small but mighty caucus," in the words of one delegate, for providing "the real opposition" to the Liberals. A feisty, fortified Cochrane was in top form, blasting "Terminator Frank" for spending cuts that he said endangered the Equal Opportunity legacy of Louis Robichaud and Richard Hatfield.

Cochrane's post-election musings about re-examining the party's language policy were forgotten. "To address the concerns that COR said upset them," Myers says, "we'd have to turn the clock back and take away rights that people had waited a hundred years for, and that wasn't doable." Besides, Tories who'd opposed bilingualism most strongly were now in COR. "They had cashed in and moved on," says Cochrane, who admits that a policy fight on bilingualism might have broken out if the PC party's survival been in doubt. But it was not. "We are," Cochrane told the cheering delegates, "the next success story in New Brunswick politics."

* * *

There was one person in the COR caucus who might have written a different ending to Cochrane's hoped-for success story.

Brent Taylor had joined COR after his mother, Helen, a long-time Conservative, had backed Pafford's 1988 federal campaign in Miramichi. Pafford "was an extremely impressive 'relator' to people, very charismatic," Taylor says. "He wasn't tied up in detail, he didn't sweat the minutiae of policy, but he knew where he wanted to go." Taylor, a political junkie with a deep, rich voice — he had once been a radio announcer — soon landed a policy job in COR's Fredericton office, doubling as master of ceremonies at party events.

With his hefty frame, balding head and thick moustache, Taylor lacked the conventional good looks of a successful politician, but in the Legislature he had become COR's most effective MLA. He'd find embarrassing quotations in Hansard from the Liberals' opposition years and throw them back in their faces. When Finance Minister Allan Maher's 1992 budget imposed wage restraint on government workers for two years, Taylor resurrected Maher's attacks on Hatfield for precisely the same thing. "This is not bargaining in good faith," the quotation read.

When COR scheduled its leadership convention for September 1992, Taylor's smooth performance led many to see him as a potential candidate. "They were right," Hargrove says. "He was smoother, and Danny was lethargic." But Hargrove suspects it was the Tories who were stoking Taylor's ambition in order to stir dissent in COR.

Some in the party saw Taylor as a young man in a hurry, too anxious to get his hands on the status — and the big salary — that went with being Opposition leader.

Taylor says he considered running because he saw the same old-style political tendencies in Cameron that others in the party were complaining about. "The two or three months of the sitting gave me quite an eye-opener as to the kind of leader Danny was and the kind of leader the party needed, and they weren't the same guy," Taylor says. "He wasn't ill-willed or malicious, but his style was top-down. I thought the leader could and should stay in touch with the membership and still be an effective leader in the House." When Cameron declared he would run for the leadership — his interim position giving him a head start — Taylor says he tried to recruit Blaine Higgs, a party member who'd run against Pafford in 1989, to challenge Cameron. When Higgs refused, Taylor says, he decided to run himself.

The relationship between Cameron and Taylor deteriorated quickly. In June, Taylor rebuked Cameron in a confidential letter, calling it "disturbing" that Cameron had issued a press release on the native fishery issue without consulting Taylor, COR's natural resources critic. But the letter turned into a broader critique, telling Cameron it was unfair that he was holding on to the interim leadership of the party while campaigning for the permanent job. "During our last caucus meeting," Taylor wrote, "when I declared my intentions I also resigned as Chairman of Caucus. You said, 'I know what your game is and I'm not going to bite.' Then you left the meeting." He urged Cameron to quit as interim leader to make the race a fair contest. Cameron refused.

Taylor's assessment proved correct: heading into the convention, which was to be held in Campbellton, Cameron was favoured to win easily. He'd managed to portray himself during the race as the steady hand, while painting Taylor as too impatient to further his own career. There was no split on policy — both men claimed to be moderates on the language issue, promising a cautious approach to dismantling bilingualism once in government. They both supported proposed revisions to the party platform, to be ratified at the convention, that would delete the vow to make English New Brunswick's only official language and replace it with a promise to have *no* official language, while retaining English as the "working language" of the provincial bureaucracy. But on the question of experience versus energy, experience had the edge, especially with Arch Pafford openly supporting Cameron on the convention floor in Campbellton.

The party members, however, were restless. They'd seen media references to the Tories as "the real opposition." A year after the election, COR was stalled in the polls. The delegates wanted to get excited about something again, and the talk of moderation, the constructive approach in the Legislature and vows to proceed with caution weren't going to do it. They had joined COR out of anger. And after Cameron delivered what one reporter called a "trademark, rambling, folksy address" with no promises and only brief references to COR language policy, Taylor gave them anger.

He opened with a denial that COR was anti-French — then attacked the fundamental, defining aspect of Acadian culture, the brutal deportation known in French as the *Grand dérangement.* "I am tired of hearing about expulsions and things from 237 years ago," Taylor thundered. "Expulsions happen. I know that! But I wasn't there then so don't blame me for it! Every New Brunswicker living today has ancestors who were expelled from some place or another. We all came here through adversity. And I think it is time the government of this province started treating us all like citizens of 1992, not just as descendants of 1755."

Digressing for a moment to call for the removal of the Acadian flag from the Legislature, Taylor quickly returned to the theme of expulsions, telling delegates his family had lived in Montreal so he knew what it meant to be part of a linguistic minority. He compared the violent torching of Acadian homes by British militias in 1755 to the mass migration of anglophones from Quebec after the election of the Parti Québécois. "I was part of that exodus," Taylor roared. "I was part of that expulsion. And I stand before you and the COR party and the people of New Brunswick right now to tell you that this boy will be expelled no more."

It was an absurd comparison, but the crowd loved it, and Taylor wasn't finished; he continued by contradicting COR's repeated insistence that the party was open to francophones. "We in the COR party of New Brunswick have built an organization that stands up for *us*," he said, leaving no doubt about the meaning of "us." "We have shown the rest of the province that if we want an organization that will look after our needs, we can build it ourselves. And I think that is a message for other organizations that are [reaching] out to government with their hand out time after time looking for taxpayers' money. We built it ourselves right here. And I have no quarrel with people reaching into their own pockets to support their own culture. But I do have a quarrel with them reaching into *my* pockets and taking money that I would want to use to support *my* culture."

This was what the members wanted to hear: that familiar COR excitement, that talk of putting French people in their place. Taylor gave it to them, and the mood in the arena began to shift. Cameron was losing votes to Taylor right there on the floor — and it began to appear that Dennis Cochrane's worst-case scenario might come true, that COR might get the shot of energy and talent it desperately needed to build on its 1991 breakthrough.

But Cameron had Arch Pafford, still highly influential, on his side, and that was enough to hold Cameron's vote — barely. The result was 570 for the steady hand and 554 for the young man in a hurry.

Cameron had won, but there was a message in those numbers for him, if he chose to heed it: despite his prominent position and all the benefits of incumbency, he was far from the unanimous choice of the membership. Taylor quickly pulled on a Cameron t-shirt and made the standard leadership convention loser's call for unity, but it was clear that the party grassroots were demanding the attention of their leader and that COR's future success would depend on his ability to repair the relationship that had started off so badly a year earlier.

There was little time to reflect on the implications of the vote, though. COR had passed two tests of democracy in a single year — a provincial election and a leadership race — and now a third was coming up fast. On October 26, Canadians would be asked to approve, by referendum, a new constitutional reform package agreed to by Prime Minister Mulroney and the premiers, a package laden with concessions to Quebec and — less noticed in the national debate — to Acadians. McKenna's Liberals, the Tories under Cochrane and the NDP would support ratification.

COR, alone in opposing the deal, could unite again behind the very reason for its existence. The party finally had what it wanted: a referendum on its issues, a chance not only to opt out of the consensus, but to destroy it for good. COR's central message — its entire history and its motivation — would be distilled into one word on the ballot: "No."

"We'll be going full speed tomorrow morning," Cameron promised the cheering delegates in Campbellton. "We're going to send the No message to the premier and we're going to send the No message to Ottawa."

* * *

The Charlottetown Accord was meant to repair the damage caused by the collapse of Meech Lake two years earlier. It included the fundamental elements of Meech, such as recognition of Quebec as a "distinct society," and added a grab-bag of other constitutional changes to make it palatable to those who'd opposed Meech. There was aboriginal self-government, a "social charter" to constitutionalize programs such as medicare, a reformed Senate to appease the West — and entrenchment of New Brunswick's Bill 88, to go beyond individual rights and guarantee that New Brunswick's two linguistic communities would be treated equally.

The disparate aspects of Charlottetown also gave critics more to oppose. COR's "No" campaign targeted the Quebec concessions, the loss of four New Brunswick Senate seats, the unknown implications of native self-government and the entrenchment of Bill 88. "Since Bill 88 pertains to government and the allocation of resources, and since the two communities have different degrees of input towards the public purse, one of the two groups will become financially overburdened in supplying 'equality' for the other," one of COR's "No" campaign documents argued.

Dennis Cochrane's Tories, meanwhile, sided with McKenna in pushing for a "Yes" vote — fully aware of the political risk involved in getting on the wrong side of the surly mood that was out there. "The fastest way to kill the deal," Cochrane said, "would be to have people believe that it's Brian Mulroney's baby."

That was exactly the strategy the "No" campaign adopted nationally, and the early optimism that the deal would get the required "Yes" vote in each province faded. The populist rage that had scorned Meech and sent eight COR MLAs to the New Brunswick Legislature overtook the campaign. By Referendum Day, it was clear the Charlottetown Accord would be defeated. It was only a question of which provinces would say "Yes" and which would say "No."

New Brunswick said "Yes" by a margin of 61.3 per cent. Support was highest in francophone areas, while most anglophone regions saw narrow "No" wins. Three days later, Cameron issued a press release claming it was now clear McKenna had no mandate to entrench Bill 88, "considering that the majority of his own constituents in Chatham rejected the Charlottetown Accord in the referendum." The release went on to break down the vote, highlighting "No" wins in other provincial ridings in the Miramichi area.

Cameron was splitting hairs and violating COR's fundamental principle of majority rule, which, he had assumed, could never benefit francophones. But a majority was a majority. New Brunswickers had voted "Yes" to Charlottetown, including Bill 88, and had rejected COR's "No" arguments. Meanwhile, the national "No" vote removed from the political agenda the constitutional process that had fuelled the spread of Prairie-style populism across Canada. New Brunswick's "Yes" and Canada's "No" was the worst possible result for COR.

The party had been defeated at its own game, an exercise in grassroots democracy centred on francophone rights.

Dennis Cochrane had gambled that he might be on the winning side of something, *anything*, for once — and he won.

Now Frank McKenna had one last move to make in this game, a gamble of his own. It would either put COR back on its feet or bring it to its knees.

Chapter Ten

PULLING IT TOGETHER

FRANK McKENNA would claim that the things he did as premier from 1991 into 1993 reflected not a political design but his wish to provide good government. This might be true — but whatever its motivation, the fundamental thrust of the premier's program also undercut the Confederation of Regions party and nudged it back towards the political fringe.

First was McKenna's fiscal conservatism. Besides his well-publicized frugality — civil servants were forced to fly economy class and pay for their own alcohol and tobacco — the premier was determined to get government spending under control. In June 1992, he extended his earlier wage freeze to all public sector workers, who staged a four-day illegal strike. New Brunswickers who wanted to know their tax dollars were being wisely spent saw that, while COR talked about small government, McKenna appeared to be doing it.

That may be why voters trusted him when he spent large sums on job creation. In a pursuit that became his trademark, McKenna pitched New Brunswick as the perfect location for call centres, the facilities at the other ends of toll-free customer service lines. The province has an excellent fibre optic phone network, he'd tell businesses. The cost of business — wages and workers' compensation coverage — was low, he'd add, and there were plenty of bilingual employees to serve callers from any region of Canada.

The first deal, with Camco, a subsidiary of GE, was cut in February 1991 at a taxpayer cost of $32,000 per job — steep, but worth it for a call centre that would be the model for future pitches. In November 1991, Federal Express brought four hundred jobs to Moncton, this time with no subsidies. Suddenly the mayor of Saint John, Elsie Wayne, who had stridently opposed the Poirier-Bastarache report, was bragging about her city's bilingual workforce.

The call-centre strategy worked on two levels. First, harkening back to the campaign McKenna had run in 1987, it took the focus off language divisions and put it back on employment, an issue on which all voters could agree. Second, it turned bilingualism itself into a selling point for the province.

When McKenna landed another big call centre deal for Moncton in June 1992, with Purolator, everyone in the area welcomed the news — with the exception of COR's economic development critic, MLA Gordon Willden. He issued a press release attacking the "fallacy of promoting the bilingual capability" of the province. "New Brunswickers are not impressed, and unilinguals are rightfully resentful of this government's stance," Willden said in a remarkable display of political tone-deafness.

McKenna's skilled communications staff kept the call centre campaign in the public eye, while behind the scenes, another anti-COR strategy went into effect: the Liberals were quietly retreating on parts of the "language profiling" policy in the civil service.

Andy Scott, who'd worked on the file leading up to the 1991 election, was now charged with finding a political "fix." He established a committee to receive and investigate complaints from civil servants about language requirements; when COR accepted an invitation to place a supporter, a former senior bureaucrat, on the committee, Scott knew he'd defused that irritant. Meanwhile, the contentious issue of "language of work" — letting government employees function in their language, thus requiring more bilingual staff — quietly faded away. It remained a policy objective, Scott says, "but it wasn't our first-phase priority." He denies the government retreated. "If you get up in the morning with a list of five things to do and you complete four," Scott asks, "are you backing away or are you limited by time?" Even francophone activists in the Liberal caucus such as MLA Bernard Richard were willing to let "language of work" go. "Language of service has always come first," he explains.

Retreat or not, the strategy was working. Even Conservatives had to admire Scott's quiet success. "He put a lot more rationale into the system than there had been before," says Fred Beairsto, a Fredericton Tory who'd been dismayed by COR's breakthrough. "The system got better, and there wasn't as much to worry about as there was before."

At the same time, other circumstances — including a host of feel-good cultural exchange programs within the province and an economic recovery that took the edge off public cynicism — lowered the heat on the language issue in 1992. But the most damaging blow to COR would unfold in the forum the party itself had chosen for its fight: the floor of the Legislative Assembly.

The morning after the Charlottetown referendum, McKenna had announced he saw the New Brunswick results as a mandate to entrench the principles of Bill 88 into the Constitution — a relatively simple step that required not the consent of seven provinces but only identical resolutions in the federal Parliament in Ottawa and in the New Brunswick Legislature. COR immediately challenged the premier to hold a referendum on it, but McKenna noted that he'd won the Charlottetown vote, plus two elections with entrenchment as part of his platform. "At some point, you have to take yes for an answer," he told reporters. "It's not like this was a side issue. This was the centrepiece of the 'No' campaign."

McKenna challenged the COR MLAs to live up to their responsibilities: Bill 88 struck at the founding principles of their party more than any other matter to come before them in the Legislature, and fighting it was the job that 88,000 voters had sent them there to do.

The leader of the Progressive Conservative party was in a more complicated position. Dennis Cochrane wanted those COR voters — his party needed them to rise again — and he knew that voting for the Bill 88 resolution was no way to win them back. Perhaps hoping to avoid the dilemma, Cochrane had warned against moving to entrench. "I'm putting the caution out there that the public is in no mood to be tampered with," he said the day after the Charlottetown vote. "They made their vote on a package, and I'm not sure if the salespersons of the package should be going out now and doing things with it. It's a question of whether the time is right."

But Frank McKenna controlled the timing, and he was in a hurry. Dennis Cochrane would have to decide.

* * *

The text of the amendment affirmed the equality of New Brunswick's two linguistic communities and their right to their own educational and cultural institutions. On December 4, 1992, four days after tabling it, Frank McKenna rose to open the debate. No other Liberal would speak. The government anticipated that COR would mount a long, drawn-out procedural battle, and McKenna's advisors wanted the messy business over with as quickly as possible.

"The time for promises is over, the time for action is now," McKenna told the chamber in his grammatically correct but robustly tortured French. "Never again will a New Brunswick government strip either anglophones or francophones of their rights. Never will equality become a luxury, nor will it become a matter of charity. . . . On linguistic issues, there are no minorities in New Brunswick, only citizens equal before the law, only equal communities, only equal treatment of individuals and communities."

McKenna was fired up. The retreat in the civil service, the call centre jobs — they were subtle ripostes, but there was nothing subtle about his speech on entrenchment. He was taking the fight directly to COR. He was getting in their face. The Official Opposition "not only opposes equality," McKenna said, "but indeed wants to march resolutely back through time and repeal the Official Languages Act, other language legislation, presumably the entire constitutional protections that were placed in the Constitution by our forefathers and all the progress that we have worked so hard to achieve in the province of New Brunswick.

"They want to divide New Brunswickers, Madam Speaker. Their course would be deceptive. In their approach, there is no magical state of grace. There is no shimmering Camelot that, once regained, would restore the harmony and the prosperity of the good old days. There is only division, hatred and regression. People are sick of hearing it, Madam Speaker. New Brunswickers want vision, not division."

When McKenna finished, all eyes shifted across the aisle for the counterattack. Ed Allen, struggling to his feet to launch the Opposition assault, opened by painting a picture of a population on the verge of violence, of families sitting around kitchen tables, or at business meetings or at church, fearful of what Bill 88 would mean for them. "When people feel this way," he said, "they become hostile and may react with aggressive behaviour. I certainly hope not."

Allen spelled out his criticisms, returning to the familiar argument that English-French relations had been harmonious back when francophones had no legal protection. He also addressed one fact he knew he could not avoid: that as a member of the Hatfield government, he'd voted for Simard's original Bill 88 eleven years earlier. He explained that the bill had been a tool for the Conservative party to win support in French New Brunswick — evidence that it had lost sight of its objectives, and one reason he eventually left. Bill 88 cost Hatfield his base in English New Brunswick, Allen said, a fate that awaited any party voting for entrenchment now.

Allen's rationale for his own 1981 vote was tortuous. "I have the courage of my convictions," he said. "I have the guts to stand behind my basic beliefs. Yes, Madam Speaker, I supported the passage of Bill 88 with reservations, because I believed it was my duty as an MLA on the government side to support my party and my leader. Thank God I no longer accept that concept of government! It goes without saying, of course, that today I will vote according to my conscience."

Allen wasn't getting off that easily. His one-time Conservative cabinet colleague, Jean Gauvin, soon rose, notes in hand. To applause from the Liberal benches, Gauvin read quotations from Allen from his time in Hatfield's government — quotations full of praise for the late premier and his bid to make New Brunswick more bilingual. "'Perhaps I will not live to see the realization of this,'" Gauvin quoted Allen from 1983, "'but I sincerely believe that my children and grandchildren will. In another generation or less, I believe most New Brunswickers, upon reading the history of this province for the 1960s, 1970s and 1980s, will likely wonder what our present differences were all about.'

"Madam Speaker," Gauvin said, looking up from his notes, "I want to tell my colleague today that he is living those beautiful moments."

The debate moved forward, each of the COR MLAs condemning Bill 88, some of them accusing McKenna of trying to make it impossible for a future COR government to change language laws in the province — a motive to which McKenna's advisors readily admit. As Opposition leader, Danny Cameron was the last to speak against the motion. The NDP leader, Elizabeth Weir, voiced her support, then it was Dennis Cochrane's turn.

Cochrane said he would support the resolution, as would his small caucus. "Our party has a long history in this regard," he said. "It went through some difficult days in the Legislature and, I suspect, in a number of church basements and meeting halls throughout the province. The party has not changed. Although we have been defeated and divided and re-elected and applauded and discredited, I feel good standing here as a leader of this party, indicating that we will be supporting the equality amendment that is being put forward by the Premier of New Brunswick today."

Cochrane recalled his own childhood in the mostly francophone town of Dieppe, where he'd attended an English school — a right at the heart of Bill 88. Still, it was clear Cochrane had agonized over the political consequences of his position. He seemed to back into it when he posed a long series of rhetorical questions about the resolution's contents — "what is in there that I could be against?" — and answering each time, "I *have* to be for it."

Cochrane acknowledged many New Brunswickers would disagree with him. In response, he cited Edmund Burke's famous rejoinder to his constituents when they'd demanded that he always reflect their views; the passage that might have served Cochrane well in the House of Commons in 1988, when, one eye on the upcoming election, he declined to vote on a new Official Languages Act. "Your representative owes you, not his industry only, but his judgment," Cochrane quoted now, "and he betrays, instead of serving you, if he sacrifices it to your opinion."

Having reminded himself of his duty, Cochrane seemed to shed his equivocations. Turning to glance at the COR MLAs, he said, "I also heard someone say today that he made no apology for leaving a party that had lost all sight of its objectives. I don't think this party, even though it was lost from sight for a while, has ever lost sight of its objectives. The objectives are as strong today as they were in 1981 or at the advent [of Hatfield's vision] in 1970. Fairness, understanding, tolerance and equality are concepts for which my party has stood and has paid a price. In spite of that, it is surviving. We haven't lost sight of our objectives, and I hope no one in New Brunswick has. When they look at this legislation, there is no question that it is the right thing to do for New Brunswickers."

When he was finished and had taken his seat, it could not be said of the Tory leader that he was soft on the language issue. Not today. Dennis Cochrane had spoken clearly at last.

McKenna closed the debate, and the Speaker called for the vote. Thirty-four Liberals, three Tories and one New Democrat voted yes; eight COR members voted no. The resolution was on its way to Ottawa for ratification.

In the public gallery, McKenna's aide, Steven MacKinnon, looked at his watch. Six and a half hours after it had begun, the debate was over. The Official Opposition had moved no amendments. It had attempted no filibuster. It had made no use of any of the parliamentary tools at its disposal. "It was almost perfunctory," MacKinnon says of COR's performance.

He turned to another McKenna staffer next to him. "This is it," he said. "They're done. They're out of gas."

* * *

The enshrinement of the constitutional amendment was marked with a ceremony in Ottawa on March 12, 1993, an event Danny Cameron would say he was too busy to attend. He told reporters COR would seek to block or repeal the amendment "somewhere down the road," but it was clear the party had lost what little fight it had put up.

The recriminations began. Austin Clark, a COR member in Moncton, wrote to Cameron the same week as the Ottawa ceremony, attacking him as a "dictator." In light of Bill 88's entrenchment, Clark said, he was resigning from COR. Cameron's executive assistant, Dorothy Brislain, replied with a two-page letter defending the leader. "Our party, although forming the Official Opposition in the House, has only eight voices and, therefore, eight votes," she said. "Every one of our Members debated the entrenchment amendment with great fervour. With fifty other members in the Legislature voting in favour of the entrenchment, I would appreciate receiving your suggestions as to how we could possibly have defeated the Motion?"

But Clark and other members weren't interested in explanations about *how* the system worked. They'd sent those MLAs to Fredericton to *change* the system, dammit, and the MLAs were letting them down. "We had to explain to them why we couldn't do some things," says Max White, the member for Sunbury, "and that was unacceptable." COR was suddenly faced with the same problem as most political parties: elected members, newly aware of the complexities of the political system, must convince fervent supporters that some things are simply not practical. "The problem with democracy is everybody wants their voice heard, and it's not possible," says Greg Hargrove, sounding for all the world like a conventional politician. "You need direction, but you can't go sixteen different ways. If you make your intentions clear and they vote for you, they should leave you the hell alone."

The defeat on Bill 88, COR's *raison d'être*, reopened the divisions of the leadership race. A feud had developed between Don Sutherland, COR's official representative on compliance with political fundraising laws, and Arch Pafford, whose job as provincial coordinator involved tending to the party's grassroots organization. Pafford says he believed Sutherland was too tied to Cameron's top-down leadership style — "I felt he was from the old school of politics" — while Sutherland considered Pafford unqualified for his job, clinging to it because of his cult-like following in the party and because of Cameron's pity. "Danny felt sorry for him because Archie had no trade," Sutherland says. But after winning the leadership and learning the Campbellton convention had lost money, Cameron had become impatient with Pafford. "When Danny told you what your job was, you did it," Sutherland says.

Pafford responds that Cameron was impatient with something else: the loyalty Pafford still inspired in COR. "I'd walk into a hall and get a standing ovation," Pafford says. "Mr. Cameron never got that reception, and I think that bothered him. It was not my intention to undermine the leader, but I was the first leader of the party and I couldn't change the perception people had of me."

Sutherland would be accused of orchestrating a series of letters from riding associations in November 1992 that demanded Pafford's dismissal. That angered Pafford loyalists on the party's board of directors, and the feud metastasized into a wider battle within COR

— a fight documented in Danny Cameron's correspondence files. One letter-writer from Carleton North — where a provincial by-election was expected in the coming year — complained that Pafford had not visited her riding and suggested that he be fired so the party could use his salary to pay its bills. A member from Riverview, writing the same week, insisted, "Arch Pafford must continue to occupy a prominent and public position in our party."

Cameron tried to soothe the party's executive and board of directors but came up short in charm. In a letter to them in January, he chastised the membership, saying the recent criticism was "nothing new" and came from people "probably ignorant of background information and the reason behind some decision-making." He asked the board members "to examine your own efforts and determine how much time do you and your district members spend on expanding membership, attending meetings, contributing financially, and how much support do you give your MLAs, or are they convenient reasons to blame things on?"

Cameron overestimated his influence on the board members — riding association presidents who jealously guarded their roles as representatives of the party grassroots. The feuding continued. At a February 20 board meeting, Pafford threatened to quit unless the board removed Sutherland as official representative. By law, that job is filled by the party leader. Cameron told the board it was powerless to remove Sutherland, and Pafford could not dictate otherwise. "The results of the personal animosity between these two individuals is now impacting on the MLAs," Cameron wrote in a February 23 letter. "There is, obviously, one solution . . . and that is to demand they both be terminated."

The letter was signed by all eight MLAs. Two, however — Brent Taylor, Cameron's former leadership rival, and Bev Brine from the riding of Albert — attached letters distancing themselves from Cameron. Brine said Cameron, though under no legal obligation, should grant the board's request to turf Sutherland, but he did not have the right to "demand" Pafford's firing. Taylor agreed, though in less direct terms.

COR's board of directors met again on February 27. Sutherland, according to the minutes, repeated his belief that Pafford "has not done his job, as he has only given one report since his term began."

Pafford reminded the directors he was "assured of a job by several people in the party" after the 1991 election. "The issue is not whether he has done his job," the minutes paraphrase Pafford as saying (a passage Cameron later highlighted with a marker on his copy), "it is the accusations made against him." Cameron acknowledged he'd promised Pafford "meaningful" employment in writing, but, the leader told the board, he should have added the phrase "but not forever." He also revealed he'd supplemented Pafford's salary out of his own expense budget for most of 1992. Now, Cameron said, he considered Pafford's job redundant because of the creation of COR regional directors around the province.

Pafford's battle wasn't just with Sutherland, the directors now saw, but with Cameron himself. They sided with Pafford, defeating a motion to fire him by a vote of twenty-four to eleven. "Mr. Pafford thanked the people for their votes," the minutes say. "He contends that there are still problems which may never be resolved. . . . He stated that because of the dissension that is still present in this party he may choose to move on to new challenges. He asked that the Board consider a proper package for him."

With the board's refusing to bend to Cameron's wishes, the clash had become a more fundamental conflict between the leader and the grassroots of the party, as represented by the board. A COR member from Riverview, A.F. Walker, wrote to Cameron on March 1 to remind him how the party was supposed to work: he and his MLAs, Walker said, "are only observers at the administrative meetings," allowed to speak "only as a courtesy." Cameron was disregarding COR's democratic principles. "It would be a grave mistake on your part," he wrote, "to assume or imply in any way, that the individuals comprising the Provincial board or District executives, do not have the competence or where-with-all to make proper and intelligent decisions or to properly manage the affairs of this Party."

As if to remind him of their clout, some board members drafted a motion to review Cameron's leadership — a power given to them by COR's constitution. They presented, then withdrew it at a board meeting March 20, hoping Cameron would take the hint. Instead he lashed back, berating the board and writing party president Jay Paradise on April 2 to accuse some riding associations of not following political fundraising laws. He also demanded to know what his critics were doing to build party support in their communities — and called the entire bottom-up philosophy unrealistic. "Everyone must realize there are circumstances where it is totally impractical and unworkable that every minor item must come to a board meeting of forty odd members once a month for criticism, redirection and commentary when those board members cannot possibly understand the rational thinking behind such routine activity."

The tension between the caucus and the grassroots peaked at precisely the worst time. The disagreement over who called the shots in COR was about to have consequences where it mattered most: at the ballot box.

* * *

Carleton North had been Tory for as long as the St. John River had flowed, it seemed, until it fell to the Liberals in the McKenna sweep of 1987. Four years later, COR had spoiled Tory comeback chances in the riding. The Conservative candidate, restaurant and bakery owner Dale Graham, came within 131 votes of knocking off the Liberal incumbent — while COR snared 857 votes, more than enough to have made the difference.

The Liberal MLA, Fred Harvey, was a businessman from Glassville, and on election day 1991 he and his campaign team worked hard to get out the vote. A little too hard, as it turned out, because later that fall the RCMP charged Harvey with one count of irregularities — arranging for an underage person to vote — under the provincial Elections Act. Convicted, Harvey launched a series of court challenges, but in March 1993 a judge declared the seat vacant, and McKenna called a by-election for June 28.

A by-election in Moncton three months earlier had been a replay of 1991: the Liberals won, COR held its twenty per cent of the vote, and the Tories were humiliated in third place — suggesting the public's mood hadn't changed and Dennis Cochrane was paying a price for having supported Bill 88. Cochrane girded for the Carleton North battle knowing the future of his party might be at stake. "McKenna was still very popular and we were kind of looked on as the upstarts," Cochrane remembers. "COR was boasting they were going to win and we were fighting very much for survival. Frankly, as leader, people would measure me by the result. A lot was riding on it." A Liberal win would represent a stalemate for the Tories, but a COR victory would probably finish the PC party.

The stakes were high for COR, too. The party was losing members at an alarming rate — seventy-seven per cent had not renewed as of June 11 — and that was creating a cash shortage. Losing Carleton North to the Tories would confirm that Cochrane was providing the "real" opposition in the Legislature, while winning would give COR the momentum it had lost after the referendum defeat, the Bill 88 entrenchment and the internal fighting.

Pafford's regular reports to the party board — which he'd started filing more often when his job as co-ordinator was in danger — record several trips to Carleton North. As the by-election loomed, however, other COR members said the party machine was all but non-existent. Just a few months earlier, there had been an executive with only two members, whose past political involvement was limited to voting "if it was convenient for us," as one of them would write in a letter to party headquarters. "We were truly Green Horns. . . . We didn't know what to do or who to turn to."

Danny Cameron thus felt that he'd been right to defy the grass-roots and try to fire Pafford. Cameron dispatched one of his caucus employees, Jerry Covey, to Carleton North to assemble an executive, convene an annual meeting, recruit a candidate, schedule a nominating convention and find a headquarters. "Danny stepped in and said, 'I will deal with this,'" Brent Taylor remembers. Cameron vetoed Pafford's choice of a headquarters, in the small village of Bath, in favour of an office in a motel on the outskirts of Florenceville. In retrospect, Taylor says, the party's organization in the riding was thin, and members there were probably glad to have the help. The eventual candidate, Phil Dunbar, would write, "The campaign was going nowhere fast. . . . The leader had to step in and do the job." But the provincial board — newly wary of Cameron's take-charge style — didn't like it. "The board looked at their own ridings," Taylor recalls, "and said, 'What if we had a by-election? Who would we want running it?'"

Even Cameron's supporters in the caucus admit he overstepped the limits in Carleton North. "The locals up there were peeved," Hargrove says. "It was seen as this group from Fredericton coming up and running everything." Max White adds, "No matter what anybody wanted to do, Danny had preconceived how that election was going to go. Danny had a lot of friends in that area, and Danny believed they were going to get behind him, and they didn't."

The Tories, in contrast, found that their old party machine still hummed quite nicely. Dale Graham was selected to run again, this time enjoying the by-election advantage of having his party pour everything it had into his race. Cochrane spent half the campaign in the riding, reminding voters his in-laws lived there. "We played every card we could find," Cochrane says. "It was that kind of campaign." Hank Myers, who had got to know many area farmers when he was agriculture minister, made two three-day trips to the riding and used his personal credibility to refute COR attacks on Cochrane. A young party worker, Charles Murray, set up a voter tracking system to identify supporters and get them out on by-election day, an operation Tories in Carleton North had never needed before.

COR president Jay Paradise, who campaigned hard for Phil Dunbar, remembers getting a sense of things on the doorsteps, where, she says, people were "always friendly — very, very friendly. I don't think we got anything cold. A lot of people said, 'We're going to vote PC, but would you like to have a cup of tea anyway?'"

Dale Graham was driving through Bath at seven p.m. on voting day when a sudden thunderstorm unleashed its fury on the St. John River Valley. As hail pounded down on him, Graham called his headquarters, fearful that the weather would affect the turnout. Cochrane, stationed back at the office, reassured him that Murray's tracking system was working. "We have our vote out," Cochrane said.

And they did: Graham won with 2,315 votes, compared to 1,439 for the Liberals, gaining a wider margin than any of the three PC MLAs elected in 1991. COR was third with 778, a drop of seventy-nine votes from the 1991 general election.

Cochrane had taken a stand for Bill 88 and he'd *still* ended up with a fourth Conservative MLA, halting any momentum COR might have had. "I knew we could hold COR down," Graham said at his headquarters as he celebrated his victory. "I saw a bunch out there who were making a lot of noise, but I didn't think they would grow any."

Carleton North was a turning point in New Brunswick politics. "COR had their chance to move ahead and gain another seat, and that didn't happen," Graham says. Cochrane saw a PC party finally climbing out from the depths of defeat. "That's when it was clear we could go back to our base," he says, "and pull it together."

And the COR party showed that, after twenty months as the Official Opposition, it had gained nothing — no strength, no momentum, no sense that it deserved to grow into a viable alternative to the Liberal government. "This doesn't prove anything as far as I'm concerned," Cameron protested to reporters in Fredericton. "We've still got eight and they've just got four." But the Tories were one MLA closer to being competitive again, and COR had been pushed one step back toward the political fringe.

A week later, on July 6, 1993, a hand-scrawled note from Andy LeSage, a party supporter in Albert County, squeaked off the COR fax machine at the office of the Official Opposition.

"Danny Cameron, MLA," it began. "This is not an official notice. However, at our executive meeting and our membership meeting it was unanimous that you must go or drastically mend your ways. COR was never born to be dictated to from the top. It is not and never will be just another political party like the P.C.'s, Liberals and NDP. Our president has been instructed to vote for review. You must let the members, through the board, run this party."

The letter concluded: "You said at the executive meeting in Fredericton June 16th if we did not win Carleton North, we could have your head on a platter. Where would you like it sent?"

Chapter Eleven

"WE THE PEOPLE"

JAY PARADISE READ Andy LeSage's fax to Danny Cameron. "I must say I am appalled!" she wrote to LeSage the next day. "I am not going to beat around the bush – I am totally ashamed of your behaviour."

As COR president, Paradise had clashed with Cameron just weeks before, but LeSage's attack went too far. "I simply will NEVER understand downright cruelty, or kicking someone when they are down," she wrote to LeSage. "I still cannot believe these words came from a fellow COR member." Because of her fervent belief in the party's democratic principles, she said she would not demand that LeSage apologize, but she pleaded with him to do so. "Remember, the Party is all that really matters — not one individual — just the party."

For many of its members, the Confederation of Regions party and its slogan "We the People" had come to matter deeply. Paradise had arrived in Fredericton in 1987 and couldn't find a job because, she says, she couldn't speak French. She ended up cleaning houses. "I was very good at it and I enjoyed it," she says, "but I wouldn't have minded something better." Living in Waasis, a rural area outside the city, she heard about COR from her neighbours. She felt that the party's message on bilingualism rang true, and its bottom-up philosophy made her feel welcome. After working on Max White's Sunbury campaign, she volunteered in the party office, became board secretary, and was elected president of COR in September 1992.

"I believed so much in the party policy then," she says. "I really felt we could make a difference. I was quite naïve and excited about this great change we were going to make in our province." What Paradise loved most about COR was its members — "the most wonderful people on earth" — and she believed that representing them and upholding the "We the People" slogan were the most important elements of her mandate.

It was thus all the more difficult for her when "We the People" became the crux of a battle that would tear COR apart.

The by-election loss in Carleton North emboldened Danny Cameron's critics to mobilize against him. To them, his hands-on management of the losing effort proved he couldn't understand that COR was ruled by the members, through their riding presidents who sat on the board of directors. "Some of the people who came to the party late in the game didn't understand the concept," Arch Pafford says, "and it was a very simple concept when you thought about it. The party executive would not interfere with the MLAs unless they deviated from policy — but the leader was answerable to the executive." Pafford's allies on the board dusted off the leadership review motion they'd introduced and withdrawn in March.

The Cameron faction saw the "We the People" slogan as a convenient excuse for Pafford loyalists, who dominated the executive and the board. They had a hard time accepting a leader other than Pafford, Don Sutherland says. "Archie had a group of followers, and they're probably just as true to him now as they were then. They'd die for him. They were jealous of Danny. He had money, and he had a following. Archie had nothing but a following."

Cameron had tried again to fire Pafford at a provincial executive meeting on June 19, just nine days before the by-election, but his request had been voted down a second time — with Paradise casting the deciding vote against. "We, at the Administrative Office, consider ourselves the ROOTS of this Party," she wrote to Cameron. "If you have any plans on trying to close us down, I suggest you think long and hard about it. I am the Captain of that ship, and NO way in hell are we going down."

Pafford, though, was forced to retreat — on doctors' orders, he would later explain. "I threw my hands up in the air," he would tell the *Daily Gleaner* of Fredericton. "I said, 'I give up.' The pressure got to me." He went on sick leave, only to learn in July that he couldn't collect unemployment insurance benefits because the UI office had been told he'd been fired. His loyalists on the board were outraged because they hadn't authorized termination. They prepared for the showdown.

As the cracks widened, Greg Hargrove — who had helped start COR because he was fed up with the way the old parties did things — looked with envy at how those parties managed their members. "We had no power for patronage," he says. "The leader could say things and anyone could look at him and say, 'Go to hell.' If you're the premier and you say something and someone says 'Go to hell,' you say, 'Okay, you don't get that road built, you don't get this, that or the other thing. You can dole out patronage if you're in power, and we didn't have that luxury."

COR's directors gathered on July 17 for the regular monthly board meeting. They quickly passed a motion to allow only voting board members to speak — thus shutting out the MLAs, most of them sympathetic to Cameron. Then they endorsed a resolution urging party members to take complaints about COR first to the person involved before going to the board. After a thank-you from Carleton North candidate Phil Dunbar and a report from riding presidents, Cameron was invited to speak.

He didn't waste any time, scorning members who were using "We the People" as a way to attack him. "It is fine for people to voice legitimate concerns and openly ask questions that have merit," he said, according to the prepared text of his remarks. "However, there has been enough of this going-to-the-media nonsense because you don't understand the facts or you're not happy with reality. . . . There are people here who question and criticize just to hear themselves speak." As he had before, he suggested the members spend less time on him and more on basic tasks, such as recruitment — COR's membership had dropped from 20,000 to 5,000 in less than two years — and fundraising. "This is not my responsibility," he told Paradise, the executive and the directors. "It is yours." And, he suggested, "all must promote the job our MLAs do in the Legislature. . . . Let's support them, rather than turning our backs on them and hanging them out to dry."

This wasn't the conciliatory tone of a man seeking middle ground. Rather, Cameron seemed intent on alienating his critics. "This board, who are supposed to be the builders and promoters of our party, are destroying it. Instead of meeting here every month to bond together for the betterment of the people of New Brunswick, you come here for a power struggle within our own ranks. . . . Right now, the COR party can ill afford to have perennial malcontents hanging around preaching doom and gloom, criticizing things they know nothing about. These are the same people who are not pulling their weight. The party doesn't need this." Cameron warned that, if he were ousted as leader, the same faction would go after his successor. "Some of you, practising a selfish personal agenda, will never be satisfied," he predicted.

Once Cameron had finished, there was a procedural interlude during which the board heard reports from various committees. Then board member Jim Goodfellow introduced a motion for a leadership review. Two members asked to table it until the next meeting so they could consult their associations, but that request was voted down. The board voted for the review twenty-eight to eleven.

Greg Hargrove, one of the MLAs who'd watched in silence, persuaded the board to let him speak. The close leadership convention result, with Cameron and Taylor just sixteen votes apart, had split the party, he said, and the caucus saw a potential solution: the board could name Taylor the deputy leader and lead spokesman for COR. The directors ignored the suggestion, however, and scheduled their next meeting for August 2, when they would hold the review vote and deliver their verdict on Cameron.

This was unusual. Most political parties allow only the members, usually at a general meeting, to hold a leadership review. COR's rules, strangely for a "We the People" party, also gave that power to the small group of people making up COR's board. If twenty-four directors — a majority of the riding presidents — agreed, the board could call a leadership convention on its own. Except for that one difference, COR might have followed the same script as any political party: Cameron would have the right to be on the ballot at the convention. If he won, he'd have a clear mandate. If he chose not to run, or if he ran and lost, the party would have a new leader and it would move on. But since the board, not the membership, was initiating the review, Cameron's supporters had the means to challenge the process, using the very "We the People" philosophy that the anti-Cameron faction claimed to uphold.

Sutherland, who as official representative owed his job not to the board but to Cameron, quickly labelled the board meeting — and

Paradise's chairing of it — "an abomination and illegal." He challenged her to prove that each director, a riding association president, had voted based on the democratic will of his or her respective local membership. And he demanded proof that each director was a fully paid up member of COR.

Sutherland was baiting Paradise, since he knew that two days earlier, a background check by Opposition staffer Jerry Covey had revealed that several directors had let their memberships lapse. In a confidential memo to Cameron, Covey said Jim Goodfellow, the man who'd moved the review, had not renewed. "Due to this, one can argue quite strongly the motion made by Jim Goodfellow was out of order as he had no authority to vote at that meeting as his current dues for 1993 were not paid. The motion voted on was illegal."

Covey also told Cameron he and others would begin lobbying the riding associations to reverse their presidents' pro-review votes. "The time has come for 'off with the gloves,'" Covey wrote.

If the COR grassroots wanted a fight, that's what Danny Cameron would give them.

* * *

Danny Cameron was taking on the membership, and the membership needed a champion: a viable replacement for the leader. They got one on July 27, when Brent Taylor entered the fray.

As early as March, in the wake of the first, aborted review bid, Cameron had accused Taylor and another MLA, Bev Brine, of instigating, through their supporters, a plot "to denigrate me and assassinate my character." In a letter, he told them to fall in line or risk being expelled from caucus. Then, as part of Jerry Covey's "off with the gloves" strategy following the July board vote, two MLAs loyal to Cameron had attended a COR meeting in the village of Harvey, in Cameron's own York South constituency. One publicly attacked Taylor for his "lack of participation" in the "No" campaign against the Charlottetown Accord and for other actions that, the MLA claimed, showed he was not a team player.

Taylor responded the next day with a blistering nine-page letter to Cameron, which he promptly forwarded — along with Cameron's March threat to expel him from caucus — to the entire COR board of directors and executive. He rejected an accusation that he was behind the review, saying two of the directors who'd pushed for it had been Cameron supporters at the Campbellton convention. "I took defeat like a gentleman," Taylor reminded him.

Now Taylor told his leader he was no longer sure he accepted the result. Cameron had revealed in March that he'd been using his expense budget to supplement Arch Pafford's salary as co-ordinator for most of 1992 — while Pafford, as party president, had been in charge of seeing that the leadership race unfolded fairly. This put Pafford's public support of Cameron at the convention in a new light, Taylor argued. "When one of the candidates is paying the referee under the table without the knowledge of the other candidate, something is dreadfully wrong." He'd opted against going to court or to the police earlier. "I think now that I made the wrong decision."

Taylor invoked COR's grassroots principles, explaining he was sharing the letter with board members so they would know why he'd run for the leadership. "Your autocratic rule has no place in a democratic party and . . . I felt there had to be a change before our movement was done great damage." But the timing of Taylor's attack — just a few days after the vote for leadership review — and the subsequent leaking of the letter to a Fredericton newspaper left no doubt in the minds of Cameron loyalists that Taylor wasn't interested in "We the People" principles as much as in positioning himself to replace Cameron.

But Cameron knew how to position himself, too. If his enemies were going to challenge him on the grounds of party democracy, he would meet them on that terrain and seize it back.

Besides their continuing attacks on what Cameron called the "unfair and undemocratic process" at the July 17 meeting, his supporters discovered another weakness to exploit: by identifying which riding presidents supported review, then comparing the number of COR members in those ridings and the votes the party's candidates had received there in 1991, they could show Cameron had the support of the ridings where COR was strongest. Thus, they argued, when people tried to measure the mood of the grassroots, those pro-Cameron votes deserved more weight.

Greg Hargrove remains adamant that it was unfair that his pro-Cameron riding — with 1,200 party members and a member of the

Legislature — could be outvoted by eleven other ridings with a *total* membership of only 1,200 and no MLAs. "If you want to have the same vote," he says, "go out and get yourself 1,200 members." Yet the logic completely contradicted the COR principle that each riding should have equal strength on the party's decision-making bodies. In the summer of 1993, however, each faction was prepared to use the democratic principles that suited it.

There were other contradictions. Although Cameron challenged directors who hadn't consulted their memberships on the review, Hargrove criticized MLA Bev Brine for claiming she backed the review because her local COR members wanted it. "You cannot or will not distinguish the difference between a caucus and a party executive," he told her in an August memo. "You are a part of a separate body which represents all the citizens of New Brunswick in opposition to the governing party." Brine's support of review, though, had nothing to do with her legislative role as an MLA, and everything to do with her membership in the COR party.

Each side twisted "We the People" so badly that summer that the slogan eventually lost its meaning. "There is no such thing as a grass-roots party," Hargrove admits now. "It sounds good and it gets your novice politicians all in a tither, thinking they're going to have their say. But it's just not workable." Even Jay Paradise now concedes that her devotion to the grassroots ignored the realities of the work MLAs had to do. "The board of directors would get very angry with them, but when you sit in the House things are different, and a grassroots person might not understand that. These people have a mandate, so let them do their job."

On August 21, 1993, however, Paradise saw things differently and, at the board meeting that day, pushed the leadership review ahead at full speed.

Cameron boycotted the meeting, but one of his surrogates, MLA Ab Rector, showed the director a lawyer's letter questioning the legality of the July 17 vote, given that some directors hadn't paid their dues. But Rector had forgotten that COR members cared first about democracy, and about getting results. Liberals and Conservatives had used technical arguments about rules and procedure to thwart public opinion; now, Rector had clearly fallen victim to the same establishment thinking. According to the minutes, Paradise ruled that, because membership forms weren't always sent from the riding presidents to the party head office right away, "it is impossible to know for certain, at any given time, who is a member in good standing." She said she would accept the word of any directors who said their dues had been paid, a ruling the board endorsed by a vote of thirty-three to twelve.

Hargrove warned the directors that they were straying into dangerous territory and that their actions might be challenged in court. They brushed aside his objections and voted on the main question: "Do you want to have a Leadership convention?" The answer was Yes by a clear margin, twenty-nine to sixteen. The board opted for a convention late in the fall, with the annual general meeting scheduled for Saint John in September to go ahead as planned.

With Paradise and other members of the executive up for re-election, Saint John would be the next skirmish in the leadership war, and Danny Cameron prepared for it carefully — seemingly at the expense of his duties as Leader of the Official Opposition. He issued no press releases that August, and his files show few policy documents from the period. He did, however, compile lengthy, detailed attacks on his opponents inside COR. His personal files contain exhaustive handwritten notes on Jay Paradise's conduct as party president, including what he saw as her failure to expand COR's membership. The notes were the basis of a letter to her that Cameron distributed to the board of directors two weeks before Paradise sought a new term as president in Saint John.

Cameron attacked Taylor even more strongly. He assembled a twenty-page response to Taylor's July 27 letter, a response remarkable not only for its length but for its methodology. Cameron numbered each of Taylor's accusations, tallying what he called "innuendoes" that Taylor couldn't substantiate (twenty-eight in all), then rebutted his rival's criticisms with his own words and with highlighted, cross-referenced denunciations by other MLAs. "Why did you not include a copy of the February 23rd letter?" Cameron asked in a typical passage. "It might clear up some of the comments in Paragraphs 13, 14 and 15 (Innuendo #7)." It is an extraordinarily meticulous document that was clearly time-consuming to draft, but Cameron did so with evident gusto. "Your comment is pure crap," he wrote of one of Taylor's criticisms.

For good measure, Cameron circulated the document with a six-page cover letter, also addressed to Taylor. He faulted what he said was Taylor's immaturity but also called him "a bright young man" who had had a great political future. Still, Cameron couldn't stay sweet for long. "You want to be number 1 now — to hell with the consequences to the Party," the letter continued. "Yet in a year or so, you might very well have had the opportunity to be number 1, if you had exercised a little patience, humility and propriety, instead of embarking on a vicious, untruthful campaign to discredit me."

The attack seemed to silence Taylor for the time being, but no sooner had he disappeared than Cameron's other tormentor resurfaced.

The COR board was still wrangling over what to do about Arch Pafford. At a meeting on September 18, it struck a committee to find a solution. A riding president's proposal that the board reaffirm Pafford's appointment as provincial co-ordinator fell one vote short of the twenty-four needed to pass. His status in doubt, Pafford gave an interview to *Telegraph-Journal* columnist Don Hoyt in which he launched his own assault on Cameron. "I worked hard to get him in there and I will work very hard to get him out of there because he's not COR," Pafford said in a front-page story published September 21, just days before the Saint John meeting.

COR was hurtling towards a cataclysm. A brand-new conspiracy theory began circulating in the party. This time, the plot came not from Paris or Quebec or the Société des Acadiens, but from the Progressive Conservative party. Danny Cameron, it had become obvious to some members, was still a loyal Tory, placed inside COR as a sleeper agent assigned to destroy it. "It was just my suspicion that he could possibly be trying to do it from the inside," says Jim Webb, one of COR's founders.

Confronted with the suggestion when it appeared in the media, Conservative leader Dennis Cochrane could barely keep a straight face. "I couldn't fabricate a plot more interesting than what is unfolding," he told a journalist. "To suggest that we might is an extension of the paranoia that obviously exists."

* * *

On the afternoon of September 25, Danny Cameron walked to the stage of the Saint John Trade and Convention Centre, the same stage on which Richard Hatfield had saved his leadership by appealing to the traditions of moderation and compromise in the Progressive Conservative coalition. But COR had no such tradition, and Danny Cameron was no Richard Hatfield.

In Cameron's world, moderation and compromise betrayed weakness. He'd always relied on his strength — to escape the poverty of Osgoode, to join the Allied fight in the Second World War, to transform himself into a millionaire businessman. He wasn't going to pull a Hatfield and go soft now.

He might have extended an olive branch to the new executive — voting had taken place, but the results were not known. Instead he attacked the incumbents, saying if they won new mandates, COR would likely collapse. "The course of destruction upon which we are embarked must change now," he insisted.

Cameron gave the membership a history lesson, reminding them of his repeated attempts to limit the board's authority over the MLAs and his warnings about what would happen without those limits. "The leader can't lead if he has to follow everyone else," Cameron said as his supporters cheered and other members sat silent. "I'm a 'We the People' man but I'm not a 'We the Directors' man." Now he'd been proven right, he said: the board was abusing its power to launch a leadership review. "You want to change leaders every six months — what's wrong with you people?" The democratic mechanisms had been co-opted by enemies like Pafford, Taylor and Paradise, he suggested. "It is perhaps coincidental that today is the last day of the moose hunting season. However, I can tell you it has been open season on Danny Cameron for the last two years!"

Cameron moved on to the thrust of his defence: the illegality of the July 17 and August 21 board meetings. "This board, by its actions, is asking me, as leader, to condone wrong-doing as a standard procedure in this party. I cannot, nor will not, agree to such a practice at any time. What has happened is the promotion of a leadership convention under circumstances approaching false pretences. For that reason, I wish to notify you that I will not participate in a leadership convention unless this matter is handled correctly."

It was a clear and uncompromising message: Cameron said he'd participate in a proper review — and meet with a review committee if one were established under the rules — but he would not recognize the leadership race the party was now organizing.

He concluded with an appeal to higher goals — "the way is open before you, therefore go with purpose" — but Cameron had taken COR to the brink of schism. The members were free to hold whatever convention they chose, but he would remain the rightful leader of the party regardless of their will.

The will of the members became clear almost immediately when the results of the executive elections were announced: they'd given Jay Paradise a second term as party president. The woman who had stood up to Danny Cameron had a mandate to keep fighting for "We the People."

* * *

Paradise's new mandate didn't last long. After Saint John, as Cameron's forces intensified the pressure, she cracked. She resigned in October, claiming her life had been threatened by other COR members. "It was emotional hell," she says now. "I was a basket case towards the end." The board itself fractured after an anonymous letter from "Concerned COR Citizens" was sent to party members. It repeated the accusation that Paradise, not Cameron, had perverted "We the People" by preventing the riding presidents from consulting their associations on the review before they voted. The letter urged COR members to boycott not just the leadership race but upcoming board meetings.

Undeterred, the rump board scheduled the convention for December in Moncton, and Taylor and Pafford entered the race. Despite gossip that one of his surrogates would declare, Cameron's faction avoided any move that might lend legitimacy to the contest. Instead, MLAs Ab Rector, Max White and Greg Hargrove announced that if Taylor became leader of the COR party, they would quit the caucus to sit as independents.

The leadership race unfolded in a surreal political netherworld. Taylor and Pafford met COR supporters in community halls and church basements, but the process did not exist to half the party members, and those who did participate seemed baffled. "What the hell has happened here?" party supporter Jack Welton asked at a debate in Minto, attended by three dozen COR members. "How did we get into this fiasco?" Taylor talked of the failure to uphold the principles of "We the People" — but he was speaking to ghosts. This business of factions and procedure was a long way from the straight, simple, easy-to-understand crusade against bilingualism — a crusade no one talked about anymore.

The convention went ahead in Moncton on December 4. In his speech, Taylor denounced "that bunch of politicians in Fredericton," but this time he was referring not to the Liberals or the Conservatives but to Cameron and the five MLAs supporting him. Pafford's tone was conciliatory, asking the convention for a "mandate to mediate" between COR's factions, but the delegates preferred Taylor's fighting words. With a margin of 437 to 232, he secured the victory that had eluded him the previous year.

But the sense of achievement was as illusory as the race he'd just run. Taylor had won the grassroots contest, the only thing that was supposed to matter in COR, but he knew he needed to be recognized as leader in the Legislature.

The COR caucus met on the Monday after the convention, but none of the five MLAs who had backed Cameron would acknowledge Taylor as leader. It was left to the Speaker of the Legislature, Liberal Shirley Dysart, to rule on whom she would recognize as Leader of the Official Opposition — a task that led to a final, bizarre contortion in COR's grassroots game.

At 10:37 that night, a fax arrived at Premier Frank McKenna's office from Albert County. "Mr. McKenna," it began, "you and you alone have a very weighty decision to make."

Andy LeSage, expelled from his beloved COR party, laid out for the premier the convoluted history of the leadership fight. Typing completely in capital letters, he recapped the various votes and meetings, and explained in detail how the board of directors represented COR's members and how Danny Cameron refused to accept this "and therefore does not believe in the tenets of COR-NB." He concluded, "I appeal to your sense of justice. . . . All I ask is that you instruct Shirley Dysart not to do anything unjust."

It was the last irony of the COR leadership war: a loyal member of the party, who had spoken out time and again about the importance of democratic principles and the dangers of autocratic rule, was now asking his mortal enemy to use the heavy hand of his office to impose his will on the supposedly independent Speaker of the Legislative Assembly.

Whether McKenna ever saw the fax is unknown. The next day, Dysart announced in the House that she had met with members of the Official Opposition caucus and had consulted both parliamentary precedents and some of her counterparts in other provinces.

"The recognition of the Leader of the Official Opposition is an internal matter for the House," Dysart explained. "For purposes of recognition in the Legislative Assembly, the Speaker can only take direction from the members of the Official Opposition caucus."

In other words, precedent forced Dysart to draw a line between the functions of the party structure and the functions of the Legislature — where parties did not exist except as groupings of MLAs. And a majority of this particular grouping of MLAs had made their choice, she said.

"Under these circumstances," Dysart said, nodding to Danny Cameron, "the honourable member for York South is recognized as the Leader of the Official Opposition."

Cameron rose to his full military bearing and, for the embarrassment and inconvenience, offered Dysart an apology "on behalf of the COR party."

But Cameron could no longer speak on behalf of the COR party, which had rejected him. He could speak only for the Official Opposition, for the two had become separate entities. None of the party meetings, the motions, the letters and the convention mattered if a majority of COR MLAs chose to ignore them and stick with Cameron.

The people who'd set out in 1989 on a mission to change politics were discovering what Tories and Liberals had long known: the parliamentary system isn't just incompatible with grassroots party democracy. It renders it completely irrelevant.

Chapter Twelve

THE COALITION WITHIN

DEFEATED IN HIS BID to become Leader of the Official Opposition, Brent Taylor now sought another way — any way — to remain a viable and valuable political player.

The day after the convention in Moncton, Denise Murray, COR's vice-president on the anti-Cameron rump board of directors, had written to the province's chief electoral officer, Barbara Landry, to tell her the result. Supported by thirty of the forty-six riding presidents — a clear majority of the board — Murray asked Landry to change COR's official registration to list Taylor as the leader.

But Danny Cameron's faction blocked the move. Party president Peter Whitebone wrote to Landry that, by law, only he, as president, could speak for the party on its official registration. "Contrary to the contents of Ms. Murray's letters, the COR Party of New Brunswick has not held a convention nor has it selected Mr. Brent Taylor, M.L.A., as its leader," he said. There was no need to change COR's registration; Danny Cameron was still the leader.

Landry had no choice but to agree. A change to the registration required the signatures of the party president and the official representative, and allies of Cameron held both positions. Cameron may have lost his power over the party machinery, but the rules of the Legislature allowed him to remain Opposition leader, and the laws governing political parties recognized him as leader of the COR party.

Now, he would bend COR to his will. Using the party leader's legal right to create and dissolve riding associations, on December 22, Cameron told Landry he was decertifying twenty-five of them — Taylor's, Pafford's, Brine's and twenty-two others that had been pro-review. In a single stroke, the associations no longer existed. Cameron transformed the board into a smaller body that supported him unanimously. Now, his allies in those twenty-five ridings could reorganize themselves as pro-Cameron associations and send friendly directors to meetings of the board.

Cameron had outfoxed the Taylor faction of COR, which had planned to renew its fight at the January 22 board meeting. Back in November, a narrow pro-Cameron majority on the party executive had expelled ten members of the party, including Jay Paradise, several directors who'd pushed for review and — most symbolically — Arch Pafford himself. "We had to get rid of the shit-disturbers," an unrepentant Sutherland explains. Those ten had planned to appeal the decision before the full board in January, but now the board was transformed from pro-review to pro-Cameron. In a reversal of the leadership race, Taylor and his supporters boycotted the January meeting, claiming the downsized board wasn't legal. "As far as we're concerned, the meeting isn't happening," Taylor told reporters. The pro-Cameron board upheld the expulsions while Taylor prepared for his last stand.

Taylor hired a lawyer, David Peterson, a former Clerk of the Legislature, to ask the Court of Queen's Bench for a quick ruling on the legality of the convention he'd won in December and, therefore, on his leadership of the party. A ruling in his favour would probably get him recognition under the Elections Act and might even revive his claim for the title of Leader of the Official Opposition.

But in April, Judge Hugh McLellan shut Taylor down. Peterson had argued that, since Cameron and Taylor weren't disputing the facts of events at board meetings, merely their interpretation, a full trial wasn't needed. The judge disagreed, saying certain "facts," including whether directors with lapsed memberships were entitled to vote, needed more scrutiny. "Justice done quickly without consideration of law is also justice denied," McLellan ruled, offering the two sides a full trial to explore the dispute in detail.

The legal cost of a full trial would be $25,000, far more than the $5,000 cost of the motion for a summary ruling and beyond the ability of Taylor's backers to afford. It would also drag the dispute into 1995, close to the next election. "I have no problem with going to trial on all the facts, but when the trial is over, the boat will be on the bottom," Taylor said, comparing COR to the *Titanic*. Reluctantly, he abandoned his efforts to become party leader.

Cameron threw his foes a lifeline, telling journalists that, if there were no more legal challenges, Taylor and Brine might eventually "come back into caucus in a meaningful way."

But the two dissident MLAs knew there was no way back. COR had plunged to single digits in the opinion polls; they would be fools to return to a sinking ship. But their status was hardly ideal. They sat together in the Legislature, calling themselves the COR caucus but knowing under the rules they were really just two independent MLAs cast adrift. Locked out of the main Opposition suite, restricted to their own small offices, they were without a party in a system in which party affiliation meant everything.

There was, however, another party in the Legislature desperate to grow.

* * *

With COR in tatters, Dennis Cochrane's moment of opportunity had arrived to repair the split in the Tory base and effect a grand reconciliation between the COR vote and the French fact — if only he could move decisively and convincingly to broker the required understanding between the two.

At first, Cochrane shied away, deploying Hank Myers, as tried and true a Tory as you could find in New Brunswick, to search for that common ground. Representing the Protestant heartland constituency of Kings East, Myers had come to understand Richard Hatfield's vision. When he became minister of agriculture in 1985, he used the benefits of that office to visit places he'd never been before, developing a fondness for the Acadian Peninsula and an appreciation of the province's diversity. In 1989, as leadership candidate, Myers had pledged to entrench Bill 88 in the Constitution.

Yet, while Myers could look beyond the Tory heartland, he was also *of* it. He'd seen his constituents' fear of the Poirier-Bastarache report. He'd challenged the bilingual designation of that NB Power linesman's job in Sussex so that his unilingual constituents could apply for the position. And, though he'd never been tempted by it, he'd seen and understood the rise of COR.

All of this made Myers a key player in the political drama that unfolded behind the scenes at the New Brunswick Legislature in 1994, as the PC party wooed Brent Taylor and Bev Brine.

"Bev and I were friendly with Hank," Taylor says. "We had a lot of casual conversations." When the two MLAs were shut out of COR for good in April, the casual chatting evolved into intense discussions. "Some of their members were very acceptable, Brent Taylor probably the most," says Dennis Cochrane, who encouraged Myers to keep the channels open. "Most of them were people who had got caught up in a cause, and they were not bad people."

The math wasn't bad, either. In late 1993 Cochrane had gained a fifth MLA when Percy Mockler — one of Richard Hatfield's recruits from the breakthrough 1982 election — won a by-election in his old riding of Madawaska South. Mockler would recall what Hatfield had told him after the 1987 wipeout: "Someday, your people will ask you to come back under extraordinary circumstances, and you will win again." Now, Mockler's comeback had put the Conservatives one MLA away from COR's total. The addition of Taylor and Brine would allow them to become the Official Opposition, with all the staff, funding and stature that came with it.

More important, it would show that Hatfield's frayed coalition could be mended, and that New Brunswickers from across the language spectrum could find a political home and build a consensus within the Progressive Conservative party. That, in turn, might restore it to power.

When rumours spread that Taylor and Brine were getting friendly with the Tories, Cochrane was evasive. He hadn't offered the pair anything, he told reporters, and besides, they'd have to ask first. They'd also have to renounce their opposition to official bilingualism — and even then, they might not be welcome. "We will have to look at the perception and what our party stands for before accepting any request," he said.

Within a month, Taylor declared that he no longer opposed the Official Languages Act. His tortuous explanation was that Danny Cameron's treatment of COR dissidents indicated how Cameron, as premier, would treat francophones — and that meant francophones needed protection. He told CBC Radio, "There obviously is still the opportunity for a heartless and suspicious government to be elected." As long as unilingual anglophones weren't prevented from competing for government jobs, Taylor said, his constituents would probably accept government services provided in French. "This wasn't done to make myself more attractive to somebody," Taylor said, claiming he wasn't even clear on what the Tory language policy was, he didn't know if it still went "overboard," as it had under Hatfield, or had become "more sensible." In a newspaper interview, though, he said, "If [my view] matches what someone else thinks is the right thing and they feel there's a way together for New Brunswickers later, then fine."

Taylor's declaration — and the perceived motives behind it — prompted a scathing editorial the next day in *L'Acadie Nouvelle*, New Brunswick's only French-language daily newspaper. Nelson Landry said Taylor "changes his conduct, his language, his opinion to suit his interests. . . . [He] wants us to believe his conversion to bilingualism and to forgive him his anti-francophone behaviour of the past." As an example, the editorial cited Taylor's vicious speech at the 1992 COR leadership convention.

Landry didn't spare Dennis Cochrane, either, reminding readers of the old questions about his stand on bilingualism. Cochrane had been a "dinosaur" in 1988, Landry wrote, when as a federal MP he'd refused to vote on Bill C-72, an update to the federal languages act. It was hardly surprising Cochrane would flirt with Taylor, the editorial continued, but the acquiescence of Jean Gauvin — who'd fought for Poirier-Bastarache and for Hatfield's vision of the PC party — was a disgrace.

Six days later, Cochrane announced that, after consulting his caucus and his riding presidents, he'd discovered a consensus that Taylor and Brine were not welcome, either to join the caucus as Tory MLAs or to run as Conservatives in the next election.

Taylor and Brine, adrift again, reverted to COR form. Taylor wrote in a newspaper column that the PC party was obviously controlled by the "Acadian minority," and Brine told a reporter, "The Tories have made it perfectly clear to anglophone New Brunswickers that the Tories aren't interested in them."

As the summer of 1994 came on, Taylor explored the idea of a new political party with supporters around his riding. Cochrane, having earned a ninety-eight-per-cent approval vote on his leadership, kept up the spadework of rebuilding the PC party at Tory picnics and barbecues. Danny Cameron prepared for a COR annual meeting in September, at which the party would take another step toward becoming like other political parties by eliminating its board's power to launch a leadership review unilaterally.

And that August, in southeast New Brunswick, at the first Acadian World Congress, thousands of Acadians from across the province collectively shrugged off COR's existence and joined compatriots from around the country and from France, Louisiana, Massachusetts and elsewhere to celebrate the survival and flourishing of their culture.

Then came Tracadie.

"Things got serious after Tracadie," says Brent Taylor. "We became much more attractive."

Tracadie is the first major town a visitor encounters on a drive up the Acadian Peninsula. It had been Liberal since the creation of single-member ridings in 1974. Before that, when it was part of the multi-member riding of Gloucester, Tracadie had last voted Conservative in 1912, before Pierre-Jean Veniot had turned the Acadians into a Liberal voting bloc. The most recent Liberal to represent Tracadie, cabinet minister Denis Losier, had left politics for a business career, opening the riding, everyone assumed, for yet another Liberal.

Cochrane, mindful of his poor French, knew he might be a liability in the by-election. "If I'm going to hurt by being present in Tracadie, let me know," he told local Tories. "I won't be there." But they wanted him, and he travelled to the riding one night to meet with a prospective candidate Jean Gauvin and Percy Mockler had scouted. Mindful of Hatfield's admonition that credible francophone Conservative candidates must have strong community ties, they'd zeroed in on Elvy Robichaud, who'd chaired the local school and hospital boards, served as principal of two schools, worked as the administrator of the hospital, and sat on town council. Cochrane persuaded him to run — and sensed an air of possibility in Tracadie.

The Liberals tried, in the by-election campaign, to capitalize on Cochrane's springtime flirtation with the COR dissidents to revive doubts about his commitment to language rights. "They're not very different," Losier, the outgoing Liberal, told a campaign rally. Robichaud, though, had a more potent use for COR's name. Elect me, he told voters, give the PC party six MLAs — precisely the same as Danny Cameron's caucus — and help knock COR out of the Official Opposition office and deprive it of the research budget and staff for which Acadian tax dollars were paying. "It was definitely something that got me many votes," Robichaud remembers. "It felt like people were joining a cause. Of course, they wanted changes, and there was disillusion with the Liberals in the area, but the COR factor was a major factor."

The opportunity to send a message to both COR and Liberal premier Frank McKenna, who had closed thirty beds at Tracadie's hospital, was hard to resist. Cochrane remembers a paving crew on one of the riding's rural backroads, their jobs owed to Liberal connections, flashing discreet thumbs-ups at Robichaud. He captured Tracadie easily, with 5,615 votes over 4,251 for the Liberals.

Little did the voters know that, far from marginalizing COR, they were moving two of its former MLAs back to the centre of Tory thinking in Fredericton.

* * *

A new session of the Legislature opened on November 29. Cochrane had moved the Progressive Conservative party into a strong second place in a new opinion poll, with twenty per cent support — well behind the Liberals at sixty-five, but far ahead of COR, which, at three per cent, was on track to lose all its seats. The moment of opportunity that Cochrane had let pass in the spring was offered to him again: he might just bury COR and win the long struggle to regain the English heartland vote. Becoming Leader of the Official Opposition would help enormously, so Hank Myers reopened secret negotiations with Brent Taylor and Bev Brine.

They would meet for coffee in the Legislature's basement cafeteria, and when they needed more privacy, go up the hill to Prospect Street for pizza. At first, "Dennis stayed away so that he wouldn't have to lie if he was asked," Myers says. But Cochrane was keeping track of Myers's progress. "He never said, 'Do it.' It was more like 'Do you think there's a possibility?' He'd say, 'Have you been talking to Brent and Bev lately? What are they thinking?' — and then he'd say, 'Leave me out of it.'"

Myers, Brine and Taylor began to sketch out a process. The PC riding associations in Southwest Miramichi and Albert would have to approve the move, since Taylor and Brine would expect to seek the party nominations for the next election. Would they sit as caucus "affiliates" until they secured those nominations? Or win the nominations first, then move?

But that was process. The question at the heart of the discussions remained the same: would Taylor and Brine endorse official bilingualism?

Taylor, who'd made his declaration in the spring, says Brine "was more principled on that than I was. She was holding out for some sort of accommodation." Cochrane says he was firm that there would be no such accommodation — but both Taylor and Brine knew he'd been flexible in the past. He'd supported Bill 88 two years earlier, true. But as a young man he'd backed Leonard Jones, the symbol of opposition to bilingualism in Moncton. And he'd skipped that vote in the House of Commons on Bill C-72. "The fact that he came from that end of the party was probably comforting to us," Taylor says, "but he never said to us, nudge-nudge, wink-wink, 'You guys are right.'"

Another participant in the secret talks, however, remembers a Dennis Cochrane willing to bend on language — willing to bend so far, in fact, that it would have twisted the PC party into something very different from what Richard Hatfield had envisioned.

Arch Pafford would drive down to Fredericton to a motel on the hill overlooking the St. John River, away from the prying eyes of the city's political downtown. Brad Green would meet him in the parking lot and usher him into a room where Cochrane would be waiting.

Cochrane recalls that Pafford needed a job and was under the impression that, if the merger came off, he'd be hired as an organizer for the Tories. "That wasn't acceptable," Cochrane says, noting that Pafford — the party he'd created in tatters, his followers looking for a new political home — had no leverage. "Arch obviously knew the score on what was happening."

Pafford remembers that it was Cochrane who needed the deal, and he was quite willing to negotiate on Pafford's terms. "The big thing at that time was a softer stand on the implementation of Bill 88," the former COR leader says. "It was going to create dualism as far as we were concerned, and this was something the province couldn't afford." But Cochrane had called Bill 88 an article of faith for his party just two years earlier. "There's such a thing as interpretation," Pafford responds, "and these things could have been interpreted in a different way. We would have been able to put a different spin on things."

Although Cochrane insists he would never have watered down Conservative language policy, Pafford is adamant: "I think he would have gone all the way if things had developed the way they should have."

And it appeared things might go "all the way." The francophone wing of the party lacked a champion in caucus, someone to remind Cochrane where the line was and what might happen if he crossed it. Elvy Robichaud was too new to become the Acadian conscience of the party, and Percy Mockler was too eager to win. The only other MLA who might play that role was Jean Gauvin, but he had health and money problems and was leaning towards not running again — hardly the makings of a champion.

* * *

Gossip reached the Liberals about the back-channel negotiations. Bernard Richard, former Acadian activist turned Liberal MLA for Shediac-Cap Pelé, referred to it one day in a member's statement. "Cochrane's jaw dropped," Steven MacKinnon recalls. "We could tell right away there was something there." MacKinnon, from his perch in McKenna's office, understood that the PC party had reached a political crossroads. "It was the defining moment," he says. "Were they going to co-opt COR or be the Hatfield coalition?"

In a speech to Acadian leaders earlier that year, Frank McKenna had vowed to "wipe out COR" in the next election. Now, faced with the possibility of COR's vanishing too early and its voters strengthening Cochrane, "it made some sense to keep them apart," Richard says, by goading the francophone PC MLAs to rebel against the overtures. "In the school of thought of 'When your enemy is drowning, throw him an anvil,'" MacKinnon says, "we raised [the issue] every time we could."

McKenna would refer to Percy Mockler as a FORy — "that's a francophone Tory with a COR member in his caucus," the premier explained. Deputy premier Ray Frenette caught Cochrane using the word "we" to refer collectively to the Conservatives and Taylor. "Where are his principles?" demanded Frenette. "Will he decide which side of the fence he is going to be on?" Richard searched the federal Hansard so he could quote Cochrane's refusal to vote on Bill C-72 in 1988. "Is this where the leader of the PC party stands on official bilingualism?" Richard asked. "He chooses not to stand. Is this the leadership he proposes to offer all New Brunswickers?"

The endless taunts roused Gauvin to action as the session continued into December. Gauvin realized, Taylor says, "that Dennis was talking to us seriously — and it would get more serious if it continued." According to Cochrane, Gauvin had endorsed reaching out to Taylor and Brine and himself had tried to persuade Max White to defect from COR to the Tories. Now, Cochrane detected a change in his French lieutenant's mood. "He had become more sullen and more distant to me."

Gauvin had moved from his riding of Shippagan-les-Îles to the Moncton suburb of Dieppe, where the two language groups were in constant contact and, Cochrane says, where francophones had to be more guarded about their rights. "I think he was hearing from a lot more people who had misgiving about the COR people," Cochrane says. "Therefore his opinions became less [those] of the pragmatic politician."

There are other theories. Robichaud believes Gauvin's shift was the result of a call-in radio show on the Acadian Peninsula in which callers condemned any thought of a Tory-COR entente. Myers remembers gossip that someone had slipped Gauvin a copy of Brent Taylor's 1992 leadership convention speech, in which he'd said, "I think it is time the government of this province started treating us all like citizens of 1992, not just as descendants of 1755." And "This boy will be expelled no more." And "We in the COR party of New Brunswick have built an organization that stands up for *us*."

Whether motivated by principle or opportunism or some stormy mix of the two, Gauvin decided to act on the morning of December 16.

The Legislature had sat the night before as a committee of the whole to consider a bill on rural zoning, and Myers and Brine had teamed up to question the minister, spelling each other off when one or the other needed a break. Gauvin didn't like it. "I think he saw that as them getting ever closer to being in our caucus," Myers says.

The House adjourned at eleven p.m. The next morning, the first item of business was Speaker Dysart's ruling on Cochrane's request to become Leader of the Opposition on the basis of his six seats. She turned him down, saying the principle of incumbency allowed the existing Official Opposition to retain that status until another party had *more* MLAs — a ruling that gave more urgency to the courting of Taylor and Brine. But that courting was about to end.

When the House moved back into committee of the whole, Myers tried to resume his questioning on the rural zoning bill, but the Liberal house leader, Ray Frenette, caught Myers on a procedural point, asserting that Myers had finished his questioning the previous night. Before Myers could protest, Gauvin was on his feet to support Frenette: "Mr. Chairman, according to Standing Rule 69, I move that the question be now put."

Gauvin had just sandbagged Myers, his fellow Conservative, by moving for a quick vote. Gauvin was, in effect, invoking closure — something opposition parties don't do because it allows the government to escape further debate. "Are you nuts?" an angry Myers demanded as the Liberals gleefully voted the bill through.

Cochrane quickly summoned his MLAs into his office. Normally slow to anger, he was enraged. "I was coaxed to run for this job," Cochrane reminded them, according to Myers. "I didn't ask for it, and I'll be damned if I'm going to put up with two of my own members fighting like schoolchildren."

"Gauvin went into a tirade," Myers remembers, "accusing me of wooing Taylor and Brine, and he said there wouldn't be a francophone vote in the province for us, and he'd see to it. Then Mockler and Elvy said 'You don't speak for us,' and Gauvin stomped out."

The party appeared to be splitting anew just as it was becoming a credible force in politics again. Cochrane's leadership was being put to the test.

He met with Gauvin on Sunday, then announced — as Gauvin had demanded — that Taylor and Brine, and any others who'd been COR MLAs, were not welcome as members of the Tory caucus or as candidates in the next election. "The answer is no," Cochrane said in a written statement. "There can be no more definitive statement on the subject than that, and from this point forward let there be no further room for speculation." Should any of the eight original COR MLAs want to run in the next election, he said, "we are not prepared to facilitate their chances by having them seek nominations as Progressive Conservatives . . . because of the symbol of intolerance they have chosen to make of themselves."

Five days later, having been accused of caving in to Gauvin, Cochrane punished him for his procedural ambush of Myers in the House by stripping him of his position as party whip. Gauvin accepted his demotion, reminding reporters, "The press has said many times he does not make a decision. Well, he's made a decision. I respect that decision."

The crisis appeared to have passed — but Cochrane soon made another decision. In February, after returning from a vacation cruise with his wife, he told the PC board of directors he was resigning as leader. He didn't want the job of premier badly enough to slog through the expected four more years in opposition, he explained at a press conference. Nor did he like what politics was doing to him: he was a positive person, but being in opposition forced him to be negative, and he didn't like it.

But there was another reason, he said, a matter of principle: he'd gone against his own beliefs in letting Gauvin convince him to ban COR MLAs from running as Conservatives. "I feel very strongly about the democratic process," he said. "I do feel in my heart that members of riding associations should have the right to choose their candidates."

It was the same principle Cochrane cited to explain his support for Leonard Jones in 1974, when the federal PC party had quashed his nomination in Moncton. Back then, Cochrane had chosen that principle at the expense of speaking clearly on language. Now he was again saying the riding organizations must be free to select their candidates — regardless of the message those selections might send. "I compromised on some things that I felt strongly about," he said of his concession to Gauvin. "I didn't get into politics to compromise my principles."

But Cochrane had also talked of principles on December 18, when he had banned Taylor and Brine "because of the symbol of intolerance they have chosen to make of themselves." It was becoming difficult to keep track of which principles were most important to Cochrane. Jerked toward riding autonomy, yanked toward speaking up for tolerance, Cochrane left politics for good, bedevilled at the end of his political career, as at the beginning, by his weakness on the language issue.

He left the Conservatives divided and leaderless with an election just months away — the same position they'd been in four years earlier when Barbara Baird-Filliter resigned. Except this time, they could wonder what might have been. Steven MacKinnon says Cochrane might have won twelve to sixteen seats for the PC party in the next election. Brad Green believes he'd have taken twenty. Hank Myers says Cochrane would have captured enough to form a government.

But such a triumph would have masked a deeper defeat, because Cochrane's caucus would likely have been drawn mostly from the English heartland, where he was popular. His legacy would have been the restoration of the traditional PC vote — and of the language-based voting split that had persisted for decades in the province. His legacy would have been a setback for Hatfield's vision of a PC party capable of competing for power anywhere in New Brunswick.

Jean Gauvin's move had saved Hatfield's vision — for another day, and for another leader better able to inspire trust across the language divide. Gauvin had allowed Cochrane to leave with a reputation for decency and for principle, even if he never quite got one principle right — the one that mattered in the brokerage politics of New Brunswick. Richard Hatfield's gravest error had been to neglect the most vociferous spokesmen of the English wing of his party. Cochrane had made the same error with the most vociferous avocate for the French side.

By every other measure, New Brunswickers could have trusted Cochrane to give them good government. By one standard, though, he fell short: after Leonard Jones, after Bill C-72 and after Brent Taylor, francophones would always have wondered about Dennis Cochrane. Even in supporting Bill 88 — his finest moment in the Legislative Assembly — he'd appeared forced into his decision.

If there had been doubts about Dennis Cochrane's ability to re-build the Hatfield coalition within his party, they arose because he hadn't proven he could build that coalition within himself.

Chapter Thirteen

WEAVING

ON THE AFTERNOON of September 8, 1995, the Progressive Conservative campaign bus chugged down the main street of the isolated logging village of Saint-Quentin. It eased into the parking lot of a sawmill, and the party leader bounded out the door. He made his way into the yard and climbed onto a pile of wood to speak to the workers. Peppering his comments with local references, Bernard Valcourt made them a promise. "I'll never forget my people," he said. "I never have. I've proven it before and I'll prove it again." The working men cheered and, for an instant, Valcourt looked like a leader being propelled to victory by the will of the citizens.

Richard Hatfield would have been delighted at the scene. Once, he'd had difficulty persuading people that a Conservative MLA could come from this francophone village in the northwest woods of New Brunswick, about as far away from the Tory heartland as one could imagine. Now, the party's leader came from here.

But Hatfield's delight would have turned to dismay as Valcourt and the PC volunteers climbed back on the bus to resume their journey, the epiphany on the woodpile quickly fading behind them. The campaign staff knew, on that final Friday of the election campaign, that they were racing toward defeat. They knew that the PC party — weaving every which way in search of a path back to power — had lurched from an anglophone leader who couldn't win the trust of Acadians to a francophone leader unable to gain the confidence of the English Tory base.

* * *

If you lived in Saint-Quentin in the 1950s and 1960s, you saw Bertin Valcourt when someone in your family died. The owner of the only funeral home in town was known as a perfectionist. "If you're going to do something," he would tell his children, "do it right or don't do it at all."

Bernard, the third of six children, took his father's advice to heart. He became a top student at the small school in Saint-Quentin and earned admission to the classical high school program at Collège Saint-Louis-Maillet in Edmundston, a couple of hours away. He stayed for undergraduate studies and, during the initiation rites for freshmen students, found himself paired with another ambitious young student, Percy Mockler. Despite their different backgrounds, they forged a friendship that would endure long after Valcourt had graduated and left for Fredericton to attend the University of New Brunswick law school. At UNB, barely able to speak English, Valcourt stumbled and bluffed his way through classes until he'd mastered his second language.

Back in Edmundston to practise law, he was asked in 1983 by Jean-Maurice Simard to help revive the federal Progressive Conservative riding organization. An election was on the horizon, and Valcourt assumed Simard planned to run for the nomination. One day during a tennis game, the young lawyer asked the provincial minister when he would announce. "You don't understand, do you?" Simard replied. "You're the candidate, not me."

Carried to Ottawa in the 1984 Mulroney sweep, the young MP caught the eye of the prime minister, who saw a bit of himself in the scrapper from the small industrial town who'd beaten the odds by attending law school in his second language. Midway through his first term, Mulroney gave Valcourt a junior cabinet post. In 1988, the re-elected Valcourt was promoted to minister of consumer and corporate affairs. The rising star earned a reputation as partisan and blunt-speaking. He told reporters, after recording the second-highest travel expenses of any minister, "Valcourt has not been sitting on his ass in Ottawa." He would offend the mayor of Saint John, Elsie Wayne, by putting his feet up on her desk during a meeting.

Valcourt soon eclipsed Gerald Merrithew, the former Hatfield minister and MP for Saint John, who'd been a senior member of Mulroney's cabinet. Noticing the portraits of his predecessors the day he arrived in his ministerial office, Valcourt remarked that he'd be the thirteenth minister of consumer and corporate affairs and joked that he must be destined for bad luck.

The bad luck was of his own making, and it arrived the night of July 4, 1989. Valcourt visited a pair of taverns in Madawaska, Maine, across the river from Edmundston. In the wee hours of the next day, he climbed onto his Yamaha 1100 motorcycle to drive across the short international bridge and return home. Not long after he crossed into Canada, a city cop noticed Valcourt's motorcycle weaving back and forth. The cop turned on his flashing lights, but Valcourt sped off — then hit a curb, lost his helmet, flew thirty feet through the air and smashed into a wooden fence.

He lay unconscious for nine days and lost an eye, but otherwise he made a full recovery — at least physically. His career was another matter. When police laid a drunk-driving charge, Valcourt pleaded guilty and resigned from Mulroney's cabinet.

But Mulroney's soft spot for the young MP remained, and Valcourt recuperated at the prime ministerial cottage at Harrington Lake, outside Ottawa. At the federal party's annual meeting that fall, Mulroney told delegates, "I've got some news about Bernard Valcourt, a young man who got himself into some very serious trouble. I can tell you that he's with me at Harrington Lake and he's looking better every day." It was a sign that Mulroney planned to put Valcourt back in cabinet. But one of Valcourt's law school friends, Brian Warnock, visiting him at the lake, told him his future was elsewhere. In five years, Warnock predicted, he'd be leading the New Brunswick Progressive Conservative party.

Valcourt returned to cabinet in 1990 as minister of fisheries and was later promoted to employment and immigration, one of the biggest departments in Ottawa. But time was running out on the Mulroney government. In the leadership race that followed the prime minister's retirement, Valcourt abandoned his friend Jean Charest to back Kim Campbell. Campbell won narrowly, but, in the October 1993 election, the Conservatives were left with only two seats.

Vanquished, but with a $42,000 annual House of Commons pension to cushion the blow, Valcourt rebuilt his law practice. His first two cases were run-of-the-mill assault charges, a long way from the nation-shaking policy debates of Ottawa. Then, in February 1995, he accepted an invitation to attend the annual meeting of the World Economic Forum in Davos, Switzerland, one of only ten Canadian members of Global Leaders of Tomorrow, a Davos sub-group made up of people under the age of forty.

On the way back to Edmundston, Valcourt and Pauline LeBlond, his companion, changed planes in Montreal. Calling home from an airport payphone, LeBlond was told by the babysitter that there were dozens of messages for her partner. Dennis Cochrane had resigned as the provincial PC leader. LeBlond passed the news to Valcourt and asked if he wanted the messages.

No, he told her. He needed only one number, that of Percy Mockler, his old college friend and one of Richard Hatfield's greatest discoveries. Mockler was now an MLA again and an influential political organizer. Valcourt had a decision to make.

* * *

On March 22, 1995, Valcourt returned to politics, kicking off his campaign for the provincial Progressive Conservative party leadership with an aggressive promise to slash taxes. His launch was attended by a large number of high-profile supporters from the party's southern, English-speaking establishment — aimed at demonstrating he was more than just a francophone candidate. But the language issue surfaced in the form of the question that had been fatal to Dennis Cochrane: would Valcourt allow COR MLAs to run as Tories?

His answer was quick and unequivocal: he'd lift the ban. "I can't tell the constituency associations on one hand that we will consult with them, and that they do matter, and then not let them choose who will be their candidate," he told reporters. "The party has fundamental beliefs, and anyone who subscribes to them is welcome in this party. And that means anyone."

Jean Gauvin rose again in the Legislature the following Tuesday. Having derailed one Conservative *rapprochement* with COR, he now aimed to halt another. "I cannot accept Mr. Valcourt's position," Gauvin said. "His position would mean that we were wrong last year when we refused to accept the COR members. . . . Accepting Mr. Valcourt's position today means that Bob Stanfield was wrong when he refused to sign Mr. Jones's nomination papers." He became increasingly emotional as he continued; soon, tears were running down his face. "What is more important, a political party without principles, or principles without a party?" Gauvin asked. "I must tell you that in a week I have had over a hundred calls from different people around the province, and I am not alone. Even if I were alone, I believe I would rather die politically and die standing up."

Unlike Cochrane, Valcourt was the kind of street-fighting politician willing to fight back. "Gauvin knows better than to think I would want to ignore or violate the Constitution of Canada, which recognizes the equality of both linguistic communities," he told a reporter that evening. "I don't need to take the back seat to anyone in terms of my commitment to this principle." He followed that interview with an open letter reminding Gauvin of his own attempts to woo COR MLA Max White. "It may now be convenient for you to regret your then-overtures, but it tells much about the depth of the position you now take."

It was one thing for Valcourt and Gauvin to shadow box in the media; the real test of Valcourt's position would come when he faced rank-and-file Acadians. The Sunday after Gauvin's attack, Valcourt was in Tracadie, the scene of Elvy Robichaud's surprising Conservative upset the previous year, for a delegate-selection meeting for the May leadership convention. These were the Tories who'd voted for Robichaud to get rid of COR.

Several Liberal MLAs had picked up on Gauvin's attack, claiming Valcourt's olive branch to COR made him a danger to francophones. In Tracadie, Valcourt, waving in the air a newspaper clipping about the Liberal charges, demolished them and Gauvin at the same time. "Acadians!" Valcourt shouted mockingly, waving his hands. "Be on your guard! Valcourt is coming!" A collective chuckle rippled through the room. "Be careful! It's Valcourt, the federal member who introduced into the House of Commons — Bill 88!"

The ripple became open laughter as everyone realized the absurdity of Gauvin's position. For Valcourt had worked with Frank McKenna to carry the Bill 88 resolution to Ottawa, where it had been ratified by Parliament and written into the Constitution. He had impeccable credentials on language, something Dennis Cochrane could never claim, and that gave Valcourt the political cover to invite COR members to rebuild the Hatfield coalition. Gauvin had lost the fight and would never recover his influence in the PC party.

With francophone Conservatives on board, Valcourt now faced a challenge on his anglophone flank: Scott MacGregor, a Riverview lawyer whose only claim to fame was losing the 1985 by-election that had signalled the end of Richard Hatfield, was quickly turning the leadership race into an English-French battle.

MacGregor would claim language wasn't an issue and he wasn't a tribune for Tories who opposed a francophone leader. His only reason for challenging Valcourt, he'd say, was the unpopularity of Brian Mulroney's legacy. "I don't think it's possible to honestly say that the connection to the Mulroney government is going to be anything but damaging," he said. Valcourt would respond weakly, "I was not the leader." He'd explain that both McKenna and Mulroney were wrong to make decisions without consulting voters, but his government would be different: "Everything will be in the way that we do it."

As the two men took their battle for delegates into the Tory heartland — into ridings held by COR MLAs — it became obvious that the Mulroney connection wasn't Valcourt's only problem. His Frenchness and his infamous motorcycle accident reminded Tories of the precise combination of factors — bilingualism and personal scandal — that had ruined Richard Hatfield. MacGregor would cite his support of the ban on COR MLAs as proof he wasn't pandering to bigotry, but he would also repeat familiar COR themes, such as questioning whether unilingual anglophones could land jobs in McKenna's call centres. At a meeting in Hillsborough he bragged, perhaps with a Freudian slip, that he could connect with COR voters because "I'm speaking a language they understand."

MacGregor no doubt tapped into a strong sentiment in the party, but the Tory establishment touted Valcourt as the man to beat McKenna, and the message was sent down to the ridings. At the convention, Valcourt swamped MacGregor, taking two-thirds of the vote on the first and only ballot. The victory was a measure of how powerful the backing of the insiders could be to a membership still inclined to defer to the party brass. But MacGregor's respectable result — one-third of the vote for a nobody who'd taken on a giant — reflected something just as telling: the segment of the party that wouldn't accept Valcourt.

"Today the Progressive Conservative party turns the page on the past and opens itself to you, and to the future," Valcourt said to his provincial TV audience in his victory speech, a handful of already-nominated election candidates standing behind him. To the delegates, he issued a plea for unity: "Let's leave confident in our future and confident in our party."

The candidates behind him appeared, however, anything but confident. Among them was Don Parent, who'd run for the Tories against Ed Allen in Fredericton North in 1991. Parent would run again, this time in Mactaquac, a riding formerly known as York North. Parent had agreed to challenge Greg Hargrove of COR when Dennis Cochrane was the leader. Now he found himself with Valcourt, who couldn't be more different from Cochrane. "In a relatively rural, anglophone riding, he was one of the biggest problems I had," Parent says now. "I didn't have a problem with him, but a lot of constituents did. People were saying, 'We just can't support you.'"

* * *

But who would "a lot of constituents" support in the end?

Many of those voters had been Conservatives most of their lives until opting for the Liberals in 1987 — the closest thing they had to a protest party in a two-party system. In 1991 they moved to COR, but by 1995 the party had all but destroyed itself.

That spring, however, COR had a final chance to right itself. Danny Cameron had quit in March, and the party's two factions began making conciliatory noises. Greg Hargrove talked of welcoming Brent Taylor and Bev Brine back into the caucus. "I would be willing to try to put this behind us and let bygones be bygones," he told a reporter. Taylor praised the "encouraging signs" and said he might abandon his attempts to start yet another protest party.

The six-member caucus chose Oromocto MLA Ab Rector as interim Leader of the Opposition as it waited for the leadership convention. Rector immediately denied that he'd been placed in the job because he'd been a Cameron backer. "I'm not a follower of anybody," Rector said, a comment that would set the tone for what was to come.

At the convention in July, Gary Ewart, a Saint John teacher with no political experience other than as a defeated COR candidate in 1991, captured the leadership over Hargrove and Max White, two MLAs who'd backed Cameron. It was a strong message that the grassroots hadn't forgiven the former leader or his allies. "The resentment against the MLAs was so strong," Hargrove remembers. The rank and file "wanted to have someone in there who would keep us in line." The factions re-emerged in full force when Ewart sought to reverse the expulsion of the ten party dissidents, including Arch Pafford and Jay Paradise. Rector said Ewart's plans might go against COR's rules. "No one will go around the constitution as long as I'm around," Rector said.

Of course, Rector should not have been "around" at all by then. In political parties, it is the prerogative of a newly elected leader without a seat to name the party's leader in the Legislature. But when Ewart named Hargrove — a gesture of unity to the man who'd come second at the convention — Rector refused to give up the position. "I'll go if the caucus wants me to go, but I'm not moving just because one person says so, no matter who that is."

Ewart responded with a move from the Danny Cameron playbook, threatening to use one of the few powers that did belong exclusively to the leader — the right to approve party candidates running for election — to veto COR members who didn't fall in line. That threat only escalated the battle. Rector accused Ewart of trying to oust him so he could claim the $5,000-a-month expense allowance granted to the Leader of the Opposition, an accusation that raised the obvious question of Rector's motivation for trying to hang on to the title.

Ewart saw the situation for what it was and resigned as leader twenty-three days after winning the job, leaving COR to its internal feuds. Greg Hargrove, who'd decided not to run again — "why go through the embarrassment?" — now found himself chosen interim leader by a group of fifteen MLAs and election candidates. COR's fourth leader in four months told a journalist he had an unusual asset. "I know all the players involved in this party," he said. "I know the personalities involved. I know who doesn't like who and why. I know who is saying things about people and why, and I can get the factions together."

In fact, Hargrove knew that COR was already finished. The split between Ewart and Rector came from the same inherent contradiction that had created the feud between the board and Cameron: the inability of a grassroots party organization to work with an elected caucus. "There's a symbiotic relationship there," Hargrove says. "They have to co-exist, and if one shuns the other and says 'We won't deal with you,' they're both going to die."

Others knew what fate awaited COR and tried to understand what had gone wrong. "I got out of it and I was fine," says Jay Paradise, the former party president. "Wal-Mart came to Canada, thank God, and gave me a job." But she regrets the party's downfall. "I think it's an incredible shame. So many people poured their hearts into something and it just went down the drain."

Paradise still talks warmly about how COR allowed her to meet "wonderful people" around the province. She admits that, of course, all the "wonderful people" she met were anglophones, and that she'd missed getting to know any of the francophones who make up one-third of New Brunswick's population.

And that was COR's fundamental problem: despite their victories in 1991, COR's members were powerless to act on the resentment they felt toward Acadians. Looking for another outlet for their anger, they found it within their own party, and drove away most of the 88,000 voters who gave them their breakthrough in 1991.

* * *

So the question remained: where would those voters go?

Bernard Valcourt knew he was starting from way behind and there was little he could do to catch up. His best chance was to run an effective campaign that might restore the traditional Tory vote and position him to win the next time around.

Even that would prove difficult. In May, the PC leader told a newspaper editorial board he'd need $500,000 to run a good campaign, but he'd managed to garner barely half that amount when Frank McKenna called the election in mid-August. "Yes, there is a money issue," Valcourt admitted. "We don't have a lot of money, and it's making it tough to advertise and communicate through that channel." It also meant they couldn't afford tracking polls to measure the minute, day-to-day shifts in public sentiment that allow campaign strategy to adjust quickly.

The Tories fell back on a riding-by-riding ground battle, a strategy hampered by Valcourt's unease with anglophone voters. "I've always felt Valcourt was not comfortable in the south," says Hank Myers, who was seeking another term. "Several of us had urged him to come down more often and let people get to know him." But other local Conservative campaign managers didn't want their candidates seen with the leader. "No one said 'We don't want him,' but they said, 'We'd prefer he didn't come,'" recalls one party insider. "If you insisted, like we had to be able to say he'd visited every riding, they'd say okay." Valcourt, the insider says, made it quite plain that he wanted to avoid the south and cursed when asked to go there.

The hope, then, was to win seats with "wedge issues" — contentious subjects that might drive some voters away but brought others to you and deepened the attachment of the loyalists. Valcourt became convinced that one such wedge issue was Frank McKenna's mismanagement of NB Power. If he could expose the corporation's wasteful spending and bloated debt, he was confident he could damage McKenna's reputation as a frugal manager. "I didn't see it," says campaign manager Craig Astle, "but he said, 'Oh yeah, it's there.'"

Midway through the campaign, Valcourt went to Saint John to unveil a study by University of New Brunswick professor Norm Betts that purportedly showed the Liberals had miscalculated the demand for power exports when they built a costly new generating station at Belledune. The utility's increased debt would lead to plant closures and layoffs, Betts predicted, or huge increases on power bills.

The event was a disaster. Liberal cabinet minister Ray Frenette turned up to shoot down the accusations as "Bernie-babble" — the phrase McKenna's team had created to demolish Valcourt's credibility. "We were very much willing to make Valcourt the issue," says advisor Steven MacKinnon. Recalling the name of a craft business in the PC leader's home county, Frenette also labelled Valcourt the "Madawaska Weaver" — a reference, Frenette explained, to his spinning of false attacks. That the nickname also conjured up memories of his drunk-driving accident was lost on no one.

Valcourt undermined his own NB Power attack when he was unable to explain to reporters covering the news conference why he was appearing in the party's French television ads but not in the English versions. He finally said he was "following the advice of our communications experts." Pressed as to why they'd give that advice, he snapped, "You ask them. I don't know" — a hollow answer, given Valcourt's claim that McKenna's track record was the invention of his communications advisors.

Valcourt was failing to gain traction. The only hope for the Conservatives was for the COR vote not only to collapse but to return to the Tory fold by default.

The signs were promising. In addition to the latest leadership debacle, Ed Allen, in poor health, had decided not to run again. Brent Taylor failed to win the party nomination in his riding. To avoid a vote split, Max White, the MLA from Sunbury, begged local Tories not to run a candidate against him and promised he'd cross to the Conservatives immediately after the election — an offer the Conservatives confidently spurned.

Hargrove, meanwhile, "was trying to hold the provincial party together," says Lynn Mason, who was parachuted into the Charlotte riding as a paper candidate, just a name on the ballot to round out COR's slate. Hargrove was often at party headquarters until three o'clock in the morning, looking for candidates and working on the election platform, Mason says, "to the sacrifice of his own riding." When he finally began campaigning in Mactaquac, two weeks into the election, a crowd at the Stanley Fair was lukewarm. "I didn't know you guys were fighting that battle," one man told Hargrove, who was explaining COR's opposition to federal gun control. Another asked, "Isn't that old leader Danny Cameron still trying to take your job away?" And in the horse stables came the most discouraging sign for the leader of a populist protest party. "We don't want no politicians in here," a man said to Hargrove. "You're all the same and you just want to line your pockets with money."

COR was collapsing, just as the Tories had hoped. But the COR voters were not going home.

The Liberals had worked hard to recruit credible candidates in the eight ridings COR had won. They were candidates with strong local profiles, like former school board member and principal Al Kavanaugh, running in Riverview. The bilingualism issue had exhausted itself, Kavanaugh remembers. "The question at the time really did not come up." And McKenna's small-government ethos resonated. "As they got to know Frank," Kavanaugh says, "they probably came to realize Frank was more of a Conservative than Hatfield had been." Candidates such as Kavanaugh were people COR members could vote for.

Then, in the final week, came an explosion in Edmundston that would deliver a last, fatal blow to Valcourt.

As he toured the province, Valcourt's supporters at home were working to win the riding for him from Roland Beaulieu, the Liberal who'd snatched it in the 1986 by-election. The unseemly local campaign saw Valcourt and Beaulieu record radio ads in which each tried to out-brag the other about the millions of dollars of government largesse they'd secured for the riding — even on projects in which the two ministers had collaborated to obtain funds from their respective governments.

The Conservative strategy in Edmundston was crafted by Jean-Maurice Simard. After a life-saving liver transplant earlier in the year, the senator was determined that the Tories would retake Edmundston. Though he was supposed to remain in the background of the constituency campaign, Simard couldn't resist showing his old fire-breathing self to a newspaper reporter. "I'm back," he said. "I'm whole. I'm happy to be back, and I will continue to be a spokesman for this region. I'm paid for that, and God willing I'll continue doing that."

But the riding of Edmundston could not long contain Simard's fiery denunciations of the Liberals — to the horror of Conservative candidates in English-speaking ridings.

In the final week of the election, Simard decided to "help" the PC campaign by addressing francophones directly in a series of advertisements in *L'Acadie Nouvelle*. The long messages attacked Frank McKenna's record on job creation, on taxation and on standing up for Acadians. The party couldn't afford the ads, so Simard raised the money himself — rendering the ads illegal under New Brunswick's Political Process Financing Act, which limits advertising to political parties. The bureaucrat in charge of administering the act ordered the newspaper not to run them.

Simard flew into a rage, claiming censorship — which caught the attention of Neil Reynolds, the libertarian editor-in-chief of the *Telegraph-Journal*. Reynolds detested state intervention as a matter of course, but he was particularly angered by government attempts to limit speech. He decided to translate Simard's messages into English and publish them, not as advertisements but as editorial content, allowing them to escape the law.

On September 7, just four days before the election, readers of the *Telegraph-Journal* across the Loyalist rural ridings of English New Brunswick sat down to breakfast with a large, front-page photograph of Jean-Maurice Simard staring back at them. As they read his denunciations of McKenna's language policies, they were reminded of all the headaches Simard had caused them. Now they had a new one.

In Conservative election headquarters across the south, candidates and campaign managers shuddered as their hopes of victory grew thinner. One candidate, who went on to lose by a handful of votes, would say he knew he'd lost the moment he saw that front page.

That same day, Valcourt's campaign bus was in Dieppe, where the PC leader campaigned in a shopping mall with his local candidate, a young lawyer named Bernard Lord. The two were called on the carpet by a man from Sackville they encountered at the food court. "I think you should take some responsibility and stay out of politics," he sneered at Valcourt. "I'm all for COR. This country is broke, and we've got bilingualism forced down our throats when the country's broke. So put that in your pipe and smoke it."

The man who'd said he wouldn't "take the back seat to anyone" in defending language equality froze. Here was a chance to show English New Brunswick the Bernard Valcourt they hadn't seen, the leader of passion and pride who'd triumphed in front of that crowd in Tracadie in April. Now, with the cameras and microphones of the English-language media in his face, he hesitated. The opportunity passed, the Tory leader unable to master a moment that might have defined him, and the angry old man stalked off. "He won't even stay for an argument," Valcourt finally joked flatly for the journalists.

The Tory bus limped north through Kent County to Miramichi and then into the sprawling ridings along the Bay of Chaleur. The final, exultant stop would be in Valcourt's hometown of Saint-Quentin. On that last leg of the tour, Valcourt admitted to reporters that he might not win the election. "I think New Brunswickers and Tories know that when I became the leader fourteen weeks ago, I did not inherit a party that was rich," he said. "We had no money, we had very little resources, bare bones, we barely had candidates selected. And in fourteen weeks we had to do all of that."

Election night in Edmundston was over quickly. At one point, the CBC reported the Conservatives ahead in ten ridings, but the numbers settled into another McKenna landslide. Of the three Conservative MLAs elected in 1991 — Cochrane, Gauvin and Myers — only Myers was running for re-election. All three of their ridings fell to the Liberals, whose popular vote increased to fifty-two per cent. The three Conservatives who'd won the by-elections in 1993 and 1994 — Graham, Mockler and Robichaud — won again and were joined by three new MLAs, including Valcourt.

But that added up to only six Conservative MLAs. The PCs increased their share of the popular vote from twenty per cent in 1991 to thirty-one per cent, but that meant the Tories had captured only about half of COR's 1991 support. The eight ridings that had voted COR four years earlier returned not to their traditional Tory voting patterns but to Frank McKenna. In most of them, Liberals won outright, gaining more votes that the combined COR-PC result. Thousands of voters who had embraced a party of revolution and resentment now lined up behind Frank McKenna, the premier who had been the focus of their anger. "Winning all those seats back," says MacKinnon, "was an incredible vindication. Having done Bill 88 — having met these guys head-on — it was an incredible feeling."

Valcourt pledged to stay on and continue rebuilding the PC party, but the clock began ticking on his leadership immediately. The party constitution required a review within two years of an election defeat, and rank-and-file members who'd supported him because the party brass had called him a winner now knew better. He was not the man to lead them back to power.

The leader they needed would have to be, like Dennis Cochrane, at ease in English New Brunswick — earnest, polite and decent enough to win back those votes. He'd need Valcourt's French credentials to be competitive in Acadian ridings, and to bring COR voters back without alienating francophones. Like Barbara Baird-Filliter, he would have to be young, fresh and energetic, with no political baggage to weigh him down. And, of course, he would have to be bilingual, preferably fluently, so he could move easily between the two language groups in the party and eventually unite them.

It was easy to draw up a description of the ideal leader. Tories knew, however, such a perfect candidate did not — *could* not — exist.

Part Three

BALANCING ACT

Former Liberal premier Louis J. Robichaud becomes emotional as he praises Bernard Lord's new Official Languages Act in the New Brunswick Legislature on June 7, 2002. NOEL CHENIER/*THE TELEGRAPH JOURNAL*

Chapter Fourteen

THE PERFECT CANDIDATE

THE ONE-TIME POLITICAL assistant leaned over the small round table, glanced outside at the passers-by on Elgin Street, took a sip of his Starbuck's and outlined the most fanciful political scenario of the year: the triumphant comeback of Bernard Valcourt.

The man was a consultant now, but once he'd worked for Valcourt on Parliament Hill, back when the Mulroney Tories were in power and the scrappy New Brunswick MP commanded an entourage of loyal advisors. These days, things were bleaker for Valcourt and for Conservatives everywhere. Yet the former assistant was certain that, eventually, the provincial PC party in New Brunswick would ask — no, *beg* — Valcourt to be their leader once again.

Only a Conservative in Ottawa, far removed from the reality on the ground back in New Brunswick, could advance such an absurd fantasy in the early autumn of 1997.

Valcourt had had no shortage of ammunition to fire at the McKenna Liberals after the 1995 election, from their decisions to eliminate local school boards and force several municipalities to amalgamate to their lucrative contract with video lottery machine owners and their secret negotiations to let private companies charge tolls on provincial highways. Standing in the Legislature day after day, Valcourt hit the Liberals with everything he had, extolling Progressive Conservative principles such as local governance and rejecting clandestine kowtowing to corporations. But Valcourt could not build a following, not among New Brunswickers nor in the party he led.

His offences against the Tory grassroots seemed minor, but they mattered. Not bothering to work an entire room at a party event and missing the funeral of former Hatfield cabinet minister Mac Macleod, who'd been interim leader after the disastrous 1987 election, showed Valcourt's lack of humility. Policy battles on the floor of the Legislature were important, but in a party that valued tradition, the leader was expected to greet and court volunteers in church basements and at picnics. "He was never around," the MLA for Carleton, Dale Graham, would tell a newspaper reporter later. "He was never seen in the ridings. We were all concerned about that."

In March 1997, two weeks before the party's scheduled leadership review vote, Jean-Maurice Simard said what few in the party were willing to say. In an opinion column in the *Telegraph-Journal*, Simard said his protégé was a victim of an anti-French faction within the Tory organization. "There are simply members of the party who do not accept to be led by a francophone," he wrote in the column, which he submitted against Valcourt's wishes. "Few will come out and say it," but those Tories "wish they could turn back the clock thirty years to the time of the St. John River Valley party, when having a French-speaking leader was unthinkable."

Ahead of the Fredericton convention, Valcourt told reporters he'd stay on if two-thirds of the delegates voted against review. But the result fell short — only 62.5 per cent endorsed him — and he left for a Florida vacation to consider what to do. "I could have stayed and fought it all," he explained later. "I could have wimped out and I could have blown the whole damn thing apart." But, he added, "the prime and fundamental responsibility of a party leader is to position his party to be election ready." Divisions over leadership made it impossible for him to do that, he concluded.

For Valcourt's former assistant in Ottawa, the review vote was a serious mistake by a membership that did not know how lucky it was to have his one-time boss as leader. He shook his head at the short-sightedness and the lack of political sophistication.

But in announcing his resignation, Valcourt demonstrated again the personal style that was to blame for his lack of support in the party. He chose not to attend his own news conference in Fredericton, recruiting party president Brian Harquail to read his resignation letter to journalists. He wrote that he had based his decision on the vote and "the subsequent non-support of half the caucus."

Two days later, he elaborated on that comment in a blistering *Telegraph-Journal* interview. "These guys have no idea of what politics is," Valcourt said of three MLAs who'd hinted after the review vote that they wanted him to go. Elvy Robichaud — who'd scored the 1994 breakthrough in Tracadie and had been re-elected in 1995 — "is concerned about his pension," Valcourt said, "so when you're in this business for securing your future with a little sweet pension and you think that your leader cannot do it, you don't support him." Carleton's Dale Graham, whose 1993 by-election win had turned the tide against the Confederation of Regions party, "was the softer of the bunch," he continued. "I could have won [him] over, I think, but he was listening to a lot of his people and again was concerned we could not win." As for Milt Sherwood, who'd unexpectedly won Grand Bay-Westfield in the 1995 election, Valcourt said, "Someone had to make up his mind for him, I guess, and someone did."

The attack on the three MLAs was hardly a sign that Valcourt wanted "to position his party to be election ready." Its timing was also unfortunate: the leader of the embattled federal Conservatives, Jean Charest, was campaigning in New Brunswick that day, hoping to pick up seats in the province in the federal election and save his party from extinction. Valcourt's comments were hardly a rallying cry for Conservatives to pull together.

Charest's final event of the day was in Saint-Jacques, in Valcourt's Madawaska fiefdom near the Quebec border. His former Mulroney cabinet colleague was waiting for him when the PC campaign bus pulled up at the local arena. The rally was a huge success. Afterward, as he prepared to leave, Charest embraced Valcourt warmly. Just two years earlier, they'd both been federal ministers with bright futures, bilingual and highly regarded. Now, a chasm had opened between them. Charest was bound for a future full of promise, while Valcourt's career in provincial politics had become a lamentable postscript to his Ottawa days. Madawaska County adored him, but the rest of New Brunswick just wanted to forget about him.

Only a former political aide sipping coffee in Ottawa, far removed from that reality, could imagine the provincial PC party pleading for Valcourt to come back.

One element of the former aide's argument was, however, compelling: the race to succeed Valcourt as leader was underwhelming. No one had heard of any of the four candidates, and none had the political skills to defeat the powerful New Brunswick Liberal machine. Worse, the four candidates shared a history of losing elections.

Fredericton lawyer Cleveland Allaby had run federally in June and been bested by first-term Liberal backbench MP Andy Scott. Margaret-Ann Blaney, of Fairvale, near Saint John, was a telegenic former broadcaster from Newfoundland who had been trounced by Liberal star Brian Tobin in 1993. Norman Betts, the business professor who'd been Valcourt's advisor on NB Power, had failed to get his name on the election ballot in 1995, losing the provincial PC nomination in the Southwest Miramichi riding.

And Bernard Lord was a scrawny, five-o'clock-shadowed lawyer from Dieppe, a suburb of Moncton. Just thirty-one years old, Lord's only distinction in a field of losers was that he'd managed to be defeated *twice* before — in the same year. He'd failed in a bid to become a Dieppe town councillor in May 1995; four months later he had lost as Valcourt's provincial PC candidate in the constituency of Dieppe-Memramcook.

Four candidates, four losers. The very lack of a high-profile front-runner in the race was a measure of how undesirable the Conservative leadership was and how inevitable the new leader's fate would be. Any one of the four unknowns might win his or her own seat and perhaps hold and gain few others in the next election. But restoration of the PC party to greatness would have to wait for another election and another leader.

* * *

Yet some saw in young Bernard Lord not just a decent candidate or a good leader but the potential saviour of the Progressive Conservative Party of New Brunswick.

Barbara Winsor, another of Valcourt's failed 1995 candidates, had met Lord at his nominating convention during that futile campaign and had been mesmerized by his speaking skills. "I said, 'My God, this kid is good,'" she remembers. "'He's kind of an interesting young man.' I wondered if he might have leadership capabilities, even then, when I first met him." Within the year, Lord became president of the federal PC riding association that covered Dieppe and Moncton. Winsor was vice-president. "I saw him as very mature, and very smart, and very *even*," she says. "He was very calm and even. He didn't have to shout. He had a way of getting people to his way of thinking."

Now, in the midst of the leadership race, other Conservatives were discovering the same qualities in Bernard Lord. "I instantly liked him," says Margaret-Ann Blaney, who got to know him as the candidates traipsed across the province to countless PC meetings. "He was very focused, very serious, very intense." Like Blaney, Cleveland Allaby began thinking that he might support Lord if he couldn't win the leadership himself. "He said, 'If you have a problem with me, tell me,'" Allaby remembers. "If you have a prospective leader, those are the kinds of things you want to hear from him." Even early in the race, Lord was seeking consensus, reaching out to his rivals to lay the groundwork for them to come together.

Lord brought other assets. As he'd told a newspaper reporter when his name first surfaced as a potential candidate, he had no baggage. "I have been in this party for about two years," he said. "I don't have any enemies. I haven't fought any of the old wars. I haven't teamed with anybody. I don't owe anybody anything and no one owes me anything. I am starting with a clean slate."

But all four candidates had clean slates — or, as the Liberals argued, were blank slates. Bernard Lord had something that set him apart: a family background that made him the perfect candidate for Tories who knew that, to win power, they needed to rebuild the Hatfield coalition.

* * *

Bernard Lord's father, Ralph Lord, had been raised in rural York County, first on the Lord Road in Beaver Dam, near Fredericton, then in the communities of Tracy and McAdam. His roots were utterly English: his mother's maiden name was Shakespeare. He spent five years in the Royal Canadian Navy before coming home to New Brunswick to learn to fly airplanes. To work as a bush pilot, he moved to Roberval, Quebec, a town on the southwest shore of Lac-

Saint-Jean that served as the jumping-off point to the vast expanses of the province's north. There, Ralph Lord boarded with the Morin family and fell in love with their daughter, Marie-Émilie, a school teacher. At twenty-seven, Ralph Lord of York County learned to speak French so that he could marry a Lac-Saint-Jean woman.

After designing and flying water bombers used against forest fires, Ralph Lord moved his young, growing family to the Quebec City area, to be one of the provincial government pilots who flew cabinet ministers and premiers — among them Jean Lesage and Daniel Johnson Sr. — around the province. Because of Ralph's long periods away from home, Marie-Émilie returned to Roberval to be with her family for the birth of their fourth and last child, Bernard, in September 1965.

The family relocated again in 1972 when Ralph Lord went to work for the federal government. They settled in Riverview, a growing bedroom community across the river from Moncton. Though the Lords continued to speak French at home, the children were exposed far more to English than they had been in Quebec, and Bernard — just seven years old at the time of the move — absorbed his second language quickly. He would grow up speaking English with no hint of a French accent.

As a child, Bernard Lord was aware of his roots in Canada's two dominant cultures. He recalls speaking French as he picked rhubarb with his Québécois grandfather in Roberval and English while fishing with his aunt and uncle in McAdam. "It was pretty common to switch," says his older brother Roger. As a boy, Bernard's fluency in both languages allowed him to take on paper routes for both English and French newspapers in Moncton. He would deliver *L'Évangéline* and the *Times* in the morning and the *Transcript* in the afternoon, moving seamlessly between the two languages and the two communities without a second thought. "When you're growing up," he says, "you don't overanalyze these things."

Lord played hockey with English friends but attended francophone schools, including the Université de Moncton, where he studied social sciences and, at a time of transition on the campus, became involved in student politics. The era of radical activism was ending, and student leaders were more willing to work with, rather than against, the university administration. In the spring of 1984, when Lord ran for president of the Fédération des étudiants de l'Université de Moncton, a debate was raging over the expulsion two years earlier of seven student leaders who'd occupied the administration building to protest tuition increases. The activists were demanding readmission, but candidate Lord struck a moderate tone and won the election by focusing on practical concerns, such as how a student government must provide quality service and represent the views of all members.

Mario Thériault, one of the expelled seven, now calls the protest "tacky. . . . We were the leftovers from the seventies. It was the last remnants of that fairly active period." To Thériault's eye, Lord represented something new on campus: the politics of personality, in which a candidate's image was more important than his or her views. Activists of the day questioned Lord's choosing of pragmatism over militancy. "We can't say he's bad-looking," Martin Pitre wrote in the student paper *Le Front* after Lord was interviewed by Radio-Canada. "Seeing him on television, you'd even say he has a future. But as president . . . he has nothing to say!" Addressing Lord directly, Pitre wrote, "I won't ask you to show leadership in your opinions — you have none of the first and don't have much of the second."

Lord never organized a single protest march or occupation, saying that strategy "had never proved to be a success in the past. It's not as if I saw it had a great impact on tuition, on student loans, or on the quality of education received. . . . I was more focused on identifying objectives and meeting the objectives." An independent, student-run teacher evaluation system was one initiative he pioneered that contributed to improving the quality of education. Another was a referendum on a fee increase to build a student centre that would house a coffee shop, store and student federation offices. "Is this student centre the perfect centre? No," Lord said at the time, displaying the same rhetorical style he would use in provincial politics. "It's obvious the perfect centre would be bigger and offer more services. But we're convinced it's impossible to do better than what we're proposing with the constraints we face."

Students rejected the fee increase, but they liked Lord's middle-of-the-road approach, re-electing him to a second term with forty-three per cent of the vote against two opponents. He remained low-key when he met Premier Richard Hatfield on behalf of the New

Brunswick Students Association to lobby for better education funding, afterward saying only that Hatfield's commitments were "ambiguous." Lord was more forceful in criticizing the association itself, of which his federation was a member, for issuing a press release in English only — but standing up for bilingualism was hardly a politically risky or bold move at the Université de Moncton.

Lord lost his bid for a third mandate, placing behind two other candidates with only twenty-six per cent of the vote. But the following fall, the woman who had bested him resigned suddenly and Lord ran against two other candidates to serve out her term, portraying himself as a safe, predictable, non-radical option. "It's ridiculous to make promises that can't be kept in four months," he said in a campaign advertisement. "That's why I'm offering myself as the candidate of continuity." The students gave Lord his first political comeback, showing him that caution and pragmatism led to success.

Lord's involvement in student affairs was matched by a keen interest in the broader world. He remembers discussions over the kitchen table about the election of the Parti Québécois and the rise of the Parti Acadien in New Brunswick. He also recalls television images of angry crowds and hurled eggs during public meetings on the Poirier-Bastarache report. "I remember thinking at the time, 'What's this all about?'" he says. "Some people seemed quite fearful, while for me it seemed quite natural to live in both languages." He would remain interested in politics — helping a friend design pamphlets for Kevin Fram's 1986 campaign for the PC youth wing presidency and volunteering for another friend running as an NDP candidate in the 1987 provincial election — but he would not join a political party for years to come.

Lord enrolled in law school, driven to succeed, he says, by values of hard work, discipline, respect for others and the importance of finishing what you started, all learned from his parents. The success of his older brothers and sister also spurred him. "They were so disciplined," he says, "and they would work hard and they would achieve. They were so successful. . . . I was probably motivated to show I could do the same. There was always this drive to keep up." Lord's sister Marie-Linda became a university professor, his brother Frank is a family doctor, and his other brother Roger is a pianist who performs around the world. "We did raise the bar for Bernard,"

Roger says, "but for him it didn't seem to be an effort because it was normal for him." Roger adds that his brother's much-commented-on evenness comes from his parents, who were similarly rational and unlikely to "get emotionally carried away. . . . We're all pretty balanced," he says.

For such a balanced young man, Lord did something relatively radical when he was admitted to the provincial bar in 1993. A change in the rules allowed new lawyers to decline to pledge allegiance to the Queen, who represented to some Acadians the British Crown that had deported their ancestors in 1755. Lord is reluctant to discuss why he chose not to swear the oath. It wasn't a political statement, he emphasizes, and it wasn't because refusing was the thing to do among young francophone lawyers. "It wasn't necessary," he says simply. "If it wasn't necessary to pledge my allegiance to someone else, I wasn't going to do it."

Lord's 1995 decision to run for town council in mostly franco-phone Dieppe would prove fateful. The earnest young candidate caught the eye of several Conservatives in the riding of Dieppe-Memramcook who were scouting potential candidates for the coming provincial election. Lord "impressed me as a young individual who would want to make a difference," says businessman Paul d'Astous, who, with fellow entrepreneur Arthur Savoie and lawyer Ron LeBlanc, made up the small Tory brain trust in Dieppe. Alyre Boucher, another Conservative, who'd been a partner in the law firm at which Lord had worked after law school, approached him on the street one day. "I don't think anyone was beating down their doors to be a candidate," Lord laughs. Neither was he: his son Sebastien was not yet a year and a half old, and his wife, Diane, had just given birth to their second child, daughter Jasmine. It was hardly a good time to jump into politics.

Still, Lord said it would be all right if Bernard Valcourt called him, and the idea of running began to grow on him. "It's easy to sit around the kitchen table, or at the bar, or at lunch, complaining about government, saying, 'What they're doing is wrong,'" he says. He was also skeptical of Frank McKenna's "New Brunswick miracle." Despite the hype, the unemployment rate was still high, and McKenna was practising a top-down style of government. Lord liked what Valcourt was saying about being socially progressive and fiscally conservative while restoring powers to local levels of government. Though he knew he had no hope of winning, Lord purchased a PC membership card and was nominated as the candidate. "I got in to offer something different, something else," he says.

Lord's estimate of his chances proved correct. He finished a dismal second with 22.5 per cent of the vote, but this result was still an improvement over 1991, when Dennis Cochrane's driver was persuaded to become a paper candidate at the last minute. And, after all, Dieppe-Memramcook was perhaps the most solidly Liberal riding in the province, having gone Conservative just once, when Richard Hatfield made his Acadian breakthrough in 1982.

PCs around Moncton thought that Bernard Lord might just have a future. In late 1996, after he'd become president of the federal riding association, some of them began talking to him about being the party's candidate in the next national campaign. Barb Winsor went to "his dumpy old office" to talk him out of it. There was no way Moncton would abandon the federal Liberals. "I said, 'You can't sustain three losses. It would be a disaster for you. I think you should think about running for the leadership of the provincial party.'" Winsor was planning ahead: she expected Valcourt to win the April 1997 review vote, then lose the next election. ("A brilliant man," she says of Valcourt. "I truly liked him, but I thought he was not electable.") Sometime after 1999, she calculated, Lord could run to succeed him.

Events unfolded more quickly than she'd expected. Valcourt fell short in the review vote at the April 1997 convention, and talk in the hall immediately turned to potential candidates. "I didn't see it as a realistic option that spring," Lord says. But on the drive back to Moncton, Paul d'Astous says, "we started toying with this idea of New Brunswickers electing young leaders." A month later, while Lord and Winsor were volunteering in the federal election campaign in Moncton, word came that Valcourt had quit.

Lord made the rounds of New Brunswick to measure potential support for a leadership bid, aiming for endorsements from at least two MLAs, two senators and fifteen riding association presidents. On the advice of Winsor and d'Astous, he immediately targeted Dale Graham, the MLA for Carleton and winner of that decisive 1993 by-election. "His riding . . . is what had traditionally been the base of the

Conservative party," Lord says. An endorsement from Graham "would be noticed," d'Astous says, "and we could build on it from there."

Lord made the trip up the St. John River Valley three times, the first on June 23, the day the Tories lost a by-election in the riding of Victoria-Tobique. "Dale," Winsor said, grabbing his arm at the campaign headquarters, "I tell you, we've got a premier here." The second trip was to talk to Graham at the restaurant he owned in Centreville, and the third was to the MLA's home, where he was scrutinized by members of the Carleton riding association executive. They liked the polite, earnest young man from Moncton, and Graham signed on. Lord called Diane at home to tell her he was in the race.

* * *

Lord's candidacy was still a long shot. Many Tories were turning to Elvy Robichaud, the MLA from Tracadie, as a potential leader. "I felt he would make a great premier," says Cleveland Allaby, the Fredericton lawyer. "He's clever, he's articulate, he's compassionate — he's all of those things you'd like to see." Robichaud was popular for a strategic reason as well. It was clear by 1997 that the Confederation of Regions party was finished and that many of its prominent supporters and organizers were poised to drift back to the Progressive Conservatives. A unilingual anglophone leader who embraced former COR members could alarm Acadians, but a francophone would be immune — as Valcourt had been — to accusations of being co-opted by anti-bilingualism extremists. "We needed a francophone," says Lisa Keenan, an unsuccessful PC candidate in Saint John in 1995.

Allaby signed on to chair Robichaud's campaign, but the Tracadie MLA eventually decided not to run. The flip side of Keenan's logic was the sentiment among some Conservatives that they'd lost one election with a francophone leader and that was enough. "For some segments, it was huge," says Barbara Winsor. "You know what the party's like."

But for Bernard Lord — born in Quebec, educated in French schools, elected student president at Université de Moncton and now a resident of Dieppe — that sentiment was not a liability. At a gathering of Conservative insiders at Senator Noel Kinsella's home in Fredericton, the prospective candidate was introduced to anglophone Tories who knew nothing about him. Greeting them in his unaccented English, he was asked, "But, Mr. Lord, can you speak *French*?"

Suddenly the magic equation contained in Bernard Lord became apparent. "A lot of people, not knowing him, didn't even realize he was bilingual because he didn't have an accent," Paul d'Astous says. For those who wanted a leader with francophone credentials who could bring COR supporters back without an Acadian back-lash, Lord was their man. Just as important, for those averse to a francophone leader, Lord could be *their* man, too.

"If I was in English New Brunswick, I would say he is a New Brunswicker," Barbara Winsor acknowledges. "I would give his father's heritage a lot. Everyone knew his mother was French, but I wouldn't stress that aspect in English New Brunswick, especially rural English New Brunswick."

Lord says the party's decade-long crisis over language had left it "struggling with its identity" and debating how to rebuild. "A lot of people were saying, 'We need an English person running this party. We need to recapture our base first and then we can try to expand.' . . . I guess that the choice I offered was a *provincial* party that could appeal to all people of New Brunswick. I could speak to virtually every New Brunswicker directly, and I could listen directly to vir-tually every New Brunswicker. I wanted to offer a leadership that would create, recreate and strengthen a provincial party."

The race took shape as the summer drew to a close. Blaney, who lived in the suburbs of Saint John, drew most of her support from the city and had no MLA behind her. With Robichaud out, Allaby jumped in himself, the Tracadie MLA becoming one of the few francophones to back him. Norman Betts, ruddy-faced, red-haired and freckled, was the acknowledged front-runner, a PhD with a knack for explaining policy in a folksy way. He was supported by MLA Milt Sherwood and former MP Jean Dubé, the son of Hatfield cabinet minister Fernand Dubé. Though Valcourt stayed neutral in public, it was believed he also was backing Betts. But his two fellow Madawaska MLAs, Percy Mockler and Jeannot Volpé, decided to get behind Lord.

Lord didn't impress at the outset. "I was surprised at how young he was," says Allaby, who first met him at the reception at Senator Kinsella's home. "He didn't seem all that committed to the idea that he could be the next premier." But, he adds, Lord grew rapidly as the four candidates criss-crossed the province to meet Conservatives.

There was little open discussion of language policy during the race. All four candidates supported official bilingualism, and all agreed the party should be open to anyone — even one-time COR members — who embraced the same principle. There was a flare-up when Jeannot Volpé accused Allaby of being anti-French. "I couldn't identify any francophone I didn't like," Allaby jokes, "other than Jeannot Volpé at that moment."

Betts says language was a factor in the race only to the extent that Lord's fluency in English and French gave him an advantage. "It was an issue in the sense that it was a card that he had that I didn't have. But I don't remember it being played." But it was played, over and over, in subtle ways; during a candidates' debate, for example, Lord joked about having delivered both English and French newspapers in Moncton as a child.

For many Tories, after a decade of tension between the English and French wings of the party, it was almost a relief to have a candidate who came from both — or neither. Those anglophone members who'd strained to make out what Bernard Valcourt was saying could sit back, uncross their arms and discover in Bernard Lord an unfailing politeness and sincerity that reminded them of Dennis Cochrane. The candidate could also journey to the francophone north and work a room of Acadian Conservatives like a native son — just as Bernard Valcourt had. This factor may have represented the Canadian ideal, as his supporters would say, or a more cynical political calculus, but it worked.

Lord's other assets on the campaign trail were his easy-going nature and his tendency to seek consensus, the skills Barbara Winsor had noticed while serving on the federal PC executive in Moncton. In Legion halls and community centres around New Brunswick, Lord befriended Allaby and Blaney. Betts, though, was less chummy. "There wasn't any talking to Norm," Allaby says. "Norm had all the answers and there wasn't going to be a relationship."

Betts planned to win the leadership outright on the first ballot, so he didn't entertain scenarios about who might back whom on the second. Lord's supporters were expecting a second ballot, perhaps even a third. "He was building his bridges all along the way," says Lisa

Keenan. In the final sprint, Lord himself was on the phone with Blaney's campaign manager, Bill Eaton, almost every other day. "It became obvious that it was a race between Norm Betts and Bernard Lord," Blaney says, "and Bernard Lord had made some overtures towards looking for second-ballot support. There were no overtures from Norm Betts's camp."

Allaby remembers being impressed that Lord negotiated without intermediaries — something Betts didn't do. Betts explains with a shrug, "I was busy going around, doing my thing." The night before Tories began gathering in Fredericton, Allaby says, he and his campaign team were invited to meet with the Betts camp at what was then the Sheraton Hotel. Finally, Allaby thought to himself, the courting is about to begin. He was wrong: "Norman's group proceeded to lecture us on the fact that we were so far behind that we just didn't matter."

The PC party had adopted a one-member, one-vote leadership system. Convention day featured five voting centres: the main convention hall at the Aitken Centre in Fredericton and four satellite locations in Moncton, Bathurst, St-Léonard and St. Stephen. In the Fredericton area, each candidate had the traditional section of seats for supporters and, down below, a "ready room" in which to rest or cut deals.

The satellite voting system was decisive. On the first ballot, Betts won the Aitken Centre, but Lord was first overall with 1,390 votes, or 36.5 per cent of the total. It wasn't enough to win, but there would be a second ballot, the scenario for which Lord had planned all along. "*On l'a, on l'a*," Lord said to his wife Diane — "We've got it." A subsequent academic study showed that Lord earned the support of two-thirds of francophone delegates on the first ballot and a healthy one-quarter of anglophones.

Allaby had planned to stay on for a second ballot if he placed a strong third, but his 663 votes were far behind Betts's 1,223. Blaney, last with 527, called Allaby's campaign manager Don Drury moments after the results were announced and told him she was moving to Lord right away. As Allaby and his top organizers left their seats to huddle in his ready room, Lord and Blaney clasped hands on the other side of the arena.

Allaby descended some stairs into a long back corridor running the length of the arena and came face to face with Norm Betts, who did not try to stop him and did not ask for his second-ballot support. The two men did not even exchange a word as Allaby entered his ready room. Soon, several Betts supporters were hovering around the door, clutching bags full of Betts buttons to pin on Allaby supporters. Inside, though, Allaby told his campaign team he was moving to Bernard Lord. "He is more attractive as a leader to the province as a whole," he said.

As Allaby emerged, a wide-eyed Betts supporter asked, "Well? Well?" But Allaby breezed by and up a ramp to the arena floor, where Lord and Blaney were waiting. They tried to move to the stage to show the entire hall — and the TV viewers in the satellite voting stations — that they'd struck a deal, but Brad Green, the party's executive director, stopped them. A stage display was against the rules. Thinking quickly, Percy Mockler arranged three chairs in a row in front of the stage. Lord, Blaney and Allaby climbed up on them and linked hands again — the payoff for Lord's bridge-building during the race. "Norman was upset he didn't win on the first ballot," Allaby says now, "but he shouldn't have been surprised at what happened after that."

Some Allaby supporters broke ranks and moved to Betts, but it wasn't enough. In three of the four satellite voting stations, Lord won handily on the second ballot; he lost by only four votes to Betts in St. Stephen. In the Aitken Centre, where Betts had had a clear advantage on the first ballot, he bested Lord by four votes on the second. The province-wide totals were 1,830 for Lord, 1,413 for Betts. "I hate politics," Betts's wife Bonnie exclaimed as she left his section of seats, tearing off her ID tag and throwing it on the floor.

"During this campaign, all the candidates said that we would be united — and we will be united," Lord said at the podium to cheers. "I will reach out to all of you so we can stay strong and united, so we can bring back good government to New Brunswick."

After his brief victory speech, Lord was fitted with a headset for an interview with CBC anchor Terry Seguin, who challenged the new leader on how he would avoid the Tory divisions that had plagued Barbara Baird-Filliter, Dennis Cochrane and Bernard Valcourt. "I'm a consensus builder," Lord answered. "I like to understand that what is good for one is good for the other and build the common ground. I know there is a lot of common ground."

Still, Seguin said, he was the second Conservative leader in a row to be a francophone. "Let's get one thing straight," Lord replied. "There are some differences between me and Bernard Valcourt. I do come from both backgrounds. My mother is francophone and my father is anglophone, and a lot of people saw that as a way we could build bridges between communities in this party and in this province."

Seguin persisted: "What do you say to the people of the party who think that this should have been the time for an anglophone to get the job?"

"Well, I tell them I am an anglophone," declared Lord, who just minutes before had said goodnight to his children in French on live television. "You know that I speak English just as well as the others. My name is English, my father grew up in McAdam, in an English area, my father learned to speak French when he was twenty-six, twenty-seven. . . . So I can say to these people, 'I am a New Brunswicker, and I am proud of that.' And I am very fortunate to have grown up in a bicultural family, and I think that is going to help me as leader of this party and hopefully will help me as premier of this province."

Lord was on to something. Previous premiers and leaders had been bilingual, but none as seamlessly. It made him the perfect candidate. Now, as he set out to become the perfect leader, it would allow people to see in Bernard Lord whatever they wanted to see.

Chapter Fifteen

A MIRACLE UNDONE

EVEN AS BERNARD LORD savoured his victory onstage at the Aitken Centre, the Liberals were preparing their first trap. Frank McKenna had retired as premier and resigned as MLA for Miramichi-Bay du Vin a few days earlier. The morning after the PC convention, the interim premier, Ray Frenette, called two by-elections to fill McKenna's old seat and that of Tantramar. Lord could move almost immediately into the Legislature — if he dared to challenge the popular and mighty Liberals. Lord refused to take the bait, and the Liberals quickly spun reporters that the new leader was afraid. It was a little smug, but they were confident that, McKenna or no McKenna, their image of managerial competence and bold innovation would overwhelm the thirty-two-year-old lawyer from Moncton. They'd chew up Bernard Lord just as they had his predecessors.

Lord believed otherwise. The public opinion surveys showed the Liberals far ahead, but some pollsters detected creeping doubts about the party's handling of key issues. The McKenna government had forced unpopular municipal amalgamations on the Miramichi area and in Edmundston. It had imposed a regional RCMP force on Moncton, Dieppe and Riverview in defiance of local councils. Even some Liberals sensed a pent-up malaise. "The government was in a bad mode," one partisan would remember. "They were clamping down, making extremely bad decisions." And Frank McKenna, the man best able to persuade New Brunswickers that a bad decision was good for them, was now gone.

Yet the Liberals' continued lead in the polls indicated, perhaps, that New Brunswickers couldn't see a viable alternative. Bernard Lord's first test as leader would be to identify the discontent out there and become its vehicle.

Speaking to the *Telegraph-Journal* when he first thought about running for leader, Lord had cited what he considered a particularly outrageous example of the McKenna method, an incident that had been in the news just a few days before. "When you send the police and the dogs after parents who are fighting for their schools," he said, "there is obviously something wrong in this province." He was referring to the events of May 2, 1997, in the tiny Acadian Peninsula community of Saint-Sauveur. There, amid a hurricane of tear gas, yapping police dogs and a roaring RCMP helicopter, the McKenna Miracle imploded.

In early 1996, Frank McKenna had abolished school boards, further burnishing his credentials with the national media. The notion of giving parents greater control of their children's schools was faddish at the time among advocates of innovation in education. The Liberals replaced the boards with parent committees at every school, made up of dedicated mothers and fathers who would, in theory, oversee the teaching of their children. In reality, the committees were powerless. The move cut out the middleman of education governance and gave the Department of Education direct control over superintendents, principals and teachers. It left no outlet for those who wanted to challenge decisions, including a December 1996 edict that two elementary schools in the Acadian Peninsula, in the communities of Saint-Sauveur and Saint-Simon, would be closed six months later, at the end of the academic year.

The logic of the decision was evident to the bureaucrats in Fredericton. École La Découverte in Saint-Sauveur and École Lorette-Doiron in Saint-Simon were expensive to maintain, and enrolment was dropping. The province could save money by busing students to newer schools with a wider range of modern facilities in nearby communities. But in northeast New Brunswick, where the economy never really shifts into high gear, the shuffling of resources and the reallocation of the public good is highly political. A modest red-brick building — a school or a post office — provides not only a few well-paying jobs but a sense of community in places where there is little else to justify a name on a map.

Early in 1997, the parents of Saint-Sauveur and Saint-Simon each set up local save-our-school committees to persuade McKenna's education minister, James Lockyer, to change his mind. Lockyer, a smoothly bilingual former law professor, was a proud member of the McKenna team, first elected in the sweep of 1987 and an ardent defender of the premier's aggressive reforms. He wouldn't budge, and parents in Saint-Sauveur responded by keeping their kids home from school and blocking buses carrying other children.

On April 17, a bonfire was set in the middle of Route 160, the main road in Saint-Sauveur and the primary link between Tracadie-Sheila and the provincial highway to Bathurst. The crowd was well-behaved — they sang songs and offered food to RCMP officers. Lockyer flew in to Bathurst to meet with the save-our-school committees from Saint-Sauveur and Saint-Simon. The RCMP, anticipating things might get out of hand, put its tactical troop — a riot squad of helmeted officers bearing shields and batons — on stand-by near the hotel. The squad wasn't needed, however, and Lockyer persuaded the protestors to open the highway by promising to respond to their concerns by April 25. He later unilaterally extended his own deadline to May 2.

On May 1, the morning after two hundred people had marched peacefully down Route 160 in Saint-Sauveur, the top-ranking Mountie in the administrative area known as District 8, Staff-Sergeant Charles Castonguay, got advance word that Lockyer would tell the parents the next day that he would not back down. Castonguay quickly summoned the RCMP Special Unit to the area.

The Special Unit was made up of the tactical troop, a tear-gas unit, the rifle-bearing emergency response team, an "arrest unit," a dog squad, an identification team to record events, and a helicopter. Believing local rumours, Castonguay was not taking any chances. "Public security was clearly at risk in the region," he would explain later. "There had been threats that the schools would be set on fire. There was a threat that they would be blown up. There had been threats against [RCMP] members." One of his officers, Castonguay later explained, had been injured during riots over crab fishing quotas in nearby

hurry to get things done, to reform, to "innovate" — that had been the key to their popularity for a decade. They signed the contract in January.

The ink dry, the contract was made public, and outrage quickly spread in Petitcodiac, Salisbury and other small communities along the Trans-Canada Highway west of Moncton. "It went really quick," Stiles says. The federal and provincial governments had just finished twinning a short section of the highway in that area using an existing infrastructure fund. Now it was transferred to the Maritime Road Development Corporation to become part of the toll highway. Tolling would begin for that section, at seventy-five cents per car, later in 1998, more than three years before the full highway would be finished. Local residents who used the highway to commute to Moncton saw that they would be paying for the road twice, once with their tax dollars through the infrastructure fund and a second time with tolls. To make matters worse, the location of the first toll booth, east of the interchange to Fredericton, meant that drivers heading to and from Saint John would also be dinged for seventy-five cents. This, the residents concluded, was proof the arrangement was really intended to be a cash cow for the government, a tax disguised as a highway.

The anger cut across party lines. Tom Taylor, a Salisbury convenience store owner who'd run for the Confederation of Regions party in 1995, and Gordon Bowser, a veteran Liberal worker, decided to put an organization together. "There were so many people saying there was no damn way they were going to pay that toll, and we just took it from there," Taylor recalls. They invited Irvin Robinson, a Petitcodiac businessman and Progressive Conservative supporter, to join their effort, creating a genuinely non-partisan movement.

The anger was localized, but the Liberals realized they had to respond. When Taylor's group scheduled a public meeting in Salisbury, the government booked a room of its own to hold an information session nine days ahead of his. The Liberals hoped their event would calm the clamour, but the event only gave the critics more ammunition. About four hundred people heard local Liberal MLA Hollis Steeves explain meekly that, as a backbencher, he was powerless to stop a project so strongly opposed by his constituents. "That was discussed by cabinet and I'm not in cabinet," he said. Then a man who was in cabinet, long-time transportation minister Sheldon Lee, explained that *he* was powerless as well. In a remarkable breach of cabinet solidarity and confidentially, Lee revealed he had fought against the idea and lost. "The decision was made by the government," he said. "I'm not the government. I'm only one member. You have no idea how many times I recommended against tolls."

Lee brushed aside suggestions from the crowd that the government exempt local residents from paying the tolls, yet he appeared baffled by the frosty reception he received. He complained about being booed despite having overseen more than $2 billion in highway construction during his decade as minister. It was as if Liberals, so popular for so long, were unable to recognize grassroots anger when it was staring them in the face.

Now Bernard Lord had his political opening if, recognizing the anger, he could find a way to channel it. Lord and the Tory MLAs in the Legislature complained loudly about the lack of consultation and the constraints the contract placed on future governments, but they weren't saying precisely what they would do if elected.

Lord met with the Progressive Conservative caucus on February 19, ahead of his trip to Salisbury to speak at Tom Taylor's anti-toll meeting. The leader and his seven MLAs — the party had won one of those two by-elections called after the PC convention — discussed once again what the party's position should be. Some MLAs argued it would be impossible to remove the tolls, and that carried the day. "The caucus agreed they wouldn't [make the promise]," says one party insider, who did not attend the meeting but who was later told about the discussion.

That was the position when Lord left Fredericton for Salisbury, accompanied by MLA Percy Mockler, but by the time he reached the podium in the high school gym in Salisbury that evening, something had changed.

The meeting opened with messages from municipal councils in the area voicing their opposition to the tolls. During a break in the proceedings, Lord — still adhering to the caucus position — told some journalists he could not promise to tear up the deal. "I'd like to say that," he told them. "To say I would cancel the deal — I can't say that. That would be irresponsible. I don't know what the cost would be."

Minutes later, at the podium, Lord was not so blunt, vowing to try to alter the terms of the contract with the Maritime Road Development Corporation — even though his party had fiercely criticized it for being iron-clad. "If you change the government," Lord said to the crowd, "we will change the tolls." But the people in the audience weren't in the mood for slogans; besides, "change the tolls" implied that, even under Lord, they would continue to exist in a different form. Two men in the bleachers began shouting down at him, demanding the specifics of the promise he'd just made.

A Tory government would renegotiate "parts" of the contract, he replied.

"You haven't answered my question," the man shouted back, and a hush fell over the crowd as if they realized that Bernard Lord was being tested.

Lord looked up at the back rows where the hecklers were sitting and said, "We will take the tolls off."

It hit the organizers of the meeting like a thunderclap.

They hadn't anticipated a definitive statement, a clear and unequivocal promise, and many would assume the inexperienced PC leader had cracked under pressure. "I don't think Bernard Lord had completely made up his mind," Wally Stiles says. "When he went in and saw how people reacted, he made his decision." Tom Taylor was surprised as well. "I hadn't expected him to come out and say that. . . . It kind of looked like they'd put him in a corner. My first impression was that he was just saying this to appease us, to get the votes."

The explanation was simple. Between Lord's departure from Fredericton and his walk to the podium in Salisbury, "Percy single-handedly convinced him to change his mind," says a Tory insider interviewed on the condition of anonymity. "Percy obviously made a public opinion calculation." The insider — perhaps realizing that it might appear Lord was inventing policy on the spot with little concern for the consequences — added in a subsequent interview, "Being the cautious person that he is, [he] would have had some idea how to do it."

Lord had been consulting people in the area, including a local businessman who'd studied the contract in detail, to see if there was a way to eliminate the tolls without a costly lawsuit against the province. Lord says those consultations had persuaded him the highway could be less expensive without tolls. Still his own account of the day does not explicitly deny Mockler's decisive role.

"There was a discussion [in caucus] that day," Lord says. "There were discussions every day for a while on that issue, and I don't remember precisely the discussions we had in caucus, but I remember talking to some caucus members about that, and it was clear to me this was the right position to take. When I arrived in Salisbury, when the meeting started, my mind was made up. . . . I felt going in that this would be the appropriate forum to express the position I was going to take on the toll highway. It was clear to me that this was the right position to take. . . . Percy was supportive of the position. He was one of the caucus members who was the most supportive. But I made the decision."

The Liberals pounced on the perception that Lord had caved in at the podium. Sure, some yokels around Petitcodiac might fall for his hasty commitment, and the riding, along with a couple of others along the highway, would probably vote Tory. They were traditionally Conservative anyway. But most New Brunswickers knew that the Liberals were competent, get-things-done managers who could be trusted. They'd see Lord for the weakling he was, someone who would make a promise without any idea how to implement it. Wally Stiles agrees the early reviews were bad. "A lot of people thought it was a rookie mistake," he says.

But Percy Mockler had again earned his reputation as a crafty strategist. Though the caucus would be outraged at what he'd done, and Lord would have to calm them down, Mockler had accurately read the mood, not just of Salisbury but of the province as a whole. People in that school gymnasium were willing to do *something* if the Liberals didn't back down, he'd surmised. The Conservatives needed to draw a clear line between themselves and the government.

The issues raised in Saint-Sauveur and Saint-Simon may have been more fundamental and more deserving of becoming a full-blown political scandal. But the toll highway deal would prove easier to understand. The road also happened to pass through a wide swath of traditional Conservative territory, including ridings where the Confederation of Regions party had done well in 1991. And it was much closer to two of New Brunswick's media centres, Fredericton and Moncton, meaning it would be easier for reporters to cover that story than it had been to file from two backroad communities in the Acadian Peninsula.

That night in Salisbury, Bernard Lord — whether inadvertently or by design, based perhaps on principle or perhaps on electoral math — haltingly grasped a position that distinguished his party from the government. The Liberals would choose a new leader in May. The winner, on becoming premier, would find himself saddled with, as Dalton Camp put it, "a record he could neither run on, boast about, nor run away from." Bernard Lord wasn't just offering voters a free highway. He was offering them an alternative. He had made himself a symbol of change.

Chapter Sixteen

SUPERMAN

TO TAKE THE NEXT STEP — to transform himself from a mild-mannered Moncton lawyer into a leader capable of rebuilding the Conservative coalition and lifting the party to victory — Bernard Lord needed certain events to fall into place.

The Confederation of Regions party had to continue its descent into political oblivion, freeing up voters who'd resented the Progressive Conservatives' support for bilingualism. Then the PC party had to prove it could be a "We the People" party, willing to listen to the grassroots voices of those who felt neglected by Richard Hatfield. And the Liberals had to choose a leader who would fail to capture the public's imagination as Frank McKenna had. At the same time, Lord had to demonstrate his own appeal by winning a seat in the Legislature, which would give the Tory base the faith that they might taste power again someday soon, and the motivation to strive for it.

The shocking completeness of COR's defeat in 1995 had created an opening for two men to try to reshape it as a party that was less hard-edged, less overtly hostile to francophones, and more focused on issues such as fiscal discipline and democratic accountability. One was Lynn Mason, who'd worked so tirelessly and so idealistically in 1991 to elect Ed Allen in Fredericton North. Mason attributed COR's disastrous leadership battles to what he called "a power disease" that befalls most politicians. "They think they're gods when they speak in front of large groups of people, and they forget where they came from." In COR, Mason says, the disease collided with a large faction that believed the MLAs weren't pushing the anti-bilingualism message enough. "When you have radicals in a party," he says, "and we had our share, and you have a party constitution that gives them the power to speak up, it can cause great difficulty."

Mason had kept his head down during the bitter wars between Danny Cameron and the party board, toiling on the Fredericton North riding executive. When Ed Allen decided not to run again in 1995, Mason sought the COR nomination in the riding but lost. Still believing in the cause, he was parachuted into the riding of Charlotte, on the Bay of Fundy about an hour south of Fredericton, as a paper candidate.

During his perfunctory campaign, Mason met Antoon Huntjens, the round-faced, thick-middled COR candidate in the neighbouring riding of Western Charlotte. Tony Huntjens had a biography different from that of the average COR candidate. He was born in Holland, where his father had mined coal in the evening and tended his farm during the day. "It was one hundred per cent sure that I would have ended up in the coal mines," Huntjens says, the lilt of his Dutch accent still audible today. In 1952, to give the children a better future, the family emigrated to Canada, selling their belongings to pay for the journey and settling in Maugerville, down-river from Fredericton, with a hundred dollars between them. Young Antoon worked on the family farm, learning the values of hard work and frugality, before attending college and becoming a high school teacher in St. Stephen.

Late in 1992, Huntjens wrote an open letter to Frank McKenna, published in his local weekly newspaper, in which he denounced the plan to entrench Bill 88 in the Constitution. Huntjens objected to many policies that benefited francophones — the Acadian flag flying at the Legislature and the lawyers' option to decline to swear allegiance to the Queen. But what angered him most was the existence of separate English and French school systems in New Brunswick, a fundamental right for which Acadians had fought hard. Huntjens was convinced Bill 88 would lead to a similarly expensive duality in all government departments. "In my opinion that makes it dangerously divisive," he wrote.

"I come from a country where a second language is second nature," he explained in a 2003 interview for this book. "Nobody thought about it. People in Holland learned three or four languages, so language was never an issue. . . . I fully support bilingualism [in New Brunswick] but we're not going at it the right way. . . . I think we need to be careful that we don't divide the province into two linguistic communities. When you separate children from each other, that puts a stigma between the two communities. As long as we keep separating English and French communities, we're not being conducive to harmonizing."

Danny Cameron saw and liked Huntjens's letter and contacted him, suggesting he get involved with COR. He did, and his 1995 campaign leaflet in Western Charlotte struck typical COR themes, promising electoral reform, including referenda, and the elimination of government waste. It also railed against provincial grants to the Acadian World Congress and the Acadian Games — and, of course, it attacked duality in education. "This is the government that promotes dual linguistic schools in the name of unity!" the pamphlet exclaimed.

Huntjens and Mason came to like each other immensely. Two weeks after the electoral debacle of September 11, 1995, they met to see if there was a way to save the party. Huntjens had stepped into the job of party president, and he and Mason decided on a two-step process to moderate COR's image. First, they would rewrite the party constitution and have their changes ratified at the next annual general meeting. "We wanted to take anything that could be determined as racist out of the constitution," Mason says. Second, within a year of the first meeting, they would convene a second to draft and ratify a new policy platform for the next provincial election. The 1995 platform, Mason says, "could be taken as extremely racist."

Mason estimates he spent three hundred hours travelling the province, attending local party meetings to shape the new constitution. One key change was to eliminate nominations from the floor at provincial and local conventions — a tactic that had been used in 1995 to blindside the sitting Riverview MLA, Gordon Willden, and deprive him of the COR nomination in the election. "You weren't altering the democratic process," Mason says. "You were doing away with the sneaks. You were taking away any possibility of them sabotaging the process."

Mason and Huntjens co-chaired the 1996 annual general meeting in Fredericton, which ratified their new constitution one article at a time. They began planning for phase two of their overhaul, the policy convention. Over the winter of 1996-97, however, they had difficulty persuading the provincial board to schedule it. The third time he attempted it, "I found the board overly stacked against the convention date," Mason says, "and when I suggested an alternative, I was turned down flat. I could not get a date for the policy convention. As far as I'm concerned, at that board meeting, the COR party died."

Huntjens confirms Mason's account. "I discovered there was a segment in the party population, so to speak, that was not willing to co-operate on that issue. They continued to make language *the* issue of the party. So I basically said that was enough. After two years as president I wasn't gaining anything in terms of unifying the party behind the platform we had established."

The two men quit the party, leaving COR dominated even more by language hardliners who would further marginalize it as a political force.

Mason would eventually accept — as the hardliners refused to — that COR had put up a good fight for its vision of New Brunswick and had lost. Separate French and English schools were here to stay. "I recognize the fact that it can't be changed at this point," he says. "It still sticks in my craw, but you can't change what's been done when it's been written into the Constitution."

Some things *could* be changed, though, such as excessive spending in government. Mason had developed a taste for politics; that fall he watched the Progressive Conservative leadership convention on television. He was particularly interested in the message of inclusiveness the new leader, Bernard Lord, seemed to be sending directly to New Brunswickers like him. "The openness of the man impressed me to no end," he says, "and the fact he was proposing a party that was open to all other parties, including COR." Mason, who considers himself a good judge of character, decided that Bernard Lord was "a genuine person." Lord's own support for linguistic rights barely registered. "His personal views on bilingualism have never been put to the front," Mason says approvingly.

* * *

As the new leader of the PC party, Bernard Lord had one resource that Dennis Cochrane and Bernard Valcourt had lacked: time.

His two predecessors had taken over with election campaigns just months away. Lord had time to work on policy, establish his profile and find the right balance among the party's factions — and perhaps even reach out to those who had left. His careful courting of the other candidates did not end at the convention. "The object of the reaching out wasn't to win the leadership," Lord says. "It was to win the election."

Lord asked leadership rivals Norman Betts and Margaret-Ann Blaney to oversee a series of policy consultation meetings open not only to PC members but to everyone. Elvy Robichaud, the franco-phone MLA who'd supported Cleveland Allaby, would join them. "The people in this province will have a chance to participate direct-ly," Lord said when he launched the process in January of 1998. "It's not a closed process, it's wide open."

At eight regional meetings, participants broke off into separate workshop groups chaired by Betts, Blaney and Robichaud, while Lord roamed from workshop to workshop. The discussions led to a draft policy document, which was sent out to the fifty-five PC riding associations. They held their own meetings to draft amend-ments to the document, which would be voted on at a full provincial policy convention. It was hard to imagine a process more expressive of COR's "We the People" rhetoric.

Margaret-Ann Blaney recalls "certain frustrations being raised" about language policy, and Betts remembers complaints from people who couldn't get bilingual government jobs, but no one tried to change the party's support of official bilingualism. "It might have been murmured in the hall," Betts says, "but in all of our workshops and at all of our meetings, I can't remember an instance where that was challenged. . . . There was a recognition that if you're going to be a modern party, that was the way it was."

Five hundred Tories gathered at the Saint John Convention Centre in mid-April to ratify the policy document. Any resolution from a riding association that earned one-third of the votes in Friday night workshops was sent to the floor on Saturday. Among those adopted were resolutions calling for tax cuts, a balanced-budget law, the return of local school boards, the creation of elected hospital boards, the elimination of highway tolls and a veto for local councils on municipal amalgamations.

On all of these issues, the members of the Progressive Conservative party would have their say — and, after eleven agonizing years, they would have their say on language policy, too.

Because the historic moment had not been contentious at all, it passed almost unnoticed: for the first time, the Tory membership endorsed official bilingualism as one of ten fundamental principles in the policy document. "We came of age in the party," says Lisa Keenan, then its vice-president, "when it was an automatic given that the party is bilingual and supported French and English equality." Headed "Equality of the Two Linguistic Communities," the section said, "We believe the diversity of our two linguistic communities is a unique strength of our province. We believe in official bilingualism and that we must protect and promote our cultures and heritage while treating each community with fairness and justice."

That seemingly innocuous statement would become a powerful political tool for Bernard Lord. Anyone who wanted to join the PC party, including former COR members, would have to sign a party card committing themselves to upholding the party's statement of principles — including support for linguistic equality — that had been voted on in an open, grassroots, "We the People" exercise.

But skeptics of language rights would also find comfort in the phrase "with fairness and justice." In ridings that had fallen to COR or that had tilted strongly in that direction, Conservatives could now point to an official party document that pledged to apply the policy fairly — that, by implication, people would not lose their jobs because they could speak only English. "Not everyone needs to speak both languages in every position in government," says Kirk MacDonald, who planned to seek the PC nomination in Mactaquac, Greg Hargrove's old riding. "That's what I stressed, and to his credit, that is what [Lord] stressed as well. It was important to reaffirm it again, publicly. Whether it was true or not, people hadn't believed it in 1991. Perhaps just to hear it being stated publicly reassured them."

"There was some uneasiness among some members of our party and of the public that some opportunities might not be open to them because they don't speak both official languages," Lord says. "It was important to ensure that everyone in New Brunswick knew we supported official bilingualism and we supported fairness." The phrasing echoed what Richard Hatfield had said in April 1969 when, as PC leader, he'd endorsed the Official Languages Act while calling on the government "to assure that no one in this province is treated unfairly" by it. The party had now come full circle, and another PC leader was assuring anglophones they had nothing to fear from bilingualism.

Tories left the Saint John convention exhilarated at what they had accomplished. "It was tangible," Blaney says. "It was contagious. There was an excitement that was there that hadn't been there for a long time." And that came in part from the confidence that the party had struck the perfect balance between staying loyal to Hatfield's vision and bringing home those voters who had strayed to COR.

"Everyone emerged from that meeting realizing we did have an open party and we had a party that knew what it stood for," Mac-Donald says. "COR had *talked* of grassroots democracy, but this is exactly what we *did*." Keith Ashfield, a New Maryland Tory who had been defeated by COR in the 1991 election, says the Saint John convention was the beginning of the renewal of the Conservative coalition. "The grassroots had felt they were being left out and no one was listening to them," he says. "And during that whole policy process, that attitude shifted. It went a long way to winning them back."

At least one Conservative did not share the enthusiasm for Bernard Lord's balancing act on language policy. In August, Senator Jean-Maurice Simard visited Lord at his home in Dieppe. Simard would tell his Provincial Archives interviewer in 1999 that he found the young PC leader was like the other post-Hatfield leaders — too timid *to do things* on the language issue, too afraid of its consequences and too willing to buy the line that Hatfield had lost in 1987 because he'd reached out to Acadians. "They all believe it," Simard said. "They listen to the Liberals too much. That's why I told Bernard Lord not to listen. . . . Richard Hatfield gave hope to the Acadians to improve their lot. . . . I have never heard [Lord] speak in favour of this fact."

"I don't know what would have given him that impression," Lord answers. While he feels tensions over the Poirier-Bastarache report contributed to what happened in 1987, he says he agrees with Simard that other issues played a bigger role.

Jean-Maurice Simard's critical assessment of the young PC leader is telling. What the Archives interview does not reveal is why he decided to keep it to himself at the precise time Lord was reaching out to the very New Brunswickers who'd so distrusted Simard.

Perhaps the original French lieutenant finally understood that the best contribution he could make to the rebuilding of Hatfield's coalition was to keep his peace.

* * *

Less than a month after the Progressive Conservatives' free-wheeling embrace of grassroots democracy at the Saint John Convention Centre, Liberals jammed the same rooms and corridors to go through the motions of a leadership convention so predictable it could have been scripted in advance.

Many felt it was. The man poised to win, Camille Thériault, had been part of Frank McKenna's sweep in 1987, and he'd coveted the top job for almost as long. He'd ascended to cabinet in 1991 and eventually taken over the Department of Economic Development and Tourism, which placed him next to McKenna at all his trademark job announcements. It also allowed party members all over New Brunswick to encounter Thériault's amiable, down-to-earth personality. By the time McKenna retired, "Camille had sewn up all the organizers," says a senior Liberal of the day. "He had assembled everybody who knew how to pull a crowd in New Brunswick. It was a team built to win."

Two other ministers — Greg Byrne from Fredericton and Bernard Richard, the one-time Acadian activist from Cap-Pelé — mounted perfunctory leadership campaigns at the urging of those Liberals who felt Thériault lacked the intellect and discipline to fill McKenna's shoes. The campaign featured the odd spectacle of all three men apologizing for the actions of the popular government they'd served as cabinet ministers. All acknowledged McKenna's top-down style. All knew that, even before McKenna left office, the lack of consultation was beginning to catch up with the Liberals. All three pledged to consult New Brunswickers more while maintaining McKenna's fiscal discipline.

When the toll highway became an issue, however, only Byrne and Richard spoke of taking a second look at the arrangement. Thériault, with his front-runner's confidence, didn't need or want to forfeit that revenue and declared the tolls would remain if he became premier. "I think it would be irresponsible to come here and be like Lord and say I'm going to tear this thing apart," he told anti-toll protestor Tom Taylor at a party meeting in Salisbury.

That, one Liberal says, was a mistake. "As a leader you need to define yourself, and that would have been an easy way." If Thériault wanted to distinguish himself from McKenna, he needed more than platitudes about being different.

Thériault secured an easy first-ballot victory in Saint John, but once he was sworn in as premier, some Liberals were unsure what he wanted to do. "He was following a premier who was very popular, albeit a premier who was developing some baggage," says the same Liberal insider. "There was a fatigue with reform. He had a tough situation." Others blame the drift on the small circle of McKenna advisors who left government for lucrative private-sector jobs when Thériault took over, then criticized his shift away from McKenna's hard-nosed style. "The old guard decided to go off into the sunset and give him all the rope he needed," says a Conservative with a soft spot for Thériault. "They were incredibly cruel. They totally undermined it."

Thériault became premier in May and was urged to call a fall election. The polls showed troubling trends: one recent survey had the Liberals ahead of the Conservatives forty-three per cent to thirty per cent — a substantial lead, but narrower than the huge margins they'd enjoyed under McKenna. An early campaign would pre-empt a continuing slide, and it would force Bernard Lord to spend much of the campaign in Dieppe, trying to win his own seat.

Thériault ignored the advice. He wanted to put his own stamp on the government. But no one could define exactly what that was, other than not being as mean or as zealous for reform as McKenna had been. He tried to demonstrate his kinder, gentler approach, his "third wave" of New Brunswick Liberalism, with gimmicks that backfired, such as linking health funding to changes in the consumer price index — a formula that would have seen less money going to health, not more, during the McKenna years, when growth in spending exceeded inflation.

In his gut, the new premier understood there was only so much distance he could put between himself and Frank McKenna. "If the issue is change, we can't win," Thériault told Dalton Camp, "and there's nothing I can do about it."

* * *

By mid-1998, COR was beyond salvation, the PC policy exercise had been a success, and the Liberals had selected a weak leader. Bernard Lord was now in a position to launch a concerted, focused assault on the Liberal government. But to do that, he needed to sit in the Legislature.

Lord had said he would run in the next election in Dieppe-Memramcook, the solidly Liberal riding where he'd been defeated in 1995. But when Thériault was sworn in as premier, the Liberals' interim leader, Raymond Frenette, left politics, giving up Moncton East, which he'd held since single-member ridings were created in 1974. The working-class constituency, principally anglophone but with a large French-speaking population, would hardly be easy for Lord: it was considered strongly Liberal, and Lord didn't live there. Still, he announced in August that he would run in the by-election Thériault was expected to call for the autumn.

"Some have said and some will say that I had no choice but to run in Moncton East," Lord told about a hundred party supporters at his announcement. "Let me tell you that I disagree. I did have a choice." Two MLAs — Percy Mockler and Dale Graham — had offered to resign to allow him to run in their ridings, he said. But he'd chosen to wait for Moncton East to open up because it was a part of the community where he'd been raised.

The fact was that Lord had to run somewhere — soon. Over the summer, impatience about his performance was growing. The mayor of Sackville, a Conservative named Pat Estabrooks, had told a reporter that "leaders have to be visible and they have to go out there and gain the support and respect of people, and I just haven't seen that happening with Bernard." She'd suggested that Peter Mesheau, the smooth-talking marketing man who'd been elected Conservative MLA for Tantramar in a by-election, might make a better leader. Mesheau quickly denied any interest, but the brief buzz showed Lord needed to assert his leadership.

At his announcement, Lord also hedged on the importance of the by-election, telling reporters — implausibly — that he'd stay on as leader if he lost. "I'm not risking my political career," he said. Lord's advisors believed otherwise. When the by-election campaign got underway in September, they picked up rumours that a group of Tories who'd supported Norm Betts in the leadership race would try to oust Lord if he failed to win Moncton East. The morning after a defeat, the rumour said, several of them would hold a news conference, demand Lord's resignation and propose that Betts take over. "A lot of people were still rallying and trying to get Norm," says one of Lord's advisors. So the Moncton East campaign represented a very real risk to the leader's political career. "Everything was riding on it," says the advisor.

The Liberals chose a formidable candidate: Charlie Bourgeois, a former NHL hockey player from Moncton, who was well known for his charity work during his pro days and for the hockey schools he'd run for area kids. More important, he'd grown up in the riding. "This is about making sure the people of Moncton East continue to be represented by a person who knows the area and who cares about the area," Thériault said at Bourgeois's nomination. Reminding voters that Lord might abandon them to run in Dieppe in a general election, Bourgeois said, "I'm not applying for a temporary job. This is a long-term commitment."

But Bernard Lord also had a long-term argument for the voters: he just wanted a chance to prove himself. "I am asking you to make a contribution to democracy to elect the Leader of the Opposition," he said in announcing his candidacy. "I want the opportunity to show the people of the riding and the province that I am capable of providing an alternative to eleven years of Liberal rule."

It was a powerful case, and Lord wouldn't be making it alone. Progressive Conservatives from all over New Brunswick poured into Moncton East when the by-election was called. Every resource the party had was deployed: party staff from Fredericton arrived, as did all the MLAs, including veterans of previous by-election campaigns such as Percy Mockler and Dale Graham. Everyone knew that, if Lord lost, the party would be condemned to more acrimony, so they mounted an aggressive, all-or-nothing campaign, a tireless push to get Lord to every house in Moncton East. "We went in as the under-dog," Mockler says, "but we knew by exposing him to Joe Public, Joe Voter, he would connect like he did at the convention." The choice the Tories presented to voters was simple: pick a guy who'll stand up for you — and who might become premier — or someone who'll be a powerless member of a team on its way out.

Another dedicated organization served Lord in the by-election. The opponents of the toll highway had formed a group called the Tollbusters and bought advertising and appeared at campaign events to push their message. They claimed not to choose sides, but their intervention could only help Lord by reminding Monctonians of the increasingly unpopular highway contract. That opening allowed Lord to repeat his vow to renegotiate the deal, which telegraphed that he was different from the government responsible for tolls and other unpopular measures.

Still, the outlook wasn't good. One poll, conducted before the by-election was called, pegged Lord's support in the riding at just ten per cent. Another survey released just before the campaign showed a rebound of Liberal support provincially, giving the party fifty-six per cent among decided voters.

When the time came for residents in Moncton East to make up their minds, though, Tory pessimism turned to optimism. "The mood of the electorate seemed to change as we were going door to door," re-calls Brian Harquail, then party president. "People seemed to think, 'Let's give this young fella a chance.'" A final poll on the Saturday before the vote reflected the shift. Asked whom they preferred to see as premier, people in Moncton East chose Thériault over Lord, a sign that the Liberal brand was still strong. Yet, in the by-election, 32.2 per cent planned to vote for Lord, but only 26.6 per cent for Bourgeois. The voters seemed to feel they could safely give the polite, earnest young PC leader an opportunity to prove himself without turfing the Liberals.

On by-election day, October 19, prominent Tories fanned out across Moncton East to deliver the vote for their leader. "He had the vice-president of the party working a poll for him," chuckles Lisa

Keenan. "You had all these Tories of significant weight working the polling stations for him." It worked; as the results came in that night, Lord moved into the lead immediately and never had to worry. He took 3,346 votes compared to 2,633 for Bourgeois.

There was more good news for the Conservatives that night. Two other by-elections were taking place, and in Fredericton South, Brad Green — the youth wing president under Hatfield who'd gone on to be Dennis Cochrane's executive assistant — also won, giving the Conservatives nine MLAs, a post-Hatfield high for any opposition party.

But the night belonged to Bernard Lord, the gangly kid in the blue suit whose stature seemed to grow as he thanked his supporters. "I look forward to the next general election because we want to offer a choice to the people of New Brunswick," he told them. "It starts here in Moncton East and will continue throughout the province."

Any threat to his leadership evaporated in that instant; the membership would trust him and fall in line behind him. "They came to see him as a potential premier," says Paul d'Astous. The potential of power — and of the spoils of power — now imposed its discipline on the party. "That in itself will keep a lot of the rumpus down because they know they have a chance," d'Astous says. "They'd been down for a long time."

For Barbara Winsor, another early Lord fan, the Liberals had erred by not following the federal tradition of allowing the Official Opposition's party leader to win a seat unopposed. By throwing a credible candidate at Lord, they'd made his victory all the more impressive. "They could have just given it to him and made fun of him," Winsor says. "That was their biggest mistake. He came in as a Superman."

* * *

Four weeks later, the new Progressive Conservative MLA for Moncton East returned to his *alma mater*, the Université de Moncton, to honour his Liberal predecessor, Raymond Frenette. The campus was in the riding, and throughout the McKenna years, Frenette had been a fierce advocate for the university at the cabinet table, securing a bit of research funding here, some infrastructure dollars there, when they were available. To thank him, the university's board decided to name a new building after him. On stage during the ceremony were Frenette, who'd just been premier, Bernard Lord, who wanted to be, and Camille Thériault, who actually was.

Normally, a university president in New Brunswick is deferential to whoever happens to be the premier — even when, as was the case that year, the government cuts funding to campuses. But the cuts had forced Jean-Bernard Robichaud to increase tuition fees by ten per cent, and angry students had criticized him for not speaking out against the reduction. So Robichaud chose to use the dedication of the Frenette Building to speak out in front of a hundred assembled guests, most of them prominent, influential Acadians. His voice filling the foyer, Robichaud lamented "the flagrant lack of resources" while Premier Thériault listened uncomfortably. The new building, named for the university's greatest champion, "is a first step in the right direction," he said, "but it's only a first step."

Embarrassing Thériault even further, Robichaud told the guests he had a question about the university's need for a new champion. "The answer may be in this room," he said, looking to the premier and then to Lord. "Who will be the next Ray Frenette among our current politicians?"

At the end of the speech, the guests applauded, but Thériault did not. He may have concluded that Robichaud was hedging his bets — calculating that deferring to the current premier was no longer as important as pleasing the new Leader of the Opposition, a young man who suddenly had the aura of victory about him.

Chapter Seventeen

THE JUMP BACK

BERNARD LORD'S IMAGE as a winner was the most important effect of his by-election triumph in Moncton East — far more important than his actual arrival in the Legislative Assembly of New Brunswick.

Granted, there was an electric atmosphere when the new session opened on November 24, 1998, and Lord took his seat in the front row of the Opposition benches. It was the first sitting since the Liberal leadership convention. Directly across the aisle, Premier Camille Thériault was getting used to his new chair as well. The game was set for the coming election.

On the first day, Lord went on the offensive, calling the government's Speech from the Throne, which emphasized Thériault's "third wave" of Liberalism, "a speech of desperation." Later in the week, he demanded the premier impose a moratorium on highway tolls until after the upcoming election. Thériault mocked the suggestion — asking if he should delay all government action until after the vote — while government members heckled Lord for a procedural error.

The sparring continued. Elsewhere, however, in the church basements and community centers of the Tory heartland, the real political drama was unfolding.

The Confederation of Regions party was effectively dead, existing only on paper and in the minds of a handful of men and women scattered around New Brunswick. Greg Hargrove, COR's unpaid, unelected leader, had applied to change the party's name to the New Brunswick Party, but was turned down by the province's chief electoral officer, who said voters might confuse the name with that of the NDP. Early in 1999, Hargrove announced he wouldn't run in the next election. "We've been brutalized so bad we can never recover," he told a reporter.

Hargrove's old riding of Mactaquac was one of the places where the implications of COR's demise first became apparent. The Progressive Conservative association had scheduled its nominating convention for August 1998, the first of fifty-five in the lead-up to the next election. Kirk MacDonald was one of four Tories selling memberships in pursuit of the nomination. "People were saying, 'You should talk to this person. I know they voted COR in the past, but you should have a conversation.'" MacDonald discovered that those voters were no longer as angry about bilingualism, and had been reassured by the PC party's promise to implement the policy "with fairness and justice." They quietly bought Tory membership cards and began attending events.

Farther up the St. John River Valley, across the fields of York and Queens counties, through the streets of Fredericton and into the hills of Kings and Albert counties — throughout the territory of the once-formidable Conservatives — the same pattern repeated itself. "One day they had to finally decide," the veteran Tory organizer Fred Beairsto says of the COR voters. "They had to make that jump back. It would not necessarily be easy for them. It would be embarrassing. It helped that the COR party was gone, so they didn't have much choice if they wanted to stay in politics."

Lynn Mason was lying in a hospital room recovering from surgery when a man he didn't know walked in and introduced himself as Peter Forbes, a lawyer who'd led protests against the federal gun registry. "I understand you have a fair grasp of politics," Forbes said to Mason. Forbes explained that he was going to be running as the Progressive Conservative candidate in Fredericton North, and he needed a campaign manager. Mason, remembering his interest in the young PC leader Bernard Lord, agreed to take on the job.

As Lord toured the heartland, shoring up the resurgent support, his anglophone roots in the back roads of York County served him well. "He was able to go in and identify with people and make them feel comfortable that this was an inclusive party," says Lisa Keenan, then party vice-president. "The fact that Bernard could express himself on both sides of the language issue helped a lot," agrees the PC president at the time, Brian Harquail. And Lord's calm, deferential demeanour reassured those who *did* see him as a francophone that he was no militant nationalist. "The fact he didn't have the attitude of Simard helped," says Paul d'Astous.

So many COR members were returning that Lord and other party officials had to soothe the bitter feelings of Tories who had remained loyal and saw what was happening as opportunism. "Anytime someone has gone on a different path than you, and then they come back and sing from the same songbook, there are suspicions," says the former leadership candidate Cleveland Allaby.

Fortunately, Lord himself hadn't been there for the trauma of the rupture over language. "I never felt that these people who left the party for a few elections and then came back had betrayed me or were disloyal to me in any way, so I didn't have any of that baggage," he says. Lord was warned the COR people would make him look bad and hurt the party in Acadian ridings. "It was more important to me to have an open party and to welcome people in than to worry about how they voted ten years ago," he says. "A lot of people viewed the former COR members just through one filter — that's the filter of language — but I believe many people supported and voted for COR for other reasons."

Even if Lord was naïve and they *had* voted COR to roll back bilingualism and crush francophone rights, he still had the Saint John policy resolutions at his disposal. "People who wanted to join us joined us knowing that those were the policies . . . adopted by the members, not imposed by the leader," Lord says. For rebuilding the Conservative coalition, principle number three, the statement on linguistic equality, was a flexible tool. While it lured COR sympathizers back with its promise of "fairness and justice," its clear endorsement of bilingualism protected Lord from accusations he was selling out to bigotry.

Still, old wounds had yet to be healed. Of the 1,110 names on the COR membership list he brought with him to the PC association in Fredericton North, Lynn Mason estimates three hundred signed up as Tories — a gain partly offset by the refusal of some long-time Conservatives to work under a campaign manager who'd supported COR.

In nearby New Maryland, the PC riding executive was divided over what role former COR MLA Max White should play at its nominating convention, scheduled for March 1999. White had bought a PC card a couple of months earlier, and some Tories had suggested he seek the nomination, but emotions ran too strong for that. "One man in particular didn't want me involved," White says. Instead, he offered to nominate Keith Ashfield, the PC candidate he'd defeated in 1991, who was interested in running again. That was contentious, too. "Half resented the idea and half welcomed the idea," says Jim Blake, a member of the executive. "Some people looked at [White's time with COR] as a desertion — you know, 'You deserted the party, what are you doing coming back now?'" The executive allowed White to speak, realizing, as Blake says, that "deep down, these people were all Conservatives, and it was only a matter of time before they came back."

White's speech at the New Maryland meeting finally gave the public a glimpse of the reconciliation taking place in the PC party. Other Conservative conventions in the former COR ridings were jammed. In Albert, six hundred people attended. In York, a thousand members pressed into Harvey High School to see Stephen Little, the COR candidate in 1995, second the nomination of Don Kinney. "A lot of these COR people basically said, if we don't get back on the same page, the Liberals will keep walking down the middle," Kinney says.

Events were moving so quickly that even Arch Pafford, the founding president and first leader of COR, got caught up in the excitement of the Conservative coalition.

Pafford's account of how he almost became a PC candidate in Miramichi Centre doesn't quite match Lord's, just as Pafford's recollection of his negotiations with Dennis Cochrane are at odds with Cochrane's. The way Pafford tells it, someone in the local PC party approached him about running, and he met secretly with Lord and Dale Graham in Miramichi. "I explained that I could live with what he was proposing," Pafford says.

With fairness and justice. That key phrase from the policy resolution persuaded the founder of COR to become a Tory again. That, and the balance he saw in the party's young leader. "I told him I liked his policies, I liked the individual, I liked everything about him," Pafford gushes.

Pafford says Lord wanted him to run but insisted he had to take it to his caucus for approval. "I don't know what kind of reaction I'm going to get," Pafford remembers Lord telling him, "but I'll do it — I'll get back to you." He says Lord later called to say the MLAs had no objection, but then, as the nominating convention approached, Pafford suffered some chest pains and was forced to call off his return to the political mainstream. "It wasn't worth the gamble for me to pursue it," he says, "even though I was welcome."

Lord's recollection is that Pafford approached him but that the idea didn't go very far. "We talked about the principles of the PC party and felt it would be more difficult for Arch to run for us than others because of the high profile," Lord says, "and eventually he decided not to run." Instead, the nod went to a young woman named Kim Jardine, who had the backing of former COR members at the convention, including Pafford. Lord, the guest speaker, acknowledged Pafford's presence from the podium, a moment Pafford remembers fondly. "I thought that was quite big of him," he says proudly.

Two weeks later, another prominent ex-COR member, Tony Huntjens, the former party president, captured the PC nomination in Western Charlotte. Though he'd railed against the Tories in 1995, Huntjens now found the party a good fit. "They had taken on some of the philosophies that COR had," he says. "That's the grassroots system — making people's voices heard. . . . I liked the whole message, the way [Lord] approached it — the inclusion issue, which I felt was absolutely necessary." Lord's francophone roots remained in the background, Huntjens says. "When I hear him talk, he's always talking about that he's originally from McAdam."

Huntjens says Tories welcomed him warmly. "I think people knew where I was coming from, and I made it very clear. . . . I was honest. I told them what I did and why I did it. I still today make no apologies for that. I think my choices even then were honourable and were right." But other Conservatives were nervous: the migration of COR voters to the PC party was becoming a media story just as an election call appeared imminent. "I was worried about it," says Barbara Winsor, then the party's executive director. "I was worried that maybe it would hurt us in the francophone areas."

That thought had occurred to the Liberals as well.

The first to attack Lord was Kevin Fram, who'd almost ousted Brad Green from the PC Youth presidency in 1986. Fram had become a Liberal in the early 1990s and took a leave from Prime Minister Jean Chrétien's office to run against Lord now in Moncton East. Admitting his continuing admiration for Richard Hatfield in front of a room full of Liberals at his nominating convention, Fram accused Lord of betraying the late premier's legacy. "If you want francophones and anglophones to live together in the spirit of harmony, then you must say no to the merged 'COR-servative' party. This province has come too far over the past thirty to forty years to go back now just because Bernard Lord thinks it's politically expedient to attract COR support."

It was a brazen attack, but Liberals were quietly delighted that Fram was saying of Lord what other Liberals would not. In fact, as Fram revealed in an interview, there was nothing maverick about it. His remarks had been carefully planned and scripted by the Liberal campaign team, and his instructions had come directly from Mario Thériault, the premier's brother and senior election strategist.

Fram's assault was only the first of many. Two days later, when the election campaign began, Camille Thériault's Liberals set out to rip apart the coalition Bernard Lord had spent eighteen months methodically stitching together.

* * *

Camille Thériault visited the lieutenant-governor on the morning of Saturday, May 8 to sign the writs, then went off to his first Liberal rally. But Bernard Lord hadn't waited for him: he'd already released portions of his election platform, "New Vision — New Brunswick," earlier in the week and had rolled out his campaign bus for a photo opportunity. It was a pre-emptive strike to seize the initiative and show voters that, after twelve long years, the Progressive Conservative party was ready to be taken seriously again.

Lord needed to make an impression quickly. The last pre-campaign poll, released in March, showed fifty-three per cent of decided voters intended to vote Liberal and twenty-eight per cent PC. Thériault's team conceded privately that Lord would gain seats — perhaps as many as fifteen or twenty in all — but a Liberal victory was inevitable.

Even so, the Liberals hammered Lord on COR. "We have the right to be worried as francophones," cabinet minister Bernard Thériault said at his nominating convention in Caraquet the first Monday of the campaign. Though the premier refused to endorse the attacks, he didn't stop them. Two days later, Greg O'Donnell, the francophone MLA for Dieppe-Memramcook, questioned Lord's acknowledgement of Arch Pafford at the Miramichi Centre meeting — though O'Donnell embellished somewhat. "You know as well as I do what he stands for," O'Donnell said. "And Bernard Lord brings this man up on the podium? . . . Anybody who [supports] the principles of Richard Hatfield cannot support Bernard Lord."

The Liberals were certain they had a wedge they could drive between the factions in the PC party. If the attacks forced Lord to speak in favour of bilingualism, he risked alienating the COR voters; if he hedged, he'd have problems in French-speaking ridings.

But Lord had already immunized himself. Whenever a French-speaking Liberal candidate vowed to protect francophone rights from the PC threat, Lord would ask why that Liberal hadn't spoken up for the parents of Saint-Sauveur and Saint-Simon. "He stayed in his seat rather than defend the people of the Acadian Peninsula," Lord told reporters after the attack from Bernard Thériault.

Each of Lord's PC candidates in French-speaking ridings hauled out the same weapon: item number three from the party's statement of principles, voted on by the entire membership. "I had to make it clear that these [former COR] people were adhering to our policies and principles, and that included support for official bilingualism," says Louis-Philippe McGraw, a young Acadian lawyer running for the Conservatives in the riding of Centre-Péninsule. McGraw would also highlight Lord's French roots, which were played down to former COR voters. "To anglophones he's an anglophone, and for francophones, he's a francophone," McGraw says. "I'd tell [voters] he's married to a girl from the Peninsula and he went to the Université de Moncton, and we don't have anything to worry about with him."

Lord had balanced his appeal so perfectly that, according to Kevin Fram, he actually welcomed the Liberal attacks. Fram says Lord told him after the election he'd been happy the Liberals went after him on COR. "He'd wanted [Camille] Thériault to come out and do it," Fram says, because — with his francophone credentials established

— the criticism only helped solidify Lord's support among former COR voters.

The Liberals quickly realized the tactic was not having much effect on Acadian voters. "We thought [Lord's reaching out to COR] would backfire more in the francophone areas than it did," says Mario Thériault. The attacks ceased altogether after Robert Pichette, a one-time aide to former premier and Liberal icon Louis Robichaud, penned columns for the *Telegraph-Journal* and *L'Acadie Nouvelle* condemning what he called "binges of demagoguery" from the Liberal candidates. He accused the party of disturbing the linguistic peace to win votes. "To me, this was most un-Liberal," Pichette says. He wrote the columns in a deliberate attempt to shut down the attacks, and it seemed to work.

Lord's coalition-building skills had passed their first test in the heat of a campaign. Ever balanced, the PC leader had assured reporters, "I'm proud that my children have both Acadian and British blood, and I'll protect that heritage" — a curious line that sounded like a tortured attempt at eloquence. The significance of the phrasing would be clear only after election day.

* * *

As the leaders raced across the province, Thériault dogged by the Tollbusters and Lord vowing to renegotiate the deal, the highway project — though it affected only about a dozen ridings — came to define both men. The Liberal premier's refusal to budge linked him to all the other controversies McKenna had left behind. And the PC challenger's willingness to eliminate the tolls made him the solution to all the grievances people had with the government. Norm Betts, knocking on doors as the PC candidate in Southwest Miramichi, would introduce himself and his party and get no reaction. But when he mentioned change, he recalls, "they'd get all enthused: 'Oh yes, it's time for a change.'" Liberal candidates felt it, too. "There was the perception that the Liberal team was not listening to people the way we should have done," says Al Kavanaugh, campaigning to keep the Riverview riding he'd won from COR in 1995.

The momentum of the election began to turn.

Midway through the campaign, at a rally in Pont-Lafrance, a small community outside Tracadie-Sheila, two hundred Liberals gathered in a community hall to cheer their candidate, a bookish law professor named Serge Rousselle. Rousselle was attempting to unseat Conservative MLA Elvy Robichaud. Despite his being mired in opposition, Robichaud had become even more popular since his 1994 by-election win. Still, logic suggested Rousselle had a chance. He'd been doing one thing the incumbent could not do: bringing home the spoils of power. He listed recent government funding decisions for Tracadie that were the result of his lobbying. "If I can do that as a candidate, imagine what I can do as an MLA," he said.

But there was an odd feeling in the room that night in Pont-Lafrance. A Liberal win was still inevitable. Yet something wasn't quite right.

The malaise grew after the English and French television debates on May 25. Having won first pick of seating positions, Thériault opted for the right side of the stage, allowing Lord to take the centre, with NDP leader Elizabeth Weir on the left. Lord was thus the focus, and his frequent gazes into the lens — right into the living rooms of New Brunswickers — made him likeable, while Thériault appeared scripted and hesitant to "look the viewers in the eye." The two men clashed about taxes, economic development and highway tolls, and though there was no real winner, Lord came off as equal to the premier, and thus a plausible aspirant for the job.

Minor irritants for the Liberals now became major portents. The day after the debate, Kevin Fram removed Thériault's picture from his billboards in Moncton East. Fram called it a coincidence, but Tories chortled. The same day, the Moncton *Times-Transcript* ran an interview with an astrologer who'd been provided with the dates of birth of the three party leaders. "All signs point to Lord victory," said the front-page headline.

A more scientific assessment — a new public opinion poll by ATV News — confirmed two days later what everyone was sensing. The Tories had moved ahead with thirty-two per cent of decided voters, against twenty-seven for the Liberals. It was the first lead the party had enjoyed in a poll since Richard Hatfield was premier. Subsequent polls seesawed back and forth, but that ATV survey changed the psychology of the election.

The exigency that had destroyed COR four years earlier — the need to be a partner in power — began to turn against the government. In francophone ridings in the north, and in former COR constituencies in the Tory heartland, the Liberals had stressed the importance of being "on the government side." Now the assumption underlying that pitch — that they would continue to govern — was evaporating. Thériault began warning that Lord would squander the prosperity McKenna had created, but his tactic only confirmed he was losing. "The public had parked their votes with [Thériault]," one Liberal says, in explaining the positive pre-election polls. "They'd given him the benefit of the doubt." But "Lord exceeded all expectations," a Tory insider says, "so he could only go up, whereas Camille and the Liberals had been there so long, so they would have had to do extremely well." Lord agrees Thériault was a victim of bad timing. "In many ways he was in the wrong place at the wrong time. Those who want to blame him are missing a lot of the picture. The McKenna agenda caught up with him."

In the final week of the campaign, Lord met Richard Hatfield's former executive assistant, Win Hackett, at a breakfast rally in Saint John. "Confidentially, Win," Lord told him, "the numbers are enormous." There was little that could stop him now.

* * *

Then, just when the last undecided voters were making up their minds — among them Acadians who were contemplating voting PC for the first time in their lives — Tony Huntjens, the former COR president turned PC candidate, chose to share his thoughts on that most cherished francophone achievement, duality in the school system, with a reporter for Radio-Canada, the French-language network of the CBC.

"People want to learn to live together; they want unity," Huntjens said in a story that aired Wednesday, June 2, five days before the election. "They don't want a dual Department of Education, for example, and spend twice as much money than they need to on the bureaucracy of education. That money could be better spent in the actual classroom. We're duplicating things. I still maintain we're segregating. We're living in a world where people must learn to live together, and — this is my personal point of view — I don't believe we can continue to segregate people and think we're going to have a healthy future."

News of the remarks, which also included a critique of government subsidies for Acadian cultural events, struck the campaigns like a torpedo. "Linguistic Duality Questioned by a PC Candidate," screamed the front-page headline in *L'Acadie Nouvelle* the following morning. Bernard Thériault, the Liberal candidate in Caraquet, quickly rejigged a half-page advertisement he'd purchased for the paper. The Liberals, the ad now said, would defend bilingualism, duality and Acadian culture "unlike other political parties." Thériault knew the Conservatives had a narrow window of time in which they might recover. His ad would appear on a Friday and *L'Acadie Nouvelle* did not publish on Saturdays, meaning Lord had only one opportunity — Friday morning's paper — to reverse the damaging perception.

The Conservatives knew it, too. Tracking polls from that Wednesday evening, taken after the Huntjens story was broadcast during the supper hour newscast, showed PC numbers dipping in French New Brunswick. Meeting voters on their doorsteps in Nigadoo-Chaleur, Conservative candidate Hermel Vienneau saw the effect immediately. "They said they would be happy to vote for me if it wasn't for that statement by one of our candidates."

Campaign strategists got in touch with Huntjens. "We had a chat with him," Barbara Winsor says, "and told him not to talk to anybody." A letter was drafted over his name — in case it was required — in which Huntjens would resign as a PC candidate. Meanwhile, Lord repudiated the comments. "The French population in New Brunswick has fought hard to have their schools," he said, "and it is protected by the Charter of Rights in the Constitution and will remain that way."

By a stroke of luck, Lord was scheduled to campaign that Thursday with his candidate Hermel Vienneau in Nigadoo-Chaleur, which was also home to the head office of the Société des Acadiens et Acadiennes du Nouveau-Brunswick, the main francophone lobby group. Vienneau cancelled plans to take Lord canvassing and invited the SAANB to meet the PC leader at the local campaign headquarters. The SAANB had asked to meet him earlier, to discuss strengthening the 1969 Official Languages Act, but he'd begged off. Now he needed them.

The society's executive director, Daniel Thériault, hadn't been sure what to make of Lord's linguistic balancing act until then. "Because he was in the Conservative party, because the previous leader was a francophone, it was like he was trying not to be seen as a francophone," Thériault remembers. "He was afraid to be seen as a francophone because, in his party, it might cause him problems. *We* see him as a francophone — more than he presents himself as one."

In the privacy of Vienneau's campaign office, Lord assured the SAANB that he wouldn't touch spending on Acadian cultural events, and that he'd study — not implement, but *study* — the upgrade of the language law they wanted. "It was reassuring, but it was still pretty timid," Thériault says. Still, SAANB president Ghislaine Foulem afterwards told reporters she was satisfied. Lord told the journalists he'd examine an overhaul of the act "very seriously" and pointed out that a strong contingent of Acadian MLAs in his government would certainly advance the issue. For good measure, he reminded them that *his* vision of duality in education included local elected school boards — "contrary to what is the case now," he said, "given that the Liberal party took away the rights of parents and communities to run their schools."

Lord had dodged the torpedo. Friday's front-page headline in *L'Acadie Nouvelle* quoted his promise to study a revision of the law, and the story highlighted his not-too-subtle reminder about Saint-Sauveur and Saint-Simon. By Monday, election day, the affair had vanished from the news. "It was an uncomfortable couple of days," Huntjens recalls now. "Although it was a hot issue in some areas, it was quickly forgotten compared to the important issue, which was to make a change in government. I can't think of another reason why people would let it go that quickly."

* * *

That last Friday of the campaign, Conservative strategists estimated they were winning in thirty-eight or thirty-nine of the province's fifty-five ridings. On Saturday morning, a last poll predicted a PC victory. Then, over the weekend, several Liberal seats in French New Brunswick moved into the PC column. "People who had never been with us said they were with us because there was going to be a PC government," Percy Mockler would say. On election day, Lord won forty-four seats, an astounding result for a leader who'd entered the campaign in distant second place. The Liberals won ten, and NDP leader Elizabeth Weir held her riding. COR's candidates averaged 156 votes in each of the eighteen ridings they contested.

The scope of the victory was stunning: all eight seats won by COR in 1991, and then by Liberals in 1995, went Tory. So did thirteen of the twenty seats with large francophone populations. All nine incumbent Tories were re-elected, while more than a dozen Liberal ministers lost. The Conservatives won every riding along the toll highway, and in the rural Tory heartland, and in the five largest cities, with the exception of Weir's. Nepisiguit, the constituency that includes Saint-Sauveur, went PC. Caraquet remained Liberal, but the polling stations in tiny Saint-Simon went Conservative, 239 to 235.

Lord's caucus would reflect the breadth of the Conservative coalition. Young men from the next generation of Acadians, such as Louis-Philippe McGraw and Paul Robichaud, who couldn't remember a New Brunswick without an Official Languages Act, would sit at the same table as two men who had once pledged to repeal that act, Tony Huntjens, elected in Western Charlotte, and former COR member David Jordan, who had defeated the Liberal deputy premier in Grand Lake. Two of Lord's leadership rivals, Norman Betts and Margaret-Ann Blaney, were also elected. Bev Harrison, who'd led the revolt against Hatfield in 1985, was returned to the Legislature after twelve years to join Percy Mockler, who'd fought to save Hatfield.

Three days after the election, voters learned something new about the young man they'd chosen to be their premier. News stories reported a burst of local pride in the Lac-Saint-Jean area of Quebec, particularly in Roberval, where Bernard Lord had been born. A few New Brunswickers had known this, but most had not. Lord's official campaign biography said only that he had grown up in Moncton. Now the import of that tortured phrasing, "my children have both Acadian and British blood," became clear. Though technically accurate — the "Acadian blood" came from Lord's wife Diane — the statement steered the curious away from Lord's origins in the hotbed of Quebec nationalism, roots that might well have alarmed former COR voters.

"I've always been clear on that fact," Lord said testily in an interview for this book, denying any political calculation. "A campaign biography doesn't include all the details of everything. If anybody would have asked me, as I'm sure many people did, I'm sure I said

I was born in Roberval, Quebec, but that New Brunswick is home."
In fact, a Conservative insider admitted that the campaign staff was
relieved that no one *did* ask.

It was a small but important reminder of the ambiguity at the
heart of Bernard Lord's appeal. To Acadians, the francophone Lord
had promised to study expanding the Official Languages Act. To
former COR voters, the anglophone Lord had implicitly promised
the status quo: adherence to the existing law — "with fairness and
justice," of course — and nothing more.

Those two groups of voters, seemingly irreconcilable, had won the
election for him. Now, having fulfilled the primary objective of any
political party leader — the acquisition of power — the new premier
would have to decide what to do with it and which Bernard Lord he
wanted to be.

Chapter Eighteen

HOLDING THE CENTRE

THE PROGRESSIVE CONSERVATIVES took power with barely concealed glee. It had been twelve long years since Richard Hatfield had led them to disaster and eight since the party had been told it might disappear altogether, a victim of the language chasm that was then opening in New Brunswick politics.

But as Bernard Lord and his cabinet were sworn in on a sunny June day outside the Legislative Assembly, all that was far in the past. New Brunswickers had voted PC across linguistic lines, restoring and expanding Hatfield's coalition to a breadth even he could not have imagined. Four French-speaking ridings in the north had francophone MLAs in the fifteen-member cabinet. If Lord were counted among them, one-third of the Progressive Conservative cabinet was francophone, a perfect reflection of the province's population.

Balance was the order of the day. Lord's patronage appointments in the months to come would include Conservatives who'd fought internal fights but had proven their loyalty in the end. Hank Myers, who'd run for the leadership in 1991, became head of the dairy regulatory commission, while Scott MacGregor, who'd sought it in 1995, was made chairman of a tax assessment appeal board. Keith Dow, one of the musketeers who'd tried to oust Hatfield, joined the hospital board in Saint John, and Max White, the former COR MLA who'd returned to the Tories, was named to the Fredericton board. The message, even if Lord didn't send it consciously, was that when the party's factions work together, the party wins, and the spoils of power are made available.

As party leader, then, Lord remained faithful to that notion of power. But as head of government, he veered boldly away from the centre with his first major initiative — and learned a potent lesson.

Lord spent his first six months as premier easily fulfilling his "200 Days of Change," an election platform gimmick that made him appear dynamic. He held press conferences at which he checked off each of twenty items with a felt marker on an oversized poster. Most were easy, like asking a committee of MLAs to devise a model for re-establishing school boards. He missed the deadline for only one, the elimination of tolls on the new highway, but soon reached a deal with the highway consortium to let the province pay the debt that would have been covered by toll revenue. The Liberals said the arrangement would cost the province far more than the tolls, but the promise was kept.

After the two hundred days days, Lord faced harder decisions. An external audit predicted budget deficits totalling $450 million over five years, forcing Lord to tilt toward fiscal conservatism. He unveiled his less centrist face in January at the annual meeting of the New Brunswick Federation of Agriculture. When he listed his government's five priorities — education, health care, job creation, government reform and better fiscal management — farming was conspicuously absent. "Some things are bound to change in the way the government will work with the agriculture industry," he warned. "We have to live within our means, and we have to meet the most important needs of New Brunswickers."

Lord reorganized his government in March, merging the departments of agriculture and fisheries into a single entity called Food Production, cutting seven programs and laying off seventy five employees, including forty specialized veterinarians. "Our department has been slaughtered," the president of the agricultural federation told reporters. But the premier asked whether the government should fund support staff, such as legal secretaries, for other sectors. "People in agriculture are really like business people and should be treated like other business people," he said.

The new, bold Bernard Lord did not go over well. A few days after the announcement, he convened an emergency meeting of his caucus to explain the cuts to backbench MLAs who hadn't been briefed yet. Like most campaigning leaders, Lord had promised to give back-benchers more power, but that wasn't in evidence now. "Some of them raised concerns in caucus that they heard from their constituents, and that's good because that is the role of an MLA," the premier told a newspaper.

A week later, Lord was in Sussex, a Kings County town at the heart of the province's dairy industry and the Tory vote. A convoy of more than a hundred tractors wound its way down the town's main street to the motel where he was speaking. "If nothing else at least the Lord government has united the farmers of New Brunswick," said one of the organizers of the protest. A crowd of farmers shouted and laughed at him and — perhaps most damaging to his image as a consensus-builder — accused him of not having consulted them.

Two days later, Lord backed down, at least temporarily, by extending the phasing in of the cuts "to ensure the consultation process takes place," he said. He also reversed himself on the name of the department, relabelling it the Department of Agriculture, Fisheries and Aquaculture. He now calls the Sussex episode "a growing experience for me as premier and as an individual," though he's vague about what he means. "People wanted to talk to me as their premier and tell me they were not happy, and that was clear to me," he says.

One of Lord's most loyal advisors says he became "diffident" for a time after Sussex, more timid and less quick to make decisions. Some committees that had been asked to study important issues missed deadlines, and the government took its time choosing how to act on the eventual recommendations. His then finance minister, former leadership rival Norm Betts, says the premier's consultative style was one of his greatest strengths, but, he adds, "I think everybody got a little frustrated sometimes with a little bit of procrastination. We'd joke about that. I'd say, 'Geez, Bernard, I'd make this decision tonight,' and he'd say, 'Between the two of us, we should have it just about right,' because I'm just the opposite. I'm impetuous. I'd have a problem the other way." Hermel Vienneau, on taking over as the premier's chief of staff in 2002, would admit to a reporter, "People think we aren't making decisions."

"It'd be a lot easier for me not to consult, not to talk to anybody, just make decisions," Lord responds in a way that burnishes his consensus-builder image. "But it's not making decisions that's important, it's making the *right* decisions. The decisions I make don't just have an impact this week or next week. They have a lasting impact for months, for years and sometimes for decades. So taking the appropriate time to allow other people to express their points of view, to get information, to understand all the different aspects of an issue is the appropriate way to make a decision."

Explained that way, Lord's cautious style is an asset, not a liability. But the rapid, no-consultation model that he criticizes is precisely the one he adopted in the agriculture department, which led farmers to jeer him and backbenchers to wonder about the clout they'd been promised. It appeared that Lord had had to relearn the merits of caution and balance after he'd seen the pitfalls of boldness in March 2000.

The premier's post-Sussex diffidence created a new problem within the government: his "impetuous" finance minister, Norm Betts, juggling myriad labour disputes and high-profile budget initiatives, began to appear more decisive than Lord. "It seemed like every week for two years I was on the panel on CBC," Betts says. "They'd call down and someone would say, 'Send Betts.' I was just doing the job that the premier wanted me to do. I really believed in what we were doing, and therefore I had a willingness to go out there and sell it."

After Lord choked up in the Legislature in December 2000 over a newspaper cartoon that took a sexist jab at Margaret-Ann Blaney, the other leadership rival he'd put in his cabinet, tongues began wagging around Fredericton that the premier was weak and Betts was in charge. "We've drawn the conclusion here that it's Mr. Betts who is calling the shots," said one union leader who negotiated contracts with the government. Donald Savoie, an expert on governance at the Université de Moncton, told CBC Radio that "there's a great deal of talk . . . that [Betts] has far too much power, far too much influence in terms of the agenda, that he shapes it and not the premier. What I do not know is if that's a problem in terms of perception or in terms of reality. Clearly, there is a perception problem, because people are talking about it."

The suggestion angered Lord's political staff. "If it caused any problem, it caused a problem with people around the premier who believed it," Betts says. "At the Norm Betts – Bernard Lord level, there wasn't an issue. But it got to the point where some of his communications people thought I was out there a little too much." One staffer counters that Betts "wanted to be the premier" and Lord, balanced to a fault, was too accommodating. "His 'strength,'" the staffer says, "is that he forgives everybody for everything. He can get past it and not everyone can. I can't." A Conservative insider adds, "It was the staff causing the trouble. . . . There was a push to ensure Betts was not too prominent. They didn't want a Paul Martin scenario," a reference to Martin's growing control of the federal agenda and of the Liberal party at the time.

The Liberals picked up the theme in the Legislature, referring to Betts as "the real premier." But Lord dismissed the talk as "an opposition tactic of division." The Liberals were becoming bullish, however, openly speculating that Lord could lose power after a single mandate.

Lord silenced them in February 2001 when the PC party — with the premier's smiling face prominently displayed on campaign brochures — won by-elections in Caraquet and Campbellton, two predominantly francophone ridings, following the retirement of two former Liberal cabinet ministers. Lord may have been seen as weak around Fredericton, but voters liked him.

In March, he recalled the Legislature to pass a bill forcing an end to a strike by hospital support workers, an attempt, the Liberals said, to toughen his image. If so, it worked: the union returned to negotiations and protestors at the Legislature focused their rage on Lord, not Betts. Taking on farmers might have been a mistake, but challenging unionized public-sector workers wasn't nearly as dangerous. A month later, the Tories won a third by-election in Kent South, the seat left vacant by Camille Thériault's resignation as Liberal leader and MLA.

In October, Lord surprised almost everyone by shuffling his cabinet and moving Betts out of finance and into Business New Brunswick, the department that oversaw economic development. Betts says his image as the axe-wielding bad guy had worn him out and he requested the move. With a fiscal plan — a hundred million dollar "rainy day fund" and a schedule of tax cuts — in place, "I had that 'been there, done that' feeling" about finance. Lord didn't want it to look like a demotion, Betts adds, but the perception stuck.

There was no more talk around Fredericton of who was in charge, though. Paradoxically, Lord had decisively imposed his cautious, consultative style on the government. Though criticism mounted among political observers that the premier wasn't doing much more than running affairs day by day, the public, after the tumult of endless McKenna policy innovations, seemed content with Lord's quiet, competent management.

Liberal bluster about a one-term government had evaporated by the time Conservative members gathered in Saint John in November 2001. Those who remembered Tory annual meetings during the lean years — the cheap posters, the low attendance — revelled in the record turnout of 1,800 delegates, the high-tech sound system and the brisk sales of PC merchandise. The party had paid off its debt, and an upbeat mood permeated the hall. Some delegates talked of repeating Frank McKenna's historic 1987 sweep of every riding in the next election.

They owed their optimism to the man at centre stage — the man who'd defied the odds to reconcile the competing interests within the party and bring them to power again. Bernard Lord basked in reflected glory in Saint John and predicted many more years of PC government. He was a consensus-builder, his one stab at boldness a forgotten mistake, and the public approved resoundingly. As Lord fielded questions in a bearpit session with Tory delegates, they applauded his answers and nodded adoringly.

Other questions went unasked however, questions of fundamental importance to the party: What existed at the core of Bernard Lord? How would his embrace of balance — and the Conservative coalition — fare in a true crisis? Was he strong enough to hold the centre?

No one expected those questions would need to be asked and answered anytime soon. No one imagined that all the strands of the PC party's long struggle over language were about to come together to test Bernard Lord.

* * *

Mario Charlebois is one of those otherwise inconsequential Canadians whose name, through a seemingly mundane brush with the lower reaches of the law, has become, in the era of the Charter of Rights and Freedoms, synonymous with the triumph of tolerance and progress.

A less likely champion would have been hard to find. Charlebois owned a duplex on Archibald Street in Moncton that he had converted into a rooming house. On February 1, 2000, a City of Moncton building inspector served him with an order telling him the conversion violated a municipal bylaw. Charlebois needed a building permit and would have to make renovations to comply with it. "I didn't apply for one, so sure, they were right in that respect," Charlebois would acknowledge. He defended himself with the one weapon he had: the Constitution.

The bylaw was written in English only, and the building inspector who'd dealt with Charlebois hadn't been able to speak to him in French. So Charlebois took the city to court, arguing that his language rights had been violated. When the trial judge dismissed his arguments, agreeing with the city that the Charter did not apply to municipalities, Charlebois, representing himself, went to the New Brunswick Court of Appeal. Given the implications of the case, the Société des Acadiens et Acadiennes du Nouveau-Brunswick, the federal Official Languages Commissioner and the Association des juristes d'expression française du Nouveau-Brunswick, a lobby group representing francophone lawyers, intervened in the hearing to support Charlebois.

The Court of Appeal released its decision on December 20, 2001. It was the court's first interpretation of Section 16(2) of the Charter, which gives French and English equal status and rights "in all institutions of the legislature and government," and of Section 16.1, which recognizes the equality of the two linguistic communities in New Brunswick. Chief Justice Joseph Daigle wrote that those sections *did* apply to municipalities, which are created by provincial legislatures that are themselves subject to the Charter. Daigle based his reasoning in part on the Supreme Court of Canada's 1999 Beaulac decision, which said language rights must be interpreted broadly and generously. Moncton's English-only bylaw, Daigle concluded, "is an outright denial of a Charter right," and a clause of Section 16.1 obligated the provincial government to protect that right.

Moncton's bylaws, and those of every other municipality in New Brunswick, were unconstitutional, Daigle continued. He froze the effect of the ruling for one year to give the province time to respond, and he suggested it consider — as a provincial government report had once proposed — a formula based on population to establish which municipalities needed bilingual bylaws.

The ruling was a political time bomb. Acadians had lobbied for years to have the Official Languages Act extend to municipalities, but such a change would be costly and contentious, particularly in heavily English cities such as Saint John, Fredericton and Miramichi. The notion had alarmed small-town anglophone mayors at the time of the Poirier-Bastarache report, and no provincial government had been willing to take the political risk. Now the Court of Appeal had dropped the decision in Bernard Lord's lap — and set the clock ticking on him and his coalition. The delicate balance he had created could be blown apart with one wrong move. "Was the premier really prepared to take that issue on?" one Tory insider asks. "Clearly, no."

"Anglophones in caucus paid attention because the language issue is always just below the surface in New Brunswick, and if you fan it, it can rise and bite you," says Norm Betts. "Francophones of the province know the Official Languages Act. It's dear to their hearts, because it's all about protecting their rights. They pay attention to the words. They pay attention to the phrases. They study it. Anglophone New Brunswickers don't, because as the majority, we have a tendency to think if it's good for them, it must be bad for us."

Now they were paying attention, watching Bernard Lord very carefully, recalling his implicit commitment to apply the existing law "with fairness and justice" and do nothing to expand its reach.

Francophones were paying attention as well. Back in March 2001, nine months before the Charlebois ruling came down, Lord had spoken at a symposium organized by the lobby group of francophone lawyers. The premise was that the 1969 language law needed an overhaul to bring it in line with the 1982 Charter. (Some elements of the 1969 law allowed the province to offer services unilingually in areas where the makeup of the population didn't warrant bilingualism, but the Charter made no such distinction.) Given Lord's promise during the campaign controversy over Tony Huntjens's remarks to study such a revision, and given that he'd repeated the promise in a Throne Speech, the lawyers' association wanted to know when he was going to deliver.

Lord had agreed to speak despite his unease with the Acadian nationalist crowd. Unlike Jean-Maurice Simard, he'd never been comfortable with them. He'd never embraced their more far-reaching goals, such as extending duality — separate linguistic branches of government — beyond the Department of Education to all government operations, as recommended by the Poirier-Bastarache report. "First and foremost, we are New Brunswickers," he says. "History has brought us together, and it's our duty to ensure we move forward as one province." Lord also questions whether Acadian nationalist organizations speak, as they claim, for all francophones. "A lot of groups out there represent different interests, but as premier my obligation is to look at the overall interests of the province. We cannot only listen to those who yell the loudest, because they may not have the right idea or the right point of view, and they may not represent everyone."

Not disposed to pander to the symposium organizers, Lord would not commit in his speech to a modernization or expansion of the language law. Instead, he echoed the promise to promote bilingualism while treating both groups "with fairness and justice," and he emphasized what he called "regional equality" — giving various areas of the province the tools to prosper economically. "That goes beyond working strictly on one law," Lord told reporters.

"People almost fell out of their seats," says Daniel Thériault of the Société des Acadiens et Acadiennes du Nouveau-Brunswick. "No one could believe it. He knew whom he was talking to. The expectations weren't very high and he didn't even meet them." Lord had been set to announce his appointment of Robert Pichette, the former aide to Louis Robichaud who'd defended him from the Liberals' COR attacks during the election, as New Brunswick's cultural ambassador to the Francophonie. But the mercurial Pichette, incensed by the speech, resigned before Lord could make the announcement. For Thériault and other activists, Lord had made his choice: he clearly didn't want to alienate the COR voters who'd supported him in 1999. "We sensed that there was this fear of a backlash," Thériault says.

Whatever the reason, a significant modernization of the Official Languages Act was not in Lord's plans. Nine months later, however, Mario Charlebois forced him to reconsider.

* * *

The Liberals, sensing Lord's caution on language policy, tried to exploit it when the Legislature reconvened on January 2, 2002, two weeks after the Charlebois decision. Reviving their campaign strategy of driving a wedge into the Conservative coalition, they demanded Lord comply with the ruling, forgo an appeal to the Supreme Court of Canada and draft new legislation. "There are basic principles at stake," said MLA Bernard Richard, the interim Liberal leader. "One is the very nature of New Brunswick as an officially bilingual province. On that position there should be no hesitation." Richard blamed Lord's inaction on the presence of former COR supporters in his caucus. "This government is very weak on language issues," he said. "The premier has a hard time taking a stand."

The government had been given sixty days to decide whether to appeal, and fifteen had already passed. Lord wouldn't be rushed. "We pondered the issues," he says, "and I certainly took the time to analyze the advice that was given to me." The justice department recommended an appeal because, Lord says, the ruling created a "very broad" definition of provincial institutions to include municipalities, something the Supreme Court might reverse.

But taking the case to the nine justices in Ottawa posed risks. Acadians, on the verge of a major legal breakthrough, might feel betrayed and abandon the PC party they'd embraced in 1999. "Legally, there may have been grounds to do it, but politically, it would have been suicide," says Hermel Vienneau, who was handling his first crisis as Lord's new chief of staff.

And going to the Supreme Court was not a simple matter of having Charlebois upheld or quashed: one of the nine justices was Michel Bastarache, the co-author of both Bill 88 and the controversial Poirier-Bastarache report that had so inflamed English New

Brunswick. His 1984 report had contained the idea of a formula on bilingual municipal services that the New Brunswick Court of Appeal had cited in its decision. "You never quite know how judges will react and what they will say," Lord says, "but we did have reports from Mr. Bastarache on some of these questions."

It was Bastarache, after all, who wrote in his infamous report that "attitudes have not evolved as they should have," then urged Hatfield to proceed anyway, ignoring his researcher's warnings that the expansion of francophone rights ought to be "founded on persuasion and not coercion." He now led the Supreme Court on language-rights cases, and his fingerprints were already all over the Charlebois decision. He'd written the 1999 Beaulac ruling, for example, which created the precedent that had forced the New Brunswick Court of Appeal to interpret the Charter broadly when it considered Moncton's bylaws. Those who knew Bastarache speculated that, given the opportunity, he might not simply uphold Charlebois but expand its reach — perhaps ordering every last city, town and village in New Brunswick to adopt bilingual bylaws and provide bilingual services.

That, Lord's advisors knew, would be a far worse political nightmare than the New Brunswick Court of Appeal ruling. The PC party had split when Hatfield had forgotten the Tory grassroots and moved too far in one direction — Bastarache's direction. Now, if Lord did what many English New Brunswickers wanted and tried to get Charlebois struck down, Bastarache might push Lord back in that direction and set the heartland ablaze again.

Lord looked to his caucus for a way out of the dilemma. If he chose not to appeal and instead drafted a new Official Languages Act, francophone members would enthusiastically support him. But he would also need to persuade those anglophone MLAs who'd been chosen as PC candidates at nominating conventions packed with hundreds of former supporters of the COR party — and who'd been elected with thousands of their votes. Those Tories thought there'd been an understanding: the linguistic status quo, "with fairness and justice," and nothing more. Now the leader who had made that implicit promise might do considerably more. "If the caucus had blown up on him," says Robert Pichette, "the entire province would have paid the price."

And yet, if anyone was suited to pull it off, if there was anyone whose style and temperament allowed him to move firmly in one direction while maintaining the balance he so cherished, it was Bernard Lord. He'd followed his instinct — go slow, consult exhaustively — on just about everything in government after the misstep of the agriculture cuts. He'd followed that instinct to the point that he was criticized for not making decisions. Now that instinct would serve him well. It would be the key to everything.

Several months earlier, in summer 2001 — after the fiasco of the symposium speech, but before the Court of Appeal had ruled on Charlebois — Lord had set up a secret consultation group within the government to explore what might be done with the Official Languages Act. At that time, his intentions were for a mere "housecleaning," in the words of one government official — the bare minimum to allow him to say he'd kept his promise, but little else, and certainly no sweeping enhancement to cover municipalities. Still, the group's early discussions were wary and tentative. The civil servants, political staffers and MLAs knew that, if they reopened the act, Acadian organizations would push the question of municipalities, risking a repeat of the turmoil of the Poirier-Bastarache process, which had been fanned in part by alarmed city and town councils.

The premier had selected two MLAs to join the group: the young Acadian lawyer Louis-Philippe McGraw, for whom francophone rights were an article of faith and an accepted reality, and Tony Huntjens, former president of COR, which had urged their repeal. "Tony was there for a strategic reason," McGraw says. "You could say, 'Look, if Tony says it's okay — he's not a big francophile — then it's probably okay." Huntjens says his role was "to make it as fair as possible for all New Brunswickers and to make it workable."

"In having those two people," says Mactaquac MLA Kirk Mac-Donald, "you had both ends of the spectrum, and bringing a diverse group together . . . lent it legitimacy."

Characteristically, Lord hadn't pushed the group to hurry during the late summer and autumn of 2001, and it had made no decisions by the time the Charlebois ruling came down in December. Now, its membership, a microcosm of the coalition in Lord's caucus, would become critical.

On January 8, 2002, the group reconvened for the first time since the ruling. Government lawyers presented the legal options, including a new law that would take its cue from Charlebois itself. The legislation, the lawyers suggested, might lay out a formula requiring municipalities to translate bylaws and provide bilingual service only if the minority language population reached a certain percentage. The New Brunswick court and, indirectly, Michel Bastarache himself in his 1984 report, had proposed such an idea, so it would have a good chance of surviving future legal challenges.

For Tony Huntjens, the formula meant that municipalities in his riding, such as St. Stephen, would not face the prospect of bilingualization. "It didn't seem feasible for communities with one or two per cent [from the minority-language group] to be bilingual," Huntjens explains. "It was an issue of how far do you go with bilingualism? It didn't seem feasible to make it mandatory to have everything done in a bilingual way." He signed off on the formula. So did Louis-Philippe McGraw, who knew that even the most militant Acadian groups saw no point in forcing a town like St. Stephen to become bilingual.

The next night, January 9, Lord had dinner at a Dieppe restaurant with francophone supporters and acquaintances in the Moncton area to canvass their views. Around the table with the premier were lawyer Ronald LeBlanc and businessman Arthur Savoie, who had first supported him in Dieppe-Memramcook during the 1995 election; Louis Léger, the son of Hatfield-era minister Omer Léger, who was now a communications consultant; Roger Ouellette, a political scientist who'd taught Lord at the Université de Moncton; Frédéric Arsenault, Hatfield's original Acadian advisor in the 1960s; Robert Pichette, Louis Robichaud's former executive assistant and a Lord defender in the 1999 election; Hermel Vienneau, the premier's new chief of staff; Marie-France Pelletier, a young advisor from his office; and Daniel Allain, Lord's constituency assistant in Moncton East.

"The premier was certainly reluctant even at that late stage" to forgo an appeal and update the law, one participant says, and "did not have an easy evening" after citing several reasons why he *should* go to the Supreme Court. Others recall Lord's leaning against an appeal and in favour of a new law. The unofficial advisors around the table were unanimous that it was the only course he could take — the only course that would show his mettle as a leader. "It wasn't a legal question, it was a political question," one guest says. "It wasn't up to the Department of Justice. It was up to the premier — and he should not appeal."

Frédéric Arsenault spoke up and, gesturing at Pichette and at himself, reminded Lord that they represented a link with more than thirty years of history. He also reminded the premier that Robichaud and Hatfield had endured far more difficult political tests than the one he faced now, and by enduring those tests, they'd moved the province to a point that made Lord's task far easier than it might have been.

Behind those words, one dinner guest detected that Arsenault and Pichette envied Lord's opportunity to do something historic.

"It helped me get a better understanding of the issues and how this had evolved over time," Lord says of the dinner. "It made me appreciate the work they had gone through and the efforts they had devoted to this question. It certainly helped me get a broader historical context for this decision that I was about to make."

"The dinner was decisive," one of the guests remembers. "That was when he decided he was going to take it on and deal with it and make it his own."

* * *

The Liberals had been certain Lord would falter in the face of the challenge Charlebois posed. But on Monday, January 21, 2002, Lord announced the choice that would define him. He would *not* appeal to the Supreme Court. He would persuade his caucus and his party that the right course was to modernize the 1969 Official Languages Act — the first such overhaul in its history — to broaden its reach to municipalities. All seven New Brunswick cities would be required to have bilingual bylaws and to offer service in English and French, as would towns and villages where the minority-language group made up at least twenty per cent of the population. The province would pay the translation costs for the cities, towns and villages covered by the act.

Lord now had to oversee the drafting of the bill — the substance, the details. Again, he was the right leader at the right time. He could sell those details to uneasy MLAs because, thanks to his own anglophone roots and his connections to York County, he understood where they were coming from. He knew his fear that Michel Bastarache and the Supreme Court might not only uphold Charlebois but expand its reach would be shared.

So the new Official Languages Act — the next great step forward for francophone rights, the historic expansion of the 1969 law that Acadian activists had been clamouring for — was sold to reluctant English-speaking MLAs as just the opposite.

"One thing Bernard communicated very well," says Norm Betts, "was that this bill was all about limiting rights. The Charlebois decision blew it wide open. The Charlebois decision said, taken to its extreme, that the village of Doaktown had to have bilingual services. So the approach that the premier took in addressing it was: 'The courts have said these rights are there. Are we willing to limit them?'"

Judicial activism — the notion that unelected judges had become too powerful and were undemocratically rewriting laws with their rulings — was a favourite complaint of the political right. Lord and his caucus would strike back at that activism with the new bill. "If we in government didn't set out some clearly defined boundaries," says Kirk MacDonald, "the courts would do it for us. There was certainly a potential that every community would have to have all their bylaws in translation, regardless of what the linguistic makeup of the community might be." The bill, however, would restore the legislature's primacy in determining rights. "It was almost beyond our control," says New Maryland MLA Keith Ashfield, who represented a former COR riding. "The courts were making decisions in the absence of clear legislation. Because our legislation wasn't precise enough, you never knew how the courts were going to interpret it. We put more clarity into it and gave less latitude to the courts in their rulings."

It was perhaps the ultimate balancing act from a politician who was proving to be a master of the art. Amazingly, the premier could expand and limit francophone rights at the same time — with the same bill.

Asked about the apparent cynicism of this approach, Lord calmly explains that, yes, as a matter of fact, the legislation can indeed be seen as both a broadening and a narrowing of language rights. "In some ways, it may do both," he says. "There are new things in the act that were not there before, so is it an expansion? . . . [But] some would argue those rights were in the Constitution anyway, so is it a limitation? Some would argue it defines a reasonable threshold."

Lord says bilingual municipal service is "a concept I can support," but he also shared his MLAs' fears of judicial activism. "I did talk about that [with the caucus]. I much prefer seeing elected officials determining what the laws are, rather than having appointed judges do it for us. That's why we're elected."

But the judges of the New Brunswick Court of Appeal were not "determining what the laws are" in the Charlebois decision. The irony of Lord's argument is that the court was relying on laws that were part of the proud history of the PC party that he himself often invoked. Section 16.1 of the Charter of Rights, which the court cited, has its roots in the Conservatives' language wars. The section, which protects the equality of New Brunswick's two linguistic communities, is the direct legal descendent of Bill 88 — drafted by Jean-Maurice Simard with the help of Michel Bastarache, passed by the Legislative Assembly on July 16, 1981, and entrenched in the Charter of Rights in 1993, when COR appeared to threaten that equality.

Judges hadn't made the law in the Charlebois decision; Jean-Maurice Simard had done it by working with Richard Hatfield to persuade a doubtful PC caucus. It was the legacy of their efforts "to build a new party . . . *to do things!*" When COR, fuelled by the backlash to those efforts, stormed into the Legislature to roll it back, the Assembly opted instead to write it into the Constitution, the supreme law of the land.

Simard had died in June 2001, six months too soon to see the courts use his beloved Bill 88 for the first time. Now his vision had been accepted, albeit reluctantly, by the same Tory heartland and the same COR faction that had so detested him. They accepted it because Bernard Lord had told them, rightly, that there was little they could do: it was in the Constitution.

But it was in the Constitution because Jean-Maurice Simard had led the fight to put it there. And Simard, despite his recklessness, had always used the tools of democracy to advance his objectives. To dismiss Charlebois as the work of "appointed judges" is to belittle that achievement. The ruling represented the reason Simard joined the PC party in the first place: to work within the system of political brokerage. *To do things.*

* * *

The caucus vetted the legislation at two long meetings held in the large conference room of the Department of Education building on King Street in Fredericton. At the first meeting, Lord presented a draft and invited feedback. At the second, the revised final version was presented to the MLAs, and Lord and his assistant, Marie-France Pelletier, walked them through each section, explaining its meaning and implications.

MLAs whose constituents might have chafed at the cost of bilingualism were sanguine because they felt part of the process. Don Kinney, who represented Danny Cameron's old riding, called the two-stage caucus review of the bill "probably one of the most open forums I've ever been involved in." David Jordan, the former COR member who'd become Tory MLA for Grand Lake, agrees: "We all had different ideas and thoughts and we could discuss that. We've always been able to speak our minds. There wasn't any 'Here's where we're going and toe the line.'"

There was no climactic confrontation those two nights, no showdown nor even a risk of one, because Bernard Lord had tended to his caucus during every step of the process and had built up a reserve of trust. "It's said that he's not flamboyant, but that was good in this case," says one of Lord's advisors. "[The MLAs] had the feeling that he would not get them into something that didn't make sense, and that he trusts them, too."

"Some of the contents that I wasn't sure of — it goes back to my trust of the premier," David Jordan says. "I felt comfortable with it."

Tony Huntjens seems to delight quietly in the fact that he'd confounded expectations with the role he played. "What we did was come up with a good compromise that is workable for the people of New Brunswick," he says. Opponents of bilingualism "think they've got an easy mark with me," he adds. "But I'm not easy on the big issue, regardless of who's talking. If an English person says something against bilingualism, I'll set them straight."

In those two caucus meetings, Lord's cautious tendency to consult and consult again allowed the Conservative party, once so badly divided over language that it had sundered, to unite behind a piece of legislation that would have a profound impact on the lives of many New Brunswickers, particularly francophones. The balance that Dennis Cochrane and Bernard Valcourt had been unable to find was there at last.

It could be argued that the legislation was *not* an achievement of leadership. The municipal provisions were forced on Lord by a court decision. Guarantees of bilingual health care service codified protections that existed in theory elsewhere. And the creation of a commissioner to investigate complaints about breaches of the act passed that hot potato away from the politicians.

And yet Lord had found a way, without creating a backlash, to correct a profound illogic: that Acadians in Moncton — one-third of the city's population — had no legal right to deal with City Hall in their own language, and that the mostly anglophone capital, Fredericton, by not offering bilingual service, had not truly been a capital for all New Brunswickers.

Lord had benefited from the relative calm in language politics, unlike the situation in 1991, but he triumphed because he had the necessary political skills to preserve that calm. "He made all the difference in how we've been able to function as a team," says Kirk MacDonald. "He understood there are certain issues in French New Brunswick and there are certain issues in English New Brunswick, and as premier you have to balance those concerns. You can't go too far towards one group or the other. I don't want to say he can be one or the other when he wants to be, but I would say of all the people I've met in politics, he has the best understanding of what makes the province tick."

"If you ask yourself what would have happened with a different leader," says Acadian MLA Louis-Philippe McGraw, "it's hard to say."

But Bernard Lord had been the leader. After the turmoil of Poirier-Bastarache and the move to oust Hatfield, after the trauma of the COR split, and after three leaders failed to reconcile the Tory base, the PC party had found redemption. The broader vision that Hatfield had had for his party had been strong enough, had been *right* enough, to endure those times. "In a way," says Louis Léger, "Bernard Lord is living Richard Hatfield's dream."

It was left to Brad Green, who at thirty-six years of age seemed to have as much institutional memory of the PC party as anyone in the Legislature, to consign those years of division to history when debate on the language bill began on June 4, 2002.

"Some observers have noted with irony that the greatest strides in recognizing the true nature of New Brunswick's linguistic character came from a Conservative politician from Carleton County whose command of the French language was, to be kind, inelegant," Green said. "Indeed, when Richard Hatfield proposed and guided through Bill 88, he did so against the history and current of his own political party, but it was precisely because he did that, without a motive of partisan advantage or favour, that his reforms took root and held legitimacy. . . . There was a time when the accepted view of many was that given the traditional support patterns of the Progressive Conservative party of New Brunswick, it could never be led by a francophone. Certainly, there were those who might have admitted the possibility, but who would have qualified it by saying that our party could never be *successfully* led by a francophone. There were even some on both sides of New Brunswick, both linguistically and politically, who argued, sadly, that it *should* never be led by a francophone.

"In this regard, the evolution and the maturity of the Progressive Conservative Party of New Brunswick parallel that of our province itself."

The debate lasted three days. Lord spoke of New Brunswick as a beacon for the rest of Canada, and Liberal Bernard Richard — who'd marched as a student in 1968 to demand bilingual services at Moncton City Hall — praised the premier's courage. Tony Huntjens told the Legislature Lord had the "genius of Solomon" for having devised such a "balanced approach" to the bill. And Percy Mockler recalled Hatfield's last mandate, from 1982 to 1987, and told the Speaker — Bev Harrison, Mockler's opponent in the bitter 1985 leadership review fight — that they shared the "common denominator" of wanting New Brunswick to be a better place. "We were here," Mockler told Harrison, "and we did the right thing."

The bill sped toward passage, with Lord and Richard working across the partisan divide to write an amendment that clarified the health care provisions and that guaranteed Liberal — and thus, with the NDP's backing, unanimous — support in the third and final vote, scheduled for Friday morning, June 7.

As MLAs gathered that morning, the government jet took off from Fredericton for Kent County. It landed at an airstrip in Bouctouche, where former Liberal premier Louis Robichaud, his wife, and his former assistant, Robert Pichette, waited. Percy Mockler bounded off the plane, greeted them warmly and ushered them aboard for the flight back to the capital.

Hermel Vienneau, Lord's chief of staff, had called Pichette to see if the former premier, now seventy-six and retired from the Senate, would attend the third-reading vote. Pichette told him only Lord himself could extend the invitation, and Lord placed the call. "Should we go?" Robichaud asked Pichette afterward. Only if the bill is to pass unanimously, Pichette told him. On Thursday, it was clear that it would, but Robichaud was reluctant: the icon of Liberalism wanted to work on his deck, and the Friday drive to Fredericton and back would ruin his plans. That was when Mockler offered the government plane. "He had already done all the calculations," Pichette says. "Who would pick up whom the following morning — it was all laid out."

On the flight to Fredericton, Mockler listened as Robichaud reminisced about his government's introduction of the first Official Languages Act in 1969. "He talked about how New Brunswick had progressed, and how each government leaves something to New Brunswick," Mockler says. "Hatfield implemented many of his policies, and Lord was putting the bar higher."

After the third-reading vote, Robichaud, his wife and Pichette were escorted onto the floor of the Legislature, taking seats along the back wall to the right of the Speaker's chair. "It is very clear, Mr. Speaker, that this new act will build upon the legacy of the former premier, Mr. Robichaud," Lord said in closing the debate. "It is a legacy that the people of New Brunswick are extremely proud of and will never forget. It is a legacy which transcends partisan politics because it goes to the fabric of who we are as a province."

Then Lord invited Louis Robichaud to take his former place on the government's front bench and address the assembly. Strictly speaking, the rules didn't allow it. "Mr. Robichaud was horrified by the thought," Pichette says. "He's a stickler for British parliamentary procedure. But Mr. Lord insisted and brought him to his former seat. It was extraordinary." Speaker Bev Harrison, another stickler for tradition, did not object.

"I am taken by emotion," Robichaud said. "I was not supposed to speak today — although I've spoken from this desk many, many times in the past." At that, the MLAs burst into applause. "I want to thank you all," Robichaud continued, "and I want to congratulate each and every one of you for the magnanimity that you've shown in your unanimity in passing this legislation, which is a masterpiece. I've read it and I'm telling you it's a masterpiece. I'm proud of all of you."

If the invitation had been a political calculation — and those around Lord insist it was not — it was brilliant: Louis J. Robichaud, a Liberal premier whose reputation had transcended partisanship, whose name was invoked by politicians of all stripes, was blessing the work of a Conservative premier, Bernard Lord.

It was a powerful symbol, for Lord owed much of his political career to Louis Robichaud. Robichaud had sown the seeds of Hatfield's Conservative success in French-speaking New Brunswick. He'd modernized Acadian communities and built a university where young francophones looked beyond the old ways, the old traditions and even the old Liberal voting patterns. And he'd created a New Brunswick where two cultures could co-exist without conflict, even within a single leader. Without Louis Robichaud, Bernard Lord might not have gone to school or studied law in French and would not have found a home in a bilingual, bicultural Progressive Conservative party.

Louis Robichaud had created Bernard Lord, and Richard Hatfield had created the coalition he led. And now Lord was building on that legacy.

The circle was complete. The centre had held.

* * *

From the most prominent opponents of official bilingualism came barely a peep. There were letters to the editor complaining about the cost of translating bylaws, notably from Jim Webb, who first brought the COR party to New Brunswick. But most who had spoken loudly against francophone rights over the years remained silent.

Max White, the former COR MLA turned enthusiastic Tory — and beneficiary of a government appointment — says of Lord's work on the language law, "I felt he did fairly well with it. We will assess it more as time goes on, but I think he's handling it fairly well." As a member of the Fredericton hospital board, White would help implement sections of the law dealing with health care. "We are trying to put it in practice," he said in 2003. "I said I would support it, but I would obviously watch it as time went on to make sure it was working effectively. I think it's going to work. I hope it's going to work."

Arch Pafford, COR's first leader, still glowing at the tribute Lord paid to him in Miramichi in 1999, said in an interview, "I think he's very sensitive to the language issue, to the plight of the French *and* English people. If there's a common sense approach to these things, you don't have a problem at all."

Even Len Poore, whose New Brunswick Association of English-Speaking Canadians had given the COR party its backbone, said early in 2003, "I like the way he's operating that government. He sets up committees and studies things. He doesn't just say 'We're doing it.' He studies things. He doesn't move too fast. He's not dictatorial." In an interview in his living room on Fredericton's north side, where he had plotted his moves against bilingualism, Poore allowed that tensions might not have spun out of control back in 1984 had Bernard Lord been in charge then. "I think he would have handled it better, not just coming out and saying, 'Here's what we're going to do.'"

"The only thing that bothers me," Poore volunteered, "and I wonder now, is why when he graduated he wouldn't swear allegiance to the Queen, and that bothers me. But," he added, his face brightening, "he did it when he became premier."

Poore was asked whether he considered Bernard Lord to be English or French. Ten long seconds went by as he pondered this.

"I would have to say —*French*," he decided at last. But he really had to think about it.

* * *

The new law was not the only milestone in New Brunswick language politics in the spring of 2002, not the only testament to Bernard Lord's political abilities.

Colby Fraser, an early COR party enthusiast who'd run federally in 1988, had taken on the all-but-irrelevant title of leader after the

1999 provincial election. By 2001, the entire party apparatus consisted of a computer and a few files in the basement of his home in Grand Bay-Westfield, outside Saint John. "Yeah, this is quite a step from when we had an office and we had a secretary," he admitted to a reporter who visited him that autumn.

In October, Fraser mailed out a questionnaire to COR's dwindling membership, asking if it was time to wind up the party. "If you can't get the workers," he explains, "and they come right out and say, 'Why continue?' — they may support you, but if they're not interested for whatever reason, you've got to say, 'Well, is it worth my while to continue as a party?'"

The results of the questionnaire were clear. On March 20, 2002, Fraser performed his last act as leader, writing to Annise Hollies, the province's chief electoral officer. "Dear Ms. Hollies," the letter began. "As of March 31, 2002, and pursuant to Section 139(2) of the Elections Act, please cancel the registration of the COR Party of New Brunswick, and the district associations of the Party. Thank you." It was signed, "Colby Fraser, Leader, COR Party of New Brunswick."

Thirteen years after its inception, the Confederation of Regions party passed into history.

Chapter Nineteen

"AN ORDINARY JUGGERNAUT"

AN OLD TRICK of organizing political events involves booking a venue not quite large enough for the number of people you're expecting. Once the place is jammed with supporters, pressed elbow-to-elbow so they can barely move, you cite this as evidence of strong support.

Lisa Keenan, the president of the Progressive Conservative Party of New Brunswick, knew that trick. But there was no way she could have orchestrated what happened in Edmonton, Alberta, on August 23, 2002, as hundreds of federal PC members crammed into a hotel suite to meet Bernard Lord.

Keenan, a Saint John lawyer, had taken over as provincial president after the 1999 election, and she'd reserved the suite for a reception following Lord's keynote speech to the federal party's annual general meeting. She'd planned on fifty or so delegates stopping in, but hundreds were coming, trundling over from the convention hall, bursting out of the elevators by the dozen, following the sounds of the crowd down the corridor, cramming into the suite, trying to meet the premier of New Brunswick. "He never even got into the room," Keenan says. "He just stood outside. I just stepped back and watched all these people. It was just amazing."

Lord hadn't been sure whether to attend the federal party meeting at all. Through the summer it had been shaping up as a showdown over the leadership of Joe Clark, the former prime minister, who had come out of retirement in 1998 to keep the party alive. Clark's credibility had helped it win twelve seats in the 2000 election, avoiding its predicted demise yet again. But there was a growing sense that he was not the man to take the next step: luring back right-wing supporters of the Canadian Alliance while preserving Toryism's appeal to moderates in the east, thereby ending the vote-splitting that had created a decade of Liberal hegemony in Ottawa. Leading up to Edmonton, where Clark faced a leadership review vote, more and more federal Tories were urging him to quit.

The convention might turn ugly, and Bernard Lord wanted no part of it. Additionally, there had been a bit of talk that he might have a future in Ottawa someday, so his presence in Edmonton would only cause Clark more headaches. And he was suffering from a cold. But Keenan and others persuaded him to attend. He also decided to publicly endorse Clark.

Then, on August 6, Clark had given in and announced his resignation — after Lord had agreed to deliver the keynote speech on the opening day of the convention. Clark's decision turned Edmonton into a "positioning" opportunity for Conservatives who might run for his job: a chance to network with hundreds of Tories from across the country.

Lord, in the keynote spot, was in the best position of all. "Our party has a tremendous opportunity ahead of it," he told the delegates in a speech he'd spent half the night writing in longhand. "The political landscape in Canada is changing even as we meet. It is at a turning point." The federal party, Lord said, could win again "by reaching out to people, by opening the doors, by inviting people in and bringing people together. It's what we did in New Brunswick." He told the story of the 1987 wipe-out and the advent of COR. "Our party was not just attacked from without," he said. "It split from within."

Now, Lord related, a former COR president had become a PC MLA who'd supported the new Official Languages Act. "Those members came back," Lord said, "because, first and foremost, we welcomed them back. But just as importantly, new voters came forward because we learned how to be a truly provincial party once again — a party that spoke for all New Brunswickers, not just a few." And that had allowed his party to surge in the polls during the 1999 campaign, jumping from nine to forty-four seats.

The delegates were sold, not just on the New Brunswick experience, but on the young man who'd made it happen. Speaking with a passion rarely glimpsed in his home province, switching effortlessly between English and French, Lord looked like exactly what the federal party needed. Tories could believe again that they might actually emerge from their decade-long stalemate with the Alliance and its predecessor, the Reform Party, to win again.

There were important distinctions between the two situations. Despite its own internal problems, the Alliance had done what COR could not, successfully transforming itself from a grassroots protest party into a serious, disciplined political machine. While COR had lost all its seats after one term, the Alliance had held its vote in consecutive federal campaigns in 1993, 1997 and 2000. Its growth might have stalled, but it was unlikely to disappear anytime soon.

Still, the broad brushstrokes of the New Brunswick story — of Lord's story — were what Tories had been dreaming of, and talk spread in the hall: *He's the one.* The vast majority of Conservatives did not know the exquisite duality of his biography — the roots in rural, English York County and in the Quebec nationalist bastion of Lac-Saint-Jean — but they sensed that this was a man who could woo voters in Red Deer and Rimouski. John Crosbie, the former federal cabinet minister from Newfoundland, told journalists Lord's speech was "a masterpiece" and said he was "obviously now the leading contender" for the leadership.

Reporters swooped in on Lord, already surrounded by adoring delegates. "I'm not running, I'm not running, I'm not running," the premier told the journalists as Tory matrons reached out to touch his hand. "The speech was good," Lisa Keenan says, "but it was the response to the speech that was so amazing." Close to 750 people jammed into the hotel hallway afterward for the reception, all of them wanting to greet Lord.

The notion of Lord's entering the race to succeed Clark had been so outlandish that Keenan hadn't given much thought to its consequences. And though he'd cast a spell over the Edmonton meeting, she was reassured by his insistence to reporters and delegates that he was staying in New Brunswick. Over dinner that evening, Keenan says, Lord tried to fathom the reaction to his speech. "He said, 'It's a desperation. People are just looking for an alternative.' And I thought, 'He's right. And his feet are well planted on the ground.'"

They would not stay there for long.

Conservatives across Canada were soon talking about Bernard Lord — about his successful mix of "progressive" and "conservative," for instance by balancing budgets while removing 40,000 low-income New Brunswickers from the income tax rolls. And about his success at bringing COR voters and activists back into the party. "He had demonstrated in New Brunswick a lot of the same things we needed to do nationally," says Peter Van Loan, a Bay Street lawyer and former president of the federal party. On the Monday after Edmonton, he began gathering the names of Tories who wanted to draft Lord into the race. An entire riding association in British Columbia pledged its support. "People realized in the PC party that we have our greatest appeal when we have a coalition-builder as leader," says Van Loan, who'd attended the 1998 provincial policy convention in Saint John. "I saw a focus there and a pulling together of things that would lead to success." While beating the Alliance would be more difficult — "COR was much more a nuisance than a force to be reckoned with" — he was convinced Lord could do it.

The entire federal party came down with Lord fever. The premier's continued protests that he would consider national politics only late in a second mandate — four or five years into the future — did nothing to cool the excitement. It peaked for the first time on August 28, five days after his Edmonton speech, when Brian Mulroney came to Fredericton.

Mulroney, though deeply disliked by the electorate, was still adored by the Tory establishment. There was a nostalgia for the winning coalition he'd built between western conservatives and Quebec nationalists, and he was still highly respected by corporate Canada: St. Thomas University in Fredericton raised funds to pay off a new $7 million building by naming it Brian Mulroney Hall.

Mulroney, in turn, had developed a liking for Bernard Lord. Earlier in the summer, he, former US president George Bush and several corporate high rollers had joined the premier for salmon fishing at Larry's Gulch, the New Brunswick government's lodge on the Restigouche River. The guest list was widely seen as having been assembled by Mulroney to give Lord some much-needed prestige, and he was reportedly telling friends that the young premier would make a fine federal leader someday.

Now, post-Edmonton, Mulroney was stepping right into the middle of the fever over Lord. In a media scrum after the dedication of the building, he heaped praise on Lord while taking care not to endorse him. "I like everything about him," Mulroney cooed. "He's knowledgeable. He's hard-working. He's got a good style. He's approachable, close to the people." But, he added, the premier "is in a group of remarkably talented people like Peter MacKay and John Tory and John Herron and Scott Brison and so on. . . . I hope they all run."

Some of the journalists probed for evidence that Mulroney, despite his assertions of neutrality, was trying to engineer Lord's ascent. The former prime minister, perhaps aware that his support might not be a blessing, swatted away the questions. "I don't [advise him]," he said. "I gave him as much advice as I could about catching salmon, but" — and here he produced a mellifluous Mulroney chuckle — "that does not appear to have been particularly successful." Lord was less discreet after Mulroney had gone inside. "We just talk about issues," he told reporters, unaware he was contradicting his new mentor's comments. "We share points of view. We share ideas, and that's what's really interesting. I enjoy sitting and talking with Mr. Mulroney."

Far more tantalizing, though, was a seemingly off hand remark Lord made as he tried to bring the scrum to a close. "I am reflecting on what this means," he said of the pressure on him to run federally. "But don't jump to the conclusion that that means I'm reflecting on changing my mind." Still, he added a comment in French — an analogy that would become the cliché of the year in New Brunswick politics: the door was closed, but it wasn't locked.

* * *

As September arrived, Conservatives felt their pulses racing, their breath quickening. The fever was taking hold.

The president of the PC Youth federation on Prince Edward Island launched a "Draft Bernard Lord" website. Another Internet site held a poll, and Lord shot into first place. Michael Marzolini, who measured public opinion for the federal Liberals, was quoted as saying that Lord posed a greater threat than any other potential leadership candidate. "Bernard Lord would attract voters away from the Liberal

Party, mainly in the Atlantic but across the country as well," Marzolini explains. "Mike Harris, on the other hand, would attract voters to the PCs away from the Alliance. Therefore we regarded Bernard Lord as the much more formidable candidate."

The growing enthusiasm for the earnest premier led Paul Wells of the *National Post* to label him "an ordinary juggernaut." He was the subject of a lengthy documentary on *Le Point*, Radio-Canada's leading TV current affairs program. In Toronto and Montreal, influential Tories organized meetings to discuss what incentives might entice Lord into the race.

Lord continued to say he was focused on his job as premier, but as October rolled around, his tone shifted. "I'm flattered and touched and it's certainly interesting," he told the *Telegraph-Journal* on October 9, "and it's prompting me to think about what it could mean to my family, and where is the best place for me to contribute." To the *Toronto Star*, he added, "You might say I'm reaching for the door handle."

Suddenly, Lisa Keenan, the provincial PC president, had to contemplate what might happen if Lord left abruptly. "I was one of the ones who caused him to go [to Edmonton], and then I said, 'Oh my God, what have I done?'" Lord had achieved a balance in the provincial organization based largely on his own appeal. The hypothetical question posed after his success with the Official Languages Act — "Could any other leader have done it?" — was suddenly real. "Where was the party left?" Keenan says. "Who would be a possible replacement? I couldn't think of anybody." The most likely scenario had Lord resigning as premier in January 2003, giving the party only a few months to pick a new leader and establish his or her profile before an election. "I realized we'd really let the genie out of the bottle," Keenan says.

Lord, characteristically, was taking his time making up his mind, to the irritation of some Tories. The slow, cautious approach had been fine in creating a consensus on the Official Languages Act, but now the party's main *raison d'être* — the acquisition and retention of power — was in play. Phone calls and e-mails from provincial members urging Lord to stay began to pile up next to the stacks of appeals for him to run. "His job is here in New Brunswick," party member Marie Starr said at a meeting of Tories in Fredericton South. Tories were divided again, this time not over language but over what their leader should do.

Journalists, meanwhile, bored with the "door" metaphor, began writing about who might succeed Lord and whether this or that person could win provincially, as he had. Every move the government made was examined through the prism of leadership politics. When Lord announced a minor cabinet shuffle on October 16, moving responsibility for labour negotiations from Health Minister Elvy Robichaud to Agriculture and Fisheries Minister Rodney Weston, he was asked if he was giving Weston "a bit more stature" for a leadership bid. Other reporters wondered if he was lessening Robichaud's workload so he could run.

The next day, with the pressure mounting within his party, Lord headed to Ottawa and boarded a federal government Challenger jet, joining Prime Minister Jean Chrétien, his officials and several national reporters for the flight to the 2002 Francophonie Summit in Beirut, Lebanon. Though Lord had expressed exasperation with the press gallery in Fredericton, he was more than willing to talk politics — off the record — with the journalists at the back of the plane. One of them, Paul Wells, says Lord held court for four hours after doing the same with Chrétien's entourage up in first class. "He left them evenly divided over whether he was going to run," Wells says. "They were making money bets. For everyone who said he's going to run, there was someone who would say, 'Oh, no, he's not.'"

Wells had met Lord in the fall of 1998 when he'd profiled the ten provincial premiers for the *National Post*. Underwhelmed by Camille Thériault, Wells paid a courtesy call on the then-leader of the opposition and had been sufficiently impressed that he recast his story as a preview of the looming election battle. Lord "is obviously not brilliant," Wells says. "He's obviously not the most well-read person in the world. But there was sort of an earnestness to him and a dignity to him."

Now, jetting across the world, he noted that Lord had developed "the most sophisticated critique of Paul Martin that I'd heard" — an asset for someone who might aspire to national leadership. Lord's argument was that "you can't run on 'change' if you've been there for ten years," the same logic he'd used to defeat Camille Thériault. "He knew the line on Martin," Wells says. "He knew how to take him on."

Wells adds the Liberal dauphin's 2004 election plan was to win in the Alliance's Prairie stronghold, on the assumption Quebec voters would abandon the separatist Bloc Québécois to jump on his bandwagon. Lord, as a native son from Lac-Saint-Jean, could mess that up, forcing Martin to play to Quebec and risk angering the West.

After the plane arrived in Beirut, Lord continued his ruminations in an on-the-record scrum with the reporters. "My first interest is especially New Brunswick," he told them. "But I'm really interested in Canada." Wells, on the phone with an editor in Toronto, was asked to write up the notes from the in-flight chat for Bob Fife, the *Post*'s Ottawa bureau chief. Fife would be breaking a story in Friday's *Post* that Lord had decided to run, the editor explained. Wells was unconvinced and declined to file his notes, arguing that the conversation had been off the record.

The *Post* headline on Friday morning blared, "Lord to Run for PC Leadership," attributing the story to "highly placed sources in Toronto, Ottawa, Montreal and New Brunswick." It quoted one as saying, "I can tell you unequivocally that Lord is going to run. The decision is made, and it is strictly a question of timing. All the pieces have been put together, right down to family situations and money." Lord would resign as premier in January, the story claimed, but would drop hints about his plans at the New Brunswick PC party's annual meeting, scheduled to open in Miramichi the following Friday, October 25.

"I wasn't pleased with that at all," Lord says of the *Post* story. "Someone jumped the gun. Someone gave the wrong interpretation to certain things I may have said, or they'd heard, or they simply fabricated the whole thing." Lord's press spokeswoman, Véronique Mercier-Dickens, who'd remained in Fredericton, told reporters, "His official response is that it was with great surprise that he read the story. It's a speculation piece, and it contains some inaccurate information." But reporters accustomed to Lord's careful choice of words saw no outright denial. The premier, in a conference call with New Brunswick reporters on Sunday, likewise would only call it "speculative."

Wells, who has since left the *National Post*, believes Fife was deliberately misled by Mulroney's associates. "I think they were telling him Lord would run in an effort to make it a done deal." If that was the gambit, it backfired. "It prompted me to put an end to it," Lord says. "If I would not have clarified it quickly, it would have led to more speculation, and I was concerned that it would distract the government from fulfilling its duties."

Flying back to Canada from Beirut, a more reflective Lord was leaning against running federally. When he reached his home on Fredericton's north side, he says, his son helped clinch the decision. Lord told reporters that, as he settled into a chair to read a backlog of paperwork on Monday evening, eight-year-old Sebastien, whom he hadn't seen for almost a week, climbed in with him. "There are a lot of titles that can be very flattering — premier, prime minister — but none more important than having my son or daughter call me papa," he would explain.

For a political animal like Bernard Lord, being premier gave him the best of both worlds. He was running a government, stepping on occasion onto the national or world stage, while still driving his kids to school most mornings. National politics would be different. "I knew what it would mean to run a federal campaign," he says. "I wasn't prepared to ask my wife, my son and my daughter to make that sacrifice. And I didn't want to make the sacrifice myself."

Lord called a news conference for Tuesday, October 22. He would not run. "Not only is the door closed, but it is locked," he said as several ministers, MLAs and supporters cheered at the back of the room. "The door is locked. Nothing will change my mind. My decision is made."

Watching Lord live on *Newsworld* from her law office in Saint John, Lisa Keenan breathed a sigh of relief. The genie was back in the bottle.

In fact, Keenan realized as she put the finishing touches on the PC party's big meeting in Miramichi that weekend, things had turned out rather well. True, the federal Tories were going back to the drawing board, wondering what might have been, hoping their party would survive. Provincially, however, Lord was more popular than ever. Even the Liberal leader, Shawn Graham, admitted he'd rather face any other opponent in the next election. "It's no secret that the premier is the greatest asset that the Conservative party has," he told journalists.

And the PC party itself — that broad coalition that Lord had assembled — knew now just how important he was to them. They'd seen it in the spring during his skilful handling of the language legislation, but they'd felt it viscerally when it appeared he might leave them. Now they travelled up to Miramichi to cheer him as they'd never cheered him before. "Four more years with Bernard Lord," Keenan told fifteen hundred ecstatic delegates. "Our work will go on. Our principles will endure, and our re-election is at hand."

* * *

Four months later, in the midst of a fierce February snowstorm, Percy Mockler settled into a quiet corner of a Fredericton restaurant to explain why the next New Brunswick election would be historic.

Mockler, the province's minister of transportation, had wanted Lord to run federally. He'd wanted it so badly that he'd drawn up a list of all the ridings in Canada that Lord could win as leader of the national PC party. But with Lord opting instead to seek a second mandate as premier, Mockler was throwing himself into preparations for the election expected in the spring.

The vote, he predicted, would spell the end of Liberal domination in francophone New Brunswick. Lord's big victories there in 1999 had been only the first step. After all, the Conservatives had won several of those ridings for the first time in 1982, only to lose them five years later. "In order to break that [Liberal] pattern of voting" in any given riding, Mockler said, "you always need a second victory for the Progressive Conservative party. To break the tradition, a Progressive Conservative needs two back-to-back victories."

Mockler cited such examples as Edmundston, Madawaska-Les-Lacs and Lamèque-Shippagan-Miscou, which had gone PC twice under Hatfield and were now up for grabs in most elections. They were no longer reliably Liberal except in a sweep — and sometimes not even then.

When Hatfield lost in 1987, the PC party had been deprived of similar back-to-back wins in all the French ridings it had won for the first time in 1982. Now those breakthroughs were within Lord's grasp. The polls indicated a second huge Conservative landslide, in which nine other heavily francophone ridings could, for the first time, re-elect a PC candidate. Until now, they'd been winnable by

Conservatives only rarely, but, according to Mockler, another Lord sweep would transform them into ridings the Liberals would never again take for granted.

A second Lord landslide, then, would do more than keep the Progressive Conservatives in power. It would drastically reduce the head start the Liberals traditionally enjoyed in francophone New Brunswick. It would rewrite the province's electoral map and permanently change its political dynamic. And it would cement the coalition of 1982 and 1999 in the PC Party of New Brunswick.

Once that task was complete, Mockler said, *then* Lord would move on to Ottawa to save the fractured Progressive Conservative Party of Canada. "Bernard Lord has finished Richard Hatfield's journey," he said, his eyes blazing with a sense of history. "Now he has his own journey. And that's why the nation wants him."

Chapter Twenty

THE IMPERFECT LEADER

LYNN MASON AWOKE EARLY on the morning of June 9, 2003. Summer was coming, but the air felt cool as he readied himself for what he knew would be a long day. He left his house on Preston Street on Fredericton's north side and set out for the campaign headquarters.

Mason's polling station was around the corner from his house, at the Church of Christ on Bloor Street, but he had known he would be busy today, so he'd cast his ballot in the advance poll. When he reached the headquarters, in a small office on Maple Street, it was already filling up with volunteers, and he began giving them orders. He'd worked hard, and he wasn't going to let that effort go to waste now, on election day.

Mason was the campaign manager for Peter Forbes, the Progressive Conservative MLA for Fredericton North he'd helped elect in 1999. Back then, he remembers, some of the veterans of the PC party in the riding had resented his history with the Confederation of Regions party and refused to help him get Forbes elected. This time, things were better. The former COR people "got a degree of respect they never had before," he says. "I think a majority of people in the PC party know they did what they did out of personal principles, and they respect that."

Bernard Lord respected it, Mason was sure. In his view, Lord was still the best man to lead New Brunswick because he'd accommodated different views within the PC party. Lord had even taught Mason a thing or two about trusting people he'd been suspicious of. "You have two ministers [in Lord's cabinet] who were members of the Acadian Society, and I respect them immensely," he says.

Mason had fretted during Lord's flirtation with federal politics in 2002. "I saw a bit of that power disease," referring to the ego and ambition so fatal to the COR party. Lord "just stepped over the line — and then he came back," Mason says. But he adds, "Don't get me wrong. I think down the road he'll be the next prime minister of Canada. I think he's one of the most intelligent men in politics today."

The premier's handling of Charlebois hadn't bothered him, either. "I think that was in line with Bill 88," he says. "There wasn't much he could do about that." Was it the influence of Mason's old friend Tony Huntjens that had kept Lord so balanced? Or was it the absence of a radical francophone such as Jean-Maurice Simard pulling him the other way? Mason shrugs. "I think he's got moderate views," he says of Lord. "That probably had more influence on him."

So Lynn Mason began directing the final sprint of the election race, the effort to get out the vote for the Progressive Conservative Party of New Brunswick and keep Bernard Lord in power.

Three hours northeast of Fredericton, in the small Acadian fishing village of Baie-Sainte-Anne, near where the mouth of the Miramichi River meets the Northumberland Strait, Jocelyne Durelle was starting her day and deciding when she would cast her vote in the riding of Miramichi-Bay du Vin.

Eighteen years earlier, Durelle had written to the committee studying the Poirier-Bastarache report to describe the lack of French-language services at the Miramichi Hospital and how her three-year-old daughter had been unable to communicate with the ambulance attendants. In 1991, when Sophie was nine, Durelle had watched with horror on election night as the Confederation of Regions party had stormed to victory in eight ridings, a message from 88,000 New Brunswickers that francophone rights — like the right to receive care in French at your local hospital—had gone too far. The promise of a tolerant, bilingual province had seemed so hollow that night.

Now things had changed. COR no longer existed, and Bernard Lord's PC government had passed the new Official Languages Act, with its guarantee of bilingual service in health care. "I have faith in him on the language question," Durelle says of Lord. "The fact he went to Université de Moncton, the fact he's perfectly bilingual, the fact that his wife is Acadian — he's someone who can represent us."

Sophie, now 21, was studying to become a nurse, a *bilingual* nurse. She was working for the summer at the Miramichi Hospital, where she was treating patients from the Acadian communities of Neguac, Rogersville, and Baie-Sainte-Anne in the French language — providing the service that had not been available to her as a child.

So, on June 9, 2003, Jocelyne Durelle went to the polling station in Baie-Sainte-Anne and cast her ballot for Bernard Lord, the same man Lynn Mason was working so hard to re-elect. Two people who had been at opposite ends of the language issue in 1991 were now voting for the same party, the Progressive Conservative Party of New Brunswick. That fact alone underscored Lord's political achievement.

But his Conservative coalition did not give him a second landslide victory on June 9, as his minister and advisor Percy Mockler had predicted. It saved him from losing power, but just barely.

* * *

Bernard Lord's troubles had started three months earlier, in March, when his government introduced reforms to regulations governing vehicule insurance. The premiums that New Brunswickers paid to private insurance companies were soaring, particularly for drivers considered high risk because they were old, or drove old cars, or lived in the economically depressed francophone north. A committee of MLAs wanted tougher regulatory powers for the province's Public Utilities Board, and, through the winter, as more and more insurance horror stories appeared in the newspapers, New Brunswickers waited for Lord to act.

His initial package, announced in March, featured a cap on the monetary awards the courts could award to accident victims for minor injuries, a change the industry said it needed to control its costs. At the same time, approval from the Public Utilities Board would be required for future premium increases above three per cent, a change designed to please consumers. It was a typically middle-of-the-road, keep-everyone-happy, Bernard-Lord-style solution. "It addresses several issues in a well-thought-out, balanced way," Justice Minister Brad Green said when he unveiled it.

It pleased no one.

Rates were already high, so a limit on future increases provided no relief. Within days, Lord's government gave the PUB additional powers to review existing rates. But by leaving the onus on the board to prove rates were excessive, Lord deprived it of the power to roll them back. That was quickly corrected as well, but the government appeared inept. There were no historic legislative debates or soaring rhetoric now, only the premier and his ministers struggling to explain how a tangled mix of regulations and free-market mechanisms would lead to lower premiums a few months down the road. Meanwhile, people hit with absurdly high premiums continued to contact reporters.

The balanced approach had been effective for Lord many times before, all the way back to his student government days. He'd used it to rebuild Richard Hatfield's coalition and to hold his caucus together with his carefully crafted compromise on the Official Languages Act.

So, on car insurance, naturally, he'd been inclined to be balanced as well — offering a little something to consumers and a little something to the industry. But this time he'd miscalculated. Not every New Brunswicker planned to vote based on insurance, but "a lot of people who did were looking for something else," Lord admits. His cautious, even-handed approach wasn't working: people wanted him to act boldly, to get tough with the industry — in short, "to do things."

Lord visited the lieutenant-governor the morning of Saturday, May 10, then went to a rally in the student union building at the University of New Brunswick to announce that the election would be held June 9. Surrounded by hundreds of cheering supporters, he invoked his steady, balanced style of government, his record spending on health and education, and his embrace of a diverse caucus of MLAs. "The most important word for us as Progressive Conservatives is welcome," Lord said. "Welcome to our party. Welcome to our team. Welcome to all New Brunswickers who want to join with us." He even singled out Tony Huntjens, standing among the candidates on the podium, as a former COR president who'd become "a great MLA."

He did not mention insurance once. "There's more to this election that just one issue," he told reporters after the rally, already on the defensive. "Because New Brunswick is not just one thing."

At the outset it appeared that Lord was right, that car insurance would be an irritant at worst. New Brunswickers didn't defeat governments after their first mandate, for one thing, and that lent the PC campaign an air of inevitability. A few days into Lord's bus tour, he returned to the University of New Brunswick for the nomination of four Fredericton-area candidates. A young girl sang "O Canada" in English and French as former COR supporters beamed with happiness at the prospect of being part of a second Conservative landslide. No one was surprised when the bilingual master of ceremonies acknowledged the presence of former COR MLA Max White, but there was a stir of approval when he also greeted Danny Cameron, putting in his first appearance at a PC event in years.

Yes, voters were talking about insurance, but no one doubted the coalition would deliver another large victory. Watching Lord campaign at a strip mall in the small town of Nackawic, Craig Astle, the manager of the disastrous 1995 campaign, recalled how Bernard Valcourt had avoided spontaneous encounters with voters in ridings where he knew he was the object of suspicion. But "when [Lord] goes into a place like Nackawic, pretty much the heart of that COR constituency, they don't see him as a francophone," Astle said. "They see him as a bilingual New Brunswicker."

Early in the campaign, polling indicated that few voters would mark their ballots based on insurance. Then that pool of citizens suddenly began to grow — and, as Lord would admit, they wanted "something else." Confronted by evidence that his lead was slipping away, Lord used his own nominating convention in Moncton to take a political gamble, announcing he'd recall the Legislature by the end of June if re-elected to force insurance companies to offer an inexpensive "no-frills" insurance policy. This second abrupt turn on insurance — policy-making on the fly — risked undercutting the premier's image as a quietly competent manager. *He's handled other issues so well*, the public might ask. *Why can't he get this right?* But that risk was outweighed by the need to stop the bleeding.

The no-frills plan quieted some of the static about insurance, and the PC campaign righted itself. But voters had been given a reason to doubt Bernard Lord, and they rather liked Liberal leader Shawn Graham's promise to legislate a twenty-five per cent reduction in premiums or adopt a government-run car insurance system. In northern New Brunswick, where insurance outranked health care as the top issue by a ratio of two to one, Graham began to gain momentum.

Lord opened the final weekend of his campaign in Fredericton, greeting the Saturday morning crowd at the Boyce Farmers' Market. He appeared tentative, granting a long scrum to reporters but hesitating at first to plunge into the crowd. Heading back to his campaign bus, he paused at the curb on Brunswick Street while traffic streamed by, and a man next to him said jokingly, "Run for your life."

"We are," Lord answered.

A trio of young female campaign volunteers turned up the music system on the bus and began dancing to the beat as the driver revved the engine. Lord headed behind a curtain at the back to take a phone call. When he returned to sit next to his wife up front, his palms tapped the beat absently on the table in front of him while his eyes stared into space. "I could tell it was bad news," one campaign worker remembers.

Lord had just been told that the overnight tracking polls — a nightly snapshot of what a small number of voters were thinking, averaged over three nights to reveal trends — showed that the Liberals had taken the lead on Friday. "We were behind enough that we knew it was going to be a challenge," Lord says. It was only one night's sample, but if it was accurate, the Tories had started bleeding votes again and were heading for defeat on Monday.

The campaign bus stopped in New Maryland, then in Mactaquac, where the incumbent MLA, Kirk MacDonald, had gathered Conservative supporters to greet Lord at Bird's Country Store in Burtt's Corner. In a small diner at the back, a woman read the premier his horoscope from *The Globe and Mail*. "Because you like to believe the best of everyone you meet, you might be tempted to overlook some obvious failings in the group of people you have to deal with this weekend," she read. "That's all very noble of you, but it won't stop them taking advantage of you the moment they get the chance."

"Oh my God," Lord laughed with mock horror, "the story of my life."

Back at the bus, Lord autographed campaign posters for some children while MacDonald convinced the tour co-ordinator to make a last-minute change to the itinerary. About 250 drivers of four-wheel all-terrain vehicles were holding a rally at the Lions' Club

Centre down the road. Lord's government had refused to crack down severely on ATVs, perceived as unsafe annoyances by urban dwellers but highly popular in rural areas. MacDonald was in a tough race in Mactaquac, but a quick stop by the premier at the rally might just save him.

At the community centre, several dozen drivers were checking their vehicles, sipping beer or preparing to drive off, some of them helmetless. The premier, wearing his blue blazer, strode into the crowd, but the urbane young lawyer from Moncton didn't fit in. "I don't think the people there wanted to see a bus," Lord says. "They were not there to see a bus with myself and other candidates. That wasn't the reason for the rally." When he approached six men working on an ATV's engine and none of them extended a hand to greet him, Lord was momentarily alone in the crowd with no one to talk to.

It was time to get out of there.

The Tory bus retreated back down Route 104, roared over the crest of Keswick Ridge to the Mactaquac Dam, then followed the St. John River upstream to the Trans-Canada Highway. Sitting near the front, watching the magnificent scenery of Tory country roll by, Bernard Lord steeled himself for a final, gruelling weekend of campaigning — and the punishing defeat that the voters seemed determined to give him.

* * *

Lord was diminished on election day but not defeated. He clung to power by winning twenty-eight seats, while the Liberals took twenty-six and the NDP one. Lord had the barest of majorities — only one seat — because two Acadian ridings that should have swung back to the Liberals instead remained Conservative.

As the results poured in, New Brunswick seemed to be lapsing back into its old voting patterns along that imaginary diagonal line — with the Liberal francophones north and east of it and the Conservative anglophones south and west — just as it had in the election of 1978.

Yet the PC party remained a contender in French New Brunswick in 2003. The party won eight of twenty ridings considered francophone — down from fifteen before the election, but still significant in the face of the Liberal comeback.

In the riding of Miramichi-Bay du Vin, Michael Malley was re-elected with the help of a strong Conservative vote in the Acadian fishing village of Baie-Sainte-Anne. In Malley's first victory in 1999, the village had voted against him, 620 to 383. But in 2003 he won the community 547 to 511 — thanks in part to the ballots cast by Jocelyne Durelle and others who trusted Bernard Lord and were grateful for his new Official Languages Act. In five additional Acadian ridings in the northeast, PC candidates lost by a *combined* margin of just 782 ballots. A switch of four hundred votes would have given Lord thirteen of the twenty francophone ridings and a comfortable majority in the Legislature. What cost him those votes, he argues convincingly, was not traditional Liberal voting patterns but his failure on insurance.

Victories in two Acadian ridings — Rogersville-Kouchibouguac and Dieppe-Memramcook — were particularly important. They had not been represented by cabinet ministers in Lord's first mandate, and they'd been Conservative only once before, in 1982. In close elections, parties fall back on traditional areas of support, so in 2003, those ridings should have gone Liberal. But the Conservatives held them. "Our support is more and more provincial," Lord says. "That is the party that I tried to build with my colleagues and the membership." The party has come a long way since Hatfield first began broadening its base in 1970, he adds. "It's still rooted more deeply in some regions, but it's not the same."

Those two ridings were also important to Percy Mockler's theory that a Conservative must win a French riding two elections in a row to break its Liberal tradition. The six other francophone seats Lord won, including Edmundston and Tracadie-Sheila, had shed that Liberal tradition before he became PC leader. Only Rogersville-Kouchibouguac and Dieppe-Memramcook gave the Conservatives back-to-back wins for the first time in 2003. And that meant — assuming Mockler was right — they had become two more francophone constituencies the Liberals could no longer rely on. Seven other ridings could have had their Liberal histories shattered in 2003, but two was better than none. It was progress.

So Lord's coalition, though battered, was not beaten in the election of 2003. In a campaign where Conservatives ran into trouble, some of the eight francophone ridings they won should have turned against them, depriving Lord of victory. They did not. "I'd be surprised if we went back to the pattern we had in the middle of the twentieth century," Lord says, "where election after election after election, the Liberal party won virtually every seat in French New Brunswick."

Conversely, Lord lost several seats in English New Brunswick. Yet the former COR members who suffered those defeats did not blame their leader. Lynn Mason, who saw his candidate in Fredericton North lose to a Liberal, remained convinced of Lord's greatness and of his destiny on the national stage. "I look at the federal leaders now and the man is just head and shoulders above them," he said that summer of 2003. "That man has the organizational ability to run a government well." David Jordan, elected as a Tory in 1999 and defeated in 2003, says, "I'm totally committed to where he's going and his outlook. I don't think anyone questions that the premier is the key."

Which raises the question, could the coalition outlast Lord? Could it survive the departure of a leader who so perfectly struck that balance at the precise moment it was needed? When that time came, as it inevitably would, the members would need to remember the lesson of 1999 and 2003: a united party is a winning party.

After all, the Conservatives held on in 2003 in a campaign in which the new Official Languages Act could have emerged as an issue but did not. Most former COR voters seemed, at worst, resigned to the fact that the major battles were over. Their home was in the PC party. Some had gone beyond resignation to acceptance. "You see the picture clearer when you're involved," says David Jordan. "Travelling to different areas of the province, you see the needs."

At the same time that former opponents of bilingualism acknowledged they had lost the argument, most francophones appeared satisfied they'd achieved a legal framework for linguistic equality. There would be minor skirmishes and grievances over details, but in two generations, the broad objectives had been realized. During the 1981 debate on Bill 88, Hatfield had said, "I suspect that one hundred years from now, those who occupy this Legislature will still have to fight for equality." Just twenty-two years later, New Brunswick was a good deal closer to that equality, and it had become a cliché to say that the province was a beacon for the country and the world.

For what region of the globe, torn by ethnic violence, would *not* prefer to see those differences settled by court challenges, parliamentary debates, and hard-fought election campaigns? What war-ravaged population would not choose a system in which political parties are the brokers that allow diverse communities to rise above divisions and develop a shared vision of society?

"He wanted to build a Tory party, a *new* party," Simard had said of Hatfield, and they'd helped build a new province in the process. Perhaps Brad Green had been right in 2002 when he'd told the Legislature that "the evolution and the maturity of the Conservative Party of New Brunswick parallel that of our province itself."

* * *

The election of 2003 had another notable result. The twenty-six Liberal MLAs came, not just from the francophone north, but also from Kings East and York and Grand Lake and Fredericton North and Saint John Fundy — traditionally Conservative ridings. These constituencies had strong COR votes in 1991 and usually went Liberal only when the party won landslides. So the Tories weren't alone in scoring breakthroughs. Both parties had won significant victories in the other's traditional territory. Each would return to the Legislature with a mix of English and French representation. Each would have difficulty calling any riding safe in the future because of the language people spoke there. Maybe, just maybe, that old diagonal line cutting across the centre of the province would no longer determine the outcome of elections.

There were many explanations for the Liberal wins. In some cases, weak Conservative MLAs who'd been carried by Lord's 1999 sweep weren't able to make a compelling case for a new mandate. Five consecutive landslide elections from 1982 to 1999, combined with COR's brief appearance, may have shaken some voters loose from their traditional parties. But something else may have driven the anti-government mood in 2003 — a new kind of discontent drawing a new line across the map of New Brunswick.

Northern voters were angriest about insurance because the region's relatively sparse population and weak economic conditions led companies to designate them as high risk and to charge them higher premiums. In Grand Lake, the end of twenty-four-hour emergency room service at the small village hospital set off protests. In Kings East, the government's lack of action on a new health care facility left residents bitter. In York, Lord's decision to enforce federal gun-control laws — a decision subsequently reversed — turned many rural citizens against the PC candidate.

Taken together, people outside New Brunswick's three relatively successful urban areas of Fredericton, Moncton and Saint John may have been protesting the widening economic and cultural chasm between those cities and the remainder of the province, the rural areas dotted with small towns and villages. Declining populations and increasingly vulnerable resource-based industries were shrinking local tax bases, squeezing the budgets of those municipalities. And it was becoming harder for the provincial government to justify spending money on hospitals, schools and roads serving dwindling numbers of people. Rural communities seemed destined to become less and less attractive places to live, pushing the cycle onward, while growing bedroom communities like Dieppe and Quispamsis inevitably would seek more clout in Fredericton. This provocative demand would leave rural voters with even less representation and power.

Politicians began to wonder if the widening prosperity gap would become the new "two solitudes" of New Brunswick politics. "Years ago, people were divided on language," says Louis-Philippe McGraw, the Conservative who lost in Centre-Péninsule in 2003. "Now it's urban and rural." McGraw found more common cause on issues affecting his rural riding with Kirk MacDonald, the anglophone MLA representing Mactaquac, than he did with his colleague from the francophone city of Edmundston.

"There's a huge urban-rural thing developing in New Brunswick," says Norm Betts, who lost his Southwest Miramichi seat. "It's more than just an uneasy feeling." His own home, Doaktown, once a prosperous forestry community, was facing rising unemployment because of mechanization in wood harvesting. As Betts found out when he became the minister responsible for economic development, few of the modern industries that governments pursue can replace those well-paying jobs. A small, out-of-the-way place like Doaktown wasn't even on the radar screens of such companies. "You try to push the stuff out there," he says. "You try to get stuff to go, but it's difficult to get them to go. If it's a choice between this business coming to Moncton or it's going to go to Ottawa, you encourage it to come to Moncton."

Lord, too, acknowledges the rural-urban divide as "a dimension that is growing. Demographics are changing. More people live in cities or very close to cities." It's a normal shift as society becomes less agricultural, he says and political parties need to adapt. In the 2003 campaign, however, Lord couldn't adapt. He'd read and understood the language sentiment in New Brunswick so well that he'd all but extinguished it as an issue. But he couldn't persuade people that he cared about their insurance premiums or their local hospital or their feeling that they'd been left behind. He would need to find another balance within himself if he was going to bridge the "new two solitudes" in New Brunswick.

* * *

On June 27, 2003, a sweltering, humid day in Fredericton, Bernard Lord's new cabinet was sworn in at the Legislature. Lord had lost four talented ministers in the election. That, and the common tendency for a premier in his second mandate to expand his cabinet, meant several new ministers would take their oaths in the heat.

As relatives, friends and supporters fanned themselves in the queue at the building's main entrance, the chosen MLAs strolled up to the door one by one, tight-lipped as reporters tried to divine which portfolios they were about to take on. Arriving together were two members who'd spent Lord's first mandate on the backbenches.

Rose-May Poirier held Rogersville-Kouchibouguac, one of the two seats that had finally been broken of its Liberal habit in 2003. One of her proudest moments in her first term had been voting for the new Official Languages Act. Now the Miramichi hospital, which many of her constituents in the Rogersville area used, was obliged to offer French-language services. "Miramichi has come a long, long way over the years," she says.

Joining her at the front steps of the Legislature was Tony Huntjens, for whom the new languages act had been a limit on francophone rights.

As the two of them, with their different understanding of the most important moment of Bernard Lord's first term, waited to go inside, they heard a loud squawking noise and saw a man walking in long semicircles around the crowd of Conservatives, keeping his distance but getting just close enough to be an annoyance.

Matthew Glenn of the New Brunswick Anglo Society was, in 2003, one of the last people in the province still speaking publicly against bilingualism. His group's membership was tiny compared to the masses that Len Poore had mobilized in 1984 and that had elected eight COR MLAs in 1991. Unwilling to acknowledge that that election had been his best shot at rolling back francophone rights, Glenn continued to make periodic solo visits to the Legislature, usually during official ceremonies, which he tried to disrupt with his bullhorn. He wore placards strapped over his shoulders, one asking, "Is New Brunswick Quebec's Branch Office?" and the other proclaiming, "N.B. Politicians Dancing to the Acadian Fiddle."

One of Lord's advisors, observing the one-man protest from a hundred feet away, looked over at Huntjens, who was about to be sworn in as a minister, and asked two reporters what more Glenn could possibly want. But Glenn didn't buy the idea of coalition-building. To him, Huntjens had become just another "gutless politician" who "doesn't dare say anything about the language problem."

Interviewed after he joined Lord's cabinet, Huntjens insisted otherwise. "I always speak my mind," he said. "I'll make my position clear with anybody at any time, and I don't apologize for my opinions. I don't believe I've compromised my position at all. If you go back to everything that I've done with COR or after COR, it's always been the same message: don't make linguistics the issue."

Though he was now a minister in a government officially committed to dual English and French school systems, Huntjens remained opposed. "Duality means two, and New Brunswick needs to be one. I haven't changed my opinion about that, and I still think we need to address some of those issues in time." Bilingual services, he said, are not a problem. But "when you look at the whole issue of education, I don't know if we're serving our children in the best way." He acknowledged that duality in education is guaranteed by the Constitution and his view cannot prevail. Still, he would have preferred to eliminate it. "In time, maybe it will come to a point where we don't separate communities and we learn to live together in harmony."

Asked about the Acadian argument that, given the domination of English in society, a single school system would lead to the assimilation of francophones, Huntjens admitted, "That's a difficult one. I don't know what the answer is to that. I just wonder why we're so concerned with assimilation when in Europe you have all these cultures living together and they're not assimilated with each other. I don't understand why we're making such a big fuss over it when other communities can work it out. I'm referring to Europe in particular. You have the Germans, the English, the French, the Dutch and the Belgians, and they're all able to learn each other's language without assimilation."

Lord was surprised to learn of his minister's apparent steadfast adherence to COR doctrine four years after his embrace of Conservative principles. "Tony has never raised that with me ever since we've been elected," Lord said in an interview for this book, momentarily taken aback. On duality in education, the premier added, "There's questions on this in caucus, because they want to understand these things. Where does this come from? What does this mean? But the policy of the government is clear, and I know that, as a minister and an MLA, Tony supports the policy of the government and he supports the principles of the PC party, and I'm satisfied with that."

That Huntjens felt free to express his dissent to a journalist may be another clue to how Lord engineered the acceptance of COR supporters in the party. Those thousands of voters opted out of the PC party when they felt their voices were no longer heard. Eventually, they came back because the need to win power was too great and because Lord let them feel they could advance their agenda, even if the Constitution prevented them from ever winning the argument.

Oblivious to these nuances and to the little dose of COR's "We the People" that Lord had injected into his party, Matthew Glenn stood alone outside the Legislature on June 23, 2003, berating the politicians through his bullhorn as they advanced up the steps.

And Tony Huntjens and Rose-May Poirier, symbolizing the two sides of the Conservative coalition — and the two sides of Bernard Lord himself — walked inside to acquire political power and, more important, to share it.

Federal Conservative leader Stephen Harper addresses the crowd while Bernard Lord looks on in Fredericton, May 25, 2004. CP (ADRIAN WYLD)

DILEMMAS

ON APRIL 24, 2004, more than five hundred people gathered in Moncton for a fundraising dinner for the Progressive Conservative Party of New Brunswick. The guest speaker was Brian Mulroney, and many of the Tories in the room were waiting to see what the former prime minister would say about the other high-profile invitee that night: the recently elected leader of the newly merged Conservative Party of Canada, Stephen Harper.

Harper, after all, had been one of the architects of the Reform Party, which Mulroney had often blamed for splitting the national conservative vote so fatally in 1993, guaranteeing Liberal hegemony in Ottawa for a decade. But in the fall of 2003, as leader of the Canadian Alliance and of the Official Opposition, Harper had engineered a merger of the Alliance and the federal PC party. Then he'd won the leadership of the new entity, and by the spring of 2004, with Paul Martin's Liberals mired in scandal, the Conservatives appeared poised to challenge for power again in Ottawa. Mulroney was fulsome in his praise. "I believe we have in Stephen Harper a new leader who can take the new Conservative party to government and restore vision, daring and achievement to Canada's national agenda," he gushed, exhorting the crowd, "Help Stephen Harper recreate Sir John's great alliance, with east and west, English and French, with a moderate, thoughtful program."

Bernard Lord listened in his seat as Mulroney dispensed compliments in his direction as well, defending Lord's "difficult decisions" as premier and predicting another PC election win in New Brunswick. It was no secret that Mulroney had felt Lord, not Harper, was best suited to recreate John A. Macdonald's "great alliance."

Just a month later, on May 25, Harper arrived in Fredericton for one of the first events in the federal election campaign. Hundreds of party members — most of them also supporters of the New Brunswick PC party — jammed into the Lord Beaverbrook Hotel to welcome him. Lord took the podium as Harper waited to make a carefully choreographed entrance. "It's an honour for me to introduce a true leader, a leader with courage and principles, a leader with the Conservative party united behind him, working for a better Canada," Lord said.

The endorsement was crafted for national reporters covering the Harper campaign, with the hope that the premier's reputation as a moderate would allay Canadian voters' suspicious of Harper's right-wing philosophy. Harper had sought it, however, just as Lord's appeal with New Brunswickers was wearing thin.

The problems began with his political near-death in the June 2003 election, which cost him his winning reputation, and there appeared to be little to look forward to as Lord began work on his second mandate. The very day his new cabinet was sworn in, his finance minister warned that the province was teetering on the brink of a deficit. When the Legislature reconvened in December 2003, hundreds of angry residents from the party's strongholds in the St. John River Valley gathered outside to protest the proposed closure of two area hospitals. Placards branded Lord a dictator, the kind of sentiment he'd exploited so effectively against the Liberals in 1999. Lord's health minister argued he had no choice but to consider hospital consolidation: the department was eating up an ever-growing share of the provincial budget.

In the midst of the turmoil, the premier himself was said to be in a funk, disillusioned by the harsh verdict of the electorate six months earlier and easily tempted by the opportunity to take his vaunted coalition-building skills elsewhere.

When the federal PC party and the Canadian Alliance began negotiating their merger in September, Lord's staff had quickly made him available to Ottawa reporters wanting his reaction. He said he backed the merger, repeating his view that a broad-based, inclusive party was the only way to win. He also said he wasn't interested in the leadership, but Lord did not top the list of potential contenders anyway. Few had wanted to lead the fifth-place Tories a year earlier; now that a new Conservative party might vie for power, the job was more appealing, and several talented candidates were expected. The new party would not hand the job to Lord as the old one would have in 2002. When Goldy Hyder, a federal Conservative strategist who'd wooed him then, asked Lord in October if there was any chance he'd run, "he paused, and he said no," Hyder remembers. The pause "told me he wanted it and he knew he couldn't have it."

Hyder, a former advisor to Joe Clark and an executive at the Ottawa office of public relations firm Hill & Knowlton, believed the ideological soul of the new federal party was at stake in the leadership race. Without a credible, moderate candidate from Progressive Conservative ranks, Hyder was certain Harper would win. The merger would be seen as a right-wing takeover of the PC party by the Canadian Alliance and not the type of broad-based, moderate coalition Canadians would support.

The PC faction looked first to former Ontario premier Mike Harris. But when Harris decided not to run and, according to Hyder, told associates Lord was the best prospect, there was a second wave of phone calls to Fredericton. Publicly, the premier again denied any interest, but many believed the only thing holding him back was the tight margin in the Legislature. "If he had thirty-five MLAs, he'd go," a New Brunswick party insider confided at the time. "As it is, the government would fall." Still, Hyder says, Lord told him and others to explore what would be required for a leadership campaign.

Hyder says a Lord machine could have been up and running quickly. The required money — two million dollars, he estimates — would be easy to raise, as would the additional millions needed for a general election. Organizers were prepared to sign on, and a forty-page platform drafted for Lord's aborted 2002 bid could be dusted off. And, Hyder asserts, at least ten Canadian Alliance MPs were prepared to abandon Stephen Harper to endorse Lord.

Meanwhile, strange things began unfolding in New Brunswick. On Friday, November 14, word leaked that Tory insiders had asked at least three Liberal MLAs to cross the floor and join the government. "It wasn't overtly stated that the premier may wish to go off for a federal run," one of the three, T.J. Burke of Fredericton North, said that afternoon. But the implication had been clear to him, he added. Lord, testy when asked about it at a news conference, refused to deny it — "How can I say that something hasn't taken place," he asked, "if I don't know if it's taken place or not?" — but repeated he had no plans to run federally. That weekend, following a Grey Cup meeting of premiers with incoming prime minister Paul Martin, Lord told Hyder to stop the clandestine organizing. "It's off," Lord said, according to Hyder. "I can't do it. It doesn't feel right. It feels dirty."

Still, efforts to chip away at the Opposition caucus continued. Liberal Bernard Richard accepted an appointment as the provincial ombudsman, temporarily increasing Lord's majority to two seats, with no legal requirement for a by-election to replace Richard for a year. In the most bizarre example, former PC leader Dennis Cochrane called another Liberal MLA, saying he'd been delegated to offer the position of Speaker of the Legislature. The Liberal tape-recorded the call and publicized it, reinforcing the perception of a government more preoccupied by tactics — or Lord's ambitions — than by important policy issues such as hospital consolidation, the looming budget shortfall and a restructuring of NB Power, the debt-ridden public energy utility.

The need for a credible mainstream PC candidate in the federal leadership race became acute in early December, when, following the ratification of the merger, several Red Tories bolted from the new party, including former prime minister Joe Clark. There were more calls to Lord, and backroom operatives including Bay Street lawyer Kevin Gallagher flew to Fredericton to meet him. Goldy Hyder arrived in town December 17, the same day *Bourque Newswatch*, an Ottawa political gossip Web site, reported Lord was getting organized to run.

Lord tried to shoot down the Bourque story. "There's nothing that has changed," he told journalists in a scrum at the Legislature. But the reporters spotted his carefully crafted verbal loopholes and challenged him to say nothing *would* change. "Well, a lot of things could change in life," Lord finally conceded, chuckling. "But you know, nothing has changed. And if something ever changes, I'll let you know. Am I getting calls? Yes, I am. I'm listening to the people who are calling me, and if something changes, I'll be happy to share that with you."

Hyder visited Lord in his office later that day and told him he had an eighty per cent chance of beating Harper. Hyder says he asked the premier if he could look himself in the mirror and say he'd given up a chance to become prime minister. When Lord said that, in fact, he could, "I was frankly shocked that it came out as easy as it did," says Hyder. He used a blunter argument. "I can tell you with virtual certainty that we can be having this conversation in Stornoway this time next year," Hyder remembers saying, "but I can't tell you with any certainty that you'll be premier in the next election." He says Lord understood that he might remain in New Brunswick only to be defeated at the polls.

The two met again that night at Lord's home, joined by cabinet minister Percy Mockler, who wanted Lord to go to Ottawa, and the premier's assistant, Marie-France Pelletier. Back at his hotel room later, Hyder telephoned another Lord booster, veteran Tory pollster John Laschinger, and predicted Lord would not run. Laschinger disagreed; things had gone too far now — Lord had to say yes.

The pressure was building. The Bourque Web site reported the next day that several Tory premiers would mobilize their organizations to ensure Lord a leadership victory and that supporters of Prime Minister Paul Martin were acknowledging the New Brunswick premier as an electoral threat. Bourque quoted one: "He can build the coalition that can trip us up."

The provincial PC party suddenly realized, collectively, that they might lose the tug of war for Lord's loyalty. At a caucus meeting on December 19, the day the Legislature adjourned for the holidays, Lord acknowledged he was considering the move. Several members reacted "emotionally," according to one MLA. "There were some tears" as caucus members told their leader he was the reason they'd run in the election. No one spoke in favour of Lord's departure, the MLA says. Percy Mockler remained silent.

Party president Lisa Keenan warned Lord that the worst-case scenario for him would not be to become Leader of the Official Opposition in Ottawa but, rather, a resounding electoral defeat at the hands of Paul Martin, leading to a move by disappointed Conservatives to oust him as leader. There might be a messy review vote, she warned, and then a humiliating return to practising law in Moncton.

At first, the pleas of the provincial party did not appear to be enough. At a year-end news conference on December 22, Lord spoke of the importance of reconciling the "factions" in the newly merged federal Conservative party, a task for which he clearly considered himself qualified. And his children — the reason he'd cited when he bowed out in 2002 — were no longer a problem. "They learn quickly," he said. "They grow quickly'; he had to think about where he could best serve people. When his federal boosters heard that, "a lot of us felt we were almost there," Hyder says.

Over Christmas, however, Lord fell back on his essential character trait: caution. If he temporarily stepped aside as premier to run and then lost to Stephen Harper, he would return to Fredericton a spent political force. If he won the leadership and was trounced in the federal election, his career might come to a quick end. Either way, the provincial PC party — the very coalition on which Lord's reputation was built — would be crippled by his departure, lose its majority in the Legislature and face possible electoral defeat.

On Monday, December 29, he telephoned his ministers and MLAs to tell them he would not be leaving provincial politics. He also called Goldy Hyder. "He said, 'I told you last time it doesn't feel right, and it still doesn't feel right. . . . I can't see my own government fall,'" Hyder recalls. "He felt an enormous obligation to the caucus and to ensure the government was secure." Lord had allowed his federal backers to map out a leadership campaign, but there was one aspect he had refused to authorize, Hyder says: a behind-the-scenes effort to bring the membership of the New Brunswick PC party on side, to manufacture or orchestrate a supposedly spontaneous groundswell of support within the provincial party for Lord's going federal. In the absence of that, the Tory grassroots wanted him to stay, and he'd listened to them. The next day, Lord's office issued a written statement: "I have decided I can best serve the public by continuing my role as premier."

Someone else would have to pull together the Conservative coalition at the federal level. The provincial party had won the tug of war. Now, its members hoped, Lord would focus on governing New Brunswick. "He's got to take control of the ship somehow," one party member said.

Ottawa wasn't completely forgotten, though. Hyder says that

during their December 29 phone call, Lord told him, "We're both young. Our chance could come again." That appeared optimistic. Several national columnists wrote that Lord's indecisiveness showed he didn't have what it takes for the federal scene. Chantal Hébert of the *Toronto Star* called his behaviour "self-destructive," and Lawrence Martin in the *Globe and Mail* labelled him the "Hamlet of the Maritimes." Paul Wells of *Maclean's* suggested on his Web site that journalists make a pact: "If Bernard Lord ever again, for the rest of his natural-born existence, flirts with the idea of taking a job in Ottawa, we must agree to laugh and throw things at him." Some federal Tories were equally unkind. One organizer who'd spent weeks assembling a list of campaign volunteers referred to Lord as a "prick."

Hyder was baffled by the attitude of provincial Conservatives who'd persuaded Lord to stay. "They've got a great premier," he says. "Why don't they want to share him?" The explanation lies in the unspoken bargain struck between the leader and the grassroots: he owed it to them to stay.

Yes, they were indebted to him. His natural sense of caution — his deep desire for balance at all times — had allowed Lord to achieve something historic: a winning coalition within the Progressive Conservative party of New Brunswick. He'd altered the province's electoral dynamic, broadened the PC base and banished the ghosts of Hatfield's final days and of the COR interlude. The party owed him for that.

Now he had a debt to pay to the party. If the close standings in the Legislature had trapped him, it was a trap of his own making. The caution that had been a strength for Lord in 2002 had become a weakness in 2003, spawning the "balanced" insurance plan that led, at least in part, to June's electoral debacle. Blocked from fleeing to Ottawa, Lord owed it to his party to repair the damage by meeting the growing list of fiscal and policy challenges facing his government, and making long-delayed decisions on issues ranging from rural taxation to the fate of the province's aging nuclear power plant.

The premier's public wavering about his future had caused many New Brunswickers — some within his own party — to wonder how committed he was to leaving his mark on the province. Hatfield and Simard, after all, had never intended their "new party" to be an end in itself, but a means to an end. They had created it to acquire and retain power — to do things. They would not have wanted Lord's greatest legacy — restoration of the Conservative coalition — to be his *only* legacy.

Yet Stephen Harper was destined to falter in the 2004 federal election campaign for being too firmly identified with a set of ideas, an accusation no one could level at Bernard Lord. And when Harper mused, the day after losing the election, about quitting as leader, Lord's name began appearing again in newspaper columns and television reports.

In New Brunswick, the premier's lack of a defining vision may have become a liability, but some federal Conservatives — facing a wrenching debate on just how conservative their party should be — could see such ambiguity as the solution to their dilemma.

The next time, they reasoned, Bernard Lord would surely answer the call.

Endnotes

EIGHTY PEOPLE AGREED to be interviewed or to provide information for this book. Interviews were conducted between February 2003 and January 2004 and ranged in length from a few minutes to several hours. A handful of people spoke to me on condition of anonymity. Quotations in the text attributed in the present tense come from these interviews, while those attributed in the past tense — with a couple of obvious exceptions in Chapters 19 and 20 — are drawn from contemporary reports, clippings, and so on.

THE INTERVIEWEES
Cleveland Allaby, Mike Allen, Frédéric Arsenault, Keith Ashfield, Craig Astle, Norm Atkins, Barbara Baird, Fred Beairsto, Norman Betts, Jim Blake, Margaret-Ann Blaney, Eric Bungay, Danny Cameron, David Clark, Janice Clarke, Dennis Cochrane, Paul d'Astous, Keith Dow, Yves Dupré, Jocelyne Durelle, Kevin Fram, Charles Gallagher, Jean Gauvin, Matthew Glenn, Dale Graham, Brad Green, Irène Guerette, Win Hackett, Greg Hargrove, Brian Harquail, Bev Harrison, Les Hull, Tony Huntjens, Goldy Hyder, Kevin Jensen, Richard Johnston, David Jordan, Al Kavanaugh, Lisa Keenan, Don Kinney, Eric Kipping, Louis Léger, Omer Léger, Bernard Lord, Roger Lord, Kirk MacDonald, Robert Macleod, Steven MacKinnon, Michael Marzolini, Lynn Mason, Louis-Philippe McGraw, Percy Mockler, Hazen (Hank) Myers, Arch Pafford, Jay Paradis, Don Parent, Marie-France Pelletier, Robert Pichette, Jim Pickett, Rose-May Poirier, Yvon Poitras, Len Poore, Bernard Richard, Elvy Robichaud, Andy Scott, Bob Simpson, Hubert Seamans, Wally Stiles, Don Sutherland, Brent Taylor, Tom Taylor, Daniel Thériault, Mario Thériault, Paul-Émile Thériault, Peter Van Loan, Hermel Vienneau, Jim Webb, Paul Wells, Max White, Barbara Winsor.

Prologue: ELECTION DAY, 1991
The narrative of election night is based on CBC Television's coverage, 1991, a recording of which was provided by my CBC colleagues in Fredericton. News-

paper clippings from the Saint John *Telegraph-Journal* and the Fredericton *Daily Gleaner* were also helpful, as were Greg Hargrove's COR scrapbook and the 1991 report of New Brunswick's Chief Electoral Officer.

Chapter One: JIM PICKETT LIGHTS A MATCH

Jim Pickett gave me a detailed interview on the famous night in New Denmark and supplemented his memories by going back into his scrapbooks to check dates and facts. I also relied on clippings from the *Daily Gleaner* and the *Telegraph-Journal*, on Richard Starr's *Richard Hatfield: The Seventeen-Year Saga* (Halifax: Goodread Biographies, 1988) and on documents relating to the Poirier-Bastarache report held at the Provincial Archives of New Brunswick.

Chapter Two: THE ACADIAN VOTE

For concepts of political party brokerage used in this chapter and throughout the book, I drew on Janine Brodie and Jane Jensen, "Piercing the Smokescreen: Stability and Change in Brokerage Politics," and David Smith, "Canadian Political Parties and National Integration," both in *Canadian Parties in Transition*, 2nd ed., edited by A. Brian Tanguay and Alain-G. Gagnon (Toronto: Nelson, 1996); and R.K. Carty, "Three Canadian Party Systems: An Interpretation of the Development of National Politics," in *Party Democracy in Canada*, edited by George Perlin (Scarborough, ON: Prentice Hall, 1988). Jeffrey Simpson's *Spoils of Power* (Toronto: Collins, 1988) makes a compelling argument that patronage is the glue that holds parties together and is thus a tool for building a stable political system.

Arthur Doyle told me the anecdote that opens this chapter, and his *Front Benches and Back Rooms* (Toronto: Green Tree, 1976) was a key source of historical background, as were Hugh Thorburn, *Politics in New Brunswick* (Toronto: University of Toronto Press, 1961) and Dalton Camp, *Gentlemen, Players and Politicians* (Toronto: McClelland and Stewart, 1970). Accounts of early political battles over language in New Brunswick are also found in George F.G. Stanley, "The Caraquet Riots of 1875," in *Atlantic Canada After Confederation*, edited by P.G. Buckner and David Frank (Fredericton: Acadiensis, 1985); and in Richard Wilbur, *The Rise of French New Brunswick* (Halifax: Formac, 1989). I referred often to *Elections in New Brunswick 1784-1984*, compiled by the staff of the Legislative Library. The quotation from Pierre-Jean Veniot was provided by his great-grandson, André Veniot, and is from Robert Pichette, *Pour l'honneur de mon prince* (Moncton: Michel Henry, 1989).

Valuable assessments of the Louis Robichaud years are in *The Robichaud Era, 1960-1970: Colloqium Proceedings* (Moncton: Canadian Institute for Research on Regional Development, 2001), in particular Robert Young, "The Programme of Equal Opportunity: An Overview"; Joseph-Yves Thériault, "The Robichaud Period and Politics in Acadia"; Chedly Belkhodja, "The Right Responds to Change"; and Michel Cormier, "The Robichaud Legacy: What Remains?" I also relied on Della Stanley, *Louis Robichaud: A Decade in Power* (Halifax: Nimbus, 1984).

Michel Cormier and Achille Michaud's *Un Dernier Train pour Hartland* (Moncton: Éditions d'Acadie, 1991) is the definitive account of Richard Hatfield's attempts to woo the Acadian vote and was a guide throughout Part One. It was published in English as *Richard Hatfield: Power and Disobedience* (Fredericton: Goose Lane, 1992). Richard Starr's *Richard Hatfield: The Seventeen-Year Saga* was also helpful here.

Chapter Three: THE FRENCH LIEUTENANT
Quotations from Jean-Maurice Simard come from interviews conducted in 1990 and 1999 by Janet Toole and Barry Toole for the Provincial Archives, and they form the backbone of this chapter. I have cleaned up some of the syntax without affecting his meaning. The books on Richard Hatfield by Starr and Cormier and Michaud were helpful with the chronology of events. The account of the fight over École Sainte-Anne in Fredericton is based in part on Bernard Poirier's memoir, *À la poursuite d'un idéal* (Moncton: Éditions de la Francophonie, 2001). The Poirier-Bastarache report, officially titled *Towards Equality of Official Languages in New Brunswick* (Fredericton: Government of New Brunswick, 1984), also provided background on key milestones in Hatfield's expansion of language rights. Newspaper clippings rounded out the account.

Chapter Four: "*ENCORE PLUS FORT*"
The Simard interviews were crucial to this chapter, as were countless stories from the *Daily Gleaner* and the *Telegraph-Journal* and the books on Hatfield by Starr and Cormier and Michaud. An analysis of the Convention d'orientation nationale des Acadiens is found in Harley d'Entremont and Philippe Doucet, "Acadian Neo-Nationalism and Political Power," in *Ethnicity in Atlantic Canada*, Social Science Monograph Series (Saint John: University of New Brunswick at Saint John, 1985). Quotations from the debates in the Legislature come from Hansard. The cabinet memo referring to equality of the "two official language groups" in New Brunswick is No. 13394, dated May 23, 1980, and found at the Provincial Archives among materials presented at a June 19, 1980, cabinet meeting. The document referring to career opportunities for unilingual civil servants being "reduced" is cabinet memo No. 15039, dated June 3, 1981.

Chapter Five: THE MIDDLE GROUND IS LOST
Frédéric Arsenault's insights into what went wrong in the Poirier-Bastarache process were of great value. The report itself was important, as was René-Jean Ravault, *Perceptions des deux solitudes: Étude sur les relations entre les deux communautés de langues officielles du Nouveau-Brunswick* (Montreal: International Centre for Research on Bilingualism, 1983); this was unearthed for me by the extremely helpful staff at the Legislative Library. Some information on the committee's workings and quotations from submissions come from the large Poirier-Bastarache file that is part of the Richard Hatfield collection at the Provincial Archives. Bernard Poirier's memoirs were also helpful. Starr, Cormier and Michaud, newspaper clippings and Hansard were also consulted.

Chapter Six: "ONE OF US"
David Clark responded to my questions by e-mail from his home in British Columbia despite his being offended by the suggestion that John Baxter plotted against Hatfield. I take Clark's point that Baxter is no longer alive to defend himself. Newspaper clippings, the Simard interviews and the Hatfield biographies by Starr and Cormier and Michaud books were helpful in shaping this account of the leadership review fight, as was Janice Clarke, despite my failure to jog her memory about the Hatfield review vote results.

Chapter Seven: WAITING
The final days of the Hatfield era are ably chronicled by Starr and Cormier and Michaud and traced in *Daily Gleaner* and *Telegraph-Journal* clippings. The account of Liberal polling on the province's language divisions is from Philip Lee, *Frank: The Life and Politics of Frank McKenna* (Fredericton: Goose Lane, 2001).

Chapter Eight: THE WEST COMES EAST
Geoffrey Martin's studies of the Confederation of Regions party were a great resource, especially "We've Seen It All Before: The Rise and Fall of the COR Party of New Brunswick, 1988–1995," *Journal of Canadian Studies* 33: 1 (1998) 22-38. His argument that COR's grassroots populism was incompatible with parlia-mentary democracy provided me with the theoretical framework for Part Two. Greg Hargrove, the former COR MLA for York North, reached many of the same conclusions as Martin, albeit from a different perspective. Hargrove spent an afternoon with me at his home, recounting the early days of the party, and loaned me his scrapbook of news clippings.

The most valuable contribution to Part Two was by Danny Cameron, who, though he did not grant me an interview, pointed me to several boxes of correspondence and records he had just turned over to the Provincial Archives. He also gave me permission to dig into them before the archives staff had catalogued the contents. Brent Taylor and Andrew Holland lent me some of their files, which allowed me to construct a timeline of the COR party. Other information on COR's early days came from newspaper accounts. The sketch of Elmer Knutson draws on newspapers and on Knutson's own Web site, which lays out some of his theories on Confederation and on the money supply. His obituary in *Alberta Report* and some other clippings contained in the Cameron papers filled in the rest.

This chapter is indebted to Barbara Baird for her interview and to Dennis Cochrane for his thoughtful, self-effacing account of his years as leader. Quotations from the Legislature come from Hansard. Jean-Maurice Simard made his comments about Barbara Baird in one of his Archives interviews. Philip Lee's book on McKenna and Susan Delacourt's *United We Fall: In Search of a New Canada* (Toronto: Penguin, 1994) provided the context of the Meech Lake battle. The description of COR supporters as "modernization losers" is quoted from A. Brian Tanguay and Alain-G. Gagnon, "Minor Parties in the Canadian Political System: Origins, Functions, Impact," in Tanguay and Gagnon's *Canadian Parties in Transition.*

Chapter Nine: HONOURABLE SKUNKS
This chapter leans heavily on Danny Cameron's papers and draws on many of the same books and sources noted for Chapter Eight. Some of Cameron's descriptions of his childhood are from a 2003 CBC Radio interview. A helpful account of the Campbellton leadership convention is Sue Calhoun, "Getting to the Core of COR," *New Maritimes* 11: 2 (November–December 1992) 7-16. The quotations from Brent Taylor's leadership speech come from a text he provided. I also consulted the 1991 report of the Chief Electoral Officer of New Brunswick and Elections Canada's summary of the 1992 Charlottetown referendum results.

Chapter Ten: PULLING IT TOGETHER
Danny Cameron's papers were invaluable and the main source of information for this chapter. The account of the Bill 88 debate comes from Hansard. *Frank*, by Philip Lee, and stories in the *Telegraph-Journal* and the *Daily Gleaner* were significant sources of information.

Chapter Eleven: "WE THE PEOPLE"
This chapter is based almost entirely on Danny Cameron's documents, supplemented with newspaper clippings, primarily from the *Telegraph-Journal* and the *Daily Gleaner*.

Chapter Twelve: THE COALITION WITHIN
A number of newspaper stories, particularly in the Fredericton *Daily Gleaner*, were important in this chapter, especially for the account of Brent Taylor's procedural and legal attempts to be recognized as COR leader. The story of Jean Gauvin's procedural stunt is based on an interview with Hank Myers; Percy Mockler later corroborated the Myers version. Quotations of the proceedings are from Hansard.

Chapter Thirteen: WEAVING
Most of this chapter is based on my own reporting of the 1995 Valcourt leadership campaign and PC election campaign for the *Telegraph-Journal*, during which I interviewed Valcourt, Scott MacGregor and other key figures several times. Biographical details come from a lengthy profile of Valcourt I wrote for the *New Brunswick Reader*. Barbara Baird lent me her videotape of the leadership convention. Jean Gauvin's attack on Valcourt is from Hansard. I consulted the 1995 report of the Chief Electoral Officer for my analysis of the election results. The section on COR's ongoing leadership feud is based mostly on newspaper clippings.

Chapter Fourteen: THE PERFECT CANDIDATE
The section on Valcourt's departure is based on newspaper clippings, including some of my own reporting. The Valcourt interview with the *Telegraph-Journal* in which he attacked his fellow Conservative MLAs was by Gary Dimmock. Jean-Maurice Simard's column in the *Telegraph-Journal* appeared on March 27, 1997.

The story of Bernard Lord's early years is based on the first of my three interviews with him. The analysis of his years as student president at the Université de Moncton is based on a *Telegraph-Journal* story I wrote in December 1998, for which I consulted three years of *Le Front*, the campus student newspaper. Barbara Winsor's interview was particularly helpful with the story of the leadership race, as were *Telegraph-Journal* stories by Giselle Goguen. The percentage of the vote Lord drew among anglophones and francophones is from data included in Jonathan Peter Bishop, "From Caraquet to Lord: Language Politics in New Brunswick," MA thesis, Acadia University, 2000. The account of the convention is based on a *Telegraph-Journal* story to which three other journalists and I contributed. Quotations from Lord's speech and the subsequent interview with the CBC's Terry Seguin are from a transcript that is part of the Legislative Library's file on Bernard Lord.

Chapter Fifteen: A MIRACLE UNDONE
The story of Saint-Sauveur and Saint-Simon is based on the March 22, 2001, report of the Commission for Public Complaints Against the RCMP (Ottawa, 2001) by commission chair Shirley Heafey. It includes a minute-by-minute chronology of both incidents. "Samuel Paulin" and "Marcel Lanteigne" are real people, but I have changed their names. I interviewed residents "Samuel Paulin," Thérèse Albert, Roger Foule, and Géraldine Hébert, along with MLA Bernard Richard and RCMP Insp. Kevin Vickers, in summer 2001 while researching the events for the CBC Television program *The Fifth Estate*. I also relied on some newspaper clippings.

Background information on the toll highway project comes from documents prepared by the government and by opponents of the project, as well as from some newspaper stories. The account of the February 19, 1999, meeting in Salisbury is from my own *Telegraph-Journal* report. Two well-informed members of the PC party who asked to remain anonymous recounted how Lord shifted his position between the caucus meeting and his speech in Salisbury.

Chapter Sixteen: SUPERMAN
The 1992 letter to the *St. Croix Courier* by Tony Huntjens was in Danny Cameron's papers at the Provincial Archives. His 1995 election brochure was given to me by a friend who thought it relevant to my research. Other information on COR's final spasms are from the Legislative Library's COR file. Bernard Lord read me the quotation from the party's statement of principles ("with fairness and justice") during one of our interviews. Jean-Maurice Simard's critique of Lord is from the Provincial Archives interviews. The account of Camille Thériault's capturing the Liberal leadership is from newspaper clippings, many of them in the Legislative Library file on Thériault. I also relied on clippings, including of some of my own reports, to tell the story of the Moncton East by-election. Giselle Goguen of the *Telegraph-Journal* broke the story of the discontent with Lord's leadership leading up to the Moncton East by-election, while the rumour of a pro-Betts coup was related to me by a Lord associate during my research. The account of the ceremony for Ray Frenette at the Université de Moncton,

including the analysis of Jean-Bernard Robichaud's comments, is from the report I filed on the event for the *Telegraph-Journal*.

Chapter Seventeen: THE JUMP BACK
Newspaper clippings supplemented a large number of interviews to tell how former COR voters returned to the PC party. Clippings also allowed me to construct a chronology of the election campaign. The quotation from Lord about his children's heritage is from a *Globe and Mail* story on June 10, 1999, by Tu Thanh Ha, who pointed out the ambiguity of Lord's words. The Tony Huntjens remark that provoked controversy at the end of the campaign is cited in Jonathan Peter Bishop's MA thesis, which, in turn, cites a *Telegraph-Journal* report. Clippings from *L'Acadie Nouvelle* tell the story of the fallout. I used the 1999 report of the Chief Electoral Officer for my analysis of the election results.

Chapter Eighteen: HOLDING THE CENTRE
The account of the early days of the Lord government is based mostly on interviews and newspaper accounts. The criticisms of Lord as a weak leader by Donald Savoie and by Tom Mann of the New Brunswick Public Employees Association are from a CBC Radio documentary I prepared in January 2001. Norm Betts made his comment about "procrastination" in our interview on August 18, 2003. The description of the optimism at the PC party's annual general meeting in November 2001 is based on my own observations at the event. Background on the Charlebois case is from the ruling itself, Charlebois v. Mowat et ville de Moncton (New Brunswick Court of Appeal, December 20, 2001, Docket No. 166/00/CA). The quotation from Mario Charlebois ("they were right") is from my January 2003 documentary on the man for CBC Radio. The fallout after Lord's speech to L'Association des juristes d'expression francaise du Nouveau-Brunswick is from stories in *L'Acadie Nouvelle*. The account of the internal discussions about Charlebois is based on my research interviews. Quotations from the debate on the Official Languages Act are from Hansard. I viewed the original March 20, 2002, letter from Colby Fraser at the office of the Chief Electoral Officer.

Chapter Nineteen: "AN ORDINARY JUGGERNAUT"
The PC party provided a text of Lord's Edmonton speech, and the account of "Lord fever" comes from newspaper clippings. The account of the Brian Mulroney ceremony is based on my own CBC Radio documentary on the event, and other quotations are from my own reporting for the CBC or from news-paper clippings. I found reports from the *Toronto Star*, Canadian Press, the *Globe and Mail* and the *National Post* on the Web site Torydraft.com.

Chapter Twenty: THE IMPERFECT LEADER
The government's multiple attempts to deal with the insurance issue and the description of Lord's first rally of the election campaign are based on my own reporting for CBC Radio and on other news accounts. As part of my research for this book, I followed Lord's campaign to Nackawic on May 23, 2003, and to

the Boyce Farmers' Market, New Maryland and Burtts Corner on June 7. The descriptions of the events there are based on my own observations and subsequent interviews. Analysis of the election is based on results posted on the Web site of New Brunswick's Chief Electoral Officer. Observations of the rural-urban demographic trends in the province are based on the 2001 federal census and some of my own reporting on the issue for CBC Radio. The scene at the Legislature before the cabinet swearing-in on June 27, 2003, comes from my own observations. Comments by Tony Huntjens are from our interview on September 3, 2003.

Epilogue: DILEMMAS

This account is based on my own reporting at the time for CBC Radio and on stories filed by other journalists at the Legislature, as well as on interviews. The description of Brian Mulroney's appearance at the PC fundraising dinner is from the *Telegraph-Journal* and the Moncton *Times-Transcript*. Goldy Hyder's account of his meetings with Bernard Lord was especially helpful.

Acknowledgements

I OWE MANY THANKS to people who have helped me develop as a reporter. Among them are teachers Ken Murphy at Moncton High School and professors Catherine McKercher and Elly Alboim at Carleton University. I am also indebted to friends and colleagues at the Moncton *Times-Transcript*, the Kingston *Whig-Standard*, *Prognosis*, and the New Brunswick *Telegraph-Journal*. Four former *Telegraph* editors — Neil Reynolds, Scott Anderson, Scott Honeyman and Philip Lee — granted me the freedom to grow as a journalist and writer. At CBC Radio, I cherish the work I am able to do as the provincial affairs reporter, a job I've been allowed to define in the most fulfilling way. I am grateful to Mary-Pat Schutta and Janet Irwin at CBC Fredericton for giving me time and flexibility to work on this book.

I owe many thanks to Conservatives and other New Brunswickers I've met over the years who have explained the workings of politics to me. Robert Macleod, Kevin Fram, Percy Mockler and Lisa Keenan have been particularly patient with my questions.

I owe a huge debt to those who gave me interviews and information for this book. I thank Danny Cameron in particular for granting me early access to his correspondence and files, which he was in the process of donating to the Provincial Archives when I began my research early in 2003. I am grateful to all those who helped me find photographs, especially Phil Andrews, of the *Telegraph-Journal*, and all the individuals who dug up old personal photographs for me.

At the Provincial Archives, Fred Farrell turned over Mr. Cameron's papers before they'd been catalogued, and Janet Toole pointed me to another treasure trove, her interviews with Jean-Maurice Simard. The entire archives staff has my appreciation, as do Margaret Pacey and the dedicated employees of the Legislative Library. They were always helpful and always greeted me with smiles.

Several communications officers and executive assistants in the Lord government helped schedule interviews with elected politicians. I thank David

McLaughlin, Chisholm Pothier and Christiane Gauvin for arranging my three interviews with Premier Bernard Lord.

Harvey Cashore of the CBC Television program *The Fifth Estate* hired me for two weeks in 2001 to research the events in Saint-Sauveur and Saint-Simon. I am grateful for the opportunity to learn more about this important episode. I also thank Anouk Hoedeman for technical support with Microsoft Word, Stevie Cameron for friendship and advice along the way, Daniel McHardie of the Moncton *Times-Transcript* for his assistance, and fellow members of the New Brunswick Legislative Press Gallery for encouragement and gossip.

I have enjoyed every minute of my work on this project, which I attribute to the support and encouragement of everyone at Goose Lane Editions. It has been an honour to be on the receiving end of the infectious enthusiasm of Susanne Alexander and Laurel Boone, and it was a pleasure to work with them. My editor, Barry Norris, was meticulous and rigorous. He made this a better book. Paul Vienneau, Goose Lane's designer, showed endless patience in our search for photographs.

I owe special thanks to my mother, Carol Poitras, and my sister, Suzanne Poitras, for support at home over the years and for allowing my imagination to roam into areas that eventually led me to journalism.

This project reflects the influence of two people more than any others. My father, André Poitras, loved politics and sparked my own interest. He died in 1989, before most of the events described here; I would like to think of this book as taking in many of the political discussions we have not been able to have.

My wife, Giselle Goguen, supported my work on this book unconditionally, with love and encouragement, during the many evenings and weekends (and one summer vacation) I devoted to it instead of to her. Her advice and help at the Archives enriched the project, and I could not have contemplated writing it — never mind getting it finished — without her constant and enthusiastic encouragement, even as the birth of our daughter Sophie approached. I can never fully express my gratitude to her.

Index